PROVERBS

THE OLD TESTAMENT LIBRARY

Editorial Advisory Board

Richard J. Clifford

PROVERBS
A Commentary

Westminster John Knox Press
Louisville, Kentucky

Book design by Jennifer K. Cox

First edition
Published by Westminster John Knox Press
Louisville, Kentucky

This book is printed on acid-free paper that meets the American National Standards Institute Z39.48 standard. ♾

PRINTED IN THE UNITED STATES OF AMERICA

99 00 01 02 03 04 05 06 07 08 — 10 9 8 7 6 5 4 3 2 1

Library of Congress Cataloging-in-Publication Data

Clifford, Richard J.
    Proverbs : a commentary / Richard J. Clifford. — 1st ed.
        p.   cm.
    Includes bibliographical references and index.
    ISBN 0-664-22131-9 (alk. paper)
    1. Bible. O.T. Proverbs—Commentaries.   I. Title.
BS1465.3.C57   1999
223'.7077—dc21   98-50850

CONTENTS

PREFACE

Two sentences from the great eighteenth-century English aphorist Samuel Johnson can serve as a motto to Proverbs and to this commentary. "Men more frequently require to be reminded than informed."[1] The book of Proverbs does not primarily provide information; its instructions are remarkably empty of "content" and its maxims, when rephrased, are often trite. Rather, it informs by giving its readers a perspective. To quote Johnson on the achievement of Alexander Pope: "New things are made familiar, and familiar things are made new."[2] Proverbs is about vision and action.

When I began the commentary, I assumed the most productive approach would be through philology, text criticism, and comparison with other literatures. These have their place, of course, but it turned out that the most productive way was through the rhetoric—how did the instructions and maxims engage its audience? By a typical Proverbs paradox, the common accusation against the book—that it is banal—turned out to be a key to understanding it. If a verse seemed banal, I knew I had not understood it, and so I returned to it. Many translations in this commentary are no doubt banal, but the blame for that belongs to the translator, not the original author.

The compression and wit of Proverbs mean that the translation is virtually a commentary in itself. Readers who do not know Hebrew may find it helpful to compare the translation with other translations. The textual notes presuppose some knowledge of Hebrew and the ancient versions; they can usually be skipped by the general reader.

The authors of Proverbs were suspicious of knowledge gained by an individual's unaided efforts and welcomed reproof as a sure path to wisdom. I wish to thank my "reprovers" and providers of information, among whom are Michael V. Fox, John Huehnergard, John S. Kselman, S.S., Jon D. Levenson, Paul V. Mankowski, S.J., Roland E. Murphy, O. Carm., Daniel C. Snell, Choon-Leong Seow, Eugene Ulrich, Raymond C. Van Leeuwen, and Jan de

---

1. *Rambler,* no. 2, cited in W. J. Bate, *Samuel Johnson* (New York: Harcourt Brace Jovanovich, 1977), 291.
2. Samuel Johnson, *Lives of the Poets,* essay on Pope.

Waard. Needless to say, they should not be held accountable for the opinions expressed in the book. I also thank Cynthia Thompson, who first proposed this project to me, and Jon Berquist, her successor. Catherine Playoust superbly edited much of the manuscript. Finally, I want to thank my fellow Jesuits and the Society of Jesus, who have always provided unstinting support and encouragement.

ABBREVIATIONS

AB	Anchor Bible
ABD	*The Anchor Bible Dictionary,* ed. D. N. Freedman (Garden City, N.Y.: Doubleday, 1992). 6 vols.
AEL	M. Lichtheim, *Ancient Egyptian Literature,* 3 vols. (Berkeley: University of California Press, 1975–80)
Alonso Schökel	L. Alonso Schökel and J. Vilchez Lindez, *Proverbios* (Nueva Biblia Española, Sapienciales I. Madrid: Ediciones Cristiandad, 1984)
ANET	*Ancient Near Eastern Texts Relating to the Old Testament,* 3d ed., ed. J. B. Pritchard (Princeton, N.J.: Princeton University Press, 1969).
Barucq	A. Barucq, *Le livre des Proverbes* (Sources bibliques; Paris: Gabalda, 1964)
BHS	*Biblia hebraica stuttgartensia,* ed. K. Elliger and W. Rudolph (Stuttgart: Deutsche Bibelstiftung, 1977)
BM	B. R. Foster, *Before the Muses: An Anthology of Akkadian Literature* (Bethesda, Md.: CDL, 1993). 2 vols.
BWL	W. G. Lambert, *Babylonian Wisdom Literature* (Oxford: Clarendon Press, 1960)
BZAW	Beihefte zur Zeiftschrift für die alttestamentliche Wissenschaft
Cant.	Canticles/Song of Songs
CBQ	*Catholic Biblical Quarterly*
Cohen	H. R. Cohen, *Biblical Hapax Legomena in the Light of Akkadian and Ugaritic* (SBLDS 37; Missoula: Scholars Press, 1978)
Delitzsch	F. Delitzsch, *Biblical Commentary on the Proverbs of Solomon,* 2 vols. (Edinburgh: T. & T. Clark, 1874–75)
Ehrlich	A. B. Ehrlich, *Randglossen zur hebräischen Bibel: textkritisches, sprachliches und sachliches* (Hildesheim: Olms, 1968; reprint of 1913 edition). Vol. 6.
E	English versions

FS   Festschrift (for)
Gemser   B. Gemser, *Sprüche Salomos,* 2d ed. (Handbuch zum Alten
              Testament; Tübingen: J.C.B. Mohr [Paul Sieback], 1963)
G   Greek translation, the Septuagint
GKC   *Gesenius' Hebrew Grammar as Edited and Enlarged by the*
              Late E. Kautsch, 2d English ed., revised by A. E. Cowley
              (Oxford: Clarendon Press, 1910).
HALAT   W. Baumgartner, *Hebräisches und aramäisches Lexikon zum*
              Alten Testament, 3d ed. (Leiden: Brill, 1967–1990). 4 vols.
IBHS   B. K. Waltke and M. O'Connor, *An Introduction to Biblical*
              Hebrew Syntax (Winona Lake, Ind.: Eisenbrauns, 1990).
JB   Jerusalem Bible
JBL   *Journal of Biblical Literature*
J-M   Paul Joüon, *A Grammar of Biblical Hebrew,* Subsidia biblica
              14/1, translated and revised by T. Muraoka (Rome: Pontifical
              Biblical Institute, 1991). 2 vols.
JPSV   Jewish Publication Society Version = *TANAKH: The Holy*
              Scriptures (Philadelphia: Jewish Publication Society, 1985)
JSOT   *Journal for the Study of the Old Testament*
KAI   H. Donner and W. Röllig, *Kanaanäische und aramäische*
              Inschriften, 2nd ed. (Wiesbaden: Harrassowitz, 1968). 3 vols.
KTU   M. Dietrich, O. Loretz, and J. Sanmartín, eds., *The Cuneiform*
              Alphabetic Texts from Ugarit, Ras Ibn Hani and Other
              Places (2d, enlarged edition; Abhandlungen zur Literatur
              Alt-Syrien-Palästinas und Mesopotamiens 8; Münster:
              Ugarit-Verlag, 1995).
McKane   W. McKane, *Proverbs: A New Approach* (Old Testament
              Library; Philadelphia: Westminster Press, 1970)
MT   Masoretic text, the text pointed (or vocalized) by Jewish
              scholars (Masoretes) from the sixth to the ninth century C.E.
Meinhold   A. Meinhold, *Die Sprüche* (Zürcher Bibelkommentare 16;
              Zurich: Theologischer Verlag, 1991). 2 vols.
NAB   *New American Bible*
NRSV   *New Revised Standard Version*
OTP   J. H. Charlesworth, ed., *The Old Testament Pseudepigrapha,* 2
              vols. (Garden City, N.Y.: Doubleday & Co., 1985)
Plöger   O. Plöger, *Sprüche Salomos* (*Proverbia*) (Biblischer Kommentar
              17; Neukirchen: Neukirchener Verlag, 1984).
Rahlfs   *Septuaginta,* ed. A. Rahlfs (Stuttgart: Deutsche Bibelstiftung,
              1939)
REB   *Revised English Bible*
S   Syriac, the Peshitta version

SBLDS	Society of Biblical Literature Dissertation Series
Skehan	P. W. Skehan, *Studies in Israelite Poetry and Wisdom* (CBQ Monograph Series 1; Washington: Catholic Biblical Association, 1971).
T	Targum
Toy	C. H. Toy, *A Critical and Exegetical Commentary on the Book of Proverbs* (International Critical Commentary; New York: Scribners, 1908).
TUAT	*Texte aus der Umwelt des Alten Testaments*
V	Vulgate
VT	*Vetus Testamentum*
Whybray	*Proverbs* (New Century Bible Commentary; Grand Rapids: Eerdmans, 1994).
ZAH	*Zeitschrift für Althebräistik*
ZAW	*Zeitschrift für die alttestamentliche Wissenschaft*

SELECT BIBLIOGRAPHY

I. *Commentaries in Series*

Alonso Schökel, L., and J. Vilchez. *Proverbios,* 1984. Nueva Biblia Española. Sapienciales I. Madrid: Ediciones Cristiandad, 1984.

Barucq, A. *Le livre des Proverbes.* Sources bibliques. Paris: J. Gabalda, 1964.

Cohen, A., and A. J. Rosenberg. *Proverbs,* 1985. Soncino Books on the Bible.

Delitzsch, F. *Proverbs of Solomon.* C. F. Keil and F. Delitzsch, Commentary on the Old Testament. Edinburgh: T. & T. Clark, 1875.

Ehrlich, A. B. "Die Sprüche," in *Randglossen zur Hebräischen Bibel,* vol. 6. Leipzig: J. C. Hinrichs, 1913.

Fox, M. *Proverbs.* Anchor Bible. New York: Doubleday & Co. Forthcoming in 1999.

Gemser, B. *Sprüche Salomos,* 1963. Handbuch zum Alten Testament. Tübingen: J. C. B. Mohr (Paul Siebeck), 1963

Kidner, D. *The Proverbs.* Tyndale Old Testament Commentaries. London: Tyndale Press, 1964.

McKane, W. *Proverbs: A New Approach.* Old Testament Library. London: SCM Press; Philadelphia: Westminster Press, 1970.

Meinhold, A. *Die Sprüche.* Zürcher Bibelkommentare 16. Zurich: Theologischer Verlag, 1991.

Murphy, R. E. *Proverbs.* Word Biblical Commentary. Dallas, Tex.: Word, 1998.

Oesterley, W. O. E. *The Book of Proverbs.* Westminster Commentaries. London: Methuen & Co., 1929.

Plöger, O. *Sprüche Salomos (Proverbia).* Biblischer Kommentar 17. Neukirchen-Vluyn: Neukirchener Verlag, 1984.

Ringgren, H. *Sprüche.* Das Alte Testament Deutsch 16/1. Tübingen: Vandenhoek & Ruprecht, 1962.

Scott, R. B. Y. *Proverbs, Ecclesiastes.* Anchor Bible 18. Garden City, N.Y.: Doubleday & Co., 1965.

Toy, C. H. *A Critical and Exegetical Commentary on the Book of Proverbs.* International Critical Commentary. New York: Scribners, 1908.

Van Leeuwen, R. C. "The Book of Proverbs." *The New Interpreter's Bible.* Nashville: Abingdon Press, 1997.

Whybray, R. N. *Proverbs.* New Century Bible Commentary. Cambridge: Cambridge University Press, 1994.

II. *Monographs*

Baumann, G. *Die Weisheitsgestalt in Proverbien 1–9: Traditionsgeschichtliche und theologische Studien,* 1996.

Blenkinsopp, J. *Wisdom and Law in the Old Testament: The Ordering of Life in Israel and Early Judaism.* Oxford and New York: Oxford University Press, 1995.

Boström, L. *The God of the Sages: The Portrayal of God in the Book of Proverbs.* Stockholm: Almqvist & Wiksell International, 1990.

Bryce, G. *A Legacy of Wisdom.* Lewisburg, Pa.: Bucknell University Press, 1979.

Camp, C. V. *Wisdom and the Feminine in the Book of Proverbs.* Decatur, Ga.: Almond Press, 1985.

Cook, J. *The Septuagint of Proverbs: Jewish and/or Hellenistic Proverbs? Concerning the Hellenistic Colouring of LXX Proverbs,* Supplements to *VT* 69. Leiden and New York: Brill, 1997.

Fontaine, C. *Traditional Sayings in the Old Testament.* Sheffield: Almond Press, 1982.

Golka, F. W. *The Leopard's Spots: Biblical and African Wisdom in Proverbs.* Edinburgh: T. & T. Clark, 1993.

Lang, B. *Wisdom and the Book of Proverbs: An Hebrew Goddess Redefined.* New York: Pilgrim Press, 1986.

McCreesh, T. P. *Biblical Sound and Sense: Poetic Sound Patterns in Proverbs 10–29.* Sheffield: Sheffield Academic Press, 1991.

Maier, C. *Die "fremde Frau" in Proverbien 1–9: Eine exegetische und sozialgeschichtliche Studie.* Göttingen: Vandenhoek & Ruprecht, 1995.

Murphy, R. E. *The Tree of Life: An Exploration of Biblical Wisdom Literature.* Grand Rapids: Eerdmans, 1996.

Perry, T. A. *Wisdom Literature and the Structure of Proverbs.* University Park, Pa.: Pennsylvania State University Press, 1993.

von Rad, G. *Wisdom in Israel.* Nashville: Abingdon Press, 1972.

Skehan, P. W. *Studies in Israelite Poetry and Wisdom* (CBQ Monograph Series 1; Washington, D.C.: Catholic Biblical Association, 1971).

Washington, H. C. *Wealth and Poverty in the Instruction of Amenemope and the Hebrew Proverbs.* Ann Arbor, Mich.: U.M.I., 1994.

Weeks, S. *Early Israelite Wisdom.* Oxford: Clarendon Press, 1994.

Westermann, C. *Roots of Wisdom: The Oldest Proverbs of Israel and Other Peoples.* Louisville, Ky.: Westminster John Knox Press, 1995.

Whybray, R. N. *Wealth and Poverty in the Book of Proverbs.* Sheffield: JSOT Press, 1990.

―――. *The Book of Proverbs: A Survey of Modern Study,* Leiden and New York: Brill, 1995.

III. *Articles*

Aletti, J.-N., "Séduction et parole en Proverbes I–IX, *VT* 27 (1977): 129–44.

Alter, R. "The Poetry of Wit," *The Art of Biblical Poetry.* New York: Basic Books, 1985.

―――. "Antologia o opera unitaria? Elementi intratestuali del Libro dei Proverbi," *Il libro dei Proverbi: Tradizione redazione teologia,* ed. A. Passaro et al., 1999.

―――. "Proverbs as a Source for Wisdom of Solomon." *Treasures of Wisdom: Ben Sira and the Book of Wisdom.* FS Maurice Gilbert. Ed. N. Calduch-Benages. BETL. Louvain: Leuven University Press, 1999, 255–63.

Barré, M. L. " 'Fear of God' and the World View of Wisdom," *Biblical Theology Bulletin* 11 (1981): 41–43.

Clifford, R. "Woman Wisdom in the Book of Proverbs," in *Biblische Theologie und gesellschaftlicher Wandel* (FS Norbert Lohfink), ed. G. Braulik, 1993, 61–72.

Crenshaw, J. "The Sage in Proverbs," *The Sage in Israel and the Ancient Near East,* 205–16. Ed. J. G. Gammie and L. G. Perdue. Winona Lake, Ind.: Eisenbrauns, 1990.

Day, J. "Foreign Semitic Influence on the Wisdom of Israel and Its Appropriation in the Book of Proverbs," in *Wisdom in Ancient Israel,* 55–70. FS J. A. Emerton. Ed. J. Day et al. Cambridge and New York: Cambridge University Press, 1995.

Fontaine, C. R. "Wisdom in Proverbs," in *Search of Wisdom,* FS John G. Gammie, 99–114. Ed. L. G. Perdue et al. Louisville, Ky.: Westminster John Knox Press, 1993.

Fox, M. V. "Words for Wisdom," *ZAH* 6 (1993): 149–65.

―――. "Words for Folly," *ZAH* 10 (1997): 4–15.

―――. "The Social Location of the Book of Proverbs," in *Texts, Temples, and Traditions.* FS Menahem Haran. Winona Lake, Ind.: Eisenbrauns, 1996, 227–39.

Gilbert, M. "Le discours de la Sagesse en Proverbes, 8. Structure et cohérence," in *La Sagesse de l'Ancien Testament,* ed. M. Gilbert, 1979, 202–18.

Greenfield, J. C. "The Wisdom of Ahiqar," in *Wisdom in Ancient Israel* (FS J. A. Emerton), 1995, 43–52.

Kitchen, K. A. "Proverbs and Wisdom Books of the Ancient Near East: The Factual History of a Literary Form," *Tyndale Bulletin* 28 (1977): 60–114.

Koch, K. "Is There a Doctrine of Retribution in the Old Testament?" in *Theodicy in the Old Testament,* 57–87. Ed. J. L. Crenshaw. Philadelphia: Fortress Press; London: SPCK, 1983.

Kugel, J. "Wisdom and the Anthological Temper," *Prooftexts* 17 (1997): 9–32.

Leeuwen, R. C. "Liminality and Worldview in Proverbs 1–9," *Semeia* 50 (1990): 111–44.

Levenson, J. D. "The Sources of Torah: Psalm 119 and the Modes of Revelation in Second Temple Judaism," in *Ancient Israelite Religion,* 566–67. (FS F. M. Cross), ed. P. D. Miller and P. D. Hanson. Philadelphia: Fortress Press, 1987.

McCreesh, T. P. "Wisdom as Wife: Proverbs 31:10–31," *Revue Biblique* 92 (1985): 25–46.

Murphy, R. E. "Wisdom and Creation," *JBL* 104 (1985): 3–11.

———. "The Personification of Wisdom," in *Wisdom in Ancient Israel* (FS J. A. Emerton), 1995, 222–33.

Newsom, C. A. "Woman and the Discourse of Patriarchal Wisdom," in *Gender and Difference in Ancient Israel.* Ed. P. L. Day. Minneapolis: Fortress Press, 1989, 142–60.

Perdue, L. "Liminality as a Social Setting for Wisdom Instructions," *Zeitschrift für die alttestamentliche Wissenschaft* 93 (1981): 114–26.

Skehan, P. W. "Structures in Poems on Wisdom: Proverbs 8 and Sirach 24," *CBQ* 41 (1979): 365–79.

Washington, H. C. "The Strange Woman (*'šh zrh/nkryh*) of Proverbs 1–9 and Post-Exilic Judaean Society," *Second Temple Studies,* vol. 2: *Temple and Community in the Persian Period,* ed. T. C. Eskenazi and K. H. Richards, 1994, 217–42.

Wolters, A. "Proverbs XXXI 10–31 as Heroic Hymn: A Form-Critical Analysis, *VT* 38 (1988): 446–57.

Yee, G. "An Analysis of Prov 8:22–31 according to Style and Structure," *Zeitschrift für die alttestamentliche Wissenschaft* 94 (1982): 58–62.

———. " 'I Have Perfumed My Bed with Myrrh': The Foreign Woman (*'iššāh zārāh*) in Proverbs 1–9," *Journal for the Study of the Old Testament* 43 (1989): 53–68.

INTRODUCTION

The book of Proverbs consists of several collections of instructions, speeches, poems, and two-line sayings. The titles of the collections are 1:1; 10:1; 22:17 (and its appendix 24:23); 25:1; 30:1; 31:1. There is no title to the concluding poem in 31:10–31, but it is clearly marked off by its alphabetic structure. The title in 1:1, "The Proverbs of Solomon son of David, king of Israel," is the heading not only of chaps. 1–9 but of the entire book, for the sum of the numerical values of its Hebrew consonants is 930, which is close to the actual 934 lines of the book.

The present book has nine sections.

Introduction to the Book (1:1–7)
  I. Collection of Wisdom Lectures and Speeches (1:8–9:18)
     1. Lecture I: The Deadly Alternative to Parental Wisdom (1:8–19)
     2. Wisdom Poem I: The Risk of Spurning Me (1:20–33)
     3. Lecture II: Seek Wisdom and Yahweh Will Keep You Safe (2:1–22)
     4. Lecture III: Trust in God Leads to Prosperity (3:1–12)
     5. Interlude: Wisdom's Benefits and Prestige (3:13–20)
     6. Lecture IV: Justice toward the Neighbor Brings Blessing (3:21–35)
     7. Lecture V: A Father's Example (4:1–9)
     8. Lecture VI: Two Ways of Living Life (4:10–19)
     9. Lecture VII: With Your Whole Being Heed My Words and Live (4:20–27)
    10. Lecture VIII: The Wrong and the Right Woman (5:1–23)
    11. Interlude: Four Short Pieces (6:1–19)
    12. Lecture IX: The Dangers of Adultery (6:20–35)
    13. Lecture X: The Deceptive Woman (7:1–27)
    14. Wisdom Poem II: Become My Disciple and I Will Bless You (8:1–36)
    15. Wisdom Poem III: The Two Women Invite Passersby to Their Banquets (9:1–6 + 11; 13–18; vv. 7–10 + 12 are assorted sayings)

Collecting, or anthologizing, traditional material in the ancient Near East was a recognized way of creating new literary works. There are many examples of artistic anthologizing. In Mesopotamia, lengthy literary works such as *Gilgamesh, Atrahasis,* and *Enuma elish* contained old stories worked into a new synthesis. Biblical examples are the Pentateuch, the Deuteronomistic History (Deuteronomy to Kings), and the Isaiah scroll. Anthologists reorganized inherited material in the light of new concepts and purposes; they altered, added, and subtracted characters, plots, and themes. In Mesopotamia, for example, legends of King Gilgamesh were reworked into an epic about a hero's search for immortality. Biblical anthologist-authors of the Deuteronomistic History (Deuteronomy to Kings) wove stories of local heroes, an account of the rise of David, and official chronicles into a long history of Israel from Sinai to the exile. Similarly, the author-editors of Proverbs not only collected instructions and sayings but also rearranged and reshaped them.

The material was given fresh meaning through the new juxtapositions. The ten instructions of chaps. 1–9, for example, resemble Egyptian and Mesopotamian instructions typically addressed to youths beginning their public careers. The instructions are now juxtaposed to speeches of a personified Woman Wisdom seeking disciples. The novel placement elevates Proverbs' instructions to a metaphorical level, making them suitable to an audience much wider than young men. Exhortations to act prudently and be faithful to home and profession (traditional aims of the instruction) are broadened into exhortations to seek wisdom before everything else in life. Once the metaphorical level has been established in chaps. 1–9, the sayings and poems in the following chapters gain depth and breadth. Traditional elements appear in a new configuration.

The configuration is dominated by a polarity. In chaps. 1–9, the most important polarity is that between Woman Wisdom and the deceptive woman. The book itself highlights this polarity by its summarizing diptych in chap. 9, where the two women are like debaters. Wisdom makes her final appeal in vv. 1–6, 11 and Folly makes hers in vv. 13–18.[1] It should be noted, however, that the

1. Woman Folly is meant to summarize the "foreign" woman in chaps. 2, 5, 6, and 7. See M. V. Fox, "Ideas of Wisdom in Proverbs 1–9," *JBL* 116 (1997): 618.

deceptive woman is only one of *two* enemies of Wisdom. As chap. 2 makes clear, her two enemies are deceptive men *and* their way (always plural, 1:8–19; 2:12–15; 4:10–19) and the deceptive woman (always singular, 2:16–19; chap. 5; 6:20–35; chap. 7; 9:13–18). There are other polarities as well: the male father (both parents in 1:8 and 6:20) *and* female Wisdom (see below). A final and pervasive polarity is the two ways—the way of the righteous *and* the way of the wicked.

By the end of chap. 2 an interpretive system has been established and the main polarities introduced. Proverbs 1:8–19 introduces the father (and mother), the deceptive men, and the two ways; 1:20–33 introduces personified Wisdom; chap. 2 introduces the quest for wisdom and identifies the twin dangers of deceptive men (vv. 12–15) and the deceptive woman (vv. 16–19). By the end of chap. 2, therefore, the major actors and concepts have been presented; they will remain in productive opposition until the end of the section. Chapter 9 closes the whole section by pitching one woman against the other.

Chapters 2 through 9 introduce no new major actor or topic. Rather one finds here elaborations of what has been sketched in chaps. 1–2: a second speech of Wisdom (chap. 8) and an encomium of Wisdom and her benefits (3:13–20), three warnings against the deceptive woman (chap. 5; 6:20–35; chap. 7), and six parental speeches to the son (3:1–12, 21–35; 4:1–9, 10–19, 20–27; 6:1–19), as well as the father's warning against the men and their way (4:10–19). By this time, readers are sufficiently familiar with the relationships to draw their own conclusions.

1. Date of Composition and Editing

Three times King Solomon (mid-tenth century B.C.E.) is said to be the author of Proverbs (1:1) or of independent collections (10:1; 25:1). The references cannot be used to date the book, however, for wisdom literature was conventionally ascribed to Solomon, as psalms were ascribed to David and laws to Moses. There is no reason, however, to doubt that some of the book is "by Solomon," for as king he would have collected, sponsored, or possibly even written, various kinds of writing, including literature (*belles lettres*), as 1 Kings 4:29–31 recognizes.

Proverbs contains an important chronological clue in 25:1: "These also are proverbs of Solomon, which the men of King Hezekiah collected." Hezekiah was king of Judah from 715 to 687 B.C.E. and was reckoned a reformer by 1 Kings 18–20 and especially by 2 Chronicles 29–32. Proverbs 25:1 states that the king added proverbs to an already existing collection under King Solomon's name. The title headed at least chaps. 25–26, for these chapters are an artistic unity (see under 25:1). To what Solomonic collection were Hezekiah's proverbs added? Probably all or part of "the proverbs of Solomon" in 10:1–22:16. Thus the book itself says that by the late eighth century B.C.E. there existed a collection of proverbs "of Solomon" to which royal scribes added a second collection.

Attempts have been made to date Proverbs from other data—its language, editing devices, and themes—but none of these provides assured results. To date Proverbs from its language one must determine to which period of the Hebrew language the book belongs. Two phases of the language are generally distinguished prior to the rise of rabbinic Hebrew as a literary language in the first or second centuries C.E.: (1) preexilic Hebrew (= pre-sixth century B.C.E.), which ceased to be a living language after the Babylonian exile; (2) Late Biblical Hebrew (in the later books of the Bible), which was to some extent an imitation of the preexilic language.[2] The majority of scholars believe that the bulk of the sayings of Proverbs are preexilic or exilic (= "Biblical Hebrew") and that most of the instructions and speeches (chaps. 1–9) as well as the final editing are postexilic (= "Late Biblical Hebrew").

One can readily see the difficulty of determining where the Hebrew of Proverbs fits within this broad classification. For one thing, Late Biblical Hebrew is often imitative of earlier Hebrew, and, for another, archaic features of aphorisms are readily modernized by copyists. An example of modernizing is the rhetorical question in 22:29 (cf. 29:20): "Do you see (*ḥāzîtā*) a man skilled in his craft?" In 26:12, the more ancient word *ḥāzîtā* is modernized to *rā'îtā:* "Have you seen (*rā'îtā*) a man wise in his own eyes?"

Proverbs contains some early linguistic features. Among possibly early features are the use of the negative *bal* (about ten times), the qal passive (e.g., 10:24 and 13:11, unrecognized by the Masoretes), and the archaic words *pā'al* ("to do" instead of *'āśāh*), *geber,* "man," and *ḥārûṣ,* "gold." Further indications of a preexilic date are the sparing use of the object marker *'et* (only fifteen times) and of the relative *'ăšer* (only eleven times). The article, which is not used in early poetry, occurs only about 53 times (compared to nearly 400 instances in the Psalms).[3]

Proverbs has some Aramaisms but these in themselves are no argument for a late date, for they are also found sporadically in preexilic texts. A large number in a book, however, would suggest a postexilic date when Aramaic became the language of commerce and government. Those listed by Max Wagner in his study do not constitute an argument for a late date for the book, for many are preexilic, as Wagner himself acknowledges.[4] There are no Grecisms in the

---

2. For a succinct and reliable exposition of the evidence, see A. Sáenz-Badillos, *A History of the Hebrew Language* (Cambridge: Cambridge University Press, 1993). Much of the research has been done in prose and not with poetry, but Proverbs is exclusively poetry.

3. Sáenz-Badillos, *History of the Hebrew Language,* 58–62.

4. M. Wagner, *Die lexikalischen und grammatikalischen Aramäismen im alttestamentlichen Hebräisch* (BZAW 96; Berlin: Töpelmann, 1966). It is interesting that the great majority of Aramaisms occur in chaps. 10–31 rather than in chaps. 1–9, which are often considered later.

book, which suggests a pre-Hellenistic date (before 333 B.C.E.). In sum, the book cannot be dated with certainty from its language.[5]

Another possible means of dating Proverbs is its consonant-numbers. The final editor(s) of Proverbs used numerology to underline the unity of the book and to let copyists know its original parameters, or perhaps simply as an encoded structure in chaps. 10 and 25–26 (see commentary below). P. W. Skehan developed an observation made by earlier scholars that the numerical values of the Hebrew letters of "The Proverbs of Solomon" in 10:1 add up to 375 (š = 300; l = 30; m = 40; h = 5), which happens to be the number of single-line proverbs in 10:1–22:16. Moreover, the superscription to the entire book in 1:1, "The Proverbs of Solomon, son of David, king of Israel," adds up to 930, which is close to the 934 lines of the present book. The numerical editing evident in 1:1 could only have been done on the complete book as we know it. Consonant-numbers are not attested before the second century B.C.E., which *might* indicate a late date for the final editing. Unfortunately, however, consonant numbers may have been used much earlier than the second century and thus cannot be used for precise dating.

Another way of dating the book is through its themes, but this approach does not provide sure results either. The argument, for example, that *tôrāh*, "law, teaching," and *miṣwāh*, "command," in Proverbs refer to the Torah of Moses, which would presuppose the missions of Ezra and Nehemiah in the fifth century B.C.E., is unconvincing. "Law" and "command" in Proverbs do not refer to the Mosaic Torah, as is pointed out under 28:4, 7, 9, 18. In Proverbs, the words lack concreteness and specificity and refer not to judicial or cultic norms but to prudent advice (which is nonetheless considered inspired and from God).[6]

Some scholars propose that the warnings to young men to avoid relationships with foreign women (*zārāh, nokrîyāh*) reflect the prohibitions in the books of Ezra and Nehemiah against marriages with foreigners who were outside the lineage of the "father's house."[7] Such warnings against the foreign woman, however, are attested in the Egyptian *Instruction of Any* and there are similar

5. A recent summary of the arguments for dating, with preference for a late date, is in H. C. Washington, *Wealth and Poverty in the Instruction of Amenemope and the Hebrew Prophets* (SBLDS 142; Atlanta: Scholars Press, 1994), 116–22.

6. J. D. Levenson, "The Sources of Torah: Psalm 119 and the Modes of Revelation in Second Temple Judaism," in *Ancient Israelite Religion* (F. M. Cross volume), ed. P. D. Miller, P. D. Hanson, and S. D. McBride (Philadelphia: Fortress Press, 1987), 566–67.

7. C. Maier, *Die 'fremde Frau' in Proverbien 1–9: Eine exegetische sozialgeschichtliche Studie* (Orbis Biblicus et Orientalis 144; Göttingen: Vandenhoeck & Ruprecht, 1995), 177–214; H. C. Washington, "The Strange Woman (*'šh zrh/nkryh*) of Proverbs 9 and Post-Exilic Judaean Society," in *Second Temple Studies, vol. 2: Temple and Community in the Persian Period,* ed. T. C. Eskenazi and K. H. Richards; Sheffield: JSOT Press, 1994), 217–42.

Babylonian warnings against unsuitable partners for moral reasons. Moreover, Proverbs' warnings are not against exogamous marriages but against extra-marital affairs. Readers in the Second Temple period may well have read the warnings against the foreign woman with exogamy in mind (it was a concern of the period), but it does not follow that the texts themselves were written with that purpose. Consequently, the prohibitions cannot be used for dating the com-position of chaps. 1–9.

Despite the difficulty of assigning a specific date for the final redaction of Proverbs, it is possible to give a very general sketch of the development of the book. With the rise of the monarchy in the early tenth century, palace scribes would have produced diplomatic and liturgical texts as well as the kind of *belles lettres* (including "wisdom" texts) current in Levantine courts. By the late eighth century, a collection attributed to Solomon was in circulation when "the servants of Hezekiah" added a second collection to it (25:1). By this time, pre-sumably, the familiar two-line saying had become a subgenre. The saying em-ployed the contrasting types of the wise and the foolish, the righteous and the wicked, the impious and the devout. "The Words of the Wise" (22:17–24:22), because of its obvious indebtedness to the Egyptian instruction *Amenemope,* was most likely written during the period of trade and cultural exchange with Egypt during the monarchy (cf. 24:21 "Fear Yahweh *and the king,* my son"). In short, it is quite probable that all (or a substantial part) of chaps. 10–29 were in circulation before the end of the monarchy.

At what period chaps. 1–9 were written and prefaced to the anthology is dif-ficult to say. There are no allusions to historical events in the chapters and lin-guistic and thematic arguments are not conclusive. The argument that the long poems are later than the brief sayings has no validity in view of the coexistence of instructions and sayings in early literatures. Given the lack of evidence for the final editing, perhaps the best course is to suppose that Proverbs was edited in the same general movement as much of Israel's other sacred literature in the early Second Temple period, that is, in the period from the sixth to the fourth centuries B.C.E.[8] The consonant-numbers in the titles suggest an editor who be-lieved the book had its own unity and wanted to give it final definition.

2. Historical Context

The authorship and the audience of Proverbs have been much debated over the last four decades. Before the 1960s it was generally assumed that the book

---

8. The argument that Hebrew *sôpîyâ* in 31:27 is a wordplay on Greek *sophia,* thus presup-posing a Hellenistic date at least for the final poem, is not a strong one. The similarity could be a coincidence, and there was also Greek influence before Alexander. See A. Wolters, "*Sôpîyâ* (Prov. 31:27) as Hymnic Participle and Play on *Sophia,*" *JBL* 104 (1985): 577–87.

was the work of sages, who were assumed to have been a distinct group in Israel on the basis of Jer. 18:18; Prov. 1:5; 22:17; 24:23; Job 15:18. In the 1960s, H. J. Hermisson proposed that wisdom literature was composed for use in Israelite schools connected to the royal court.[9] A competing theory, represented by C. Westermann and F. W. Golka among others, proposes that the middle section of Proverbs (chaps. 10–29) were mostly oral sayings originating in the daily life of ordinary people such as farmers, artisans, laborers, slaves, and housewives in preexilic times.[10]

Neither theory is adequate as a complete explanation. Proponents of a school origin for Proverbs point to Egyptian analogies. However, Egyptian wisdom literature was used in schools, not composed for them.[11] Egyptian authors were not school teachers, but fathers teaching their sons. Likewise, the teacher in Proverbs is not a school teacher but a father (with the mother in 1:8 and 6:2), an identity that is especially evident in 4:3–4.

The theory that holds chaps. 10–29 were originally oral sayings of villagers and farmers correctly highlights the origin within the family for some proverbs. A village or family origin cannot be inferred from the contents of the proverbs, however. Though some topics are at home in farm and field, the perspective is that of a royal court. Proverbs 11:26 speaks of farming from the view of the wealthy: "Who holds back grain the people damn, / but blessings are on the head of one who sells it." The perspective is often that of kings and courtiers (16:14; 23:1–11; especially 25:2–7).

What is the most likely social location of Proverbs? As 25:1 suggests, "the men of Hezekiah" collected them. They were employees of the palace charged with writing and recording—in other words, scribes. The best proof is the sophistication of the writing and the familiarity with foreign literature evident in the sayings and instructions. The statement of M. Fox puts the matter well: "Learned clerks, at least some of them the king's men, were the membrane through which principles, sayings and coinages, folk and otherwise, were filtered. The central collections of Proverbs are their filtrate, an essentially homogeneous one: In the end, it is *their* work and

9. *Studien zur israelitischen Spruchweisheit* (Wissenschaftliche Monographien zum Alten Testament 28; Neukirchen-Vluyn: Neukirchener Verlag, 1968). For a judicious survey of the debate, see R. N. Whybray, *The Book of Proverbs: A Survey of Modern Study* (History of Biblical Interpretation Series 1; Leiden: Brill, 1995), 1–33, and M. V. Fox, "The Social Location of the Book of Proverbs," in *Texts, Temples, and Traditions* (M. Haran volume), ed. M. V. Fox et al. (Winona Lake, Ind.: Eisenbrauns, 1996), 227–39.

10. C. Westermann, *Roots of Wisdom: The Oldest Proverbs of Israel and Other Peoples* (Louisville, Ky.: Westminster John Knox Press, 1995); F. W. Golka, *The Leopard's Spots: Biblical and African Wisdom in Proverbs* (Edinburgh: T. & T. Clark, 1993).

11. H. Brunner, *Die Weisheitsbücher der Ägypter: Lehren für das Leben* (Zurich: Artemis, 1991), 62–75; Fox, "Social Location of the Book of Proverbs," 229–32.

their idea of wisdom that we are reading, and it is, not surprisingly, quite coherent."[12]

In sum, the book of Proverbs is an anthology of collections of sayings (some of which were folk in origin) and instructions. The authors were scribes of the royal court who were responsible for the production of literature for temple and court. As Fox suggests, one should not think of them as courtiers but as working scribes, clerics or "clerks" in the medieval sense.

3. The Wisdom Literature That Proverbs Inherited

The authors of Proverbs were heirs to a centuries-old tradition of wisdom literature.[13] Included in the tradition were the two major genres found in Proverbs—the instruction of a father to a son and the concise saying. Father-son instructions are attested as far back as the third millennium both in Mesopotamia and in Egypt, and proverbs are well-nigh universal. In Mesopotamia, more than twenty-eight collections of Sumerian proverbs are attested (third and second millennia) as well as Akkadian collections. Though Egypt does not have any proverbial collections as such, some proverbs are found within the instructions.

Three Assumptions of Ancient Wisdom

Before examining the instructions and sayings, we should note three assumptions of ancient authors: Wisdom was (1) practical, (2) mediated through a hierarchy of agencies, and (3) "institutional."

1. Wisdom had to do with practical rather than theoretical knowledge—knowing how to do something, *savoir faire*. A king was wise because he knew how to govern well (*ars gubernandi*, "the art of governing"), wage war effectively, and give the right decisions. A jeweler was wise because he knew how to cut and set gems; a woman was wise because she knew how to manage a household.

Wisdom could also refer to culture as well as to craft. The beliefs, social forms, and material traits of a particular group were considered as given, part of the order of creation. They were thus informed by wisdom, for God made the world "in wisdom."

2. Wisdom belonged to the gods and was mediated through a succession of agents to human beings.[14] The process of mediation was particularly clear in

12. Fox, "Social Location of the Book of Proverbs," 239.

13. W. G. Lambert notes that "Though [the term "wisdom literature"] is thus foreign to ancient Mesopotamia, it has been used for a group of texts which correspond in subject matter with the Hebrew Wisdom books, and may be retained as a short description" (*BWL*, 1).

14. The following remarks are indebted to C. Wilcke, "Göttliche und menschliche Weisheit im Alten Orient," in *Weisheit*, Archäologie der literarischen Kommunikation 3, ed. A. Assmann (Munich: Fink, 1991), 259–70.

Mesopotamia. All the gods were wise but one god in particular was preeminently so. This god, Ea (Enki in Sumerian), shared his expertise and clever proposals with the other deities. The gods created the human race as their servants and gave to them the knowledge and culture (e.g., writing, metallurgy, farming, rituals) they needed to live properly as human beings and be good servants of the gods.

Mesopotamian mythological texts speak of seven sages (*apkallu*) who brought knowledge and culture to the human race in the period before the Flood. After the Flood they were succeeded by seven sages (*ummānu*), according to some ritual texts. Human participation grew progressively greater in the transmission of divine knowledge to the human race. At the end of the chain of transmission was the Babylonian school that was run by learned scribes.

Human beings needed wisdom from the gods to be civilized and to be good servants of the gods. Some Mesopotamian creation accounts even depicted the creation of man in two stages. In the first stage, the race lived in an animal state; only in the second stage did human beings receive the necessary culture (writing, farming, kingship, tools) to live at a human level.[15] Wisdom was thus thoroughly religious. The point needs stressing because some scholars have asserted that biblical wisdom literature was originally secular, only later becoming religious by being linked to "religious" traditions such as the exodus, Sinai covenant, and the prophets.[16] The fact is, rather, that ancient Near Eastern wisdom was always part of a religious worldview.

3. Heavenly wisdom comes to the human race mediated by earthly institutions or authorities such as the king, scribes and the literature the scribes write, and heads of families. In Proverbs, the mediating institutions or authorities are the king, wisdom writings (cf. 1:2, 6), and the father (with the mother in 1:8 and 6:20).

Mesopotamian Wisdom Instructions and Proverbs

The oldest and most widely known Mesopotamian instruction is the *Instructions of Shuruppak,*[17] in which the primordial hero Shuruppak gives rules

---

15. R. J. Clifford, *Creation Accounts in the Ancient Near East and in the Bible* (CBQ Monograph Series 26; Washington, D.C.: Catholic Biblical Association, 1994), 42–49. Two-stage creation accounts include The Sumerian Flood Story, How Grain Came to Sumer, and The Rulers of Lagash.

16. Exponents of the view include H. D. Preuss, *Einführung in die alttestamentliche Weisheitsliteratur* (Stuttgart, 1987) and McKane in his commentary.

17. A partial translation is given in *ANET,* 594–95. See also *BWL,* 92–95. The Old Babylonian version is in *TUAT* 3.1, which is the source of our translation. For discussion, see B. Alster, *The Instructions of Shuruppak: A Sumerian Proverb Collection* (Mesopotamia 2; Copenhagen: Akademisk Forlag, 1974).

of behavior and wise counsel to his son Ziusudra, the Sumerian equivalent of biblical Noah, the survivor of the Flood. Shuruppak gives the race wisdom so it will not again offend the gods and be destroyed by another flood. The *Instructions* was composed in Sumerian in the mid-third millennium and revised in subsequent editions and in Akkadian translations.

> [1]In that [day], in that far off day,
> in that [ni]ght, in that far dista[nt] night,
> in that [year], in that far distant year—
> at that time there lived one who possessed wisdom, who (with) artful words,
>   who knew the (right) word, in the land of Sumer,
> [5]Shuruppak lived, who possessed wisdom, who (with) artful words, who knew
>   the (right) word, in the land of Sumer.
> Shuruppak counseled his son,
> Shuruppak, the son of Uburtutu,
> [10]counseled Ziusudra, his son:
> "My son, I will counsel (you), may my counsel be accepted,
> Ziusudra, a word will I s[ay] to you, may it be heeded!
> Do not neglect my counsel,
> the word that I have spoken, do not change,
> the counsel of a father is precious, may your neck bow before it.

The individual counsels that follow this introduction are one to three lines in length. The Old Babylonian version (ca. 1800–1600 B.C.E.) has 281 lines and is divided into three sections (lines 1–76, 77–146, and 147–281).

The elaborate introduction, repeated twice, serves to place the sayings under the mantle of the hero Shuruppak and his son Ziusudra. The counsels are quite diverse. Some are humorous, others are admonitions; most are metaphorical in the sense of saying one thing in terms of another.

> [18] Do not build a house in the square; the crowd is (there).
> [19] Do not make a guarantee (for someone); the person will have a hold on you.
> [22–23] Do not go to a place of strife; / the strife will make you a witness.
> [30] The thief is a lion; after he is caught he is a slave!
> [51] You should not curse with violence: it comes back to the hand!
> [63] Do not rape a man's daughter; she will announce it to the courtyard.
> [64–65] Do not drive away a strong man; do not destroy a city wall; / do not drive
>   away a *guruš*-worker, do not turn him away from the city!
> [66–67] A slanderer spins his eyes as if with a spindle; / do not stand before his eyes:
>   he changes the judgment of his heart again and again.
> [98–101] With regard to another man's bread, "I will give it to you" is near,[18] / (but) to
>   give it is far heaven's span. / (Even if you say) "I will urge upon the man (the
>   promise) 'I will give it to you,'" / he will not give it to you: the bread has
>   already been consumed.

18. "Near" seems to correspond to English "to speak rashly."

$^{132-34}$Regarding harvesttime, the very precious days, / collect like a slave girl, eat like a lady, / my son, eat like a slave girl, eat like a lady—thus shall it be indeed.

$^{171-72}$Fate is like a wet riverbank; / it makes a person's feet slip.

$^{173-75}$The older brother is actually (like) a father, the older sister is actually (like) a mother! / May you heed your older brother, / may you bend your neck to your older sister for the sake of your mother.

Most of the sentences are counsels to perform, or not perform, a specific action for a stated reason (lines 18, 19, 22–23, 51, 63, 64–65, 132–34; 173–75). Several are observations (lines 66–67, 98–101, 171–72). Generally, the advice is not as specific and detailed as those of Egyptian instructions. Some counsels are blunt (lines 18, 19) but most are indirect and metaphorical. Most of the commands explain why, or give a reason for, the recommended behavior: for example, "Do not rape a man's daughter; she will announce it to the courtyard" (line 63). As is very clear from the example, the rationale need not be moral but can be based on pure self-interest—the trouble that comes from criminal behavior.

A Babylonian collection written in Akkadian, called the *Counsels of Wisdom,* originally consisted of perhaps 160 lines, at least one part of which is addressed to "my son." It was written in the Kassite period (ca. 1500–1200 B.C.E.).[19] The "son" is the typical recipient of instructions in the ancient Near East, though the expression "my son" is a regular address only in biblical and Mesopotamian literature. *Counsels of Wisdom* offers advice on a series of topics: improper speech, avoiding strife and placating enemies, kindness to the needy, the danger of favoritism to a slave girl, the danger of marrying a prostitute, the trustworthiness required of a representative, the importance of courteous speech, and the duties and benefits of religion. One topic—avoiding bad companions—is a theme of all wisdom literature and deserves examination.

^{21}Don't stop to talk with a frivolous person,
Nor go consult with a [   ] who has nothing to do.
With good intentions you will do their thinking for them,
You will diminish your own accomplishment, abandon your own course.
You will play false to your own, wiser, thinking.
. . . .
^{26}Hold your tongue, watch what you say.
A man's pride: the great value on your lips.
Insolence and insult should be abhorrent to you.
Speak nothing slanderous, no untrue report.
The frivolous person is of no account.

---

19. The translation is from *BM,* 328–31. Translations of several lines are from *BWL,* 96–107.

Lines 21 and 26 give the motive: frivolous companions harm one's standing in the community by lessening the value of what one says. Similarly, Proverbs counsels the avoidance of evil companions for many of the same reasons (22:24–25; 23:17; 24:1, 19).

Counsels of Wisdom (lines 31–55) warns against getting embroiled in strife and concludes with advice on how to deal with an enemy. We quote lines 42–49 here:

> ⁴²Do no evil to the man who disputes with you,
> Requite with good the one who does evil to you.
> Be fair to your enemy,
> Let your mood be cheerful to your opponent.
> Be it your ill-wisher, tre[at him generous]ly.
> Make up your mind to no evil,
> Suc[h is not] acceptable [to the] gods,
> Evil [   ] is abhorrent to [   ] Marduk.

Make peace with your enemies and forswear revenge. Planning evil against another offends the god Marduk. Similar advice against vengeance is given in Prov. 24:17–18 and especially 25:21–22: "If your enemy is hungry give him food to eat, / if he is thirsty give him water to drink, / for you will scoop fiery coals upon his head, / and Yahweh will reward you." Proverbs gives a pragmatic reason for not exacting vengeance oneself—it is a divine task and human beings could short-circuit the process to their own hurt (cf. especially 24:17–18).

Because finding a suitable marriage partner is a major theme in Proverbs, it is worth quoting *Counsels of Wisdom* on the topic (lines 72–79).

> ⁷²Don't marry a prostitute, whose husbands are legion,
> Nor a temple harlot, who is dedicated to a goddess,
> Nor a courtesan, whose intimates are numerous.
> She will not sustain you in your time of trouble,
> She will snigger at you when you are embroiled in controversy.
> She has neither respect nor obedience in her nature.
> Even if she has the run of your house, get rid of her,
> She has ears attuned for another's footfall.

The implicit criteria for a marriage partner are loyalty, affection, and obedience; none of the candidates is capable of unlimited loyalty to one husband. Proverbs does not warn against marrying a specific *class* of woman, however, as does the *Counsels.*

In addition to the instructions noted above, there were also many collections of proverbs—more than twenty-eight of Sumerian origin alone. The collections include material that would not today be considered proverbial in the strict sense—fables, witty expressions, raillery, and jokes. The collections were used to teach the Sumerian language and its rhetoric and, in the process, inculcate wisdom to the students who studied and copied them. The proverbs are notoriously difficult to interpret because scholars do not understand fully the Sumerian language and because the context escapes us. Some Sumerian proverbs from collections 1 and 7 show some of their concerns and rhetoric.[20]

> 1.102He who drinks beer drinks water.
> 1.160Marrying is human. Getting children is divine.
> 7.14The manicurist is himself dressed in dirty rags.
> 7.15Let me drink diluted beer, let me sit in the seat of honor.
> 7.33He gathered everything for himself, but had to slaughter his pig. He gathered everything for himself, but used up his wood.
> 7.70Fate is a dog, well able to bite. It clings like dirty rags.
> 7.77He said, "Woe!" and the boat sank with him. He said "Alas!" and the rudder broke. The young man said, "Oh god!" and the boat reached its destination.
> 7.98The pleasure—it is the beer! The discomfort—it is the expedition.

These "proverbs" are obviously broader than modern proverbs. They range from a vignette with a moral to an enigmatic saying. Several display sardonic humor; others seem deliberately mysterious.

Collections 7.14 and 7.15 are comic contrasts—a manicurist who does not attend to his own appearance, and a poor person drinking the drink of the poor while harboring grandiose ambitions. Collection 7.33 illustrates the folly of preferring luxuries over essentials and squandering precious resources. Collection 7.77 is a little story showing reliance on the gods is more effective than reliance on self. Collection 7.98 is a humorous quotation of someone's preference for staying home over going on an uncomfortable expedition. ("Expedition" is either military or commercial.) Collection 1:160 is an aphorism on human limit and on divine power.

The Sumerian proverbs apparently did not interest Akkadian scribes of a later era. At any rate, they did not copy the repertory but only certain types. It is unlikely that they would have been known to Levantine scribes.[21] A few bilingual proverbs (in the Sumerian and Middle Assyrian languages) survive from the Kassite period (ca. 1500–1200 B.C.E.), and there are bilingual proverbs (in the Sumerian and Babylonian languages) from the late period, as well as some independent Akkadian examples.[22]

---

20. Translations are from B. Alster, *Proverbs of Ancient Sumer,* vol. 1 (Bethesda, Md.: CDL Press, 1997) Alster has translated excerpts in *The Context of Scripture,* ed. W. W. Hallo (Leiden: Brill, 1997), 1.563–68. Excerpts are also in *TUAT* 1.24–30, 33.

21. Lambert notes "the curious phenomenon that [proverbs] do not seem to have become part of stock literature" (*BWL,* 275).

22. For the material, see *BM* 1.337–48 and *BWL,* 222–75. Independent Akkadian examples can be found in *ANET,* 595–96 and *BWL,* 96–107, 213–21, 275–82.

Egyptian Instructions

The instruction was a popular genre throughout the entire history of ancient Egypt. Seventeen examples from different periods have been collected by Hellmut Brunner.[23] The genre seems to have influenced Proverbs. The oldest is the *Instruction of Prince Hardjedef,* composed ca. 2450–2300 B.C.E. (*AEL* 1.58–59) and the latest is *Papyrus Insinger* of the first century C.E. (*AEL* 3.184–217). The *Instruction of Amenemope* of ca. 1100 B.C.E. (*ANET,* 421–25; *AEL* 2.146–63) influenced Prov. 22:17–24:22.

Egyptian instructions[24] were written to assist young people to live happy, prosperous lives and avoid difficulties and mistakes. They give concrete and pragmatic suggestions rather than hold up abstract ideals; for example, "Don't lie to a judge, for telling the truth will render the judge benevolent the next time around; in the long run lies do not work in any case."

The pragmatism and self-interest of such counsels do not mean, however, that Egyptian instructions were secular. On the contrary, they were always religious, for Egyptians believed that the gods implanted an order or dynamism in the world, which they called *maat.*[25] *Maat* can be translated by different English words—truth, order, justice. It is found in nature (the seasons, fruitfulness) no less than the human world (civic and social order, laws, right relationships within families and professions, among neighbors, and in relation to the king). In Egyptian mythology, *maat* is personified as the daughter of Re, the sun-god; she is portrayed crouching with a feather on her knees or head. *Maat* was not revealed but "read off" the course of the world and communicated through maxims and instructions. To help readers fulfill the demands of *maat* in every walk of life was the aim of the instructions. Some scholars suggest that *maat* was the model for personified Wisdom in Proverbs. Some influence is certainly possible, but personified Wisdom in Proverbs has a vigor and personality that goes far beyond the abstract Egyptian goddess.

A final point: the aim of the instructions is to guide the individual rather than to reform society; its readers accepted the world as it was and sought to live according to its rhythms. The instructions do not advocate changing the world but urge individuals to adapt to it.

Some aspects of the instructions are explained by the practices of Egyptian

---

23. *Weisheitsbücher der Ägypter.* See also Lichtheim's introductions to each instruction in *AEL* and R. E. Murphy's remarks in *The Tree of Life,* 2d ed. (Grand Rapids: Eerdmans, 1996), 159–71.

24. The following remarks owe much to Brunner, *Weisheitsbücher der Ägypter,* 11–98.

25. For a summary of research on *maat* and a critique of its relevance for the Bible, see M. V. Fox, "World Order and Ma'at: A Crooked Parallel," *Journal of the Ancient Near Eastern Society* 23 (1995): 37–48.

society. The career of the young man to whom they were addressed was played out, at least initially, within the *famulus* (private secretary) system. Youths entered the households of high officials who trained them in the household. The system was known also in Syria-Palestine: Joseph in the book of Genesis and Ahiqar in *Ahiqar* began as such private secretaries. The young man served the great personage, establishing a relationship of mutual trust, like Joseph with Potiphar (Gen. 39:2) and Pharaoh (Gen. 41:40). In the world of apprenticeship, fidelity to one's master was paramount. The *famulus* system explains the emphasis on some recurrent themes in instructions: delivering messages accurately, avoiding (domestic) quarrels, and guarding against entanglements with women of the household.

In discussing human beings, the instructions use "heart" as the seat of intelligence. A "hard-hearted" person lacks good sense, not compassion. The instructions render character dramatically. One's *actions* reveal one to be either wise or foolish, "heated" or "cool." Fools do not follow the advice of their father or teacher and thus do not behave according to *maat*. Wisdom is the result of education and experience as well as of nature. One learns to be wise by "hearing" (= heeding), an important verb in the exhortations. Egyptian society in most periods was quite open, allowing poor youths to rise to high positions, provided they were teachable and shrewd. For young men from the provinces or from poor households, the instructions were guidebooks to success in the new environment of wealthy households.

The content and tone of the instructions reflected changes within Egyptian society. Instructions of the Old Kingdom (2650–2135 B.C.E.) revolved around the king; but with the decline of kingship and the onset of social disorder in the First Intermediate Period (2135–2040 B.C.E.), the instructions shifted from royal affairs to private concerns. With the restoration of stable monarchy in the Middle Kingdom (2040–1650 B.C.E.), instructions once again stressed loyalty to the king. New Kingdom (ca. 1550–1080 B.C.E.) authors came from all levels of society, for daily business was now conducted by a broad range of people. With the *Instruction of Any* in the Eighteenth Dynasty (ca. 1550–1305 B.C.E.), concern for the individual and the acquiring of inner peace reappears and dominates the genre down to the Hellenistic and Roman eras. A good measure of societal change is the way success was interpreted. In the Old Kingdom, when courtiers were the intended readers, success meant getting ahead at court. When the readership of instructions became less tied to a particular class, exhortations became more general and more personal—how to live peacefully, avoid suffering, and handle conflicts and disappointments. The *Instruction of Amenemope* (ca. 1100 B.C.E.) is a good example of this kind of "humanism." Relevant portions of it will be commented upon in the commentary under 22:17–24:22.

Syro-Palestinian Wisdom Literature

The most important nonbiblical Syro-Palestinian wisdom text is *Ahiqar,* which is a narrative of the fall and restoration of the courtier Ahiqar, followed by a collection of about a hundred aphorisms, riddles, fables, instructions, and graded numerical sayings. Ahiqar's fall at the hands of his treacherous nephew Nadin and restoration to his former office may well have been based on historical fact, though the story has been shaped by the well-known plot of the vindicated courtier, which is found also in the biblical stories of Joseph, Esther, and Daniel. The narrative framework was composed in Aramaic in the seventh century B.C.E. and probably circulated among Aramaic speakers in the Neo-Assyrian court. The sayings seem to be older than the tale. J. Greenfield believes the sayings "must be considered a remnant of the lost legacy of West Semitic literature."[26] It is noteworthy that Ahiqar, who has experienced many things and suffered much, is celebrated as the author of sayings, exhortations, and wisdom poems. He has been through "discipline" or *paideia,* a process of deprivation and reproof that is often the first step to wisdom.

The following excerpts from the sayings give an idea of their range and style.[27]

> [107]A king is like the Merciful;
> even his voice is haughty.
> Who is there who could withstand him,
> but one with whom El is?

Similar awe toward the king is expressed in other passages: [100]"Quench not the word of a king; / let it be a balm [for] your [hea]rt." [101]"A king's word is gentle, but keener and more cutting than a double-edge dagger." Such sentiments are the standard view of the king in the ancient Near East. The Bible subjects kingship to sharp critique in the prophets but Proverbs, reflects the traditional view:

> Fear Yahweh and the king, my son,
> with those of a different view have nothing to do.
> For disaster will issue suddenly from the two,
> and calamity from both—who knows when.
> (24:21–22)

---

26. "The Background and Parallel to a Proverb of Ahiqar," in *Hommages à André Dupont Sommer* (Paris: Librarie d'Amérique et d'Orient, Adrien Maisonneuve, 1971), 59.

27. Only one saying in *Ahiqar* (82–83) occurs also in Proverbs: "Spare not your son from the rod, otherwise, can / you save him [from *wickedness*]? / If I beat you, my son, / you will not die; / but if I leave you alone, / [you will not live]." Prov. 23:13–14: "Do not withhold discipline from a youth. / If you strike him with a rod he will not die. / Strike him with a rod / and you will save his soul from Sheol." All translations are from J. M. Lindenberger in *OTP,* 2:499–501.

Inspired decisions fall from the king's lips;
  his mouth does not err in giving judgment.
(16:10)

Ahiqar has a personification of Wisdom (6.94–7.95), which is comparable to those in Proverbs 1, 8, and 9:

From heaven the peoples are favored;
Wisdom is of the gods.
Indeed, she is precious to the gods;
her kingdom is *et[er]nal*.
She has been established by Shamayn;
yea, the Holy Lord has exalted her.

The work contains graded numerical sayings, which are a feature of West Semitic style:

There are two things which are good,
  and a third which is pleasing to Shamash:
one who drinks wine and shares it,
  one who masters wisdom [*and observes it*];
  and one who hears a word but tells it not.
(line 92)

Such numerical sayings belong to the age-old West Semitic poetic repertory as in *KTU* 1.4.III.17–21:

Two kinds of feasts Baal hates,
  three, the rider on the clouds,
a feast of shame, a feast of meanness,
  and a feast where maids behave lewdly.

Proverbs has a series of such graded sayings in 30:15–33 and one instance in 6:16–19:

Six things Yahweh hates,
  seven are an abomination to him.

Proverbs' Adaptations of Ancient Near Eastern Wisdom Literature

The previous sections provided a glimpse of the wisdom literature of Israel's neighbors. This section sketches how Proverbs adapted to its own purposes two of the genres—the father-son instruction and the concise saying. For more details, see the commentary.

It is generally agreed that "The Words of the Wise" (Prov. 22:17–24:22), drew upon the Egyptian *Instruction of Amenemope*. The Commentary notes the Egyptian influences. Proverbs borrowed selectively and has put its own stamp on what it did borrow, recasting the material into the characteristic Hebrew bicolon, or two-line verse. Proverbs' debt to the Egyptian instructions in chaps. 1–9 is less obvious. Its warning against the "foreign woman" (2:16–19; chap. 5; 6:20–35; chap. 7) is also found in the *Instruction of Any* (Eighteenth Dynasty, ca. 1550–1305 B.C.E.).

> Beware of a woman who is a stranger,
> One not known in her town;
> Don't stare at her when she goes by,
> Do not know her carnally.
> A deep water whose course is unknown,
> Such is a woman away from her husband.
> "I am pretty," she tells you daily,
> When she has no witnesses;
> She is ready to ensnare you,
> A great deadly crime when it is heard.
>   (*AEL* 2.137)

Taken as a whole, the instructions in Proverbs 1–9 are distinctive in two ways. First, they are less specific than their Egyptian and Mesopotamian prototypes. They urge readers to seek wisdom rather than to do or not do particular actions. To put it another way, Proverbs emphasizes character rather than acts. Second, the strong personification of Wisdom in Proverbs 1, 8, and 9 and its vivid descriptions of Wisdom's two enemies—deceptive men (1:8–19; 2:13–15; 4:10–19) and the deceptive woman (2:16–19; chap. 5; 6:20–35; chap. 7; 9:13–18)—creates a metaphorical level of discourse that was unknown in earlier wisdom literature. Personified Wisdom asserts her trustworthiness, benefits, and closeness to God, and seeks receptive disciples and companions. Other voices, however, invite the youth into contrary relationships—men (always plural), a woman (always singular). The "son" in chaps. 1–9 is invited to choose a life companion. The search for a suitable wife (or properly relating to the wife one has) and founding (or maintaining) a house—characteristic tasks of young manhood—become metaphors for acquiring wisdom and virtue and rejecting their opposites.

The metaphorical use of seeking wisdom ensures that the instructions now address a broad class of readers. Even in the introduction (1:1–7), Proverbs envisioned more than the traditional audience of the *pĕtāyîm*, "simple, inexperienced," and the *na'ar*, "young man, boy" (1:4), for v. 6 has in view old and experienced people: "the *wise person*, hearing them, will grow in wisdom, / and *the prudent* will grow in skill." Elders and sages, therefore, are among the intended readers. By its carefully established metaphor system, the book addresses a wide spectrum of readers.

The other borrowed genre, the concise saying, has been distinctively reshaped. Akkadian and Syro-Palestinian sayings were extremely diverse and included witty sayings, observations on life, jokes, wordplays, humorous or ironic maxims, and proverbs. Proverbs 10–31 is less inclusive and, more important, has made all the sayings bicolon in form. Though some earlier sayings were already in parallel lines, many of them were not. Israelite authors created a subgenre, the bicolon proverb, which attained definitive shape well before the late eighth century, when King Hezekiah's clerks added their collection to an already existing one.[28]

4. Distinctive Ideas

Though Proverbs is not primarily a book of ideas, some of its basic ideas are distinctive enough to require comment. Five can be singled out here: (1) the world as self-righting ("retribution"), (2) wisdom as including justice and piety (and folly as excluding them), (3) its psychology of human freedom, (4) the two ways, and (5) its use of paired types.

The world is self-righting. God made the world in justice and it is not inert or indifferent to justice or injustice. It has the capacity to reward good deeds and punish wicked deeds. The usual term for the link between a human act and its consequences (or character and its consequences) is retribution.[29] Retribution is not an entirely satisfactory term, however, for the English word connotes punishment rather than reward, and immediate rather than gradual consequences. Proverbs sometimes speaks of more-than-human agency directly as when it mentions the proper name Yahweh (over eighty times; LORD in English translations) and God (*'ĕlōhîm* six times) as agents. At other times, it speaks of more-than-human agency indirectly by the use of passive verbs (the so-called divine passive) and impersonal constructions. The indirect approach seems to view the world almost as self-righting; justice prevails "just because." An example of an indirect statement is "Plans are foiled for want of counsel, / but succeed with many advisors" (15:22).

Wisdom includes justice and piety. Wisdom in Proverbs has a threefold dimension: sapiential (a way of knowing reality), ethical (a way of conducting oneself), and religious (a way of relating to the divinely designed order or to

---

28. It is interesting to note that most of the poetic artistry (assonance, wordplay, humor) is found in the first colon of the bicolon. One can perhaps infer that, in some cases at least, old folk proverbs were artistically extended and given new depth by the addition of the second colon.

29. The question of retribution in Proverbs and other wisdom writings is a complicated one. A fundamental starting point is K. Koch, "Is There a Doctrine of Retribution in the Old Testament?" reprinted in *Theodicy in the Old Testament,* ed, J. L. Crenshaw (Issues in Religion and Theology 4; Philadelphia: Fortress Press, 1983), 57–87.

God). The first three sayings in the Solomonic collection of 10:1–22:16 illustrate, respectively, the three dimensions.

> ¹A *wise* son makes his father rejoice,
>   but a *foolish* son is his mother's heartache.
> ²*Ill-gotten* treasure is of no avail,
>   but *righteousness* saves from death.
> ³*Yahweh* will not let the throat of the righteous go hungry,
>   but rebuffs the craving of the wicked.

Verse 1 is sapiential, having to do with knowing; it places in antithesis two sapiential types, the wise and the foolish person. Verse 2 is ethical in its concern that the wealth has been acquired by unjust means; unjust and righteous actions are contrasted. Verse 3 uses the righteous and unrighteous contrast but explicitly names Yahweh, the God of Israel, as the guarantor of justice. As Alonso Schökel has noted in his commentary on the verses, the sayings collection at its very beginning consciously relates the three spheres of knowing, acting, and piety.

The corollary to the fullness of wisdom is that folly is not simply ignorance but perversity and impiety. It condemns God's world and takes action against God and God's creatures. Wisdom is thus a serious virtue with the most serious consequences.[30]

The psychology of the human person as knower and doer. Proverbs assumes an extraordinary psychological freedom in the human person. Life is conceived as action, and human beings are defined through their organs of action—perception, decision, expression, and motion. Proverbs uses concrete images such as eye, ear, mouth (tongue, lips), heart, hands, feet. The book has such confidence in human freedom that it virtually equates knowing the good with doing the good. The ignorance of the fool is not a simple lack of knowledge but an active aversion to it, an aversion arising from cowardice, pride, or laziness. Ignorance has an ethical dimension, and knowing is a moral obligation for human beings. The wise person is morally good; the fool is wicked. This blending of ethical and sapiential language seems to be an original contribution.

Proverbs 4:20–27 is a good example of a human being viewed as a free and energetic moral agent. The italicized words in the translation below designate the organs of perception, decision, or action. By metonymy,[31] the organ stands for the act: for example, the eye for sight, the foot for walking (or activity).

---

30. M. Fox has shown the range of wisdom and folly in word studies: "Words for Wisdom," *ZAH* 6 (1993): 149–65; and "Words for Folly," *ZAH* 10 (1997): 4–15.

31. Metonymy is "a figure in which one word is substituted for another on the basis of some material, causal, or conceptual relation," e.g., container for thing contained, agent for act, product for object possessed, cause for effect. See Alex Preminger and T. V. F. Brogan, *The New Princeton Encyclopedia of Poetry and Poetics* (Princeton: Princeton University Press, 1993), 783.

[20]My son, pay attention to my words,
  give your *ear* to my utterances.
[21]Do not let them out of your *eye*sight,
  hold them in your *heart,*
[22]for they are life for those who find them,
  healing for his whole body.
[23]More than anything you guard, guard your *heart,*
  for from it comes the source of life.
[24]Rid yourself of a lying *mouth;*
  deceitful *lips* keep far from you.
[25]Keep your *eyes* gazing straight ahead,
  direct your *eyelids* unswervingly before you.
[26]Attend to the path of your *feet*
  so that all your ways turn out well.
[27]Turn neither to the right or the left;
  hold back your *foot* from evil.

The process of learning, deciding, and acting in Proverbs involves perceiving through seeing or hearing, storing the perceptions in the heart, making decisions, and expressing one's heart in words (mouth, lips) and actions (eyes, feet). As in Egyptian instructions, the heart stores and processes data and is often best translated as "mind." The above poem views the human person in action, straining every sense to its limit: extending the ear like an antenna, letting nothing escape the eyes, preserving words in the heart, keeping false speech away from the mouth and lips, holding the eyes and eyelids undeviatingly on the goal, keeping the feet from stumbling or taking detours. It is assumed that the disciple is extraordinarily free, *disponible* in the French sense. A corollary of Proverbs's presumption of psychological freedom is its contempt for sluggards who refuse to act (e.g., 6:6–11; 26:13–16). The criticism is levelled, of course, not at the energy level of such people but at their refusal to act.

The most important organ in Proverbs is the mouth (or tongue or lips). Words express the person better than anything else and words are the medium through which discipline and knowledge are imparted. Speech must be truthful and reliable; lying is vehemently denounced (17:4; 19:22; 30:6), particularly in the law court (6:19; 12:17; 14:5, 25; 19:5, 9, 28; 21:28). A key difference between Woman Wisdom and her enemies in chaps. 1–9 is the "truth," or reliability, of the words of each. In a metaphor that holds good in Hebrew as well as English, Wisdom's words are straight, "on the level" (8:6–11), whereas the words of her enemies are crooked (5:3; 9:17) and slick (2:16; 6:24; 7:5).

The two ways. The emphasis of the book on personal freedom, and its equating wisdom with virtue and ignorance with malice, is only one side of the story, however. Proverbs is keenly aware of the social consequences of individual acts, and expresses these consequences by the metaphor of the way. One's choices place one on a path that has its own dynamic.[32] By one's choices one ends up walking in "the way of the righteous" (e.g., 2:20; 4:18) or "the way of the wicked" (e.g., 4:14, 19; 12:26; 13:5, 6; 15:9; 25:26). Each has its inherent dynamic, toward death or toward life. The two ways are not permanent states; one can get on and off either path by one's conduct. One joins a community of people on the same path and shares their fate, as in the opening scene in 1:8–19. Proverbs thus balances personal freedom and social consequences.

The most extended treatment of the two ways in Proverbs is 4:10–19. Verses 18–19 add the images of light and darkness to the metaphor of the way.

> [18]But the path of the righteous is like the radiant sun,
>   shining ever more brightly until midday.
> [19]The way of the wicked is like thick darkness;
>   they are not aware of what they stumble over.

Later writings employ the contrast of light and darkness in combination with the two ways. Examples are the children of darkness and the children of light at Qumran and in the Gospel of John.

The use of antithetical pairs to describe behavior and its consequences. A major contribution of Proverbs is its use of antithetic types. The main types are the wise and the foolish, the righteous and the wicked, the lazy and the diligent, the rich and the poor. Each set of polarities has its own concerns. For example, pairings of the wise and the foolish show little interest in retribution with Yahweh as agent, whereas divine retribution is a major interest with the opposition of the righteous to the wicked. Rich and poor, as noted by a number of recent publications, are related uniquely: "Riches are traced back particularly to the commitment of the rich person, but the wise are well aware that diligence by itself is not responsible; on the other hand, poverty is not solely to be laid at the door of laziness."[33]

In addition to the antithetical pairs, certain groups and persons are singled out—father, mother, slave, son, friend, neighbor, and king. Father, mother, slave, and son together constitute the household, an institution that is of central importance in Proverbs not only because of the metaphor of founding/maintaining a

---

32. For "way," see R. C. Van Leeuwen, "Liminality and Worldview in Proverbs 1–9," *Semeia* 50 (1990): 111–44. For the metaphor of walk as living and conducting oneself, see F. J. Helfmeyer, "*Hālakh,*" in G. J. Botterweck and H. Ringgren, eds., *Theological Dictionary of the Old Testament* (Grand Rapids: Eerdmans, 1978), 3.388–403.

33. J. Hausmann, *Studien zum Menschenbild der älteren Weisheit (Spr 10ff.)* (Forschungen zum Alten Testament 7; Tübingen: J. C. B. Mohr, 1995), 342. See also R. C. Van Leeuwen, "Wealth and Poverty: System and Contradiction in Proverbs," *Hebrew Studies* 33 (1992): 25–36, and R. N. Whybray, *Wealth and Poverty in the Book of Proverbs* (JSOT Supplementary Series 99; Sheffield: JSOT, 1990).

house in chaps. 1–9, but also because the household is so important in human life. The household is viewed exclusively from the experience of the male.

5. The Background and Function of Personified Wisdom and Her Rival

The personification of wisdom as a woman is strong and persistent. She gives two lengthy speeches (1:20–33, chap. 8), builds a palace, and gives a dedicatory feast (9:1–6 + 11). She has formidable enemies: deceptive men (1:8–19; 2:13–15; 4:10–19) and a deceptive or "foreign" woman (2:16–19; chap. 5; 6:20–35; chap. 7). The deceptive woman in the form of Woman Folly makes her final appearance in chap. 9.

Modern scholarly research on the background of Wisdom in Proverbs began early in the twentieth century, part of Hermann Gunkel's project of viewing the Bible against its ancient Near East literary background.[34] Prior to Gunkel, personified Wisdom had been of interest chiefly to philosophers and ethicists. Parallels to Wisdom, when they were sought, tended to be from the Hellenistic world. Research since Gunkel can be summarized under four headings: (1) Wisdom as a hypostasis of Yahweh; (2) Wisdom as a Syro-Palestinian or Egyptian goddess; (3) Wisdom as the Mesopotamian divine or semidivine *ummānu;* (4) Wisdom as a pure literary personification.

The first theory views personified Wisdom as a hypostasis of Yahweh. In a hypostasis, a property of a deity, such as his or her anger or wisdom or cultic presence, is considered an entity in itself. For example, in the fourth century B.C.E. Jewish colony in Elephantine Island in Upper Egypt, Yahweh (Yahu) was worshiped under the surrogate name Bethel or "House of God." Similar deities were Herem-Bethel ("the Sacredness of Bethel"), Eshem-Bethel ("the Name of Bethel") and Anat-Bethel ("the Sign of Yahu.")[35] The theory that Wisdom is a hypostasis of Yahweh is not an adequate explanation, however, for Prov. 1:20–33 and 8:22–31 underlines her utter distinction and subordination to Yahweh.

The second theory proposes that a Syro-Palestinian goddess served as the model for Woman Wisdom. Bernhard Lang, for example, suggests that early Israel worshiped a daughter of El, Astarte, as the patroness of its schools until

---

34. The most recent summary of research is G. Baumann, *Die Weisheitsgestalt in Proverbien 1–9* (Forschungen zum Alten Testament 16; Tübingen: J. C. B. Mohr [Paul Siebeck], 1996), 1–57. See also R. E. Murphy, "The Personification of Wisdom," in *Wisdom in Ancient Israel* (FS J. A. Emerton), ed. John Day *et al.* (Cambridge: Cambridge University Press, 1995), 222–33, and M. V. Fox, "Ideas of Wisdom in Proverbs 1–9," *JBL* 116 (1997): 613–33.

35. P. K. McCarter, "The Religious Reforms of Hezekiah and Josiah," *Aspects of Monotheism: How God Is One* (Washington, D.C.: Biblical Archaeology Society, 1997), 71–72.

the Yahweh-alone movement forced a "reading" of her as a mere personification.[36] The proposal is not impossible in itself, but solid evidence for such a goddess does not exist. Others suggest the Egyptian goddess Maat, who represents divine order in the world. Maat, however, is a pale and nonspeaking abstraction of "order." Moreover, there is no "order" in biblical religion comparable to the order of Egyptian religion.[37]

The third theory, that personified Wisdom in Proverbs is derived from mythical bringers of culture in Mesopotamian mythology, is the most likely.[38] It is also compatible with the fourth theory (personification is purely a literary creation), for the author of Proverbs created a brilliant portrait of Wisdom. The background is the mythology of the *apkallu* and *ummānu,* respectively, the pre- and post-Flood sages and bringers of culture to the human race. The mythology was known in the Levant, for in the van Dijk list (see below), the last *ummānu* is explicitly identified with Ahiqar, the hero of the Aramaic tale *Ahiqar* (see above under Syro-Palestinian literature). Further, Philo of Byblos, a first- or second-century C.E. savant, transmits Phoenician traditions of one Sanchunathion that allude to the *ummānu* traditions of Mesopotamia.[39]

Two texts especially attest to the *ummānu*—the *Babyloniaca* of Berossus and the van Dijk list of kings and their sages. The *Babyloniaca* of Berossus (third-century B.C.E. Babylonian author) was digested by Alexander Polyhistor (first century B.C.E. scholar) and preserved in the *Chronicle* of the church father Eusebius of Caesarea (ca. 260–ca. 339). It mentions a composite fish-man named Oannes who has long puzzled readers. The puzzle has been solved by the van Dijk list, published in 1962, which makes it virtually certain that Oannes is derived from the Sumerian U_4-^{d}An(a) who is the first *apkallu* in the list. The *apkallu* were sometimes depicted as composite beings, having the features of a human being and a fish.

[2]A great mass of foreign folk had settled in Babylon, in the land of the Chaldeans, and they lived without restraint like irrational animals and wild beasts.

---

36. *Wisdom and the Book of Proverbs: A Hebrew Goddess Redefined* (New York: Pilgrim Press, 1986) and more recently in "Wisdom," in *Dictionary of Deities and Demons in the Bible,* ed. K. van der Toorn et al. Leiden: Brill, 1995), 1692–1702.

37. Fox, "World Order and Ma'at," 37–48.

38. This runs slightly contrary to statements in my "Woman Wisdom in the Book of Proverbs," in *Biblische Theologie und gesellschaftlicher Wandel* (Lohfink volume), ed. G. Braulik, W. Gross, and S. McEvenue (Freiburg: Herder, 1993), 64.

39. Sanchuniathon refers to secret works from the sanctuaries, "composed in the letters of the Ammoneans," which seems to be a reminiscence to the *ummānu.* See J. C. Greenfield, "The Seven Pillars of Wisdom (Prov. 9:1)—A Mistranslation," *Jewish Quarterly Review* 76 (1985): 19–20. The biblical figure of Enoch has also been influenced by Mesopotamian material. See most recently J. C. VanderKam, *Enoch: A Man for All Generations* (Columbia, S.C.: University of South Carolina Press, 1995).

[5]In the first year there appeared out of the Red Sea in the territory of the Babylonians an awesome beast named Oannes, as also Apolodorus reports in his book: that his whole body was that of a fish and under the fish's head another head was joined; and at the tail, there were feet like a man's; and his voice was a man's. A picture of it is still preserved. And concerning that beast [Berossus] says that the beast spent the day with human beings and did not eat any kind of food; and it taught human beings writing, various crafts and arts, the building of cities, and the founding of temples; also it taught laws and operations, as well as the measurement and division of land; also it explained seeds and the harvesting of fruits; and it transmitted to human beings everything necessary for civilized life. Since that time nothing further has been discovered. When the sun set, the beast plunged back into the sea and spent the night in the depths in preparation, so that in a certain sense it led a double life. Later, still other similar beasts appeared, about which [Berossus] says he will report in the book of the kings. And he says that Oannes wrote about creation and politics and imparted language and technical skill to human beings.[40]

According to the text, the first *apkallu,* Oannes, a divine or semidivine composite being, came to the human race when it lived an animal-like existence. He brought intellectual skills and civilized life and wrote about creation and politics. Claus Wilcke suggests the mention of creation and politics refers to other chapters of the *Babyloniaca,* the cosmogony, and the king lists,[41] but it is worth noting that Wisdom in Proverbs 8 says she guides kings (vv. 15–16) and she describes a cosmogony (vv. 22–31).

The second text relevant to the *ummānu* and the transmission of wisdom was published in 1962 by Jan van Dijk.[42] Fragments had been published before but the Warka text made a fuller reading possible. The text is a list of seven pre- and seven post-Flood kings and the *apkallu* or *ummānu* that accompanied each king. The text confirms that Oannes was the first *apkallu* and it also shows that the work of the *apkallu* was continued in the post-Flood era by the *ummānu.*

---

40. This is my translation of J. Karst's German translation of the Armenian text of Eusebius's *Chronicle,* which appears in *Die griechischen christlichen Schriftsteller der ersten drei Jahrhunderte: Eusebius fünfter Band* (Leipzig: J. Hinrich'sche Buchhandlung, 1911), 7. The superscript numbers are from Karst's edition. For another English translation, see S. M. Burstein, *The Babyloniaca of Berossus* (Sources from the Ancient Near East, vol. 1, fasc. 5; Malibu, Calif.: Undena, 1978).

41. "Göttliche und menschliche Weisheit," 263.

42. "Die Tontafeln aus dem *rēš*-Heligtum" (W 200030,7) in H. J. Lenzen, ed., *XVIII. vorläufiger Bericht über die von dem Deutschen Archäologischen Institut und der Deutschen Orient-Gesellschaft aus Mitteln der Deutschen Forschungsgemeinschaft unternommenen Ausgrabungen in Uruk-Warka, Winter 1959/60* (Berlin: Verlag Gebr. Mann, 1962), 44–45. The translation is that of R. Caplice, *Background of Old Testament History: Mesopotamian Texts* (Rome: Pontifical Biblical Institute, 1982), 35–36. The text is dated to 164 B.C.E.

[In the tim]e of Ayalu the king, U'an was *apkallu*.
[In the tim]e of Alalgar the king, U'anduga was *apkallu*.
[In the time of] Ammelu'anna the king, Enmeduga was *apkallu*.
[In the time of] Ammegalanna the king, Enmegalamma was *apkallu*.
[In the time of] Enme'ušumgalanna the king, Enmebulugga was *apkallu*.
[In the time of] Enmeduranki the king, Utu'abzu was *apkallu*.

[After the flood(?)], in the reign of Enmerkar, Nungalpiriggal was *apkallu*,
[whom Ištar] brought down from heaven to the Eannna. The bronze lyre
with . . . of lapis lazuli: it was he who made it,
with the craft of Ninagal. They placed it before Anu in . . . , the abode of god
  and man(?)

[In the time of Gilgam]eš, Sin-liqi-unninni was *ummānu*.
[In the time of Ibb]isin the king, Kabtu-ili-Narduk was *ummānu*.
[In the time of Išbi]erra the king, Sidu (variant Enlilibni) was *ummānu*.
[In the time of Abi'eš]uh the king, Esagilkinapla was *ummānu*.
[In the time of] Adadapaliddina the king, Esagilkinubba was *ummānu*.
[In the time of] Nebuchadnezzar the king, Esagilkinubba was *ummānu*.
[In the time of] Esarhaddon the king, Aba'Enlildari was *ummānu*, [whom the]
  Ahlamu (the Aramaeans) call Ahuqar.

The kings named in the second part of the text are historical and their *ummānu*s
are attested as actual authors. Sin-liqi-unninni, for example, is the author (or
redactor) of the Gilgamesh epic. In this list, the *apkallu*s are divine beings and
the *ummānu*s are human scribes.

The two texts illustrate the mediation of heavenly wisdom to human kings
through semidivine mediators. The reference to Ahiqar shows the tradition was
known in Syria-Palestine. The mythology is the general background for personified Wisdom in Proverbs. Like the Mesopotamian *apkallu* and especially
the *ummānu*, Woman Wisdom brings culture to human beings, enabling them
to live a civilized life, that is, with writing, farming, metallurgy, kingship, and
thus to be divine servants. This interpretation finds support in the Hebrew word
in Prov. 8:30a, *'āmôn*, which is generally translated "nursling." The word
seems to have been misunderstood by early scribes and misvocalized by the
Masoretes. It is actually a loanword from the Akkadian *ummānu* and should be
vocalized *'ommān* or the like in Hebrew. The proper translation is "I was at his
side as a (heavenly) sage," that is, as a heavenly figure mediating to humans the
knowledge they need to be good and blessed servants of God.

In Proverbs, Wisdom's role and her message is embodied in human institutions just as in Mesopotamia. In Mesopotamia, the culture bringers took part in
a process of transmission of heavenly wisdom to the human race. At the source
was the god of wisdom, after which came the divine beings, the *apkallu*. The
human component gradually increased in the course of transmission. As the van

Dijk text shows, the post-Flood *ummānu* can be human beings. At the end of the chain in Proverbs stand the institutions of the king, the scribe, and the family, over which stands the father. Personified Wisdom is the wisdom handed on by these institutions. Personified Wisdom says, "Accept *me,*" and the father says, "Accept the *wisdom* that I teach you." Woman Wisdom authenticates the educational process and makes it attractive and creative. In the instructions, the father initiates the process.

The antithesis of Woman Wisdom, the foreign woman, also has antecedents. The invective against her is traditional, being found, for example, in the New Kingdom *Instruction of Any,* which warns against "a woman who is a stranger, one not known in her own town." The Babylonian *Counsels of Wisdom* also criticizes unsuitable marriage partners. Unlike Proverbs, however, the woman in the Egyptian warning lacks any metaphoric dimension and choosing her is not part of a life or death scenario. Where did such an association come from?

The life or death scenario in Proverbs, which is different from the traditional warnings against the *femme fatale* in ancient wisdom writings, may have come not from the wisdom tradition but from the genre of epic. The encounter between the young man and the deceptive woman, about which Proverbs is so concerned (2:16–19; chap. 5; 6:20–35; chap. 7; 9:13–18) may have transposed a typical scene in ancient epics in which a goddess offers love or marriage (deceptively it turns out) to a young hero.[43] Examples of such deceptive women are Ishtar in *Gilgamesh* (VI.1–79), Anat in the Ugaritic legend *Aqhat* (*KTU* 1.17.VI.2–45), and Calypso and Circe in the *Odyssey* (V.202–209; X). In each scene, a goddess of love offers love or marriage to a youth—Gilgamesh, Aqhat, or Odysseus—which in fact will bring death or transform his human life. To borrow a term from Homeric scholarship, the scenes are similar enough to be termed type-scenes, or "certain prominent elements of repetitive compositional pattern . . . that are a conscious convention."[44]

The encounter of the goddess and the youth differs in each epic, but there are three constants, which occur in Proverbs as well: (1) at stake is marriage or a long-term relationship, not simply a one-time sexual seduction; (2) the young man's choice means life or death, literally so in *Gilgamesh* (the death of his companion Enkidu) and *Aqhat* (the death of Aqhat), or transformation of mortal life (*Odyssey*); (3) the goddess's deceitful offer is recognized as spurious by the hero and spurned. Proverbs seems to have transposed the epic type-scene to its own metaphorical context and dramatized the age-old warning against unsuitable marriage partners. Woman Wisdom is now the alternative to the deceptive woman.

43. For details see my "Woman Wisdom in the Book of Proverbs," 61–72.
44. R. Alter interprets encounters at the well in Genesis, Exodus, and Ruth as type-scenes in chap. 3 of *The Art of Biblical Narrative* (New York: Basic Books, 1981). The quote is on p. 50.

The figures of the two women and the persistent metaphor of finding a wife, or relating properly to her, and founding a household or maintaining it, provide a lens for reading chaps. 1–9. Chapters 5–7 at one level warn against adultery because of its high personal and social costs. Metaphorically, the texts now warn against allowing seductions of any kind to disturb one's fundamental relationship to wisdom. Wisdom invites people into a long-term, marriage-like relationship with her. The relationship is founded on her truthfulness, bounty, and closeness to God. Her appeal is to anyone who wishes to be her companion and enjoy the blessing reserved for God's friends. Personification makes her appeal emotionally more attractive and serious.

6. The Hebrew Text and Versions of Proverbs[45]

The original Hebrew manuscripts of Proverbs have not survived. The oldest manuscripts are two fragments from Cave Four at Qumran: 4QProv[a] (= 4Q102), written in an early Herodian formal script (ca. 30–1 B.C.E.), contains 1:27–2:1; 4QProv[b] (= 4Q103), written in a late Herodian formal script (ca. 50 C.E.), preserves vestiges of two columns: 13:6–9; 14:5–10, 12–13; 14:31–15:8; 15:20–31. Both fragments seem to be protorabbinic, that is, to reflect the text that the rabbis in the late first or early second century C.E. chose as the one to be copied. The text chosen by the rabbis was reasonably sound, with a relatively small number of corrupt and displaced verses (e.g., 6:22; 8:23–34; 10:10). It is, however, expansionistic, having attracted additions and repetitions (e.g., 1:16; 3:3; 28:18).

Evidently, a different Hebrew recension of Proverbs was the basis for the Greek translation of the second century B.C.E., which is known as the Septuagint. It was part of the great project of making the Bible available for Greek-speaking Jewish communities outside Palestine. In the process of translating the biblical books into Greek, a new ideal of translation came into being: *verbum e verbo,* "word for word," replacing the classical ideal of *sensus de sensu,* "sense for sense." Many readers were conscious, however, that the translations did not render the Hebrew with sufficient accuracy. Their dissatisfaction inspired corrections to the Greek text to make it conform more literally to the Hebrew text (which was itself still developing). The Septuagint bears the marks of the ongoing revision. Its free translation style is the work of the earliest translators. Only after the original translation had circulated for a time could the next stage have occurred: correcting verses and half-verses back toward the Hebrew text. One result of this correcting process is the famous Septuagint doublets,

---

45. For a complete account, see my "Observations on the Texts and Versions of Proverbs," in *Wisdom, You Are My Sister* (R. E. Murphy volume), ed. M. L. Barré (Washington, D.C.: Catholic Biblical Association, 1997), 47–61.

some seventy-six in Fritsch's count.[46] These include double translations of entire verses (e.g., 1:7; 2:21; 3:15; 18:22; 29:25), of single cola (e.g., 1:14, 27; 6:25; 8:10; 29:7; 31:27, 29, 30), and of phrases and words. The more literal rendering is judged by scholars to be a later correcting of a free or inaccurate earlier rendering. Unlike modern text critics, scribes copied the original rendering as well as its correction.

The Hebrew of Proverbs, by definition compressed and elliptical, often baffled the Greek translators. Evidently, they had no interpretive tradition to guide them. To make sense of puzzling verses, translators used several techniques: (1) borrowing from another verse; (2) metathesis or rearrangement of consonants; (3) changing the triconsonantal root; (4) substituting graphically similar consonants; (5) translating the same word twice; (6) inventing or heightening antithetic parallelism.

In sum, the Septuagint is a fairly free translation of a recension slightly different from the protorabbinic one. Though the translators' own culture and interests were inevitably reflected in their renderings, it is important to realize their primary intent was to render the Hebrew text as accurately as they could.

In the second century C.E., Proverbs was translated into Syriac and became part of the Peshitta, the Bible of Syriac-speaking Christian lands. The book of Proverbs was probably translated by Jews, for the Targum is dependent on it. S of Proverbs is a literal but not slavish translation of the Hebrew text into clear and idiomatic Syriac. Frequently S finds the Hebrew text difficult, in which case it turns to G for help. Ordinarily, S keeps an eye on G to check its own translation, just as T translates the Hebrew with an eye on S, and V translates the Hebrew with an eye on G. Though following G dozens of times, S nonetheless regards its Hebrew text as the authoritative text. There are several indications of its respect: when the Hebrew is clear, S translates it straightforwardly; S follows G with a certain freedom and sometimes corrects it in the light of the Hebrew; S follows the Hebrew order rather than the G order of sections after 24:22 and of verses in chaps. 15–17, 20, and 31. In all the other biblical books, S draws on T but in the case of Proverbs alone, T draws on S.

The Targum to Proverbs is a literal translation of MT, occasionally relying on S for interpretation and phrasing. T nonetheless assigns priority to MT, for it often corrects S back to the Hebrew and follows the MT sequence of sections and verses. Its text-critical usefulness lies chiefly in its reading of the Hebrew in the light of S and its implicit assessment of the S interpretation. Its precise function and provenance are unknown. It cannot be dated exactly. Dates from the third century B.C.E. to the eighth century C.E. have been proposed.

In 398 Jerome translated the received Hebrew text of Proverbs into a literarily

---

46. "The Treatment of the Hexaplaric Signs in the Syro-Hexaplar of the Proverbs," *JBL* 72 (1953): 170.

polished Latin that, along with other translated texts, formed the Vulgate. As was his custom, he took account of the Greek versions and followed them when he considered them superior. He knew the Peshitta but rarely followed it independently. He did not know T, which is apparently of a later date. His achievement, especially when compared to the other versions, is impressive. The text-critical value of the Vulgate is threefold: (1) Jerome had direct access to important textual witnesses (some no longer extant) and had the training and talent to use them properly; (2) he was heir to ancient interpretive traditions, especially Jewish lore from his rabbi teachers; (3) as an educated man, he was familiar with aphoristic literature generally and with the genres of the Hebrew wisdom tradition. Time and again, he is able to make sense of what the versions mangle.

7. The Influence of Proverbs on Later Literature

Proverbs contains Israelite scribes' appropriation of the centuries-old wisdom literature of the ancient Near East. In the process, they invented new genres and wrote unique compositions. The process went on for centuries—as long as the monarchy lasted and beyond. It was pseudonymous, being done in the name of Solomon, by scribes working for the king, writing in literary forms laid down from old.

In its wide variety of genres and of individual poems, incorporation of foreign material (e.g., 31:1–9), royal sponsorship over centuries, and reliance on the authority of Solomon rather than on the actual authors, Proverbs differs from later wisdom literature, which is related to specific authors and contexts. Job is the case of a man suffering particular travails. Qoheleth was written by one author in the fourth century B.C.E.; though it retains the traditional attribution to Solomon, it gives him a specific persona on the basis of which he proposes his own new teaching. Sirach is also the work of a man who wants us to know that he is its author (see 24:30–34; 38:34b–39:11; 50:27; 51:13–30). Wisdom of Solomon musters all elements to argue for the nobility of Judaism at a particular moment of crisis about national identity.

Authors of the late Second Temple period were aware of a corpus of sacred texts (including Proverbs) and "reread" these texts for new situations (French *relecture*). A good example of this intensely exegetical reading is Sirach 24, which rereads Proverbs 8 with Torah and Temple in view.

Wisdom literature is well represented in the library of the Qumran community.[47] There are fragments of Proverbs (as noted in Section 5 above), Job

47. The following remarks are strongly indebted to D. J. Harrington, "Wisdom at Qumran," in *The Community of the Renewed Covenant: The Notre Dame Symposium on the Dead Sea Scrolls,* ed. E. Ulrich and J. VanderKam (Notre Dame, Ind.: University of Notre Dame, 1994), 137–52. See also D. Harrington, "Ten Reasons Why the Qumran Wisdom Texts Are Important," *Dead Sea Discoveries* 4 (1997): 245–54.

(4Q99–101) and Targums of Job, Qoheleth (4Q109–110), and Sirach (2Q18 and 1PsªSirach [= 51:13–20b, 30b]). There are other wisdom texts as well, one describing the evils of Woman Folly in the tradition of Proverbs 5, 7, and 9 (4Q185), a poem on Wisdom making known the glory of God to a community animated by wisdom (from Cave 11, previously known as Psalm 154), a kind of instruction in a text called Sapiential A (extant in fragmentary copies 1Q26; 4Q415–418; 425). In addition to wisdom texts, wisdom themes appear in sectarian documents such as the *Community Rule* (1QS), for example, the head is called the *maśkîl,* a wisdom term meaning "one who enlightens or instructs." Other texts strongly stress knowledge and illumination. The sectarian thinkers used themes from wisdom literature to develop their own thought.

In Hellenistic Judaism, Proverbs influenced Wisdom of Solomon, written in the first century B.C.E. (possibly in the first century C.E.). The Wisdom of Solomon borrowed several themes: personified Wisdom, Solomon the wise king, the righteous person as the point where divine action becomes visible in the world, God as a father who teaches his son (the righteous person or Israel) through a process of education (*paideia;* see Prov. 3:12), the world (cosmos) protecting the righteous and punishing the wicked.[48]

Proverbs seems to have influenced *Pirqe Abot,* the *Sayings of the Fathers,* a collection of sayings from the "men of the Great Assembly" (between the late fifth to the third century B.C.E.) down to the descendants of Rabbi Judah the Prince in the third century C.E. It is one of the treatises in the Mishnah, where it became the object of commentary in *Abot de Rabbi Nathan.* Its opening sentence places the men of the Great Assembly in a line from Moses, Joshua, the elders, and the prophets. In Judaism of a much later date, Hebrew ethical wills, in which parents hand on to their children their wisdom, used Proverbs as a model.

Early Christians saw Jesus as a wisdom teacher and employed traditions about personified wisdom to express his incarnation. Some sayings in the Q tradition (a presumed source of both Matthew and Luke) present Jesus as an emissary of Wisdom (see Luke 7:35 and 11:49–50). In other Q sayings, Jesus seems to embody wisdom (see Luke 13:34 // Matt. 23:37; Luke 10:22; Matt. 11:29).

The only extended example of the genre of instruction in the New Testament is the letter of James. The work is a series of instructions using the familiar exhortatory verbs (imperatives, jussives) followed by reasons for the recommended behavior, which are often sayings or proverbs. Old wisdom themes appear: the danger of an unbridled tongue (chap. 3; cf. Prov. 10:18–21), of

48. See my "Proverbs as a Source for Wisdom of Solomon," in *Ben Sira and the Book of Wisdom* (FS M. Gilbert; Bibliotheca ephemeridum theologicarum lovaniensium), ed. N. Calduch-Benages and J. Vermeylen (Louvain: Leuven University Press, forthcoming in 1999).

presumptuous planning (4:13–17; Prov. 16:1), of ill-gotten wealth (5:1–6; cf. Prov. 10:2–3). James exalts "wisdom from above" (3:13–18 and cf. 1:17), continuing the tradition of a wisdom that is beyond human capacity but graciously given to human beings (Proverbs 8; Sirach 24). The genre is broadened by the addition of prophetic denunciations of the callous rich (1:27; 2:1–13; 4:1–10; 5:1–6).

Of the four Gospels, John draws most explicitly on Proverbs to present Jesus as incarnate wisdom descended from on high to offer life and truth to human beings. The Gospel expresses Jesus' heavenly origin by using the categories of personified Wisdom to describe him. As Woman Wisdom was with God from the beginning, even before the earth (Prov. 8:22–23), so Jesus is the Word in the beginning (John 1:1), with the Father before the world existed (17:5). As Wisdom shows human beings how to walk in the way that leads to life (Prov. 2:20–22; 3:13–26; 8:32–35), so Jesus functions as revealer in John. Jesus speaks in long discourses like Woman Wisdom (Prov. 1:20–33; chap. 8). Wisdom invites people to partake of her banquet, where the food and drink symbolize life and closeness to God (Prov. 9:1–6, 11). Jesus does the same: "I am the bread of life. Whoever comes to me will never be hungry and whoever believes in me will never be thirsty" (John 6:35). As Wisdom seeks friends (Prov. 1:20–21; 8:1–4), so Jesus recruits disciples (John 1:36–38, 43), though the possibility exists of rejecting Wisdom (Prov. 1:24–25; chaps. 7 and 9) and Jesus (John 8:46; 10:25).

Two early Christian hymns identify Jesus with God's creative word and with heavenly wisdom: Col. 1:15–20 and John 1:1–18. The Greek word *logos* ("word") in John 1 owes as much to wisdom traditions as to traditions of the word. Sirach 24:3 ("From the mouth of the Most High I came forth") and Wisd. 9:1–2 had already made wisdom and word parallel. Proverbs 8:22–23 ("The Lord created me at the beginning. . . . From of old I was knit.") and Sir. 1:1 affirmed that wisdom comes from the Lord and remains with him forever. The Johannine prologue states that the Word was always with God.

8. The Meaning of Proverbs Today

Five contributions of the book of Proverbs to wisdom reflection can be briefly mentioned. First, Proverbs is concerned with wisdom as a fundamental option in life rather than with specific wise actions. So intense is its focus on wisdom that it reifies and even personalizes it, giving Wisdom a voice that she might invite people to become her companions and disciples. She urges her hearers to seek her over everything else. Wisdom is with God, and God's blessings come to those who follow her.

Second, the quest for wisdom is depicted as a drama that is charged with conflict. The book acknowledges another voice that resembles Wisdom's and uses the same language of relationship. That voice belongs to another woman (or group of men), and it promises fellowship and life. In the end, however, the promises prove empty and even fatal. Whoever seeks wisdom must, therefore, discern whose voice is speaking, and must reject as well as choose.

Third, acquiring wisdom is both a human achievement and a divine gift. Chapter 2 states the point with succinct logic:

> If you call out to understanding,
>   raise your voice to insight,
> if you seek it as you do silver,
>   search for it as for treasure,
> then you will understand the revering of Yahweh,
>   you will find knowledge of God;
> for Yahweh gives wisdom,
>   from his mouth come knowledge and insight.
>
>   (vv. 3–6)

Though wisdom is a free gift, the way to it is through discipline, which is the willingness to learn from others and the capacity to bear pain and contradiction if need be. One acquires wisdom by making oneself open to receive it as a gift.

Fourth, the concise sayings in chaps. 10–31 do not so much convey information as impart a perspective as the reader struggles to understand them. In a sense, the sayings are the world in miniature, concealing in themselves a dimension of reality that we easily miss or rush past. As we ponder them, we learn discernment and acquire insight into God's world.

Lastly, the quest for wisdom is a universal quest, not limited only to Jews and Christians. The book enables its readers to engage in a great common quest with men and women of all faiths and in every land.

Proverbs 1

Introduction to the Book

1:1 The Proverbs of Solomon son of David, king of Israel:
2   for learning wisdom and instruction,
        for understanding learned sayings;
3   for acquiring discipline, for success,
        righteousness, justice, and equity;
4   for imparting prudence to the inexperienced,
        knowledge and discernment to the young—
5   a wise person, hearing them, will gain more wisdom,
        and a prudent person will grow in skill—

6   for understanding a proverb and a riddle,
     the sayings of the sages and their riddles.
7   The beginning of knowledge is revering Yahweh;
     only fools despise wisdom and instruction.

Like Egyptian instructions, which typically open with "the beginning of the instruction of X for his son Y," Proverbs 1 gives the title, names the author, and states the purpose of the book and its benefits to the reader. Apart from instructions in Egyptian literature and the wisdom books in the Bible, Egyptian and most biblical writings were ordinarily anonymous.

The literary unit is vv. 1–7. Though most commentators isolate v. 7 as a leitmotif, it is best taken as the culmination of vv. 1–7, for (1) revering Yahweh is an appropriate culmination to the introduction of a book that makes Yahweh the source of blessings; (2) the similar introduction of 22:17–21 makes trust in Yahweh the goal of instruction (v. 19a); and (3) the phrase "wisdom and instruction" in v. 7b reprises the same phrase in v. 2a, thus forming an inclusion marking out a section. The mention of fools despising instruction in v. 7b serves as a transition to the following section.

While the author prefers the accumulation of near-synonyms of wisdom rather than differentiation here, as Alonso Schökel notes, there is a discernible structure in vv. 2–7: vv. 2–3 are concerned with learning, v. 4 with teaching, v. 5 with the sage-teacher, v. 6 with written wisdom, and v. 7, in climactic position, with revering Yahweh. An alternative structure is also visible, which is noted by Alonso Schökel: v. 2a introduces wisdom as a general virtue, which is developed in vv. 3–5; v. 2b introduces wisdom as the capacity to interpret learned writings, which is developed in v. 6. Verse 7 is the climax of the introduction.

The purpose of the book is thus to make its hearers wise, that is, to instruct them how to live successfully, which means living in "fear of the Lord" or revering Yahweh. Another aspect of becoming wise, represented in the alternate structure, is knowing how to read the wisdom writings (vv. 2a, 6). Because v. 5 stands apart by its syntax (imperfect verb rather than infinitival), many commentators (Toy, Plöger, Alonso Schökel) rightly judge it an ancient addition. The addition took place before the Greek translation of the third or second century B.C.E., for G has v. 5. There are seven different verbs expressing wise action and fourteen different nouns for wisdom, but there is little point in differentiating them here, since the passage underscores the unity of wisdom.

[1:1] "Proverbs" in v. 1 describes the contents of the entire book and is broader in scope than in v. 6, where it means a saying. 1 Kings 5:12 (4:32 E) classifies Solomon's literary output under the heading "saying" (*māšāl*) and "song." The Bible, and indeed ancient Near Eastern literature generally, never developed clear and consistent terms for literary genres; ancient usage is broad and imprecise by modern standards. Wisdom literature was attributed to Solomon as psalms were to David and laws to Moses.

The number value of the Hebrew consonants in the three names, "Solomon," "David," and "Israel," add up to 930, just short of the 934 lines of MT. The name Solomon in 10:1 has a value of 375, which is the exact number of lines in that collection (10:1–22:16).[1]

[2] As Alonso Schökel points out, the language is open-ended, taking on different colorations in different settings. "Discipline" (*mûsār*) is an important word in Proverbs. The term has a dual meaning, referring both to a *process*—obedience to teachers and openness to correction—and to the *content*—what they teach, the tradition.

[3] While the virtues listed here are ordinarily associated with legal and prophetic teaching, biblical wisdom has an ethical dimension as well. Wisdom is knowing how to *act* rightly. Folly is not mere ignorance, but acting wrongly.

[4] "Inexperienced" (*pĕtî*) can sometimes be translated "simple" or "untutored." It is sometimes used neutrally, as it is here, to describe people without experience of life; they are young, liable to be seduced by smooth talk; they need to listen to their parents, their teachers, and wisdom. Occasionally, the word has a negative connotation, as in chap. 7, for a person who is led by impulse, rejects wise voices, and is contemptuous of community and tradition.

[5] The finite verbs interrupt the series of infinitive verbs. The book is intended not only for the young, but for the mature and those advanced in their grasp of the tradition. The book is not just for one age group.

[6] The syntax of verses 2–4 (the preposition *lĕ* + infinitive verb), which was interrupted by the finite verbs of verse 5, is resumed in verse 6. Verse 6 states that it is part of wisdom to understand aphorisms and wise sayings, presumably those in chaps. 10–31. "To understand" here means not only to comprehend the sayings but to apply them appropriately to particular situations.

[7] The phrase "fear of the Lord" is an unsatisfactory translation of *yir'at YHWH,* which occurs fourteen times in Proverbs. For one thing, "Lord" is a title and "Yahweh" is a proper name. Second, "fear of a god" does not refer primarily to an emotion or a general reverent attitude. Rather, it means revering a particular deity by performing the god's rituals and obeying the god's commands.

"Fear of the Lord" has a specific background. In the view of ancient Near Eastern peoples, the world was established by the gods exclusively for their own benefit. Human beings were created as the gods' servants. Individuals had to learn to live optimally within a hierarchized world where the gods occupied the highest tier and human beings the lowest, as slaves of the gods. The first step in living happily and avoiding trouble was to know one's place—to "fear the god(s)" in obedience and reverence. Such an attitude, with variations

---

1. Such headings suggest a single final editor of Proverbs according to P. W. Skehan, "A Single Editor for the Whole of Proverbs," *CBQ* 10 (1948): 115–130, revised in *Studies in Israelite Poetry and Wisdom* (CBQ Monograph Series 1; Washington, D.C.: Catholic Biblical Association, 1971), 15–26.

according to culture, characterized Mesopotamia and the Levant.[2] Modern readers may need to recall that ancient religion was regarded as something one did rather than something one felt. Doing one's duties were part of fearing God. How obvious these convictions were to the sages is shown by v. 7b: To scorn wisdom is to fall into the class of the foolish, whom the book virtually equates with the wicked.

The introduction conceives wisdom in more general terms than is customary in the introductions to Egyptian instructions, which vv. 2–7 resemble in other respects. Wisdom embraces several dimensions of life: the sapiential (vv. 2a, 4–6), the ethical (v. 3), and the religious (v. 7). Wisdom is a virtue (vv. 2a, 4) that enables one to act wisely; it can also designate written wisdom, which the virtue of wisdom is able to interpret (vv. 2b, 6). Like the Egyptian instructions, some of the material was originally addressed to young men of promise (by birth or talent), but the introduction expands the audience and broadens the context. Verse 5 includes in the readership those already wise, by definition those no longer young. Women are part of the audience because they could be considered wise in Israel (cf. 2 Sam. 14:2; 20:16) and would have been among the original hearers. Further, the Scriptures were intended for all Israel. Thus, the Bible itself broadens the readership to include everyone in the holy community.

Lecture I: The Deadly Alternative to Parental Wisdom

1:8   My son, hear the instruction of your father,
         do not disdain the teaching of your mother,
9   for they are a handsome diadem for your head
         and a pendant for your neck.
10   My son, if sinners entice you,
         do not consent if they say,
11   "Go with us, we will set an ambush for blood,
         lie in wait for the innocent without cause.
12   We will swallow them alive like Sheol,
         still living as they fall into the Pit.

2. M. Barré, "'Fear of God' and the World View of Wisdom," *Biblical Theology Bulletin* 11 (1981): 41–43. St. Hilary of Poitiers (ca. 315–367), commenting on Psalm 127, makes a pertinent observation: "Fear is not to be taken in the sense that common usage gives it. Fear in this ordinary sense is the trepidation our weak humanity feels when it is afraid of suffering something it does not want to happen. . . . This kind of fear is not taught; it happens because we are weak. . . . But . . . the fear of the Lord . . . has to be acquired by obedience to the commandments, by holiness of life and by knowledge of truth."

13   We will get all kinds of precious treasure,
       we will fill our houses with the loot.
14   Throw in your lot with us,
       we all have a single purse."
15   My son, do not walk on the way with them,
       keep your foot from their path,[a]
17   for senselessly would a net be held high
       in the sight of any winged creature.[b]
18   As for them, they are setting an ambush for their own blood,
       lying in wait for their own lives.
19   Such is the path of everyone who is greedy for gain;
       it takes the life of its possessor.

    a. We omit v. 16, "for their feet run to wickedness, and they hasten to shed blood," as a later addition to MT. It is taken from Isa. 59:7 to explain the puzzling v. 17 (see below). Two of the best Greek manuscripts (Vaticanus and Sinaiticus, first hand) do not have it (see commentary). The verse appears in Rom. 3:15.
    b. The earliest interpretation of the elliptical v. 17 is G, which took it allegorically of evildoers caught in God's net: "for not undeservedly are nets prepared for birds." S, on the other hand, took the same words to refer to the deceitful intent of the wicked: "and deceitfully [the wicked] spread the nets before the bird (= the innocent)." T and V read MT.

    Though vv. 8–9 could make sense as a separate piece (honor results from fidelity to parental instruction), the verses make better sense as the introduction to vv. 10–19. The syntax of v. 8, "my son, do/do not . . . (for) . . ." recurs in vv. 10 and 15. Of the unity of vv. 10–19 there can be no doubt. The intentions of the wicked in vv. 11–14 are undone in vv. 15–19. Words or phrases in vv. 11–14 are used again in vv. 15–18: the Hebrew verb *hālak* (translated "go" and "walk") appears in vv. 11 and 15; "set an ambush" // "lie in wait" appears in vv. 11 and 18; *ḥinnām* (translated "without cause" and "senselessly") appears in vv. 11 and 17. In the case of the last word (*ḥinnām*), no single English word catches the Hebrew wordplay, killing without a reason (= killing the innocent, as in 1 Kings 2:31) and holding a net up high without a reason (= senselessly). To quote the malevolent talk of the wicked is conventional (see Ps. 10:4, 6, 11; Wisd. 2:1–20).
    A single drama is played out in the verses: The young man is faced with two ways of life—acquiring wealth (or building a house) by murderous robbery with the danger of retribution, or honorable fidelity to his parents with the promise of long life, that is, without a retributive sword hanging over his head.
    As 2:12–19 points out, there are two hindrances to acquiring wisdom,

deceiving men (as here) and the deceiving woman. The contrasts (male and female, singular and plural) are a merism—the totality of people intent on hindering the quest for wisdom. The men (and their way) will be mentioned again in 2:12–15 and 4:10–19. The woman will be introduced in 2:16–19 and appear again in chap. 5, 6:20–35, chap. 7, and 9:13–18. It is not quite true, therefore, that the deceptive woman is the only block to wisdom.

[**1:8–9**] "Instruction" (*mûsār*) can mean a process ("discipline" in a modern sense) or a body of knowledge that must be "kept," which is the meaning here and in vv. 2, 3, and 7. "Teaching" (*tôrāh*) is essentially an interpretation of the tradition by an authority. The attractive jewelry symbolizes fidelity to parents; elsewhere it symbolizes Wisdom's favor (4:9), the riches that come to the wise (14:24), and the numerous progeny of the wise (17:6).

[**10–14**] The parents warn the young person, evidently leaving home on the way to adulthood, about the folly of unjust gain and the seduction of sinners' speech. The sinners recruit not just for a crime but for a way of life: "go *with us*"; "*we* will . . . "; "cast your lot *with us*"; there will be a single purse for all.

The passage illustrates the ethical dualism of Proverbs; that is, people join one of two groups by their actions. The calls of parents and sinners are similar to the calls of personified Wisdom and Folly later in the book. Verse 11: "for blood" means to shed blood; the word "without cause" means that the victims have done nothing deserving of death; they are innocent.

Verse 12 conceives of Sheol as a power rather than a place, like Isa. 5:14, "Therefore Sheol has widened its jaw, opened its boundless mouth, and [Jerusalem's] glory and multitude descend." The wicked identify their goal with that of death, like Num. 16:30–33: "And the underworld swallowed them . . . and they went down alive to Sheol." Colon B is governed by the verb "swallow" in colon A. Verse 14, "a single purse," means the robbers will divide the loot evenly (Delitzsch). The great difference between the two ways is their result: long life or unexpected death (vv. 18–19).

[**15–19**] The opening "my son, do not . . . " reprises vv. 8 and 10. "Way" is one of the great metaphors of the book. *Derek*, usually translated "way," occurs over seventy times; *'ōrah*, "path," occurs twenty times; *nĕtîbāh*, "path, road," occurs six times; the phrase "to walk on the path" (= to conduct oneself), occurs six times.

The invitation of the deceptive men has remarkable similarities to the invitation of the deceptive woman in chap. 7, which shares its vocabulary: "Come!"; "to lie in wait"; "to find"; and "Sheol." Both attempt to persuade people to be their companions or to walk on their road. The men (and their path) will appear again in 2:13–15 and 4:10–19.

[**16–17**] Both verses begin with "because" (*kî*). Normally, there is only one *kî* after a warning such as that in v. 15 (e.g., 1:8–9; 3:1–2, 11–12, 25–26, 31–32; 4:1–2, 21–22; 5:1–3).[3]

Verse 16 must be judged a secondary explanation from Isa. 59:7, which was inserted because a copyist did not understand v. 17. Verse 16 is missing in two important Greek manuscripts. The inserted verse gives as a reason for keeping away from an evil path the too obvious one that sinners' feet race to evil and therefore will incur wrath. Verse 17 is the original explanation for the warning of v. 15. Hunters netted birds in Palestine by placing two vanes of netting on either side of a clearing or hole strewn with bait, while they hid behind a wall, holding onto the cord. When the birds alighted the vanes were quickly pulled toward each other.[4]

What is the meaning of the metaphor? Several interpretations have been proposed. A common view, originating with Rashi, and supported by Ehrlich and D. W. Thomas, suggests the net is baited with grain: "for it is to no effect that the net is strewn (with seed for bait) in the sight of any winged fowl." In this view, birds watch the trap being set but, unable to control their appetite, walk into it. So also robbers, unable to control their appetite for gain, disregard warnings of their destruction and walk into punishment (McKane 271). This interpretation, however, misinterprets the verb *zārāh,* "to throw high" (for winnowing grain), which does not mean to cast a hunting net over birds (*pāraś* is the normal verb for casting a net) but to lift it up so it can be clearly seen. The piel passive participle, *mĕzōrāh,* "thrown high," is a "divine passive," a customary way of stating divine or customary agency. Verse 17 can be paraphrased: God does not hold up to the view of the wicked the net set to entrap them. Divine retribution ("a net") operates invisibly.

Verse 18, with its twice-repeated suffixal endings *-ām,* "their," refers back to the same endings in v. 15. In v. 19, the subject of "takes the life of" is the unjust gain (*beṣa'*) of colon A. Paradoxically, the wealth that is possessed kills its possessor (10:2; 11:4).

In summary, the inexperienced person, as yet untaught by wisdom, is instructed about the two paths in life, one characterized by seductive words and glittering prizes (though in reality strewn with traps), and the other honorable and safe. Voices summon to each. One voice tells lies, saying nothing about the danger of sudden death. The other is truthful. The real topic is the two ways lying before every person. Greed is an example rather than the main issue.

3. Proverbs 4:15–17 has two instances of *kî.*

4. O. Keel, *The Symbolism of the Biblical World: Ancient Near Eastern Iconography and the Book of Psalms* (New York: Crossroad, 1978), 89–95.

Wisdom Poem I:
The Risk of Spurning Me

1:20 Wisdom cries aloud in the streets,
      in the squares she lifts up her voice,

21 at the head of the bustling street she calls,
      at the portals of the city gate.
  In the city she speaks her message:

22 "How long, O simple ones, will you choose ignorance,[a]

23   will you turn away at my reproof?
  Here I have been disclosing my thoughts to you,
      speaking my words to you.

24 Because I called and you refused,
      stretched out my hand without anyone heeding,

25 because you spurned all my counsel,
      did not welcome my reproof,

26 I will laugh at your disaster,
      will mock when terror comes upon you,

27 when terror comes upon you like a storm,
      disaster reaches you like a hurricane,
      when trouble and woe come upon you.

28 Then they will call but I will not answer,
      they will look for me but not find me,

29 because they hated knowledge,
      and chose not to revere Yahweh,

30 they did not welcome my counsel
      and brushed aside all my reproof.

31 Well, then, they shall eat the fruit of their ways,
      they shall be sated from their own plans.

32 Indeed, the turning away of the simple kills them,
      the self-sufficiency of fools destroys them.

33 But the one who listens to me will dwell secure,
      will be at rest, past fearing disaster.

a. We omit v. 22bc: "(How long) will scorners join in scorning, will fools hate knowledge," as an early and intrusive addition to the Hebrew text (see commentary).

Verses 20–23 comprise the first of three addresses by Woman Wisdom. The two others (chaps. 8 and 9:1–6, 11) conclude chaps. 1–9 on a note of promise, while this speech opens the chapters on a note of threat. Wisdom's three speeches have common features: the setting of crowded city streets; the same audience (the untaught as well as a more general audience, 1:22; 8:4–5; 9:4); a competing appeal by another woman (when chap. 7 is taken with chap. 8); an invitation to enter into a relationship with Wisdom that brings long life, riches, and repute. The literary context broadens the scope of her address: The hearer is summoned to flee destructive folly and follow the life of wisdom, which is sanctioned by God.

The speech is carefully crafted with a vivid setting, lively personification, and rhetorical questions. Arguments are linked and rounded off with examples, and are amplified by parallel (though nonprogressive) syntax.

A Setting	vv. 20–21
B Wisdom's Withdrawal	vv. 22–32
Rebuke and Announcement	vv. 22–23
I Reason and Rejection	vv. 24–27
II Reason and Rejection	vv. 28–31
Summary	v. 32
C Wisdom's Presence	v. 33

Verses 24–27 use the second person plural, and vv. 28–31 use the third person plural. Alternation of grammatical person is a feature of Hebrew style and not necessarily an indication of diverse authorship. There are an extraordinary number of repeated words: eight are repeated twice, and four ("call" [*qārā'*], "reproof" [*tôkaḥ*], "terror" or "fear" [*'êd*], "come" [*bô'*]) are repeated three times. Two words in the questions of vv. 22–23a appear again in the penultimate verse ("turn from" [triliteral root *šûb*], "untaught" [*pĕtî*]) and bring the questions to a proper conclusion.

A persistent problem in the interpretation of the poem has been the proper translation of vv. 22–23a. Our translation follows in general JPSV and NAB, which differ from most in taking v. 23a as governed by the interrogative adverb, "How long?" of v. 22a. Woman Wisdom in v. 23, in our view, is not asking for a change of heart but announcing the consequences of disobedience that has already occurred. Most translations take the imperfect verb in v. 23a (*tāšûbû*) as an imperative, and join it to the following verse: "Give heed to my reproof; I will pour out my thoughts to you" (so REB, NRSV, and NJB). But why would Wisdom ask her hearers for obedience in v. 23a and in the very next verse declare disaster inevitable?[5] Alonso Schökel recognizes the temporal problem and suggests that vv. 23–31 is a future conditional statement that Wisdom will speak if her hearers do not immediately take her appeal to heart. His solution is contrived, however.

Interpreting v. 23a as a call to repentance ("Turn to my reproof!") is unsatisfactory for other reasons as well. First, *tāšûbû* + *lĕ* does not mean "turn to" as some translators render it. It can mean "to *re*turn to, come back to" (Ehrlich)

---

5. For this point and other matters, we are indebted to R. E. Murphy, "Wisdom's Song: Proverbs 1:20–33," *CBQ* 48 (1986): 456–60, and M. Gilbert, "Le discours menaçant de Sagesse en Proverbes 1,20–33," in *Storia e tradizioni di Israele* (J. A. Soggin volume), ed. D. Garrone and F. Israel (Brescia: Paideia, 1991), 99–119.

but this rendering makes no sense in the context.[6] Second, given the importance of word repetition elsewhere in the poem, one would expect *tāšûbû* in v. 23a to have the same meaning as its cognate *mĕšûbat* in v. 32, "turning away from, rejection." Third, v. 23a fits well with the preceding three cola, since its second person address matches in chiastic form the second person address in v. 22a. Fourth, no version except V certainly interpreted the verse like MT. Accordingly, we omit vv. 22bc as secondary, make a couplet of vv. 22a and 23a, and take the verb in v. 23a as an imperfect ("turn away at my rebuke").

[1:20–21] Like 8:1–3 and 9:1–3, the setting is described in rich detail: the teeming streets and the gate, where people congregated, the elders met to govern (Ps. 107:32; Prov. 24:7), and the law court sat. The site is the upper city, where business and government were carried on. It is possible that Wisdom's authoritative speaking reflects the behavior of certain women in Israel whose uncommon wisdom gave them authority to address the public in crises, as when the rebel Sheba took refuge in Abel Beth-maacah and put the city in danger.

> A wise woman called from the city, "Listen! Listen! Pray, tell Joab, 'Come here so I can speak to you.'" He came up to her and the woman said, "Are you Joab?" He said, "I am." She said, "Listen to the words of your servant." He said, "I'm listening." She said, "They used to say in the old days, 'Let them hold an inquiry in Abel.' . . . . . I am one of the peaceful and faithful in Israel. You seek to destroy a city that is a mother in Israel. Why are you swallowing up the heritage of Yahweh?" (2 Sam. 20:16–19; see also 2 Samuel 14).

The woman listened to Joab, judged his request to be proper, and ordered the townspeople to cut off Sheba's head and throw it over the wall. Wisdom seems to act like such a wise woman, deciding and acting authoritatively in a crisis. Such a possible real-life setting should not make one forget, however, the literary nature of this poem.

[22–23] Wisdom finds her audience guilty of preferring folly to wisdom; specifics follow in vv. 24–32. "How long?" implies the audience is rejecting Wisdom, which justifies the announcement of punishment that follows. "Simple" here means unresponsive and reckless.

[24–27] The section is marked off by the use of the second person plural verb form in contrast to the third person plural of vv. 28–31. Verses 24–27 are intensely personal. In v. 26 Wisdom laughs derisively with total awareness and power, as Yahweh laughs in scorn of the nations in Ps. 2:4. Vv. 26–27 are chiastic in their placement of "disaster," "come," and "terror." Wisdom, it is im-

---

6. The absolute use of *šûb* is common (Judg. 2:19; 8:33; Josh. 23:12; Jer. 8:4; Ps. 78:41). The verb never occurs in the Bible with the preposition *l* in the sense of turn or return to a word or idea. In Ugaritic *ṯwb hwt* means "to return to [my] word" (*KTU* 1.4.VII.24–25; 1.4.VI.1–2). Thus *lĕ* in *lĕtôkaḥtî* in v. 23a is a kind of locational use of *l,* "with regard to," hence "as regards my reproof" (see *IBHS* §11.2.d).

portant to note, does not cause the disaster, which simply "comes." Wisdom simply withdraws when it does come. According to the poetic justice operative in the book, Wisdom does not answer her clients, just as they did not answer her.

Some scholars point out similarities to the language of the prophets in Wisdom's harsh words (e.g., Isa. 65:2, 12; 66:4; Jer. 7:13; 11:11; 23:19), but her words use the language of personal life rather than of national life.

[28–31] The shift from second to third person address in v. 28 (and also in v. 31) shows Wisdom distancing herself from her hearers. Her message is that people must bear the consequences of their own actions and plans (v. 31).

[32–33] A summary of the rebuke (reprising two words from vv. 22–23a) underscores the life-death consequences of Wisdom's offer. Wisdom's speech ends not with a threat but with a promise of peace and security to her disciples. Her friends will not be haunted by the specter of sudden reversal and the trouble that comes from sinful actions (*rā'āh,* as used in 22:3 and 24:16).

In her speech, Woman Wisdom appears in the upper part of the city, where public business was conducted. She abruptly confronts "the simple" and narrates the story of their refusal to listen to her. The poem presumes prior neglect and obstinacy, which surprises readers (and certainly confused translators). Wisdom does not threaten in the traditional sense but simply announces she will not be there when the inevitable calamity comes. Punishment will come of its own accord; she is not its instrument. To reject wisdom is to reject Yahweh (v. 29), illustrating the opening statement that the beginning of wisdom is the revering of Yahweh. (v. 1) At the end (v. 33), her tone softens, and she implies that it is not too late to repent. Those who listen to her will dwell secure. Chapter 8 reverses the tone, devoting nearly all of its verses to promises, threatening only in its final line.

Chapter 1, considered as a whole, displays a progression in its three sections. The purpose of the book is to make it possible for its readers to live in wisdom and fidelity to Yahweh. The parents of the young person leaving home on the way to adulthood warn against bad companions and violence and point out the hidden and ineluctable "law" of divine retribution. In third and climatic place, Wisdom herself speaks where all can hear and respond to her. She warns against foolish autonomy and invites her hearers to a relationship with her.

It is worth noting how close Wisdom's voice is to the voice of the parents in 1:8–19 and to the voices of the father and mother in later chapters. They all speak with the same accents. As noted in the Introduction, personified Wisdom is partly modeled on the Akkadian *ummānu.* These heavenly sages gave divine wisdom to human beings in a chain of mediation that ended with human mediators such as kings, scribes, teachers, and heads of families. Heavenly wisdom is embodied in institutions, hence the common voice.[7]

7. Cf. C. Wilcke, "Göttliche und menschliche Weisheit im Alten Orient," in *Weisheit,* Archäologie der literarischen Kommunikation 3, ed. A. Assmann (Munich: Fink, 1991), 259–70.

Proverbs 2

Lecture II: Seek Wisdom and Yahweh
Will Keep You Safe

2:1   My son, if (*'ālep*) you accept my words,
         store up my commands within you,

2   turning your ear to wisdom,
         directing your heart to insight,

3   yes, if (*'ālep*) you call out to understanding,
         raise your voice to insight,

4   if (*'ālep*) you seek it as you do silver,
         search for it as for treasure,

5   then (*'ālep*) you will understand the revering of Yahweh,
         you will find knowledge of God;

6   for Yahweh gives wisdom,
         from his mouth come knowledge and insight;

7   he stores up[a] resourcefulness for the upright
         and is a shield for those who walk in integrity;

8   he protects the paths of justice,
         safeguards the way of those loyal to him.

9   Then (*'ālep*) you will understand righteousness and justice,
         and equity—every good path,

10   for wisdom will come into your heart,
         knowledge will be at home in your breast;

11   prudence will safeguard you,
         insight will protect you,

12   saving (*lāmed*) you from the evil way,
         from the man who speaks falsehoods,

13   from those who have abandoned right paths,
         to walk in dark ways,

14   from those who delight in doing evil,
         rejoice in malicious utterance,

15   who make their paths crooked,
         pervert their tracks;

16   saving (*lāmed*) you from the forbidden woman,
         from the stranger who uses smooth words,

17   who has abandoned the partner of her youth,
         forgotten the covenant of her God,

18   for her path[b] leads down to Death,
         her tracks lead to the Rephaim.

19 None who go to her ever return,
   none ever regain the path of life.
20 Thus (*lāmed*) you will walk on the way of the good,
   keep to the paths of the righteous.
21 For the upright will dwell on the land,
   and those with integrity will remain on it.
22 But the wicked will be cut off from the land,
   and the treacherous will be uprooted from it.

a. We read qere *yiṣpōn,* "he stores," which accords with T and V.

b. In MT, "For her house sinks down to death," a masculine noun, (*bayit*), is the subject of the third feminine singular verb. Moreover, it is not clear how a house (even if understood as "household") could "sink into death." The versions all read MT but interpret it with such variety as to offer little help to commentators. With many translators, we emend MT *byth,* "her house," to *ntybth,* "her path," which contains the same letters, plus *n,* but in a different order.

A Ugaritic funerary text (*KTU* 1.161.18) reads *išḫn špš,* which may shed light on the underworld context of the Hebrew verb *šāḥāh,* "to sink." The Ugaritic phrase can be taken as an imperative verb in the niphal conjugation, "Sink down, O Sun (into the netherworld)." For the text, see W. T. Pitard, "RS 34:126: Notes on the Text," *Maarav* 4 (1987): 75–86.

The chapter is a single poem, an acrostic of twenty-two lines (the number of consonants in the Hebrew alphabet). Acrostic poems use the Hebrew alphabet in a variety of ways. Some merely have twenty-two lines, whereas others begin each line with a successive letter in the alphabet (as 31:10–31). Our poem makes use of only two letters, the first letter, *'ālep,* and the first letter of the second half of the alphabet, *lāmed.* In the first half of the poem (vv. 1–11), an initial *'ālep* (') predominates, appearing in *'im,* "if " (three times) and *'āz,* "then" (two times). In the second half (vv. 11–22), an initial *lāmed* (*l*) predominates, appearing in *lĕhaṣṣîlĕkā,* "saving" (vv. 12 and 16) and in *lĕma'an,* "thus" (v. 20). The significant occurrences of the initial *'ālep* and *lāmed* are indicated in the translation. According to the placement of the two letters the poem can be divided into two equal parts.

A. vv. 1–4	four bicola	B. vv. 12–15	four bicola
vv. 5–8	four bicola	vv. 16–19	four bicola
vv. 9–11	three bicola	vv. 20–22	three bicola

The movement in the poem from one letter to the other reflects a semantic movement from one topic to another. In vv. 1–11 the emphasis is on "wisdom"; there are twenty-one substantives or pronouns for wisdom in the first section but none in the second. Verses 12–22 emphasize "way"; "way" or its synonyms appear ten times in the second section but only three times in the first. The shift from one theme to the other begins in vv. 7–8, where words for "way" first appear.

The speech is one enormous sentence. Meinhold translates it by a single German sentence. A single syntactic thread runs through the whole: *if* (') you search (vv. 1–4) . . . *then* (') Yahweh/Wisdom will (vv. 5–11) . . . *save* (*l*) *you from* (vv. 12–19) . . . *so that* (*l*) *you may walk* (vv. 20–22) . . . A purpose clause in vv. 20–22 brings vv. 12–15 and 16–19 to their conclusion. Verse 8, the concluding line of the first "then" section (vv. 5–8), is the key verse in the structure: its verbs "to protect" and "to safeguard" recur in reverse order in v. 11; its nouns "paths" and "way" recur in v. 13 and again (in reverse order) in v. 20. Verses 12–15 // 16–19, the two negative portrayals of danger, correspond to vv. 5–8 // 9–11, the two positive portrayals of protection.

Some scholars suggest the poem has been expanded from an original short poem. For R. N. Whybray the original core is vv. 1, 9, and 16–19; for D. Michel it is vv. 1–4, 9–15, and 20. In the course of the "Yahwehizing" of wisdom literature (attributing to Yahweh the direction of all human activities), the poem attained its present shape.[1] Such analyses are unconvincing, however, for they presuppose mechanical symmetry and neglect the poetic techniques noted above.

M. Fox rightly calls attention to the pedagogy presupposed in the poem. The father encourages his son to persevere in striving for wisdom by holding out the assurance that God will guarantee the quest. "[E]ducation has two phases. It commences with the father's teaching and its rote incorporation by the child, but this must be complemented by the learner's own thought and inquiry. *Then* God steps into the picture and grants wisdom. . . . Education is thus a cooperative effort of child, parents, and God."[2] When God grants someone wisdom, God also grants that person protection, for it is "the wise man's knowledge of the right and his desire to do it, which will preserve him from the perils of sin."[3] Education in ancient Israel consisted not only in imparting knowledge but also in eliciting the desire to persevere in the search despite difficulties caused by the wicked. Education and instruction are about virtue and character.[4]

---

1. Whybray, "Some Literary Problems in Proverbs 1–9," *VT* 16 (1966): 486–92; Michel, "Proverbia 2—ein Dokument der Geschichte der Weisheit," in *Alttestamentlicher Glaube und biblische Theologie* (FS H. D. Preuss), ed. J. Hausmann and H.-J. Zobel (Stuttgart: Kohlhammer, 1992), 233–43. W. McKane, though disagreeing with some of Whybray's conclusions, sees the poem as worked over by later moralistic editors who have given it "a diffuse, rambling style of preaching" (279).

2. "The Pedagogy of Proverbs 2," *JBL* 113 (1994): 242. Fox's italics.

3. Ibid., 239.

4. On character in wisdom literature, see W. P. Brown, *Character in Crisis: A Fresh Approach to the Wisdom Literature of the Old Testament* (Grand Rapids: Eerdmans, 1996).

[2:1–4] The speaker is an anonymous wisdom teacher who assumes a Solomonic (1:1) and parental (1:8) mantle. The teacher constantly appeals to the student's reasoning power. Verses 1–4 encourage the young student to pursue wisdom by promising the benefits that come from its acquisition; the teacher initiates the search for wisdom by asking the hearer to "accept my words," that is, the tradition as mediated by the teacher (v. 1). Having established the teacher-disciple relationship, the teacher urges the seeker to use ears, heart (v. 2), and tongue (v. 3) with the energy and single-mindedness one uses in seeking wealth (v. 4). The son begins by memorizing his father's words and then reflects on them in his heart. As if in response to the learner's desire, God grants wisdom, a gift that includes the shrewdness to keep safe on the road.

[5–8] The tension generated by the repetition of "if" in vv. 1–4 is resolved in v. 5 with "*then* you will understand . . . " The verb *bîn* normally means "to understand" or "to analyze" (as in 1:2, 6) but its pairing with "knowledge of God" in colon B suggests a more concrete meaning here, something like "to grasp through experience."

The two triliteral roots in v. 5, "to understand" (*tābîn*) and "knowledge" (*da'at*) occur again in v. 6b in *da'at* and *tĕbûnāh*. The phrase "knowledge of God" has the meaning it has in Hos. 4:1 and 6:6, where it is parallel to *ḥesed*, "loving kindness"—devotion or loyalty to God. The search for wisdom brings one into a right relationship with Yahweh. The search does not end with the seeker grasping it but in Yahweh bestowing it (v. 6). These verses hold in perfect balance divine initiative and human activity.

In vv. 7–8, wisdom is more than theoretical knowledge, for by it one walks on the road of life in safety. In v. 7 "stores up" reprises the same word occurring in v. 1; to the person who stores up the teacher's commands, God dispenses from the divine treasury. The verb has the sense of setting something aside for a favorite, who alone will benefit from it come what may (Job 21:19; Prov. 13:22; Cant. 7:14).[5] In v. 7, the metaphors of shield and of walking in integrity introduce the themes of protection and of the path. Verse 8, as already noted, is pivotal in the structure; its two verbs ("to protect" and "to safeguard") are reprised in v. 11 and its two nouns ("paths" and "way") are reprised in v. 20.

[9–11] Equally important is the quest for wisdom vv. 5–8. The prize in vv. 9–11 is wisdom itself and ethical behavior. The words "righteousness and justice, and equity" are synonyms of wisdom in 1:3b. The full dimension of personal life is envisioned—the sapiential, ethical, and religious. The sequence of actions in vv. 5–8 is like the sequence in vv. 9–11: an experience of wisdom (v. 9), the coming of wisdom to the seeker (v. 10) and its protection of the person on life's path (v. 11).

---

5. Fox, "Pedagogy of Proverbs," 239.

What kind of protection is promised here (and earlier in v. 8)? Protection from violent and deceitful men in vv. 13–15 and from the seductive woman in vv. 16–19. The oppositions (male and female, plural and singular) suggest totality. The ultimate purpose of the protection is, according to v. 20, that the seeker can walk safely along the path of life and come to enjoy the benefits promised to the wise.

[12–15] The second or "*lāmed* part" of the poem begins here. Proverbs is always realistic about the dangers the virtuous must face. The dangers are two: deceptive men and a deceptive woman; each invites the student to walk on a wrong path. The oppositions (male and female, singular and plural) form a merism, like high and low, right and left; here it means all possible dangerous people. Both the men and the woman have left virtue behind: the word "abandoned" occurs in v. 13 and v. 17. "The man" in v. 12 is collective as can be seen from the plural verbs and pronouns in vv. 13–15. Their wickedness is deeply ingrained; they take pleasure in luring others to follow them. Nothing is said of the final fate of the evildoers, for the text is concerned with the dangers posed to those who seek wisdom.

[16–19] The verses offer a parallel to the picture of the men in vv. 12–15. The deceptive woman makes her first appearance in the book; she will appear again in 5:1–6; 6:20–35; chap. 7; and 9:13–18. As proposed in the Introduction, Proverbs' portrait of the female deceiver and the youth combines traditional warnings against a foreign woman (one not known in the town) with the epic type-scene of the goddess inviting the young hero to start a new life by marrying her. Verse 17 alludes to those whom the woman has earlier betrayed (cf. 7:26–27 and 9:18).

The betrayer seeks another victim. "Her covenant with God" in v. 17b most probably refers, because of its parallel in colon A, to an earlier union sealed according to the rituals of her god. "Death" (v. 18) is a place as in Prov. 5:5, where it is parallel to "Sheol," and in 7:27. "Rephaim" is a term for the inhabitants of Sheol. There is no second chance if one accepts the forbidden woman's invitation, for Death is the land of no return (v. 19). "To go to her" has a sexual meaning: "to go into" is a Hebrew idiom for sexual intercourse. The woman's seductive words are a metaphor for the words of anyone who promises a "wisdom" that is counter to God's wisdom.

[20–22] Verse 20, syntactically, is a purpose clause that completes the vast and complex sentence of the poem. If you seek wisdom sincerely, Yahweh will give to you a wisdom that shields and protects you from violent men and seductive women, *so that* you can walk on the path of the good and enjoy the land. The verse completes the theme of protection on life's way mentioned in vv. 8 and 11. Verses 21–22 echo the ending of Wisdom's speech in 1:32–33, where refusing Wisdom's call meant death and obedience meant life. The land as an image of bounty is found in Psalm 37 (e.g., vv. 3, 9, 11, 22, 29, 34, 38): to dwell on (or inherit) the land or to be uprooted from the land are images for God's retributive action. While there may also be an allusion to the land of Canaan of Israel's historical traditions, Psalm 37 and Proverbs 2 use dwelling on the land more generally, as metaphors for living in peace and dying prematurely. Our passage contains a further nuance: living wisely assures that one will remain on this earth rather than descending to the underworld before one's time.

The father, or teacher, encourages his son, or student, to persevere in the quest for wisdom. If the young person seeks wisdom wholeheartedly and with persistence, Yahweh will come into the process, and grant wisdom. God will give the resourcefulness one needs to live securely. Wisdom will come to one and keep one safe from the two great dangers of wise living—deceiving men and women. The young person will be armed against their deceptive words by the shrewdness given by God, the teacher, and the student's own study, and so will be able to walk with the good (i.e., be among those God has guaranteed to protect) and enjoy life. Enjoyment of life is portrayed under the image of remaining on the land.

Proverbs 3

There is scholarly consensus that vv. 1–12 form a literary unit, but there is considerable disagreement on the boundaries of the literary units in the rest of the chapter. Zimmerli and Alonso Schökel divide the chapter into vv. 1–12, 13–26, and 27–35. McKane and Plöger make the divisions vv. 1–12, 13–10, 21–26, and 27–35. We follow Meinhold, Whybray, and M. Fox[1] in taking vv. 1–12 and 21–35 as the third and fourth of the ten instructions in chaps. 1–9. Verses 13–20 are a separate wisdom poem. In this view, vv. 1–12 are an instruction on the disciple's relation to God and vv. 21–35 are an instruction on the disciple's relation to other people. The topic of God dominates the first section; the divine name (if one counts the independent pronoun *hû'*, "him," in v. 6b) occurs seven times. In vv. 21–35 there are twelve substantives meaning "neighbor" or "the other" (including *hû'*, "he" in v. 29b). In the first poem the vetitive particle *'al*, "not," occurs six times, and in the second poem, seven times.

Lecture III: Trust in God
Leads to Prosperity

3:1 My son, do not forget my teaching,
     let your mind retain my commands,

2 For they will increase the days and years of life,
     and bestow prosperity upon you.

---

1. "Pedagogy of Proverbs 2," *JBL* 113 (1994): 235.

3   Do not let love and fidelity depart from you;
        bind them about your neck,[a]
4   and you will find favor and good repute
        in the eyes of God and human beings.
5   Trust in Yahweh with all your heart;
        do not rely on your own understanding.
6   In all your ways acknowledge him:
        he will make your way straight.
7   Be not wise in your own eyes;
        revere Yahweh and turn from evil;
8   it will mean health for your body,
        strength for your bones.
9   Honor Yahweh with your wealth
        with the first fruits of your crops,
10   and your barns will be filled with grain,[b]
        your vats will overflow with wine.
11   My son, do not reject the discipline of Yahweh,
        do not disdain his correction,
12   for anyone he loves he reproves,
        like a father the son whom he favors.[c]

a. "Write them on the tablet of your heart," is not in the important Greek manuscripts Vaticanus and Sinaiticus and can be regarded as an addition to the Hebrew text. It seems to have been attracted into this verse from 7:3.

b. Hebrew *śābā'*, literally, "satiety, plenty" acquires the concrete meaning "grain" when paired with *tîrôš*, "wine," as in the eighth century B.C.E. Phoenician Karatepe inscription III.7 and 9: "May this city be the possessor of plenty (of grain) and wine (*śb' wtrš*)" (*KAI* 26.iii.9).

c. G has "for whom the Lord loves, he corrects, / and scourges (*mastagoi*) every son whom he receives." G reads the Hebrew consonants *yk'b* (= *yak'îb*, "he [God] will scourge"). MT interprets the consonants as *wk'b* and points them *ûk'āb*, "like a father." G and MT probably read the same letters, for the letters *y* and *w* were often confused in the script. Scholars are divided on which is the better interpretation of the Hebrew consonants.

We follow MT, for (1) *yak'îb* in Job 5:18, which is cited in support of the emendation, is not relevant, for it means "to injure" rather than reprove; (2) MT preserves the inclusion of thought: The poem began with a call to "my son" to heed his father and ends with God correcting like a father.

The instruction or lecture consists of a series of six four-line exhortations, in which the second bicolon of each mentions a reward or benefit. In the first five exhortations (vv. 1–10) the father promises the son a reward for righteous conduct—long life, a good name, divine protection, health, and abundant crops. The last statement (vv. 11–12) departs from the exhortation-reward scheme, perhaps implying that being Yahweh's "son" or disciple does not by that fact alone bring unalloyed bliss. Yahweh may use the occasionally harsh methods of a father to reprove.

The exhortations reveal a process like that in chap. 2. The father (or teacher) first invites his son (or disciple) into a relationship with him by asking the son to memorize his teaching (v. 1). Next, he asks him to enter a relationship of trust (v. 3), and finally to trust in God who takes up the parental task of education (v. 5). Trust in Yahweh means giving up confidence in oneself (v. 7), honoring God with one's wealth (v. 9), and allowing Yahweh to become one's teacher and father (vv. 11–12). The human father or teacher begins a process that is brought to completion by God and the learner.

The educational process described in the verses is drawn from real life, from the way teaching was done in an ancient Israelite household. The father-son relationship can stand for the teacher-disciple relationship (cf. 1 Sam. 3:6, 16; 2 Kings 2:12). The metaphor can be applied to any teacher-learner relationship where one human being helps another to seek wisdom in the face of difficulties and brings the person into a relationship with God. The context—motivating an inexperienced student—forbids us to interpret these verses as a naive and mechanical doctrine of divine reward. Proverbs is realistic about the dangers and difficulties faced by those who seek after wisdom. These have been sketched in the first two lectures. The teacher here wants to underline the benefits of the search and the help one can expect from God.

[3:1–2] The teacher urges his son to memorize his teaching, the traditional way of learning in antiquity. The father does not specify any content of his commands, but we may suppose they are the basic teaching of chaps. 1–9: to seek wisdom first, to revere the teacher's words, to trust God's action.

[3–4] The verses urge the student to exercise loyalty and faithfulness to the teacher. Education is not just a matter of memorizing words and relaying information, but involves trust and respect between two people. Acting according to the revered teacher's counsels will eventually bring the learner a good reputation. One's reputation in the community is an important social good. Public shame, on the other hand, destroys one's place within the community.

The appearance here of vocabulary characteristic of Deuteronomy, such as "teaching," "commandments," "do not forget," "length of days," affixing written teaching to one's body (Deut. 6:8), suggests that the exhortatory rhetoric of Deuteronomy and Proverbs had a common origin in the scribal class of Jerusalem responsible for their writing. Deuteronomy 6:5–9 (reprinted below) has many similarities to this section and to the next poem, 3:21–24.

You shall love Yahweh (cf. Prov. 3:5–9, "trust," "acknowledge," "revere," "honor" Yahweh) your God with *all your mind* (lit., "heart"; Prov. 3:5a) and with all your soul and with all your strength. Let *the words* (cf. Prov. 3:1, "teaching," "commands") I command you this day *be upon your heart* (Prov. 3:1b). You shall impress them on your children and speak of them *when you sit* (Prov. 3:24a) in your house and *when you walk on the way* (Prov. 3:23a) and *when you lie down* (Prov. 3:24b) and when you get up. *Bind them* (Prov. 3:3b) as a sign upon your hand and let them serve as a frontlet between *your eyes* (Prov. 3:21a).

One should not conclude from the similar language that Proverbs is talking about law, but rather that there was a common tradition of exhortatory rhetoric among the scribes of Jerusalem.

[5–6] The words spoken by the teacher aim at making the student wise. Wisdom includes knowledge, ethical action, and piety. The teacher now assures the student that the quest for wisdom is not a solitary venture. Yahweh comes into the picture to aid in the acquisition of wisdom, which brings many benefits. Trust in Yahweh, however, is not easy. It means giving up trust in one's own understanding exclusively. The perspective is dramatic: Place your full trust in Yahweh rather than in your own understanding. The metaphor of straight and crooked is employed to show that God makes the learner's path of life straight, that is, righteous and safe.

That reverence prolongs life is also found in the Babylonian *Counsels of Wisdom:* "Reverence begets favor, / Sacrifice prolongs life, / And prayer atones for guilt. / He who fears the gods is not slight by [. . .] / He who fears the Anunnaki [gods] extends his days (lines 143–47)."[2]

[7–8] Verse 7 repeats the sentiments of vv. 5–6 but reverses the order of cola in the first bicolon. To be wise in one's own eyes is a serious fault in Proverbs (26:5, 12; 28:11) and implies an unhealthy self-sufficiency and unwillingness to hear others. Its opposite here is revering Yahweh, which implies turning away from evil. The result is health, renewed physical energy.

[9–10] Another step in one's relationship with Yahweh is honoring him with one's wealth and first fruits. This is the only verse in Proverbs that commands a liturgical offering. To give the best of one's crops to God will assure that one's crops are blessed and that one's barns and wine vats will be full. Note that the hearer is assumed to be a member of a community, observing its ceremonies and its rituals. The search for wisdom and God is not a purely private and inner quest but communitarian and celebrated in ritual.

[11–12] The final step in the learning process is now described. The student has begun with the words of his father, become active, and discovered that God has entered the process. Verses 11–12 ask the student to allow God full scope, and state that God's entry means discipline and "reproof."

2. *BWL*, 105.

Deuteronomy 8 describes God educating Israel through the hardships of the wilderness journey from Egypt to Canaan: "You know in your heart that as a man disciplines his son, Yahweh your God disciplines you." It is necessary to warn students that ease and security are not automatic results of divine favor. Ancient Near Eastern clients of a god were inclined to reckon their status with their god through their prosperity. The status of the client or disciple ("my son") of Yahweh, however, cannot be so easily reckoned, for the disciple enters into a teacher-disciple, or father-son, relationship with Yahweh, and that relationship just might entail suffering. The suffering, however, is purposeful education. The analogy grounds the discipline in God's love. Though this text gives no reason why discipline involves suffering, Proverbs elsewhere assumes that one cannot become wise on one's own or inherently; one must follow a teacher and give up preconceptions, hence "suffer." God is a pedagogue and works like a father.

Interlude: Wisdom's Benefits and Prestige

3:13   Happy is the one who finds wisdom,
      the one who acquires understanding,
14   for her profit is worth more than silver,
      her yield is worth more than gold.
15   She is more precious than rubies;
      no treasure[a] can compare with her.
16   Length of days is in her right hand,
      in her left hand are riches and honor.
17   Her ways are pleasant ways,
      all her paths are peace.
18   A tree of life is she to those who embrace her,
      those who hold on to her are deemed happy.
19   Yahweh by wisdom founded the earth,
      established the heavens by understanding.
20   By his knowledge the deeps surged upward;
      the clouds dropped down dew.

a. We omit the second-person singular suffix on "treasure" with all the versions. The suffix probably arose from the confusion of the letters *k* and *m*.

As noted in the introduction to the chapter, there is considerable divergence of opinion on the boundaries of chap. 3 apart from vv. 1–12. The major question is whether the poem consists of vv. 13–20 or vv. 13–26. With most commentators, we take vv. 13–20 to be a single eight-line poem. Formally, three inclusions unite the poem: the triliteral root *'šr* occurs in v. 13a ("happy") and v. 18b ("are deemed happy"); "wisdom" and "understanding" are paired at the beginning and the end (vv. 12 and 19); the third person feminine independent pronoun *hî'* functions as a copula in a verbless clause in v. 15a (in the sixteenth place from the first word of the poem) and again as a copula in v. 18a (in the sixteenth place from the last word). Thematically, vv. 13–18 are incomplete without vv. 19–20, for the latter verses provide the explanation for why wisdom can confer such benefits. Those who acquire wisdom will be prosperous, for they live in accord with the principle by which God created the world.

The poem is an encomium of Wisdom through the listing of her benefits to human beings and the depiction of her role in God's act of creation. The encomium of wisdom remarkably foreshadows the encomium of the wise woman in 31:10–31, even to the singling out of the hands (31:19–20). Like the lectures of chaps. 1–9, the poem provides motives for hearers to pursue wisdom with all their heart. Wisdom has much more value than the trading capital of the time (gold, silver, and jewels), for she gives what money cannot buy—long life, wealth, and reputation, and makes the path of life both pleasant and secure. She is a tree of life. Why is Wisdom so powerful? Because the world in which we live is constructed by wisdom. Whoever lives in accord with wisdom will not go against but with the grain of the world. Such a person will receive all the goods a wisely constructed world can offer.

[3:13–15] The first verse is a declaration that the person who has found wisdom is happy and is in possession of what a human being most desires. Verses 14–15 contain the most developed of Proverbs' comparisons of wisdom with wealth (2:4; 8:10, 19; 16:6); the commerce metaphor is dominant in the chapter. The profit from wisdom is greater than can be got from silver and gold (v. 14), and more precious than any treasure (v. 15). The verses contain an implied comparison between finding wisdom and finding a spouse as a life companion. The verbs used in v. 13 of finding wisdom (cf. 3:13; 8:17, 35) are also used of finding a wife (18:22 and 31:10); "happy" is also said of the person who waits as a disciple at Wisdom's gate (8:34); the wife in 31:10 is also said to have a value beyond rubies.

[16–18] Verses 14–15 declared wisdom better than another thing, and now vv. 16–18 mention wisdom's value and power in itself, in progressively more metaphorical language: giver of long life, riches, reputation (v. 16), giver of a pleasant and prosperous course of life (v. 17), and an abiding source of life as a tree of life (v. 18). Wisdom's benefits in v. 16 are what people most want: long life (which implies health and vitality), wealth, and reputation. The latter was especially important in ancient Mediterranean societies, which saw individuals primarily as members of families and groups, and put great value on honor and reputation and on the avoidance of public shame.

Verse 18 declares Wisdom a tree of life, a tree that occurs in the Hebrew

Bible outside of Proverbs only in the Genesis story of the man and woman in the garden. God forbids the man to eat of the tree of the knowledge of good and evil (Gen. 2:16–17; 3:11) but not of the tree of life (Gen. 2:9), which remains in the background. The divine soliloquy in Gen. 3:22 is apparently not heard by the human couple: "and now, he might reach out his hand and take also from the tree of life, and eat, and live forever." The Genesis story ends with the tree of life guarded by angelic figures (Gen. 3:24). Proverbs reverses Genesis and ends the sequestering of the tree of life. On who finds wisdom finds life.[3]

The origins of the tree of life are obscure. Outside the Bible, there are no explicit references to it in ancient literature, though there are plants that bestow life as in *Gilgamesh* XI. The tree of life is found in 1 Enoch 25:4–5: 4 Ezra (2 Esdras) 2:12 and 8:52. Fourth Maccabees 18:16 quotes Prov. 3:18. Revelation 2:7 and 22:2, 14, and 19 connect the tree of life to the health-giving tree in Ezek. 47:12.

[19–20] The cosmogony gives the reason why Wisdom can offer such benefits to those who find her. Since the world was created by wisdom, anyone who lives in accord with it lives in accord with the structure and purpose of the universe. The cosmogony is the same as 8:22–29: God sinks pillars into the primordial waters on which he places the flat disk of earth (v. 19a); he creates an atmospheric dome over the earth by setting up a great plate (called a "tent" in Isa. 40:22; Ps. 104:2) to hold up the waters above (v. 19b); he provides exactly the right amount of this encompassing water for the earth by sinking channels down to the subterranean waters (v. 20a) and by having clouds bring the upper waters in rain (v. 20b). God's masterful handling of the waters displays his wisdom in a special way. Wisdom is after all the capacity to *act wisely,* which God has done by mastering the primordial waters and delicately tapping them to make the earth fertile.

The Bible elsewhere associates creation with the divine attribute of power as well as wisdom. In Jer. 10:12 (= 51:15; see 32:17; Ps. 65:7), God is praised: "He made the earth by his might, established the world by his wisdom, / and by his understanding he stretched out the heavens." Proverbs associates creation with wisdom for the purposes of the poem. The very wisdom by which Yahweh created the world is available to all who seek it.

In the ancient Near East, accounts of creation (often brief and stylized) have as their purpose to ground or explain an element of culture, and so with vv. 19–20. In this instance the issue is a way of life—living in accord with wisdom. The one who finds wisdom will find every human good—long life, wealth, honor, beauty, shalom.

3. See R. Marcus, "The Tree of Life in the Book of Proverbs," *JBL* 62 (1943): 117–20. On the general background, see H. N. Wallace, "Tree of Knowledge and Tree of Life," *ABD* 6.658–60.

Lecture IV: Justice toward
the Neighbor Brings Blessing

3:21 My son, do not lose sight of these,
          hold onto proficiency and shrewdness,

22   it will be life for your spirit,
          adornment for your neck;

23   you will walk your path safely;
          your feet will never stumble.

24   When you lie down, you will not be fearful;
          when you sleep, your slumber will be sweet.

25   You will not be afraid of sudden terror,
          the disaster that comes upon the wicked.

26   For Yahweh will be at your side
          and guard your feet from the snare.

27   Do not withhold a benefit from someone with a claim on it
          when it is in your power to do it.

28   Do not say to your neighbor, "Come back again;
          tomorrow I'll give it," when the thing is in your possession.

29   Do not plot evil against your neighbor
          when he lives trustfully with you.

30   Do not quarrel with someone without cause
          when he has done you no harm.

31   Do not emulate a violent person,
          do not adopt any of his ways,

32   for a devious man is an abomination to Yahweh;
          but his friendship is with the upright.

33   The curse of Yahweh is upon the house of a wicked person,
          but the house of the righteous is blessed.[a]

34   To the scorner he is scornful
          but to the humble he shows favor.

35   The wise will inherit honor,
          but fools will possess[b] disgrace.

a. We read *yĕbōrak*, "is blessed," with G and V.

b. We read *mršym*, "coming into possession of" (*mōrîšîm*, hiphil conjugation of *yāraš*) for MT *mrym* (*mērîm*, hiphil conjugation of *rûm*), "exalting." In Isa. 57:13 *yinḥal* is parallel to *yîraš*, "those who trust in me will inherit the land / and come into possession of my holy mountain."

The poem is the fourth of the ten wisdom instructions of chaps. 1–9. As noted in the introduction to chap. 3, there is some disagreement on the demarcation of the unit. Some reckon vv. 13–26 and 27–35 as distinct sections. The reasons for regarding vv. 21–35 as a single literary unit are: (1) vv. 13–20 make better sense as an independent encomium of wisdom than as part of vv. 21–26 (see the first paragraph of commentary); (2) "my son" in v. 21, though not invariably the marker of a distinct section (cf. 1:15; 3:11), marks a beginning here, for there is no addressee in the previous speech; (3) the admonitions in vv. 27–35 require an introduction; (4) the wisdom virtues in v. 21b (*tušîyāh* and *mĕzummāh*) have an operational sense well suited to the highly specific exhortations in vv. 27–35.[4]

The lecture evokes the previous lecture, vv. 1–12, which also contains seven prohibitions, each beginning with the vetitive particle *'al*, "not." Its topic is one's relationship to the neighbor, in contrast to one's relationship to God (vv. 1–12). The logic of the speech is coherent: (1) conduct toward a neighbor to whom one has an obligation (vv. 27–28), (2) conduct toward a neighbor with whom one lives on good terms (vv. 29–30), (3) conduct toward neighbors who are wicked and prosperous (v. 31–32). At v. 33, the vetitive particle "not" disappears and the righteous-wicked contrast is developed: In contrast to the wicked, the righteous are urged not to cross over to the circle of the wicked (v. 31–32); their dwellings are blessed (v. 33); they alone experience divine favor (v. 34), and obtain ultimate honor, a great name after their death (v. 35).

God favors and protects the wise, those who live shrewdly and avoid all forms of violence. The wise are righteous and avoid all violence and malice toward their neighbor. They are thus friends of God and enjoy his protection.

[3:21–26] As in the other lectures, the father (or teacher) asks the son (or disciple) to seek wisdom, in this case to practice two virtues, "proficiency and shrewdness." The two virtues connote clear thinking about acting in situations, a more concrete meaning of wisdom than in other lectures, such as chap. 2. The specific situations are mentioned in vv. 27–32. The specificity is notable only by Proverbs' standards; counsels in Mesopotamia and in Egypt ordinarily have in view specific actions.

Virtue brings prosperity in the form of protection from violent crime (vv. 22–26) and of friendship with God (vv. 32–35). Psalm 91 is remarkably similar in promising divine protection to those who trust in God: God will rescue you from the snare (Ps. 91:3 and Prov. 3:26); you will not fear the terror of the night (Ps. 91:5 and Prov. 3:24); you will see the punishment of the wicked and the blessings of the righteous (Ps. 91:8 and Prov. 3:33–35); you will walk life's path in safety (Ps. 91:11–12 and Prov. 3:23). Both pieces are cut from the same cloth.

The happy results of practicing wise behavior accrue to the body of the doer—eyes, spirit ("throat" as the source of breath), neck, side, and feet. In

4. M. Fox defines the first term as "clear, proficient thinking in the exercise of power and practical operation, as distinct from thinking as an intellectual act," and the second term as "private, unrevealed thinking and the faculty for it," "Words for Wisdom," *ZAH* 6 (1993): 149–69.

essence, practice of wisdom brings her gifts—long life (v. 22a), public honor (v. 22b), protection from crime and violence (vv. 23–25). As in the second and third instructions, the pursuit of wisdom soon brings the student to Yahweh; the opening duo of father and son becomes a trio of father, son, and God.

[27–32] The verses form a small subsection, six prohibitions on the topic of one's neighbor with one motive clause in v. 32; the verses are united by the anaphora *'al* ("not").

[27–28] The phrase "someone with a claim on it" (*bĕbālāyw*) is, literally, "owners," for the plural is a so-called intensive plural, which connotes "a singular individual . . . so thoroughly characterized by the qualities of the noun that a plural is used" (*IBHS* §7.4.3). The meaning is not the owner of a good but rather someone with a right to it. The Greek text and subsequent Jewish tradition interpret it as charity upon which the poor have a claim. Alonso Schökel compares Deut. 15:9: "Be careful not to harbor the wicked thought, 'The seventh year, the year of remission is approaching,' and you become mean to your poor kinsman and give him nothing; he will cry out against you to Yahweh and you will be held guilty." In short, one's kin had a claim on the land but it could be ignored by someone who had it in his power to grant it. Sirach 4:1–6, on giving to the poor, is similar in sentiment. Verse 28 is related in theme. Alonso Schökel suggests that Ex. 22:25–26 may illustrate the urgency of restoration before sunset: "If you take your neighbor's garment as pledge, you shall restore it before the sun goes down, for it is his only clothing, the covering for his skin; what else shall he sleep in?" In vv. 27–28 "proficiency and shrewdness" (v. 21) find expression not in self-promotion but in recognizing another person's claims on us (v. 27) and in being sensitive to that person's needs (v. 28).

[29–30] As the prohibitions in vv. 27–28 recognized the claim of people whose claims were likely to be forgotten by those more powerful than they, these verses forbid plotting against innocent neighbors. These verses underline the innocence of the neighbor and the initiative and malice of the quarreler.

[31–32] With the repetition of "not" and the motive clause, the verses bring the string of prohibitions to a climax. The command not to envy sinners in the sense of choosing their way of life is common (23:17; 24:1, 19). The sinner is specified in v. 31 as "a person of violence," which is the kind of person depicted in vv. 27–30—someone who violates the rights of the innocent neighbor. The motive clause in v. 32 is exactly appropriate for all the prohibitions: One who plots against others, "the neighbor," ends up crooked and an abomination to Yahweh, whose friendship is with "the straightforward." The metaphor of straight and crooked is a familiar one in Proverbs. One who destroys human relationships will experience the loss of the relationship with God.

[33–35] What is the relationship of these verses, which formally diverge from the previous verses, to vv. 27–32 and indeed to the whole poem? Evildoers have been present throughout the poem. God's provident protection in vv.

23–26 presupposes their malign presence; vv. 27–32 are warnings against their violent way of proceeding. It is only fitting that the lecture end with divine judgment upon them. Judgment is exercised in a biblical way; it is not an impartial pronouncement but a raising up of the righteous and a putting down of the wicked. Here it affects the "house" of the two groups (v. 33), God's manner toward each (v. 34), and their glory or shame, that is, whether and how they will live on in the memory of the living (v. 35). "Glory" in v. 35 has been taken by some Christian interpreters as referring to eternal life.

Proverbs 4

There is widespread agreement that there are three lectures in chap. 4: vv. 1–9, 10–19, and 20–27. These form the fifth, sixth, and seventh instructions in the series of ten in chaps. 1–9. In each, a father (or teacher) exhorts a son (or disciple) to heed "the discipline of a father" (v. 1) or "my words" (vv. 10, 20). The fruits of obedience are expressed with distinctive metaphors: in vv. 1–9, protection and honor; in vv. 10–19, the right way that protects the person walking in it; in vv. 20–27, life and health. A common process is discernible in all three metaphors: Heeding the words of the human teacher brings the learner to a position where wisdom itself (or the right way) bestows its benefits. The topics and themes of the three instructions are traditional: the way as a metaphor for life; the necessity of obedience to the father/teacher; wisdom's gifts of protection, life, wealth, and honor; the dialectic of student and teacher that yields wisdom (4:18–19). The deceitful woman, who was introduced in 2:16–19, does not appear in this chapter, though the parallel to the woman, wicked men (mentioned in 1:18–19 and 2:12–15), is developed in 4:14–19.

The lectures are delivered by a father to persuade his son to pursue a life of virtue (not simply to perform particular good actions). Such pursuit will bring the son to a new stage—contact with Wisdom herself (or the right way)—which will bestow protection, life, and honor. The transaction between father and son serves as a model for any teacher.

Lecture V: A Father's Example

4:1   Heed, O sons, the discipline of a father,
      pay attention to learn discernment;
2   beneficial teaching do I bestow on you;
      do not turn away from my instruction.
3   When I was a son with my father,
      the tender and beloved son of my mother,

4   he taught me and said to me:
      "Let your heart hold on to my words;
      guard my commandments and live.
5   Acquire wisdom, acquire understanding!
      Never forget, never stray from the words of my mouth.
6   Do not turn away from her and she will guard you;
      love her and she will protect you.[a]
8   Prize her and she will exalt you;
      she will give you honor if you embrace her.
9   She will place on your head a graceful wreath,
      bestow on you a glorious crown."

a. Verse 7 ("The beginning of wisdom: acquire wisdom; / at the cost of all your other acquisitions, acquire insight!") has been added to the Hebrew text. It is not in G and ill suits the context, for it interrupts the personification of wisdom in vv. 6, 8–9 (see commentary). REB omits it. The verse is made up of phrases from elsewhere: "beginning of wisdom/knowledge" is found in 1:7 and Ps. 111:10; "acquire wisdom" is found in Prov. 4:5; 16:16; 17:16.

Verses 4–7 in MT and G are textually confused. G does not have v. 5a, "acquire wisdom, acquire insight," offering instead a shorter text: *šmr mṣwt 'l tškh w'l ṭṭ m'mry py,* "guard the commandments, do not forget, and do not deviate from the words of my mouth." S does not have "never forget." In v. 5, MT is superior to G, for v. 6 ("Do not turn away from *her.* . . . ") requires a feminine singular antecedent, which can only be *ḥokmāh* (or *bînāh*) of v. 5a. In the absence of compelling evidence, we follow MT.

The teacher urges "sons" to heed his words (vv. 1–2), drawing a parallel between his own instruction as a youth and his teaching his sons now (vv. 3–4): What my father taught me about wisdom is what I am teaching you. Having heeded the teaching of his own father, he can be a model of the blessings of wisdom to his present hearers. His father's command to "live" in v. 4a has come true, for he has married and come to an age where he has sons to instruct. His status as authoritative teacher means that he has received the protection and honor that are the traditional gifts of wisdom. This father-teacher possesses the authority of one who has been under wisdom's tutelage since earliest youth.

The poem has two main parts: the call to attention and the introduction of the speaker (vv. 1–3), and the father's citation of his own father's teaching (vv. 4–9). The father's speech can be further divided: vv. 4–5, in which the father's words are highlighted as the objects of the son's search; and vv. 6, 8–9, in which the father's words are no longer mentioned and wisdom itself becomes an active agent—the subject rather than the object of the verbs. Three verbs are repeated in both parts of the poem: "to turn away" (*'āzab*) in vv. 2b and

6a; "to guard" (*šāmar*) in vv. 4c and 6a; "to bestow" (*nātan*) in vv. 2a and 9b. Each verb in its first appearance has the father's words as its object; in its second occurrence each verb has Wisdom as its object (v. 6a) or subject (vv. 6a, 9a). Verse 5 forms a transition: After v. 5 the father is no longer mentioned and Wisdom begins to be personified. As in the introduction (1:1–7) and instructions (2:1–22; 3:1–12), heeding the words of a father or teacher puts one in touch with Wisdom, who bestows her gifts of safety, honor, and wealth (vv. 6, 8–9).

[**4:1–2**] The singular-plural contrast (the teacher and his students) is a common device in Proverbs. The instruction begins, like other wisdom instructions, with a call to pay attention to the father's teaching. Listening is the first step in acquiring wisdom. Acquisition of wisdom begins with listening to the ancestors (Job 8:8–10; Ps. 78:2–6).

[**3–5**] The sage sketches his docility and immaturity as a child, a reminiscence resembling Solomon's in 1 Kings 3:7: "And now, Yahweh my God, you have made your servant king in place of my father David, though I am only a little child; I do not know how to go out or come in." Sirach 51:13–30 likewise portrays the sage as a youth seeking wisdom directly from Yahweh, though without mentioning the parental mediation that is so strong in Proverbs 4. In Wis. 7:1–14, wisdom is also given to Solomon without human mediation.

In Proverbs, the phrase *šāmar miṣwôt*, "to guard the commandments," differs from its usage in the Pentateuch and Deuteronomistic History, where the phrase means "to keep, observe the commandments (of the covenant)." Here it means "to retain" in one's consciousness, "to remember" (cf. 4:21; 5:2; 7:1, 2; 8:32). "Live" in the same verse means to have a long and healthy life, a traditional benefit of wise living.

The command, "acquire wisdom, acquire understanding" (v. 5a) is the rhetorical center of vv. 3–5. It is framed on one side by the two positive verbs of v. 4bc and, on the other, by the two negative verbs of v. 5bc. The verb *qānāh* has a range of senses, from purchasing merchandise to acquiring a wife. Verse 5 is also the transition point for the entire poem, for colon A refers for the first time to *ḥokmāh*, "wisdom," and colon B refers for the last time to the father's teaching ("the words of my mouth"). After v. 5 wisdom is personified and remains so for the rest of the poem. The father's teaching, memorized and put into practice by the son, becomes Wisdom.

[**6, 8–9**] Verse 7 is an addition (see textual notes). In vv. 6, 8–9 Wisdom is no longer the object of a quest but the acting subject, being the subject of a verb in every colon. She protects (v. 6) and gives honor (v. 8–9) to the disciple; protection and honor are traditional fruits of wisdom. Wisdom is also personified as a woman or wife. Traditional love language is used to describe the relation of the seeker and Wisdom: "prize her and she will exalt you; she will give you honor if you embrace her. She will place on your head a graceful wreath, /

bestow on you a glorious crown." "To embrace" in v. 8b means to embrace a woman, as in Cant. 2:6 and 8:3 and elsewhere. "Crown" in v. 9 may be an allusion to marriage ("the crown that his mother gave him on his wedding day," Cant. 3:11). Verses 5–9 are characterized, in the words of Meinhold, "by the speech and imagery of a love relationship between man and woman, which is applied figuratively to the relationship of the student and wisdom." The pursuit of wisdom is the pursuit of a life partner, who will be a companion bestowing all manner of benefits.

Lecture VI: Two Ways
of Living Life

4:10 Listen, my son, and accept my words
       that the years of your life may be many.
11 Let me point out to you the way of wisdom,
       help you walk on straight paths.
12 When you walk your step will not be hindered;
       when you run you will not stumble.
13 Hold fast to discipline; do not let it go;
       guard it, for it means life for you.
14 Do not go on the path of the wicked!
       Do not walk in the way of malefactors!
15 Leave it! Do not go forward on it!
       Get off it and do not go forward!
16 For they cannot sleep until they have done evil;
       they cannot sleep until they have made others stumble.
17 They eat the bread of wickedness,
       and drink the wine of violence.
18 But the path of the righteous is like the radiant sun,
       shining ever more brightly until midday.
19 The way of the wicked is like thick darkness;
       they are not aware of what they stumble over.

The process of attaining wisdom in this poem, as in the other instructions, begins with putting the teacher's words into practice and ends with the gift of wisdom or its benefits. Distinctive here is the prominence given to the metaphor of "the way." In other lectures, wisdom is the goal and climax of the quest, but in this lecture the way of the righteous is the climax. Keeping the words of the father (or teacher) puts the son on the right path. The way functions like wisdom elsewhere in Proverbs: the straight (or right) way is inherently safe and enjoys the protection of God. It is called a "way," for one must stay on it; hence the urgent exhortations of vv. 14–15.

The mention of wicked men in this poem recalls the gang of men in 1:8–19 who invited the youth to join them, and in 2:13–15, a passage that singles out wicked men and their way as one of the two great dangers to the acquisition of wisdom.

By its chiasm in vv. 10–13 (see below), the poem puts "the way" in the position usually occupied by "wisdom." It equates following the teacher's *words* with following the teacher's *way*. If one accepts the teacher's words, if one walks in the way shown by the teacher, one will walk on the path that is blessed by God and flooded with light (vv. 10–13, 18). One should therefore avoid the doomed road of the wicked (vv. 14–17, 19).

Structurally, the poem consists of two quatrains (vv. 10–13, 14–17) and a closing doublet (vv. 18–19). The first quatrain is chiastic, in which vv. 10 and 13 are the outer layer and vv. 11 and 12 are the inner layer.

v. 10 imperative verb + object ("words") + result ("life")
  v. 11 Let me point out the way,
  v. 12 I will bring you to walk on the straight path
v. 13 imperative verb + object ("discipline") + result ("life")

The second quatrain (vv. 14–17) has two couplets: vv. 14–15 forbid entering and remaining on the way of the wicked, and vv. 16–17 characterize the wicked. The last two lines (vv. 18–19) are two bicola, one describing the path of the righteous and the other the way of the wicked. Despite the structural complexity, the reality being described—choosing good and avoiding evil—is simple. The son, the seeker, begins with trust in his father. The son reveres his father's words and puts them into practice. The father's words are not simply his own insights but are communitarian and ancestral. If the words are put into practice by the learner, they generate a new reality. That new reality, which in the other instructions is wisdom, in this poem is the straight way ("straight" being a metaphor for righteous). The "straight way" is a way of living, protected and blessed by God. It is not a definitive state. Those who walk on it can leave it by poor choices.

[4:10–13] As already noted in the analysis of the structure, the chiastic relation of vv. 10 and 13, and of vv. 11 and 12, serve to put into parallel the ideas of heeding the teacher's words and walking the teacher's path. The result of heeding the words is a long and healthy life (vv. 10b, 13b). Walking on the path means not stumbling (v. 12b). The full import of v. 12—the way of wisdom is passable and safe—will become clear in the final line (v. 19), where the reader learns the road of the wicked is dark and dangerous.

[14–17] The lecture singles out the path of the wicked as something to be avoided at all costs (vv. 14–15) and describes the wicked as people devoted to harming their neighbor (vv. 16–17). Verses 16–17 give the reasons for avoiding the wicked path: those who walk on it cannot sleep unless they harm their neighbor, and their food and drink is violence. They are thus in danger of sudden retribution; they form a doomed group. The peremptory tone of vv. 14–15 and bitter characterization of the wicked in vv. 16–17 spring from the father's deep feelings for his son.

[18–19] The metaphor of the way is developed into a teaching of the two ways. The ways are characterized by light and darkness. The path of the righteous is lit by the brightest possible light—the morning sun as it rises to its zenith. Travelers on that road need never worry about unseen perils. Not so with the way of the wicked. The word for "darkness" (*'ăpēlāh*) in v. 19 always has a negative connotation in the Bible; it is the opposite of welcome light. In this verse it symbolizes ignorance and danger. Those who take this path cannot see the trap into which they inevitably will stumble. The verb "to stumble" is a leitmotif of this situation, occurring in vv. 12b, 16b, and 19b: the righteous will not stumble even if they run; the wicked make others stumble. One day they themselves will stumble, for their path lacks the light for them to see their way. The distinction between the two ways and between light and dark will be developed in later literature, as in the children of darkness and the children of light found in the Qumran and Johannine writings (cf. John 8:1: "I am the light of the world. Whoever follows me will not walk in darkness, but will have the light of the world.")[1]

Lecture VII: With Your Whole Being Heed My Words and Live

4:20 My son, pay attention to my words,
          incline your ear to my utterances.

21   Do not let them escape your view,
          hold them in your mind,

22   for they are life for those who find them,
          health for the whole body.

23   Above all that you guard, guard your heart,[a]
          for it is the source of life.

24   Rid yourself of a perverse mouth;
          deceitful lips keep far from you.

25   Keep your eyes gazing straight ahead,
          direct your eyelids unswervingly before you.

---

1. For the two ways in ethical usage, see G. Nickelsburg, *Resurrection, Immortality, and Eternal Life in Intertestamental Judaism* (Harvard Theological Studies 26; Cambridge, Mass.: Harvard University Press, 1972), 144–66; W. Rordorf, "Un chapitre d'éthique Judéo-Chrétienne: les deux voies," *Recherches de science religieuse* 60 (1972): 109–28; J. Duhaime, "Dualistic Reworking in the Scrolls from Qumran," *CBQ* 49 (1987): 32–56.

26   Attend to the path of your feet
          that all your ways may be right.
27   Turn neither to the right nor the left;
          hold back your foot from evil.[b]

a. Verse 23, (lit., "From all guarding guard your heart") has troubled ancient and modern translators. G, followed by S and V, reads the Hebrew as if it were *bkl mšmr,* "with utmost guarding, keep your heart; for from them [the "words" of v. 20?] are the issues of life." T takes the verse as a warning against avarice, "From all treasure guard your heart, for from it is the departure of life (= death)." A clue to the idiom is provided by *Ahiqar* 98, *mn kl mnṭrh ṭr pmk,* literally, "more than all watchfulness watch your mouth" (= "watch your mouth more than anything").

b. G has sayings not in MT: "For God knows the ways of those on the right, / but those on the left are perverted. He will make your paths straight, / will guide your ways in peace."

The seventh wisdom instruction begins, like the others, with the father exhorting his son to heed his words on the grounds that anyone who finds these words will have life and health (vv. 20–22). One should guard one's heart (= the storehouse of those words) as a font of life (v. 23) and keep one's mouth, eyes, and feet from wicked behavior (vv. 24–27). In short, one should keep (in the sense of preserving and acting on) the father's words to enjoy vitality.

The poem mentions no less than seven organs of the body—ear, eyes, heart ("mind"), mouth, lips, eyelids, feet. Heart, eyes, and feet are mentioned twice. The disciple is to strain every sense to its limit: one is to "extend" one's ear like an antenna, let nothing escape the eyes, preserve words in the "heart" (= mind), keep lying speech from mouth and lips, hold eyes and eyelids undeviatingly on the goal, keep one's feet from stumbling or taking detours.

[4:20–23] As elsewhere in Proverbs and in Egyptian instructions, the opening lines urge memorizing the teaching (vv. 20–21). Of the seven bodily organs the heart is the key one in the poem; it stores up the teaching and examples from outside (vv. 20–21) and decides upon action (vv. 24–27). Since the heart is so central, one must guard it above every other treasure, for it contains the words of life from the teacher. The phrase of v. 23b, "for it [the heart] is the source of life," has the same meaning as "spring of life" (*měqôr ḥayyîm*) elsewhere in Proverbs.

[24–27] Just as the faculties of hearing ("ear," v. 20b) and seeing ("eyes," v. 21a) in the first part of the poem *took in* the teaching and example of the father, so in the second part of the poem, the faculties of speech ("mouth" and "lips," v. 24), seeing ("eyes" and "eyelids," v. 25), and walking ("foot," vv. 26a, 27b) enable the disciple to *express* the teaching contained in the heart.

The instruction assumes the disciple has an extraordinarily strong sense of self and aims to lead that strong self to live according to wisdom.

Proverbs 5

Nearly all commentators view chap. 5 as a unit, though McKane and Plöger regard vv. 21–23 as an addition intended to connect the unit to 6:1–19. Chapter 5 is the eighth wisdom instruction, longer than any met heretofore except chap. 2. It is the first lecture to develop in detail the threat of the seductive woman first mentioned in 2:16–19. Proverbs 6:20–35 and chap. 7 will further develop the theme. Proverbs 1:8–19; 2:12–15; and 4:10–19 earlier elaborated the danger to the learner from violent men.

Lecture VIII: The Wrong and the Right Woman

5:1	My son, attend to my wisdom,
	incline your ear to my insight;
2	that you might keep foresight,
	hold on to knowledge.[a]
3	For the lips of a forbidden woman drip honey,
	her mouth is smoother than oil,
4	but her aftereffect is bitter as wormwood,
	cutting as a two-edged sword.
5	Her feet go down to Death,
	her steps take hold in Sheol.
6	She has never seen the path to life;
	her course meanders, for she is without knowledge.
7	And now, my son,[b] listen to me,
	do not turn away from the words of my mouth.
8	Keep your way far from her,
	do not go near the door of her house,
9	lest you give your vigor to others,
	your years to someone unfeeling,
10	lest outsiders take their fill of your wealth,
	and your hard-won gains go to a stranger's house.
11	You will lament at the outcome,
	when your flesh and body grow feeble.
12	You will say, "How could I have spurned discipline,
	how could my mind have scorned correction?
13	I did not heed the voice of my teacher,
	nor incline my ear to my instructor.

14   I am at the brink of ruin
         in the assembly and community."

15   Drink the water of your own cistern,
         the flow from your own well.

16   Should your springs flow into the street,
         streams of water into the squares?[c]

17   Let your fountain be for you alone,[d]
         not for outsiders to share with you.

18   Have joy of the wife of your youth,

19   a lovely hind, a graceful mountain goat.
     Let her love sate you at every moment;
         be enthralled by her love continually.

6:22   [e]When you walk, she will guide you,
     when you lie down, she will watch over you,
     when you awake, she will converse with you.

5:20   Why be enthralled, my son, by a foreign woman,
         why embrace the bosom of an alien woman?

21   For the ways of everyone lie open to the eyes of Yahweh;
         he sees the paths of every person.

22   His own sins catch a wicked person;
         in the trap of his sins is he taken.

23   He dies from want of discipline,
         is lost through his great folly.

a. MT, literally, "your lips will guard knowledge," makes no sense, for in Proverbs it is the heart, not the lips, that keeps and guards knowledge. The versions support MT (except G, which reads *d't śpty 'swk,* "the knowledge of my lips *I have commanded you*"). To judge from other introductions to wisdom instructions (1:8–9; 4:1–2, 10, 13, 20–21; 6:20–21), v. 1 probably urged the learner to heed the words of the father, and v. 2 to memorize them in the heart. The most economical solution to the textual problem is to delete *śptyk* as an early dittography from v. 3. The dittography caused copyists to parse the verb *nāṣar* as a finite verb rather than the infinitive it originally was. In MT colon B, the masculine verb has a feminine subject, which is to be explained by scribal dislike of the third plural feminine imperfect (GKC §145u).

b. The MT plural "my sons" and the plural verbs are at odds with the singular number elsewhere in the poem. G and V have the singular. The plural may have arisen from an original enclitic *mem* (*bny-m,* "my son") that was erroneously read as a plural. The plural noun would have led scribes to interpret the surrounding verbs as plural.

c. The jussive verb in MT, "Let your springs flow into the streets," seems to contradict the aim of the instruction to confine sexual activity to one's household. The apparent contradiction has given rise to three major interpretations of v. 16: (1) "*lest* your springs (= wife) overflow in public / like rivulets in the open streets" (Scott; similarly

Gemser and Plöger)—that is, the wife will commit adultery, provoked by her husband's adultery; this interpretation either adopts from G the negative particle *mē*, "lest," or simply assumes the verse is a question ("Should your springs . . . ?"); (2) G, S, T, and V, Ibn Ezra, and H. Ringgren take v. 16 as a result, "(and so) your springs will flow . . . ," with "springs" and "streams" referring to offspring: If you restrict your generative activity to your own wife, you will have many legitimate children (not bastards) in the community; (3) the most common interpretation is that the water symbolizes the male semen spent outside the domestic sphere; the verse is a rhetorical question ("Should your springs flow into the streets . . . ?").

The first interpretation is unlikely, for it proposes as an everyday motive the relatively unlikely possibility (in that culture) of the wife's adultery. Further, the negative particle may not be original in G, being absent in the important manuscripts Alexandrinus and Sinaiticus (first hand). The second interpretation is even less likely, for nowhere in the Bible do springs and streams of water symbolize descendants. The third is the most probable. "Springs" and "streams" in v. 16 are plural, in contrast to the singular "well" and "cistern" in v. 15. Springs and streams symbolize male potency in contrast to female potency. Such singular-plural opposition is common in Proverbs. Verse 16 has to be interpreted as a question in order to make sense; for example, "Should your springs . . . ?" Perhaps the interrogative particle *hă* has dropped out, or perhaps one should adopt Skehan's suggestion that *'êk*, "how" (already in v. 12) has dropped out through haplography with the last consonants of v. 15, *'rk*.[1]

d. We delete MT *yhyw lk lbdk*, "let them be for yourself alone," on the grounds it is an ancient variant of v. 18a, "let your fountain be blessed."

MT 17a: *yhyw lk lbdk*, "Let them be for yourself alone."

MT 18a: *yhy mqwrk brwk*, "Let your fountain be blessed."

The *Vorlage* can be reconstructed from G ("let your spring of water be proper to yourself") as *yhy mqwrk <l>bdk*. The *d/r* confusion in some ancient scripts accounts for the confusion of "yourself alone" (*bdk*) and "blessed (*brk*)," which generated a new colon. There are several reasons for our emendation: vv. 18a and 18b in MT are not truly parallel; "blessed" in MT v. 18a does not make good sense in the context and is without a parallel; G offers some support for the emendation; vv. 18b and 19a are parallel, and Cant. 2:9, 17; 8:14 show "pet names" were common in Hebrew thought; Augustine's Latin text is *et fons aquae tuae sit tibi proprius et nemo alienus communicet tibi*, "and let the fountain of your water be proper to yourself and let no foreigner share [it] with you."[2]

e. We follow Skehan[3] and Scott in inserting 6:22 here. The verse is awkward in its present position in chap. 6, for nothing in 6:20–21 prepares the reader for the sudden and strong personification of wisdom. Further, the three finite verbs of 6:22 are all in the third singular feminine, which does not fit the context. The verse fits naturally after 5:19, which presents the wife as the counterpart to the other woman in 5:3–6, guiding, protecting, and conversing with her husband. Most persuasive is the fact that 5:19 in G preserves vestiges of 6:22 (the vestiges are italicized in the English translation): *elaphos*

---

1. Skehan, "Proverbs 5:15–19 and 6:20–24," *Studies* 6.
2. Ibid.
3. Ibid.

philias kai pōlos sōn charitōn homileitō soi, hē de idia hēgeisthō sou kai synestō soi . . . , "Let [your] loving hart and your graceful colt *accompany you, and let her be considered your own and be with you* at all times . . . " The Hebrew verb *śāgāh,* "to wander unknowing; to be enthralled," repeated three times (vv. 19, 20, 23), makes a fine contrast with the guidance offered by the woman.

Chapter 5 is divided into four sections (vv. 1–6, 7–14, 15–19 + 6:22, and 20–23) by "my son" (vv. 1, 7, 15 [implicitly],[4] 20). The dominant contrast is between the wrong woman (vv. 1–14) and the right woman (vv. 15–19 + 6:22). The difference in lines is compensated for by the intensity of feeling in the portrait of the wife (Alonso Schökel).

> I. Vv. 1–14 (14 cola). Exhortations to keep the father's teaching and warnings against the forbidden woman.
>   1. Vv. 1–6 (6 cola). Attend to my wisdom and avoid her lips (= words) and feet (= path), which will lead you to death.
>   2. Vv. 7–14 (8 cola). Attend to my words and avoid the forbidden woman who will scatter your resources abroad and make you end your days in self-recrimination.
> II. Vv. 15–23 (10½ cola). Love and prize your wife as a delight and safeguard, and beware the forbidden woman.
>   1. Vv. 15–19 + 6:22 (6½ cola). Love your wife who will satisfy you, be yours alone, and prove a trustworthy guide.
>   2. Vv. 20–23 (4 cola). Beware again the forbidden woman, for Yahweh sees all, and evil deeds trap those who do them.

The speech is united through word repetitions, some of them ironic contrasts: "my son" in vv. 1, 7, and 20; "to incline the ear" in vv. 1 and 13; "forbidden woman/outsider" in vv. 3, 10, 17, and 20; "aftereffect/outcome" (*'aḥărît*) in vv. 4 and 11; "to take hold of, take (*tāmak*)" in vv. 5 and 22; "to see" in vv. 6 and 21; "tracks" in vv. 6 and 21; "path" in vv. 8 and 21; "house" in vv. 8 and 10; "discipline" in vv. 12 and 23; "to be enthralled, lost" (*śāgāh*) in vv. 19, 20, and 23.

Like other wisdom instructions, chap. 5 begins with an exhortation to hear and memorize the teacher's words. The chapter then introduces a new character beside the teacher and learner. In other instructions, the new character is Wisdom, Yahweh, or the way (4:10–19), but here it is the wife of the disciple (vv. 15–19 + 6:22). It is she who, when appreciated by her husband, is the best protection from the seductive woman. The central contrast of the poem is between the wrong woman (vv. 3–14) and the right woman (vv. 15–19). The

---

4. "My son" would fit awkwardly with the emphasis of v. 15 to act like a husband (i.e., to have relations with his wife). The singular imperative that opens the verse links it unmistakably with vv. 1, 7, and 20.

contrast can also be expressed as that between the dangers from outside (represented by the "foreign" woman's taking away the man's strength and resources) and the security from inside (represented by the wife's safeguarding the man's love and seed). In both depictions, the language is realistic: it describes what can happen in adultery. Adultery can lead to loss of health (v. 9), family wealth (v. 10), reputation (v. 14), and become the cause of bitter regret. The losses can be beyond recovery (vv. 11–13). The remedy is similarly down-to-earth and practical—prizing one's own wife.

In addition, the instruction has a metaphorical level that is established in the opening description of the forbidden woman: Her lips drip honey and her feet lead to death. The quest for true wisdom, which begins with heeding the teacher's words, can be ruined by another's deceit and one's own uninstructed passions.

[5:1–6] The exhortation begins conventionally with the father (or teacher) urging his son (or disciple) to listen to his wisdom and commit it to memory. The motive for learning is the mortal danger of the "foreign" or forbidden woman: She will seduce with sweet words and inflict death. "Foreign" meant "one not known in her town" in the Egyptian *Instruction of Any* of the Eighteenth Dynasty (1550–1305 B.C.E.). Her words are honeyed and smooth, but their aftereffect is bitter and cutting. "Aftereffect" (*'aḥărît*) is the outcome that determines the worth of the preceding events.

The woman is portrayed impressionistically: She is all "lips" (vv. 3–4) and "feet" (vv. 5–6); she is described solely by her capacity to speak and walk. Her speech is smooth and deceptive as, in Ps. 55:22: "Smoother than oil were his words, but they were unsheathed swords." Honey is applied to words in Ezek. 3:3, where the words on the scroll eaten by Ezekiel tasted like honey. The woman's course ("feet") are as deceptive as her lips; she guides people to the realm of Death. Death comes prematurely to those who become her disciples, for the evil life she advocates invites retribution (cf. vv. 21–23).

Several words in this section occur again in the poem: "My son" begins other sections (vv. 7, 20); the bitter "aftereffect" of heeding the woman (v. 4a) will be acknowledged by the man at the end of the affair (v. 11); the verb describing how the woman's strides "take hold of" (*tāmak*) Sheol (v. 5a) is the same that describes the person "taken" by chains; the woman does not "see" the path of life (v. 6a) but God "sees." The irony is that the woman who wishes to control the youth is not the one actually in control of events; her words and actions have consequences of which she is unaware. Her knowledge is false.

[7–10] "And now . . . " resumes the opening exhortation (vv. 1–2). As in vv. 3–6, remarkably little information is given about the woman. She is portrayed only as someone draining away the man's vigor, the best years of his life (v. 9), and his wealth (v. 10, *kōaḥ* in the meaning it has in Job 6:22). The woman has a house (v. 8b) and associates ("others" and "outsiders" in vv. 9a and 10a), but remarkably little other information is given about her social location. The best commentary on vv. 8–10 is the description of her opposite in vv. 15–19 + 6:22: the wife is genuine, loving, and protects her husband. In vv. 8–10, the woman is all manipulation, counterfeit feelings, and thievery.

[11–14] The exhortation continues, turning from the woman to the man, using the device of an imagined soliloquy of the man at the end of the affair. "Outcome" (*'aḥărît*) is the same Hebrew word as "aftereffect" in v. 4a, meaning the final event in a series that enables one to judge the meaning of the whole. The man suffers a premature weakening of vigor (v. 11b), just as the teacher warned (v. 9). Presumably, he loses wealth and standing in the community. Perhaps the best (inverted) illustration of v. 14 is the scene in 31:23: "Her husband is respected in the city gates / when he sits among the elders of the land." The verse is not about a judicial sentence on adultery but assesses the general loss of "place" (cf. 27:8) that comes from immoral behavior and bad judgment.

[15–19 + 6:22] The singular imperative ("drink") and the abrupt change of topic (the wife) signal a new section. Water has an erotic meaning here, as in Cant. 4:15: *ma'yan gannîm bĕ'ēr mayim ḥayyîm wĕnōzĕlîm min lĕbānôn*, "You [the woman] are a garden spring, a well of living waters, and streams from Lebanon." The metaphor of eating and drinking expresses the mutuality of love. The verses tell the husband that the best way to avoid other women is to maintain a genuine relationship with his wife. The wife is no outsider, no unfeeling stranger, no squanderer of his self and goods; she protects her man, guides him, and converses with him. In short, she is the very opposite of the woman of vv. 7–10, who is attractive at first but deadly in her effect.

There are three textual problems in vv. 15–19, which are discussed in detail in the textual notes. Verse 16 in MT, literally, "Let your springs flow into the streets, streams of water into the squares," has been a problem to interpreters from antiquity. Verse 15 commands sexual relationships to be restricted to one's wife but v. 16 seems to say the opposite, to allow one's streams to flow into the public square. The best, and the most common, solution is to refer the plural "springs" and "streams of water" to the man's sexuality and to assume a rhetorical question expecting the answer "No": "Should your springs flow into the street?" The verse builds on v. 15 by encouraging the husband to satisfy himself at home. The second textual problem is that vv. 17a and 18a seem to be duplicates, though most scholars retain MT, "Let them [the waters] be for yourself alone," and "Let your fountain be blessed." For reasons given in the textual notes, we render "Let your fountain be for you alone." The third textual emendation is to move 6:22 from its original location, where it seemed at odds with the context, to a position after 5:19. The verse develops the role of the wife as trustworthy helper to her husband, providing a nice contrast to the forbidden woman.

In the love language of the poem, the wife is portrayed as unique, like no one else, to be treasured for herself alone, to be shared with no other. Comparing the woman to an animal is conventional in love poetry; in the Song of Songs the woman is called a dove (Cant. 5:2) and the man a gazelle (Cant. 2:9, 17). If the husband can appreciate the companionship of his wife, the attractions of the outside woman will disappear. Another instance of erotic language is "Have joy of" (śamaḥ), which in Cant. 1:4 refers to the physical pleasure of gastronomical excess.[5]

[20–23] The concluding verses ask the key question of the entire poem: Why be enraptured with an *outsider* when it is unnecessary and entails such massive risk? Retributive forces are at work in the universe. Verses 10–21 state that clandestine affairs cannot be hidden from God, who will take action. Retribution is expressed in the poem in two ways: through the direct action of God (v. 21), and through the inherent self-correcting action of the universe (v. 22). The Bible often affirms both agencies without attempting to bring them into theoretical unity. Though Plöger and McKane believe these verses are not original, they form a suitable conclusion to the poem. The final verses reprise several words already used. Yahweh sees (pallēs) every person's way or conduct, unlike the woman who did not see her own path. One's own misdeeds trip one up; the verb in v. 22b (tāmak) is the same used of the woman's steps taking hold in Sheol (v. 5). There are other reprises in v. 23: "he will die" (yāmût) picks up "Death" (māwet) in v. 5; "discipline" reprises the same word from v. 12; yiśgeh, "is lost," is the same verb as "be enthralled with (love)" but now in its literal and negative sense.

Proverbs 6

The chapter consists of two separate sections, vv. 1–19 and 20–35. The second section is the ninth wisdom instruction in the series of ten in chaps. 1–9. The first section, consisting of four independent pieces (vv. 1–5, 6–11, 12–15, 16–19), is judged by many commentators to be a later addition, which has been attracted to its present position by surface resemblances to the other instructions. This section cannot, however, be judged intrusive solely on the grounds that it is not an instruction, for ancient anthologies did not always live up to modern standards of symmetry. Meinhold, for example, regards vv. 1–19 as part of the design of chaps. 1–9, one of three "interludes" in these chapters (the others are 3:13–20 and 9:7–12). The editor(s) may simply have wanted to include the material and found this section a suitable place to do so.

---

5. G. Anderson, *A Time to Dance, A Time to Mourn: The Expression of Grief and Joy in Israelite Religion* (University Park, Pa.: Pennsylvania State University Press, 1991) 36.

A case can be made that the material has a function in chaps. 1–9. Thematically, it shows the inner obstacles to acquiring wisdom, in contrast to the extrinsic ones of violent men and seductive women. These inner obstacles include faults from one's own character (poor judgment, vv. 1–5, and laziness, 6–11). The sketches of the wicked types (vv. 12–19) fill out the catalog of the wicked in 1:8–19; 2:12–15; 4:14–19. Verbally, the word "caught" in v. 2 links back to "catch" in 5:22 in the preceding instruction.

Interlude: Four Short Pieces

1. Standing Surety for One's Neighbor

6:1   My son, if you have stood surety for your neighbor,
      given your hand on behalf of another,
2   you have been trapped by the utterance of your lips,
      caught by the words of your mouth.[a]
3   Do this to free yourself, my son,
      for you have come under the power of your neighbor:
    go, put aside dignity, implore your neighbor;
4   allow no sleep to your eyes,
      no slumber to your pupils.
5   Free yourself, like a gazelle from the hunter,[b]
      like a bird from the hand of the fowler.

2. The Ant and the Sluggard at Harvest

6   Go to the ant, O sluggard;
      study its ways and become wise.
7   Without a chief,
      an overseer, or a ruler,
8   it garners its food in the summer,
      gathers its provender at harvesttime.[c]
9   How long, O sluggard, will you lie there,
      when will you get up from your sleep?
10   A bit more sleep, a bit more slumber,
      a bit more hugging of the arms in repose,
11   and the poverty of a vagabond will come upon you,
      the destitution of a beggar![d]

3. The Scoundrel

12   A scoundrel, a villain
      goes about with lying mouth,

13   shifty in his eyes, his feet ever moving,
          gesturing with his fingers;
14   perversity is in his heart, planning evil;
          at every moment he stirs up strife.
15   Therefore, suddenly will disaster come upon him;
          in an instant will he be broken beyond healing.

4. What Yahweh Rejects

16   Six things Yahweh hates,
          seven are an abomination to him:
17   Haughty eyes, a lying tongue,
          hands that shed innocent blood,
18   a heart that devises malicious plans,
          feet eager to run to wickedness,
19   a false witness who gives lying testimony,
          an inciter of quarrels among family members.

a. With many commentators, we follow S in reading "the words of your lips" in place of MT "the words of your mouth." MT's exact repetition of colon A would be unusual in poetry.

b. With many commentators we emend MT *myd*, "from the hand," to *mṣyd*, "from the hunter" (*miṣṣayyād*). G, S, and T read "from the snare" (Hebrew *mimmāṣôd*), which is also possible.

c. After 6:6–8, G has an encomium on the bee: "Or go to the bee, and learn how diligent she is, and how seriously she performs her task. Kings and commoners take of her labors for their health. They are desired by all and held in honor. Though of slight strength, she is given preeminent honor for wisdom." Gerleman suggests that the sequence of ant plus bee in G was borrowed from Aristotle.[1]

d. The usual translation is, "poverty will come upon you like a *robber,* and want like an *armed warrior.*" The Hebrew for "armed warrior" ('*îš māgēn*) occurs elsewhere only in the duplicate passage in 24:34. The translation "armed warrior" comes from the hexaplaric and V interpretation of '*îš māgēn* as "man of the shield" (= "armed warrior"). The translation "robber" (lit., "one who walks about") seems to be simply an inference from the parallel "armed warrior." Thus the traditional translations do not rest on a solid base.

Ehrlich suggested "vagrant" instead of "robber" for *mĕhallēk* and "beggar" for "armed warrior" on the basis of the triliteral root *mgn,* which in Arabic and Syriac means "(unearned) gift." His suggestion now finds support in Ugaritic, *šqrb [bhntk] bmgnk,* "present [your plea] with your entreaty" (*KTU* 1.16.I.44–45). The root meaning "beseech, entreat" fits Prov. 6:11 and 24:34.[2]

1. *Studies in the Septuagint 3: Proverbs Studies* (Lunds Universitets Årsskrift N. F. Avd. 1, Bd 52, Nr 3; Lund: Gleerup, 1956), 30–31.
2. For a concise summary of the evidence, see Cohen, 138–39.

[6:1–5] The section opens with "my son" but, unlike the instructions, does not urge the hearer to keep the father's words. Rather, it makes a plea to avoid a specific act—standing surety for someone outside the family. The warning is intensified by several rhetorical devices: the repetition of the words "neighbor" (three times) and "free yourself" (two times), the mention of bodily organs ("hand" two times, "mouth," "lip," "eye," "pupil"), and the imagery of hunting (vv. 2, 5). To add even more vividness, the father imagines his son has already made the legally binding gesture of surety and is liable for the debt of another.

The legal practice of standing surety is not mentioned in the biblical law codes but wisdom texts show the practice was common. Nonbiblical law codes mention it. The verb "to stand surety" (*'ārab*) is, literally, "to intervene" with a creditor on behalf of a debtor. The details of the practice are not well understood, but Prov. 22:27 makes it clear that the pledge was financial—if the debtor defaulted, the guarantor's own furniture could be seized. Possibly, persons could be seized for nonpayment (cf. 2 Kings 4:1–7). The practice can be extended to situations of taking responsibility for others: Judah gave himself to Joseph as surety for Benjamin, "For your servant pledged himself for the boy with my father in these words, 'If I do not bring him back to you, I will be liable to my father forever'" (Gen. 44:32).[3]

Proverbs rejects the practice of giving surety for another (11:15; 17:18; 20:16; 22:26; 27:13), though not all wisdom books follow Proverbs.[4] Sirach 29:14–20, for example, is cautiously open to the practice. Possibly the reason for Proverbs's opposition is that it puts one's property and even one's person under the power of another person (22:26–27). Proverbs normally prizes personal freedom and responsibility. The warning does not primarily arise from lack of sympathy with the poor, for the book elsewhere urges almsgiving.

This passage forbids providing surety for someone outside one's own family, "your neighbor," "another" (*zār*). In the hypothetical case proposed by the father, the son must go to his neighbor and beg to be released from the obligation he has assumed. The verb *'ārab lě* in v. 1a means the son "entered on behalf of," that is, guaranteed, his neighbor's debt. Groveling before the neighbor and loss of face are nothing in comparison to the danger. He should get out from under the obligation now!

[6–11] The sluggard, (*'āṣēl*) is a type in Proverbs. The other extended texts about laziness are 24:30–34 and 26:13–16, and individual sayings are to be found in 10:4, 26; 15:19; 19:24; 20:4; 21:25; 22:13. Sometimes the sluggard is

---

3. For a summary of the biblical evidence, see R. de Vaux, *Ancient Israel: Its Life and Institutions* (New York: McGraw-Hill, 1961), 170–73.

4. The Qumran wisdom text known as Sapiential A also inveighs against it: "If your treasure purse you have entrusted to your creditor on account of your friends, you have given away all your life for its price. . . . For no price exchange your holy spirit, for there is no price of equal value to it." See D. J. Harrington, *Wisdom Texts from Qumran* (London: Routledge, 1996), 42.

contrasted with the diligent person (12:24, 27; 13:4). The sluggard and the diligent are one of four paired types in Proverbs, the others being wise and foolish, righteous and wicked, and rich and poor. Proverbs is less harsh on the
sluggard than on the fool and the wicked, often simply dismissing the sluggard
with condescension and sarcastic humor: "The sluggard says: 'There's a lion
in the street, / there's a lion in the square!' The door turns on its hinges, / and
the sluggard on his bed!" (26:13–14).

In our verses, the tone is sharper than usual, perhaps because the context is
harvest, which is so crucial for the community's welfare. Concern about people
shirking their harvest duties was not confined to Israel. The second-millennium
Mesopotamian *Instructions of Shuruppak* presumes everyone will join in
harvesting: "Regarding harvesttime, the very precious days, / collect like a
slave girl, eat like a lady, / my son, collect like a slave girl, eat like a lady—thus
shall it be indeed" (lines 132–34).[5] Proverbs 10:5 also finds laziness during harvest reprehensible: "Who gathers in summer is a wise son, / but who slumbers
at harvest is a despicable son." Proverbs 24:30–34 depicts the dire consequences of laziness upon field and vineyard, and its conclusion (vv. 33–34) is
identical to 6:10–11.

The foil to the sluggard in the exhortation is not the diligent person, as we
might expect from similar texts in Proverbs, but the ant. Verses 6–8 are not a
fable (though fables are well represented in nonbiblical wisdom literature), for
the ants do not talk and act like human beings. Rather, the verses are observations about ant behavior, like the observations about the four tiny animals in
30:24–28, one of which is the ant: "ants are a species not strong, / yet [they]
garner their food supply in summer" (30:25). The point is that ants instinctively
spring into action at any opportunity of gathering food.

[12–15] Proverbs often deals with types such as the righteous or the lazy
person, rather than with specific persons. The verses describe the wicked person, in his essence (v. 12a), demeanor (vv. 12b–13), inner life (v. 14a), effect
upon society (v. 14b), and destiny (v. 15). The result is an intensified portrait
of wickedness. The precise significance of the gestures in v. 13 escape us.

The type is totally depraved. Hence all his activity, represented by its
source—mouth, eyes, feet, fingers—is at the service of evil. The phrase "in his
heart" in v. 14 is climactic by its position after the naming of the external organs and by its position in the middle (fifteenth of thirty words). The heart
is the engine that drives a person and in this case the heart is perverse. Verse
14 can also be translated as a tricolon, "perversity in his heart, / planning evil
at all times, / he incites quarrels" (so JPSV and JB). The final point is the social damage caused by the evil person who incites quarrels. The description of

5. W. H. P. Römer and W. von Soden, *Weisheitstexte 1* (Texte aus der Umwelt des Alten Tes-
taments 3/1; Gütersloh: Gerd Mohn, 1990), 58. My translation.

the type is not complete without a mention of its destiny—to be destroyed "suddenly," that is, by an intervention rather than by natural causes.

Stylistically, the sketch is notable in containing only one *wāw*, ("and"). The conception of an acting person through the mention of body parts is like Rom. 6:13: "And do not present the parts of your bodies to sin as weapons for wickedness, but present yourselves to God as raised from the dead to life and the parts of your bodies as weapons for righteousness" (NAB).

[16–19] These verses contain the only numerical saying in the book outside of chap. 30. Sirach 25–26 also contain numerical sayings, for example, nine // ten and three // four. "Six" and "seven" is an instance of parallelism in numbers, near but not identical. The word "abomination" means something contrary to proper religion—improper worship or improper action.

After the opening line, the sentiments and the development are similar to vv. 12–15: a person acting perversely, concluding with the act of inciting quarrels. The vocabulary in v. 18a is similar to that in v. 14a. The first five evils are associated with a particular organ. The sixth and seventh abominations, perhaps to underline their climactic place in the series, break with the previous syntax.

The phrase "haughty eyes" occurs in the prayer of Ps. 18:28 ("you [Lord] humble haughty eyes") and in Ps. 131:1 ("Yahweh, my eyes are not haughty"). Cf. also Sir. 23:4: "O Lord . . . do not give me haughty eyes." The phrase "a lying tongue" occurs in 12:19; 21:6; 26:28; and Ps. 109:2. The final verse returns to the faculty of speech in the form of a false witness; the sages emphasize the importance of words as human expression. The phrase "false witness" occurs in 14:5, 25; 19:5, and the phrase "lying testimony" occurs in 12:17; 14:5; 19:5, 9. The several traits add up to a certain unity: a self-regarding, manipulative, violent, and inherently malicious person. Indirectly, the verses offer a portrait of Yahweh—the kind of God who cannot abide such deep-seated malice in human beings.

Lecture IX: The Dangers of Adultery

6:20 My son, keep your father's commandment;
      do not reject your mother's teaching.

21   Fasten them on your breast,
      bind them to your throat,[a]

23   for a commandment is a lamp, teaching is a light;
      and the reproofs of discipline are the way to life.

24   It will guard you from the neighbor's[b] wife,
      from the smooth tongue of the forbidden woman.

25   Do not covet her beauty in your heart,
      do not let her capture you with her eyes.

26   To a prostitute may go the last loaf of bread,[c]
      but a married woman hunts down a precious life.

27 Can a man rake embers onto his breast
      without his clothes catching fire?
28 Can a man walk on blazing coals
      without scorching his feet?
29 So with the man who sleeps with his neighbor's wife:
      no one who touches her will escape unpunished.
30 People do not regard a thief as disgraced
      if he is starving and steals to fill his maw.
31 But if he is caught he must restore sevenfold,
      pay out all the wealth of his house.
32 Anyone who commits adultery with a woman lacks sense,
      only one intent on ruining himself does such a thing.
33 He will get a beating plus disgrace
      and his shame will never be removed.
34 For a husband's anger turns into jealousy
      and he will not soften when the time comes for revenge.
35 He will not agree to payment of money
      will accept no settlement, no matter how large.

   a. As explained in the textual notes under 5:19, 6:22 was judged out of place in chap.
6 and restored to 5:19.
   b. With many commentators, we follow G in pointing the Hebrew consonants *r' rēaʻ*,
"neighbor," rather than *rāʻ*, "evil." Cf. "his neighbor" in v. 29a.
   c. Rendered word for word, MT is "for on behalf of a woman, a prostitute, unto a
loaf of bread, / but the wife of a man hunts a precious soul." Either because of textual
corruption or because of our ignorance of Hebrew idiom, the exact meaning escapes us.
G, "for the price of a prostitute is as much as one [loaf of] bread, / but the wife of men
hunts precious souls," follows MT except for its omission of *'šh*, "woman," in colon A.
G may have got "price" by rearranging the Hebrew consonants *ky b'd*, "for on behalf
of," to *kbwd*, "glory, worth," which it renders "price" in 26:1. The versions adopt "price"
from G (though S and T have their own confusions), but otherwise support MT. Some
emend MT to *ky bqšh 'd kkr lḥm*, "for she seeks a loaf of bread," though *biqqēš* is not
elsewhere parallel to *ṣûd*, "to hunt." No emendation has won broad support. Tentatively,
we suggest that a copyist glossed the verse *ky zwnh 'd kkr lḥm / w 'št 'yš npšt ṣ wd*, "for
a prostitute [costs] to the last loaf of bread, / but the wife of a man hunts down life." The
glosses were: *b'd 'šh*, "on behalf of a woman," in colon A and *yqr*, "precious," in colon
B. "Precious" does not otherwise modify "soul," though the usage here is similar to Pss.
49:9 and 116:15. Ezekiel 13:18–20 accuses prophetesses of hunting souls and profan-
ing the divine name for morsels of bread, but that context is too unclear to be helpful.
Though the present overloaded verse cannot be completely understood, some parallels
are clear: loaf of bread // precious life; prostitute // married woman.

Verses 20–35 comprise the ninth of the ten lectures in chaps. 1–9. This lecture begins with the father and mother (last mentioned as a pair in 1:8–19) exhorting their son to keep their teaching before his eyes. Their teaching will light

his path (the metaphor of 4:10–19) and make it a path to life (v. 23). The parents' teaching will bring life by preserving the son from the dangers of adultery, guarding him against the alluring words of a married woman (v. 24). Do not be seduced, they tell their son, for unlike a prostitute, whose hire is entirely a matter of money, a married woman destroys one's life (vv. 25–26). Like fire, she burns your bosom and your feet; none who touches her escapes punishment (vv. 27–29). A thief who steals only to relieve physical hunger loses only money if he is caught (vv. 30–31), but an adulterer ruins his life as a member of the community by incurring loss of reputation, threats to his physical safety, and the vengeful hatred of the aggrieved husband (vv. 32–35). (As pointed out in the textual notes, v. 22 in MT is out of place and has been moved to its original place in instruction eight, after 5:19.)

The instruction is earthy to a degree not even found in chap. 7, and the motives are unapologetically practical and self-regarding. Will you risk your position in the community by an adulterous affair? The motives would have been particularly compelling in an ancient Mediterranean culture—avoiding shame, physical beatings, and an angry husband. It is helpful to remember that wisdom instructions are intensely practical: how to avoid trouble and enjoy life.

As in other instructions, the father (and mother) instruct the son to live by their words and avoid the alluring obstacles to wisdom. The enemy to wisdom in this case is a sexual relationship with a married woman. The remedy proposed here is not, as in chap. 5, appreciation of one's wife, but the prospect of horrible penalties.

The poem has two sections.

I. Vv. 20–21, 23–24 (4 lines). Exhortation to the son to heed his parents and keep their words in view; their teaching will light his path and protect him from an affair with a married woman.
II. Vv. 25–35 (11 lines). Warning against an affair with a married woman.
1. Vv. 25–29 (5 lines). Warning against a married woman on the grounds that an adulterous affair hurts one's self (*nepeš*, vv. 25–26). Sex with a prostitute costs money but involves no other loss; sex with a married woman harms one's self (vv. 27–29).
2. vv. 30–35 (6 lines). A comparison: getting caught for satisfying one's appetite for food (euphemism for the sexual appetite) versus getting caught for adultery. In the first case, a monetary payment makes everything right; in the second, no monetary payment is possible. Instead, one loses one's life as a member of society.

Many scholars regard this instruction as disjointed and suggest that verses were added or that the author was not intent in making a single statement. Unclear to them are the translation of v. 26 (see the textual notes for our solution), the function in the poem of the verses on the hungry thief (vv. 30–31), the translation of v. 30 (a statement or a question?), and the coherence of vv.

32–35. In our view, the instruction is coherent and realistic, if a bit blunt by modern standards.

A major device is the comparison between sexual relations with a prostitute (vv. 26a, 30–31) and sexual relations with a married woman (vv. 26b, 27–29, 32–35). The first relationship is entirely a matter of money; with money one hires a prostitute (v. 26a) and with money one pays the penalty if caught (v. 31). Verses 30–31 draw an analogy between prostitution and theft: strong appetites (sex or hunger) are satisfied by each. Why does the author use the analogy of theft instead of staying with prostitution? One cannot say for sure, but perhaps prostitution did not have a legal penalty that would make an effective contrast with adultery. The second relationship, that with a married woman, is far more serious, for it harms one's *nepeš*, "throat; being, life, soul" (vv. 26b and 32b).

[20–21, 23–24] The father and the mother are the source of teaching for their son (as in 1:8), an indication of the family setting of the instructions. Verse 23 reprises "commandment" and "teaching" from v. 20, and "guard" in v. 24 completes the fixed pair ("guard" // "keep") begun in "keep" of v. 20. Verse 21 is metaphorical, like Deut. 6:8–9: "Bind them as a sign on your hand and let them be a pendant on your forehead; write them on the doorpost of your houses and gates." The meaning is to keep them before one's eyes. Like 4:14–19, vv. 23–24 combine two metaphors—light and dark for moral and immoral. These verses are similar to 2:16–19, where the quest for wisdom keeps the son on the right road, safe from the wicked woman.

[6:25–29] The imperative mood of the verb in v. 25 reprises the opening imperative (v. 20) and the topic continues transposed to a negative mode. Be led by your parents and do *not* be led by the seductive beauty of the married woman! The weight falls on how adultery harms the very being of a man. Prostitution is only mentioned as a rhetorical foil to the main point, adultery.

Verses 27–28 contain wordplays and double meanings. "Bosom" has an erotic meaning, as in the phrases "wife of your bosom" in Deut. 13:7 and 28:54 and "embrace the bosom" in Prov. 5:20b. "Feet" are a euphemism for the male genitals (cf. Ex. 4:25; Isa. 6:2; 7:20; Judg. 3:24; 1 Sam. 24:4). The point is that, far from experiencing sexual satisfaction, the man will be wounded, for the woman is a fire. The adulterous woman is identified with fire in v. 27a by similar pronunciation: "Can a *man* (*'îš*) rake *embers* (*'ēš*)" refers back to v. 26b, "the wife of a man" (*'ēšet 'îš*). The phrase, "no one who touches (*nōgēaʿ*) her will escape unpunished," points forward to v. 33a, "the humiliating blow (*negaʿ*)" inflicted on the adulterer.

[30–35] The poem compares the consequences of hunger-driven theft (vv. 30–31) and adultery (vv. 32–35). Some scholars translate v. 30 as a question: "Is not a thief contemptible if he steals, / even to satisfy his appetite when he is hungry" (REB, Alonso Schökel, Meinhold). Their argument is a fortiori: If a starving person steals just for food and is punished severely, how much more severely should an adulterer be punished? Such an interpretation, however, mutes the contrasts of prostitution/adultery and money/*nepeš,* and isolates vv. 30–31.

In the case of appetite-driven theft, a money payment completely resolves the difficulty.[6] In the case of adultery, a money payment is refused and the perpetrator has to bear severe penalties.[7] As in v. 26, the Hebrew word *nepeš,* "throat; self, soul," is important. The "soul" of the thief is unaffected by the purely monetary penalty, but the "soul" of the adulterer is severely affected: He is given a beating, which diminishes his honor (v. 33) and he must remain in fear until "the time comes for revenge" (v. 34b, literally, "day of vengeance"). The meaning of "the time for revenge" has given rise to considerable discussion. Leviticus 20:10 and Deut. 22:22 make the death penalty mandatory for adultery, but the law codes cannot be used as guides to everyday legal practice.[8] Most scholars assume the offended husband took matters into his own hands. Perhaps something more general is meant: The man is subject to the wrath of an enraged husband (and his family) and is not safe from beatings that diminish his dignity, lessen his weight in the community, and ruin his reputation for discretion and good judgment. One who touches a married woman will himself be "touched." His very self (*nepeš*), not just his property, will be irreparably harmed.

6. Verse 30 attends to the motivation of the perpetrator more than the law codes customarily do. The covenant code mandates a fivefold penalty for stealing bovines and a fourfold penalty for stealing ovines (Ex. 21:37 [22:1 E]; cf. 2 Sam. 12:6). Sevenfold restitution is found only here and in the Greek text of 2 Sam. 12:6.

7. Delitzsch suggested that 6:20–22 was based on Deut. 6:4–9. A. Robert developed similar ideas in "Attaches littéraires bibliques de Prov. I–IX," *Revue Biblique* 42 (1934): 44. M. Fishbane regards the verses as an "inner biblical midrash on the Decalogue" in which the foreign woman represents the "seduction of false wisdom" in contrast to the true wisdom of chaps. 8–9. Decalogue topics would be honoring parents, adultery, stealing, coveting the neighbor's wife, the debate on whether stealing and committing adultery inflicts greater harm on the perpetrator, and binding the words on the body. See M. Fishbane, "Numbers 5:11–31: A Study of Law and Scribal Practice in Israel and the Ancient Near East," *Hebrew Union College Annual* 45 (1974): 44, and briefly, *Biblical Interpretation in Ancient Israel* (New York: Oxford University Press, 1985), 288.

Such views presume that in the early Second Temple period the Pentateuch enjoyed the same authority it did later. It also presumes a late date for the material in Proverbs. Neither can be presumed, however. Obedience to parents (especially the father) is part and parcel of the instruction genre; the metaphor of wearing commands could have been borrowed in the other direction; fornication and theft are mentioned only to underline the danger of adultery. The logic of the instruction is highly original in comparison with the Decalogue. For the relation of "law" (*tôrāh*) in the Pentateuch and in Proverbs, see J. D. Levenson, "The Sources of Torah: Psalm 119 and the Modes of Revelation in Second Temple Judaism," in *Ancient Israelite Religion* (FS F. M. Cross), ed. P. D. Miller, P. D. Hanson, and S. B. McBride (Philadelphia: Fortress Press, 1987), 566–67.

8. E. A. Goodfriend, "Adultery," *ABD* 1.83; H. G. L. Peels, "Passion or Justice? The Interpretation of *beyôm nāqām* in Proverbs vi 34," *VT* 44 (1994): 270–74.

Proverbs 7

Lecture X: The Deceptive Woman

7:1 My son, keep my words,
       store my admonitions within you.[a]

2   Keep my admonitions and live,
       keep my teaching as the apple of your eye.

3   Bind them on your fingers,
       write them on the tablet of your heart.

4   Say to Wisdom, "You are my sister,"
       and call Understanding "Friend."

5   She will guard you from the forbidden woman,
       from the stranger whose words are alluring.

6   Through the window of my house,
       through the lattice, I looked out.

7   I spotted a simpleton,[b]
       noticed a youth without sense.

8   He was passing through the market, near her corner;
       he was walking on the street toward her house.

9   It was twilight, in the eventide of the day,
       at the onset of night darkness.

10   A woman goes out to meet him,
       garbed as a prostitute, with shrouded breast.[c]

11   She is restless and forward,
       her feet no longer stay in her own house.

12   Now in the street, now in the square,
       at every corner she lies in wait.

13   She grabs him and kisses him,
       she faces him boldly and says to him:

14   "I am obligated to make a sacrifice of well-being,
       today I fulfill my vow.

15   That is why I have come out to meet you;
       I searched for your face and I have found you.

16   I have spread linens upon my bed,
       colored linen from Egypt.

17   I have sprinkled my bed with myrrh,
       with aloes and with cinnamon.

18   Come, let us drink our fill of passion till morning,
       let us feast on love.

19   For the man of the house is away,

he has gone on a long journey.
20 He took a bag of money in his hand
and will not return home till the full moon."
21 She steers him away by her grand speech,
with her smooth talk leads him off.
22 He follows her steps all unwitting,[d]
like an ox to slaughter he goes,
like a fallow deer bounding toward a corral[e]
23 until an arrow pierces its entrails,
like a bird hastening into a net,
not knowing its life is at stake.
24 And now, O sons,[f] listen to me,
pay heed to the words of my mouth.
25 Do not let your heart incline to her ways,
do not stray into her paths,
26 for many are those she has felled,
numerous are all those she has slaughtered.
27 Her house is a path that leads to Sheol,
going down to the chambers of Death.

a. G has a verse not in MT: "Honor the Lord and you will be strong; / fear none other than him.)" It is an obvious addition, for it interrupts the tight structure of vv. 1–2.

b. MT *'ābînāh babbānîm na'ar ḥăsar lēb*, "I noticed among the sons a youth without sense," though attested in S and T, is overly long and seems to have been affected by dittography. G omits *'ābînāh* and V omits *babbānîm*, which suggests that one or the other word is secondary. Tentatively, we excise *babbānîm* on the grounds that it was generated by a misinterpretation of *bappĕtā'yim*, "naive person," as plural; the word may be singular with a misunderstood *mēm* enclitic (*IBHS* §9.8). The verbs *rā'āh*, "to see," and *bîn*, "to perceive, notice," are parallel in Ps. 94:7 and Job 9:11.

c. The phrase "with shrouded heart" (*nĕṣurat lēb*) puzzled the versions, for the idiom "to guard the heart" is elsewhere positive in Proverbs. G. R. Driver suggests that Hebrew *nāṣar*, "to guard," had the same semantic development as Syriac *ṣn'*, i.e. from "guarded, reserved," to "crafty, sly."[1] Or the phrase may simply be wordplay on prostitutes' characteristic clothing, such as a shawl over their face and upper body like Tamar in Gen. 38:14–15. In this scene, the woman may cover her breast ("heart") with a shawl, while at the same time covering her heart (= mind, intent).

d. MT, followed by V and T, has *pt'm*, "suddenly." Most translators follow MT, rendering "impetuously" or the like. G reflects *pt'ym*, "simple, stupid" (plural). The reading of G ("unwitting") seems preferable because it reprises the same word in v. 7, and ignorance is more suitable for a doomed animal than impetuousness.

e. Colon C is corrupt and requires emendation. MT pointed the consonants to read,

1. "Hebrew Notes," *VT* 1 (1951): 250.

"and like an anklet to the discipline of a fool (?)," or, as JPSV renders, "like a fool to the stocks for punishment." G (followed by S and T) seems to have read the consonants of MT except *klb* for MT *k'ks: kklb 'l mwsr 'yl,* "like a dog to fetters [or like] a deer." Symmachus ("like one skipping to the fetters of fools") and V (*agnus lasciviens*) interpret *'ks* as a verb, "to hop."[2] We tentatively emend *mûsār,* "discipline," to *môsēr,* "fetters," and *'ĕwîl,* "fool," to *'ayyāl,* "fallow deer."

f. The plural noun ("sons") and imperative verbs in v. 24 are troubling, for the preceding verses were addressed to the son (see v. 1) and v. 25 is also in the singular. G and V have the singular. Plural-singular alternation is not unknown in Hebrew, but usually it is more subtle than this. If the plurals are not a misreading based on v. 7b (see textual notes there), then they function to generalize the warning for others.

Chapter 7 is the tenth and final lecture in chaps. 1–9 and the fourth of five explicit warnings against the forbidden woman (the preceding four are 2:16–19, chap. 5, and 6:20–35). It serves as a foil to the speech of Woman Wisdom in chap. 8, for the first line of its peroration (7:24) is picked up by the first line of the peroration in chap. 8 (v. 32). Chapter 2 introduced the deceptive woman in vv. 16–19 as one of the two external dangers to those searching for wisdom. Proverbs 5:1–23 and 6:20–35 elaborated the warning. Chapter 7 is the climax of these warnings. It should be noted that the deceiving woman is parallel to the deceiving men and their way in 2:12–15. The men appear in 1:8–19 and 4:10–19. The parallel of dangerous woman and dangerous men is continued in chap. 7, which repeats the vocabulary of 1:11–14: "Come!"; "to lie in wait"; "to find"; and "Sheol."[3]

Chapter 7 begins conventionally with the father urging his son to keep his teaching as a protection against the forbidden woman. The introduction is virtually identical to 6:20–21, 23–24 except for the father's advice in 7:4: "Say to Wisdom, 'You are my sister,' and call Understanding 'Friend.'" "My sister" and "Friend" is the language of courtship and love (see below). The verses urge the son to make Wisdom his companion and lover; she will protect him from the forbidden woman. The point is the same as in chap. 5—the right woman will protect you from the wrong woman. In chap. 5, the right woman is the wife; in chap. 7, the right woman is Woman Wisdom.

In vv. 6–23 the father tells his son an event that he once observed through the window of his house: A woman whose husband was away went out to meet a young man and took him to her bed, an act that killed the youth. The father's report is a masterpiece. The woman is all activity and awareness, speaking and acting, whereas the youth is silent and unsuspecting, led rather

2. G. R. Driver proposed "to hop, mince," on the basis of Arabic in "Hebrew Notes," 241. For further discussion, see McKane.

3. As pointed out by G. Yee, "'I Have Perfumed My Bed with Myrrh': The Foreign Woman (*'iššâ*) in Proverbs 1–9," *Journal for the Study of the Old Testament* 43 (1989): 56.

than leading. The text uses images of night and darkness, a bed covered with expensive linens redolent of perfumes, animals of sacrifice and of the hunt, and Sheol. Having finished his description, the father exhorts a group of "sons," perhaps disciples, to heed his words in order to avoid the death-dealing woman.

Like the other warnings against the deceiving woman, this one is not primarily an exhortation to young men to control their sexual appetites. Its details—the purposeful woman, the silent youth, the vow, the perfumed bed, the comparison of the youth to doomed animals, Sheol—suggest a metaphorical meaning and lift this lecture to a high literary level. The lecture is about two kinds of love, two ways of life.

Modern interpretation has been influenced by G. Boström's 1935 monograph,[4] which concluded that the reference is to the wives of urban merchants in Palestine (generally foreigners) who arrayed themselves as brides, representing the love goddess, and invited Jewish youth to ritual sex. The instruction thus warns young people against foreign cults combining sex and worship as in Num. 25:1–7; Ezek. 16:23; and Hos. 4:13. The foreign woman owes something to Babylonian love goddesses or the Canaanite Astarte. Boström adopts the Septuagint reading of 7:6, which assumes the person looking through the window is the woman herself. She is "the woman in the window" attested in literature (Judg. 5:28; 2 Sam. 6:16; 2 Kings 9:30:33) and in artistic representations of a woman behind a window looking outward.[5] The mention of the full moon in v. 20 suggests to Boström that the conjunction of the sun and the moon is near, which he interprets as the coitus of the sun god and the moon god.

Boström's highly specific suggestions rightly moved interpretation away from allegory (e.g., the foreign woman represents Greek philosophy), but it runs into problems, such as the lack of contemporary evidence for such ritual sex, an overly literal understanding of "foreign," and the unlikelihood that such encounters would be so common as to provoke an entire lecture.

It has been suggested that the woman's vow was a completely ordinary one. The time had come to pay it, but her husband had taken the money with him (v. 20). The woman turns to prostitution to come up with the money. The situation, it is suggested, was common enough for Deut. 23:18–19 (17–18 E) to forbid the practice of fulfilling vows from the proceeds of prostitution.[6]

---

4. *Proverbiastudien: Die Weisheit und das fremde Weib in Spr. 1–9* (Lunds Universitets Ärsskrift. N. F. Avd. 1. Bd 30. Nr 3; Lund: Gleerup, 1935).

5. There are several biblical scenes of someone looking through a window, and they involve not only sexual seduction but deception and a threat of death. See R. H. O'Connell, "Proverbs VII 6–17: A Case of Fatal Deception in a 'Woman and the Window' Type-Scene," *VT* 41 (1991): 235–41. A recent summary of the discussion is J. B. Burns, "Proverbs 7:6–27: Vignettes from the Cycle of Astarte and Adonis," *Scandinavian Journal of the Old Testament* 9 (1995): 20–36.

This interpretation is quite possible as far as it goes, but does not take into account the deceptive nature of the woman's words (see below).

Some recent scholars interpret the scene sociologically and symbolically: The woman represents women outside the acceptable circle of marriage partners for Jewish men in Second Temple Judaism.[7] The text would no doubt have evoked concerns about exogamy in readers, but it does not follow logically that it was written to inculcate endogamy. For one thing, wisdom literature was not concerned with such national issues, and, for another, the issue in the text is not marriage but foolish conduct that entails fatal consequences.

Our interpretation focuses on the vow, which is the woman's instrument of deception. The young man thinks the woman is inviting him to feast on the freshly killed animal, while in fact he himself will be the victim. Having rejected wisdom, he will be deceived by the other woman. For a detailed examination of the vow, see under vv. 14–20.

To understand the central issue, it is helpful to compare chap. 7 with the Song of Songs, for both pieces draw on the traditions of erotic poetry.[8] From that tradition come themes and conventions such as the invitation "Come, let us drink our fill of love till morning" (Cant. 7:18) and "Drink deep of love!" (Cant. 5:1), the mention of spices (Prov. 7:17; cf. Cant. 1:13–14 and 4:13–14) and the language of seeking and finding (Prov. 7:16; cf. Cant. 3:1–4).

The great difference between Proverbs 7 and the Song of Songs is that the Song exhibits reciprocity of action and mutuality in speech. Of the one hundred seventeen verses in the Song, sixty-one and a half are spoken by the woman, forty by the man, and six and a half by choruses of either sex; the remaining nine are headings or are impossible to attribute with certainty.[9] Statements are interchangeable; few passages can be called exclusively masculine and feminine. Proverbs 7, on the other hand, has no mutuality whatsoever. Only the woman speaks and she uses veiled language, "with shrouded heart." Another contrast is that in the Song the relationship of the lovers is exclusive ("My lover is mine and I am his," Cant. 2:16) and each views the other as unique ("Only one is my dove," Cant. 6:9) whereas in Proverbs 7, there have been "many" others (v. 26), though the woman professes to be searching only for him (v. 15).

6. K. van der Toorn, "Female Prostitution in Payment of Vows in Ancient Israel," *JBL* 108 (1989): 197–201.

7. C. Maier, "Im Vorzimmer der Unterwelt: Die Warnung vor der 'fremden Frau' in Prov. 7 in ihrem historischen Kontext," in *Von der Wurzel getragen: Christlich-feministische Exegese in Auseinandersetzung mit Antijudaismos* (Bible Interpretation Series 17), ed. L. Schottroff and M.-T. Wacker (Leiden: Brill, 1996), 179–98.

8. The following remarks owe much to D. Grossberg, "Two Kinds of Sexual Relationships in the Hebrew Bible," *Hebrew Studies* 35 (1994): 7–25.

9. A. Brenner, *The Israelite Woman: Social Role and Literary Type in Biblical Narrative* (Sheffield: JSOT Press, 1985), 47, cited by Grossberg, "Two Kinds of Sexual Relationships," 13.

The foreign woman in Proverbs 7, described from the father's decidedly male perspective, is a deceiver to be sure, but the speech should not be dismissed as misogynist. The ideal against which she is so judged is the ideal of the Song of Songs—mutuality. The woman in Proverbs 7 does not invite the young man to speak. Her words have a double meaning. As in chap. 5, the surest protection against the wrong kind of love is the right kind of love ("Wisdom, 'You are my sister.'").

Had the man made Wisdom his lover and life companion, she would have enabled him to discern the deceit of the foreign woman's words. He would have seen that her words meant death, that he was the sacrifice rather than the guest.

[7:1–5] Verses 1–3 are tightly knit: "keep" in v. 1a recurs in v. 2a; "admonitions" in v. 1b recurs in v. 2a; the imperative verb "live" occurs at the very center of the first three lines; v. 3, which is about preserving the teaching externally, matches vv. 1–2, which is about preserving the teaching internally (= memorizing). *And live:* the meaning is virtually "survive!" In Gen. 20:7; 42:18; Jer. 27:12, 17; and Ezek. 18:32, the imperative "live!" is uttered in the context of avoiding death; for example, Gen. 42:18: "On the third day Joseph said to them, 'Do this [leave a brother as hostage] and live!'" The imperative verb dramatizes the choice between life and death.

In v. 4, "sister" and "friend" are expressions of love. In the Ugaritic Aqhat epic, the goddess Anat, attempting to take the young man Aqhat as her lover, says 't 'ḥ w'n '[ḥtk], "you are my brother and I am your sister" (*KTU* 1.18.I.24). "Brother" and "sister" are used in Egyptian love poetry and Mesopotamian marriage songs. In Cant. 4:9, 10, 12; 5:1, the man calls the woman "my sister, my bride." "Friend" in Ruth 2:1 and 3:2 designates Ruth's future husband Boaz. That the father exhorts his son to *declare* his love to Woman Wisdom ("Say to Wisdom, 'You are my sister'") is extremely significant, for in the following narrative the youth says nothing and is led away to his death.

[6–13] In MT the father watches through the window of his house and tells the story. The word *bêt*, "house" (translated "home" in v. 20b), occurs six times in the chapter. G, followed by S, switches the person of the verbs in vv. 6–7 from first person singular to third person feminine singular; the narrator is the woman watching the youth through her window. Most scholars rightly regard G as secondary, for it abruptly and without notice changes the narrative voice from the father, who has been talking in vv. 1–5, to the woman who entraps him. The reading of G has been adopted by Boström and others who force vv. 6–7 to conform to the motif of the woman in the window.

Verse 9 states that night is falling. Night is a motif in erotic poetry, the time of longing for the lover (Cant. 3:1, 8; 5:2). Verses 10–13 sketch the woman entirely through her actions and gestures, like the sketches of the scoundrel in 6:12–15 and 6:16–19 and the wife in 31:10–31. The deceiving woman comes toward the youth, dressed as a prostitute, walking through the streets in an excited and aggressive manner. Having arrived at the corner (*pinnāh,* vv. 8, 12), she waits in ambush until she is able to grab and kiss him. The phrase, "he makes her face bold," perhaps means facing him without the veil customary for a married woman appearing in public.

[14–20] The woman tells the youth that she has already or is about to fulfill her vow (vv. 14–15). She says that she has made her bed with beautiful spreads and costly spices (vv. 16–17), invites him to take his fill of love with her (v. 18), and assures him that her husband will be away for some time (vv. 19–20). Her vow and her statement about her husband have been the subject of much discussion.

According to Lev. 7:11–21 and 22:21, a sacrifice of well-being to Yahweh could be made from the herd or flock in fulfillment of a vow. An example of such a vow is 2 Sam. 15:7: "At the end of four years, Absalom spoke to the king, "Let me go to Hebron and fulfill the vow I made to Yahweh. For your servant made a vow when I was living in Geshur in Aram, 'If Yahweh brings me back to Jerusalem, I will worship him in Hebron.' "[10] The sacrifice of well-being is payment to Yahweh for granting the object of the vow. In Prov. 7:14, we are not told what was the object of the woman's vow.

In v. 14b, the verb in the perfect tense can designate a result in past time, "I have paid my vow." It also can have a modal meaning—an action that belongs to the near future but which is represented as being performed at the moment of utterance—"I am going to fulfill my vow."[11]

As a conversation starter, "Today I fulfill my vow," seems strange to a modern ear, but the youth understands it as an invitation to a feast where meat from an animal killed in fulfillment of a vow was on the menu. Leviticus 7:15–17 stipulates that the meat must be eaten on the day of the sacrifice or on the next day. To consume the quantity of meat, guests would ordinarily be invited to the meal.[12] The young man interprets her words as "I have paid my vow, let's feast on the meat," but she means, "I am going to fulfill my vow," that is, she has not yet slain her offering.

That the youth is to be the offering is suggested by three pieces of evidence. First, the woman's vowing an animal she does not yet possess has a parallel in the vow of Jephthah in Judges 11. Jephthah also vowed whatever came out to meet him on his return home in victory. As can be seen from the two texts, there are lexical and thematic similarities, though the subject ("what comes out") differs in the two scenes. Proverbs 7 is explicit: I fulfill my vow, *therefore* I have come out.

---

10. The phrase "in Hebron" is found only in G.
11. J-M §112g, and van der Toorn, "Female Prostitution in Payment," 198.
12. J. Milgrom, *Leviticus 1–16* (AB 3; New York: Doubleday, 1991), 420.

Judg. 11:30–31: And Jephthah vowed a vow (*neder*) to Yahweh. . . . [H]e said, "If you give the Ammonites into my hand, then whoever comes out (*yēṣē'*) of the door of my house to meet me (*liqrā'tî*) on my safe return from the Ammonites shall be Yahweh's and shall be offered by me as a burnt offering.

Prov. 7:14–15: I an obligated to make a sacrifice of well-being, / today I fulfill my vow (*neder*). / That is why I have come out (*yāṣā'tî*) to meet you (*liqrǎ'tî*); I searched for your face and I have found you.

Second, vv. 22–23 compare the youth to animals led off to slaughter. Third, the woman's language is ambivalent, capable of referring to death as well as life. Her linens and spices in vv. 16–17 are ambivalent symbols. Myrrh was used for incense (Cant. 3:6) and was an image of sexual love (Cant. 4:6, 14). Lign-aloes, a spice from southeast Asian eaglewood, was also an image of sexual love (Cant. 4:14), as was cinnamon (Cant. 4:14). Yet, as R. H. O'Connell points out, linen and the spices were also used for funerals.[13] New Testament evidence indicates that linen was used for burial cloth. Myrrh and aloes are attested in funeral practices (Mark 16:1; John 19:39). Unspecified spices were used in Old Testament burials (2 Chron. 16:14), suggesting that the New Testament texts preserve an ancient practice. "Bed" (*miškāb*, v. 17) is a term for the place of burial in Isa. 57:2; Ezek. 32:25; 2 Chron. 16:14 and in the fifth century Phoenician Tabnit inscription.[14] The Introduction suggested that the deceptive woman's ambivalent offer of life to the youth is borrowed from the epic type-scene. In *Gilgamesh*, Ishtar's marriage offer to Gilgamesh conceals a threat of death as does Anat's offer to Aqhat in the Ugaritic epic *Aqhat*.

In vv. 19–20, the woman's words are matter-of-fact; no symbolic meaning need be read into them. The wife knows from the amount of money that her husband took and his expected return date that he will be away long enough for her to dally with the youth and enmesh him in her nets.

[21–23] The story ends in tragedy. The young man dies. The voice of the father-narrator makes explicit reflections. The verbs in v. 21, "to steer away," and "to guide away," can be used of leading animals such as a donkey (Num. 22:23) or sheep (Jer. 23:2 and 50:17). The animal imagery continues as the youth is compared to an ox, a fallow deer, and a bird in the moment before they are slaughtered. None of the animals is aware that it is about to die. Like the youth in v. 7, they are unsuspecting and they pay for their "simplicity" with their lives.

Verse 22 may refer to an ancient method of hunting—chasing a wild animal

13. "Proverbs VII 16–17: A Case of Fatal Deception," 238.
14. *KAI* 13.8.

through a gradually narrowing stone fence into an enclosure, called a kite, where it can be easily slaughtered. Hundreds of such kites have been detected by aerial surveillance in the Judean desert, the southern Negeb, and desert fringes of Transjordan.[15] The practice is only attested for gazelles. To judge from bones recovered from Bronze and Iron Age sites, deer and gazelle constituted only a small percentage of the meat supply, but they were regularly hunted.

[24–27] The final address to the audience begins with "And now," a word that begins perorations. The father addresses "sons," not just his own, making clear that the typical story is for others not immediately referred to in the story. Returning again to the singular number (v. 25), the father urges avoiding the woman's streets, or ways, and not to imitate the youth in the story. Verses 26–27 reveal that many have already died at the woman's hands and that the way to her house leads to Sheol, the place of the dead (cf. vv. 8, 12). The house where the youth engages in the rites of love with the woman turns out to be an entryway to death. The youth who was killed never called Wisdom "my sister" and, as a result, he was deceived, with fatal consequences.

Proverbs 8

Wisdom Poem II: Become My Disciple
and I Will Bless You

8:1 It is Wisdom who calls,
      Intelligence who lifts her voice.
2 On the highest elevation, at the side of the street,
      at the crossroads she stands;
3 By the gate to the upper city,
      by the entry of the portal she cries:
4 "To you, O people, I call;
      I lift my voice to all human beings:
5 O simple ones, acquire prudence;
      O foolish ones, acquire knowledge.

---

15. E. Firmage, "Zoology," *ABD* 6.141–42. The kites date as early as the Neolithic Age (8000–4500 B.C.E.). The practice of hunting gazelles in this manner is attested into modern times. Mishnaic Hebrew *ṣād lĕ* has the technical sense of "to hunt (by driving game) into an enclosure." *M. Šabb.* 13:5, reads "he who hunted a bird (by driving it) into a tower or a gazelle (by driving it) into a house." See M. Greenberg, "Two New Hunting Terms in Psalm 140:12," *Hebrew Annual Review* 1 (1977): 149–53.

6   Listen, for I speak noble things;
         straightforward discourse comes from my lips.
7   My mouth utters what is trustworthy;
         wickedness is abhorrent to my lips.
8   All the words of my mouth are true;
         none of them are twisted or perverted.
9   All of them are clear to anyone with sense;
         they are right to those who have attained knowledge.
10   Take my instruction over silver,
         my message over choice gold,
11   For wisdom is better than pearls,
         and no precious goods can match it.[a]
12   I, Wisdom, dwell with prudence;
         I have attained knowledge and foresight.
13[b] Pride, arrogance, evil conduct,
         a mouth that speaks perversity — these I abhor.
14   Mine are counsel and resourcefulness;
         mine are intelligence and strength.
15   Through me kings reign
         and rulers issue just decrees.
16   Through me officials govern,
         princes and just judges.
17   I love those who love me;
         those who seek me find me.
18   Wealth and honor are with me,
         lasting possessions and rich rewards.
19   My fruit is better than gold, even fine gold,
         and my yield is better than precious silver.
20   I walk in the way of righteousness,
         in the paths of justice,
21   endowing those who love me with riches,
         and filling their treasuries.
22   Yahweh begot me as the first of his tasks,[c]
         before his deeds of ancient time.
23   I was formed of old,[d]
         at the beginning, before the earth.
24   When there was no deep I was brought forth,
         when there were no fountain or springs[e] of the waters.
25   Before the mountains were sunk into place,
         before the hills, I was brought forth,
26   when he had not made the earth and fields,
         the loamy surface of the world.

27   When he set the heavens in place, I was there,
         when he fixed the horizon upon the deep.
28   When he made firm the vault of heaven above,
         when he established[f] the springs of the deep,
29[g]   when he gave the sea its boundary
         lest the waters go beyond his command;
      when he fixed the foundations of earth,
30   I was at his side, a sage.
      I was daily taking delight,
         rejoicing before him at all times,
31   rejoicing in his inhabited world;
         I take delight in human beings.
32   And now, O children, listen to me:[h]
33   do not reject discipline and wisdom.
      Happy are those who keep my ways,
         and happy the one who heeds me,
34   watching daily at my gates,
         waiting at the doorpost of my gates.
35   For whoever finds me finds life,
         and wins favor from Yahweh.
36   But whoever passes me by harms himself;
         all who hate me love death."

   a. Verse 11 may be a borrowing from 3:14–15, as suggested by P. W. Skehan, "Structure in Poems on Wisdom: Proverbs 8 and Sirach 24," *CBQ* 41 (1979): 368, but the evidence is not sufficient to excise it.
   b. MT, "revering Yahweh is hating evil," makes no sense in the context and is a gloss from 3:7. So also Alonso Schökel.
   c. "His tasks" (*darkô*) is, literally, "his way." *Derek* can mean a way on which one walks or, metaphorically, a way one takes in bringing something to completion. The second sense of "way" is equivalent to "task, work." That "task" is the meaning here is suggested by its parallel, "his deeds."
   d. For the verb, see *HALAT*, 754.
   e. With many commentators, we emend MT *nkbdy mym* to *nbky mym*. Cf. Job 38:16, *nibkê yām*, "the sources of the sea." G supports the emendation. Cf. Ugaritic *mbk nhrm*, "the source of the two rivers" (e.g., *KTU* 1.2.III.4) and Job 28:11, *mibkê nĕhārôt*, "the sources of the rivers." Here its meaning is determined by its juxtaposition to "fountains."
   f. MT *ba'ăzôz* is taken by G, S, and V as transitive, and thus is to be pointed as the piel conjugation (*bĕ'azzĕzô*).
   g. G does not have v. 29ab. It is difficult to judge whether G omitted it through haplography (all the cola of vv. 27–29a begin with the preposition *b*) or whether the verse in MT is an addition. Semantically, the verse seems redundant and the two parts of this section (vv. 22–26 and 27–31) are better balanced without it. If v. 29ab is omitted, there

are thirty-three words in the first part and thirty-six in the second. In the absence of compelling evidence, however, we retain MT.

h. There is considerable confusion in MT. The cola of v. 32 in MT are not parallel. Our translation assumes as the original of v. 32, *w'th bnym šm'w ly / mwsr wḥkm<h> 'l tpr'w.* The fixed pair in the reconstructed line—*šāma'* // *pāra'*—occurs (in reverse order) in 15:32, as does the phrase *pāra' mûsār.* The dislocation in the MT of Proverbs 8 may have been caused by the repetition of *šimĕ'û* in vv. 32a and 34a. The pairing of *'ašrê,* "happy," in a single verse is rare but not without parallel (1 Kings 10:8 and Ps. 144:15).

Chapter 8 is Wisdom's longest speech in the book. Appearing in the busiest part of the city, she addresses everyone there, singling out the inexperienced and the foolish (vv. 1–5). She assures her audience she is worthy of trust (vv. 6–11), promises those who heed her riches, honor, and governing skill (vv. 12–21), and ascribes her authority to her unique position with Yahweh at the time of creation (vv. 22–31). She ends by urging her hearers to wait at her door as disciples (vv. 32–36). The poem is the most majestic and revealing portrait of personified Wisdom in the book.

The poem is structured in four sections, each (except the fourth) having two parts of five lines each:

I.   A. vv. 1–5   B. 6–10   III. A. vv. 22–26   B. 27–31
II. A. vv. 12–16 B. 17–21   IV.   vv. 32–36

Formal features support this division. Verse 1 is linked to v. 4 by the repetition of "call" and "[raise] the voice,"[1] and is linked to v. 5 by the repetition of the triliteral root *byn* (v. 1, *tĕbûnāh,* "intelligence") in *hābînû,* "learn," in v. 5. Verse 5 points forward to v. 10 by its plural imperative in the initial position of the verse.

The first three sections divide into halves (A and B) by their style or their subject matter. In section I, Wisdom assembles the people (vv. 1–5), then speaks (6–11). In section II (vv. 12–16), Wisdom identifies her companions and shows how kings and rulers rely on her; in vv. 17–21, she lists her gifts to all her friends. Formally, section II is united by the thrice repeated emphatic pronoun "I" (*'ănî*) and recurrent /ī/ sound. Verses 17–21 are framed by the word "love." Section III consists of two complementary cosmogonies, vv. 22–26 and 27–31.

Within chaps. 1–9, chap. 8 is the companion piece to 1:20–33, Wisdom's first speech in which Wisdom spoke harshly, threatening to walk away from anyone who rejected her. Only in the last verse did she offer a promise ("But

---

1. The full idiom in v. 4b is *nātan qôlî,* "to raise my voice," as is shown by v. 1b.

the one who listens to me will dwell secure, / will be at rest, past fearing disaster"). Perhaps her abrupt harshness is a reaction to the seductive proposal to youth in 1:8–19. In chap. 8, on the contrary, Wisdom speaks nothing but assurances and promises, threatening only in the final verse ("But whoever passes me by harms himself; all who hate me love death"). Chapter 8 balances the first speech; it also provides an effective foil to the deceptive woman in chap. 7. Further, chap. 8 prepares for chap. 9 in which Wisdom completes her palace and invites passersby to the dedication feast.

Wisdom speaks in her own name, promising to transform the life of anyone who seeks her. She is powerful because she is with God as his most honored creature. She brings to human beings the knowledge they need to be good and blessed servants of God. The background to Woman Wisdom is the Mesopotamian mythology of the *apkallu* and *ummānu,* bringers of civilization and culture to the race. To receive this precious wisdom, one must be open to it and desire it more than anything else. To render hearers open and desirous is the purpose of the poem.

[8:1–5] Wisdom appears commandingly in the poem: "Wisdom" is the very first proper noun to appear. The setting of this speech, like her first (1:20–33), is the city, specifically the upper part of the city where the buildings of government and commerce were found.[2] Though the mention of several urban locations in vv. 1–3 (cf. 1:20–21 and 7:8, 12) might suggest Wisdom moves from place to place, it is probable she stands in only one place—the central crossroad of the city. The mention of multiple sites conveys a sense of the crowded and bustling city. In contrast to the deceptive woman's nighttime encounter with the lone youth in the privacy of her home (7:7–9), Wisdom speaks in broad daylight in the public square where everyone can hear her. Like Absalom attempting to win a following in 2 Sam. 15:2, she stands by the *road* leading through the *gate* and *calls* to people passing by (words that appear in both passages are italicized).

The fixed pair "people" and "human beings" in v. 4 designates human beings generally (Num. 23:19; 2 Sam. 7:14; Jer. 49:18). Though inviting all, Wisdom focuses on "simple ones" and "foolish ones." "Simple ones" can be a neutral term in the sense of untaught or inexperienced (Pss. 19:8; 116:6; Prov. 1:4; 9:4), but its parallel noun here, "foolish ones" suggests culpable ignorance. Wisdom invites even the perverse. Those on the wrong path are invited to leave it for the path of wisdom.

[6–10] Unlike Egyptian and Mesopotamian instructions that normally counsel specific actions, Wisdom urges no specific act beyond trusting her words and becoming her disciple. She presents herself as trustworthy and credible. Her words are totally reliable (vv. 6–9) and worthy of acceptance (v. 10).

2. Z. Herzog, "Cities," *ABD* 1.1040.

She uses the familiar metaphors of straight and level for true and trustworthy. The metaphor is pervasive: v. 6, "straightforward" (or "level" as in Isa. 26:7); v. 8, her words are not "twisted or perverted"; v. 9, "clear" (i.e., accessible, what lies straight ahead, as in Isa. 57:2), "right," i.e., straight, "level [way]" as in Jer. 31:9). Given the proximity of chap. 7 and its similar peroration, Wisdom's appeal is an implied rebuke to the other woman's twisted and lethal words. Unlike the deceiving woman, she does not exploit the youth's naïveté but rather heals it by her noble companionship. Verse 10 exhorts listeners to accept discipline (or reproof). In occurrences outside wisdom literature (Jer. 17:23; 32:33; 35:13; Zeph. 3:2; 3:7) the phrase means accepting divine reproof. Here it means accepting Wisdom's teaching. It is not specific counsel that she offers but herself as a trustworthy guide.

[12–16] Wisdom now tells who she is, explaining her loves (vv. 12, 14) and her hates (v. 13). Her avowal of her associates and disavowal of her enemies is like the king's avowals in Psalm 101, in which he defines himself as righteous by pledging to walk with the upright and spurn (lit., "hate") evildoers.

Verses 14–16 develop the traditional association of wisdom with kings and the art of governing. Kingship was one of the institutions through which divine wisdom was mediated to human beings (2 Sam. 14:20; 1 Kings 3; 4:29–34; 10:1–10). In his famous dream at the beginning of his reign, King Solomon did not ask for the conventional gifts of long life, riches, and the victory but for a "listening heart (= mind)" and the ability to make wise decisions (1 Kings 3:5–14).

[17–21] Verse 17 is linked to v. 21 by an inclusio ("love"). The *mutual* love of Wisdom and her disciple, and her bestowal of riches, honor, and substance on her client is the opposite of the manipulative acts of the adulterous woman in chap. 5. That woman walked on the wrong path (vv. 5–6), squandered the man's potency and money (vv. 9–10), took away his honor, and embittered his old age (v. 14). What the adulterous woman took away, Wisdom bestows as lasting gifts.

The relationship between Woman Wisdom and her client is stated in the traditional biblical language of love: seeking and finding (8:17).[3] Already possessing limitless wealth and prestige (v. 18), Wisdom needs nothing from her clients. Moreover, her benefits transcend the category of money (v. 19).

[22–31] Wisdom now explains where her authority comes from and why she is to be trusted: She has a special relationship with Yahweh, which is shown by her having been created before everything else. Her status is expressed in two complementary cosmogonies, vv. 22–26 and 27–31. The first cosmogony emphasizes the birth of Woman Wisdom *before* all else, and the second underscores Wisdom's being *with Yahweh* during the creation of the universe.

---

3. R. Murphy, "Wisdom and Eros in Proverbs 1–9," *CBQ* 50 (1988): 600–3.

The first cosmogony describes precreation through a series of negations.[4] The author presents precreation as a mirror image of present existence—when the basic elements of the universe did *not* exist. There were no cosmic waters (v. 24), no pillars of the earth (= mountains and hills, v. 25), and no habitable surface of the earth (v. 26). Both the first and the second cosmogonies end with the mention of "the earth" (*'ereṣ*, vv. 26a and 29c) and "the world" (*tēbēl*, vv. 26b and 31a). Before the universe came into being, wisdom was born.

[22–26] All four verbs used of Wisdom's origin describe it in the language of birth ("begot" [*qānāh*], "formed," "brought forth" [twice]). "Earth" in v. 23b is reprised in v. 26a, forming the boundaries of this section. Biblical cosmogonies often began with the channeling of the cosmic waters to their proper sphere. Even before that first act, Wisdom existed.

Some scholars question whether the first verb mentioned in v. 22a (*qānāh*) means anything more than "to acquire, to possess," but the evidence from Ugaritic, Phoenician, and Hebrew is clear that "to create" is one of its meanings.[5] In Ugaritic, the fivefold repeated epithet of Asherah, *qnyt 'lm*, can only mean "creator of the gods." In Phoenician, *'l qn 'rṣ (KAI* 26.iii.18) can only mean "El, creator of the earth." A similar epithet appears in Gen. 14:19, 22, where El Elyon is called "creator of heaven and earth." In Deut. 32:6 *qānāh* is parallel to "to make" and "to establish." Thus, the Hebrew verb *qānāh,* in addition to the meaning "to acquire, possess," can also mean "to create." Its semantic range is similar to the Akkadian verb *banû,* which means "to build, create, beget."[6]

[27–31] The second cosmogony is complementary to the first, but describes creation in positive terms rather than through negations. God raises up a great plate, "the heavens," to hold back the encompassing waters (v. 27a) and fixes the blue horizon at the boundaries of the cosmic waters (v. 27b). Verse 28 is parallel to v. 27, describing essentially the same act. The cosmic waters are controlled both by the "the vault of heaven" above (holding them back) and by the springs of waters below (safely bringing them up to irrigate the earth).

---

4. For the use of negation in describing precreation, see R. Clifford, *Creation Accounts in the Ancient Near East and in the Bible* (*CBQ* Monograph Series 26; Washington, D.C.: Catholic Biblical Association, 1994), 36–38 and 62–64. The same technique is also found in the Bible: "When there was *no* plant of the field in the earth and *no* herb of the field had sprung up . . . and there was *no* one to till the ground . . . then Yahweh God formed man." (Gen. 2:5).

5. A vigorous argument against *qānāh* meaning "to create" is found in B. Vawter, "Prov. 8:22: Wisdom and Creation," *JBL* 99 (1980): 205–16.

6. In Biblical Hebrew, *qānāh* had two distinct senses—"to possess" (by far the most common meaning) and "to create, beget." G rendered *qānāh* by *ktizō,* "to beget, create." S also translated *qānāh* "to create," and was followed by T. The Greek translations of Aquila, Symmachus, and Theodotion (first and second centuries C.E.) rendered the verb by *ktaomai,* "to acquire, possess." V followed this interpretation with *possedit,* "to possess." Hence, the early church had to deal with two renderings of Prov. 8:22a—"The Lord created me" and "The Lord possessed me."

The thrust of the second cosmogony is that Wisdom was with Yahweh as he created the world. Verses 27a and 30a form an inclusio, "I was there" and "I was at his side."[7] As vv. 22–26 stressed Yahweh's honoring Wisdom by making her first, so vv. 27–30a stress Yahweh's presence and even intimacy with Wisdom. The final two lines (vv. 30b–31), on the relationship between Woman Wisdom and Yahweh, are particularly important. The chiasm is particularly clear.

I was daily taking *delight*,   *rejoicing* before him at all times,
(*wā'ehyeh ša'ăšu'îm yôm yôm*   *měśaheqet lěpānāyw běkol-'ēt*)

rejoicing in his inhabited world;   I take *delight* in human beings.
(*měśaheqet bětēbēl 'arṣô*   *wěša'ăšu'ay 'et-běnê 'ādām.*)

The verb *śāḥaq* in the piel conjugation has several meanings: "to rejoice" (Jer. 15:17; 30:19; 31:4), "to jest" (Prov. 26:19), "to play with," "to entertain," "to play" (of children, Zech. 8:5),[8] "to dance [before God]" 2 Sam. 6:5, 21). The surest indicator of the meaning of *śāḥaq* is its parallelism to *šā'ăšu'îm*, "delight," which occurs in Psalm 119 in the meaning of delight in God's word or teaching (Ps. 119:24, 77, 92, 143, 174). The parallelism in Proverbs suggests the meaning of the feminine participle *měśaheqet* is "rejoicing." Wisdom enjoys being with God and her position of honor. Her joy is especially intense as she watches God create. The scene is reminiscent of the heavenly beings in Job 38:7 who sang as they watched God create: "when the morning stars sang together / and all heavenly beings sang for joy."[9]

The chiastic placement of "delight" and "rejoicing" binds vv. 30b–31 together and highlights the parallel between Wisdom delighting in Yahweh and Wisdom delighting in his creation, the human race. A parallel is drawn between the two acts of delight. As Wisdom delights in God "daily" in v. 30b, so the disciple is to wait upon her "daily" in v. 34. The relationship between Wisdom and her disciples on earth in vv. 32–34 mirrors the relationship between Wisdom and Yahweh in heaven. Wisdom is the most honored heavenly being and is therefore an apt mediator of heavenly gifts to the human race.

---

7. For the chiasm, see G. Yee, "The Theology of Creation in Proverbs 8:22–31," in *Creation in the Biblical Traditions* (*CBQ* Monograph Series 24), ed. R. J. Clifford and J. J. Collins (Washington D.C.: Catholic Biblical Association, 1992), 88.

8. Translators who render *'āmôn* "child" (rather than "sage") usually translate the verb "to play," but it should be noted that "to play" in this sense is attested only once. As pointed out below, the translation "child" is unlikely.

9. O. Keel suggests that the verb should be translated "dance," and refers to the ancient Egyptian custom of entertaining the gods with semierotic acrobatics, a practice that has some connection to the Maat (see *Die Weisheit spielt vor Gott: Ein ikonographischer Beitrag zur Deutung des měsahäqät in Sprüche 8.30f* [Göttingen: Vandenhoeck & Ruprecht 1974]). Maat is an unlikely model, however, and acrobatic dancing is unrelated to the work of Wisdom.

[**32–36**] The peroration of Wisdom's speech has suffered some textual confusion (see textual notes) but the meaning is clear enough. The phrase "and now" introduces her final appeal. She repeats the call with which she opened her speech (v. 4). She has a house (v. 34), where she will issue her great invitation in chap. 9. The final two lines (vv. 35–36) make accepting or rejecting her a matter of life and death.

The opening line of the peroration, "And now, O children, listen to me," is identical to the peroration of the father to his son in 7:24, but, unlike that passage, the disciple is invited to genuine life. Wisdom invites her disciples to have a relationship with her analogous to the one she has with Yahweh.

Excursus I: The Interpretation of Prov. 8:22
(Yahweh begot me as the first of his works)
in Early Judaism and Christianity

The portrait of personified Wisdom in Proverbs 8 fascinated early Judaism and Christianity. The earliest known interpretations of Proverbs 8 are Sir. 1:4, 9, and chap. 24, composed ca. 185 B.C.E. Sirach 24 imitates the thirty-five lines of Proverbs 8[10] and reprises Prov. 8:22 in v. 9: "Before the ages, in the beginning, he created me." Sirach 24 tells how Wisdom left her heavenly home to dwell with the people Israel in Zion and now is found in the "book of the covenant of the Most High God, the law that Moses commanded us" (v. 23). Subsequent Jewish interpretation followed the lead of Sirach in declaring that Wisdom was to be found in the Torah.

Seeking to express the ancestral tradition in the terms of Hellenistic Judaism, Wisdom of Solomon in the first century B.C.E. (or perhaps the first century C.E.) affirms a strong role for Wisdom in governing the world. The book alludes to Prov. 8:22 in 8:3, "She glorifies her noble birth by living with God, / and the Lord of all loves her," and in 9:9, "With you is wisdom, she who knows your works / and was present when you made the world."

Early Christians gave their own answer to the question where wisdom is to be found—not in the Torah, but in Jesus. They sought a warrant in the Jewish Scriptures for their belief that Jesus was the Son of God. They saw personified Wisdom as an inspired persuasive harbinger of their belief. The Gospel of John, for example, drew on 8:22 to portray Jesus as Wisdom incarnate. As Wisdom was with God "at the beginning," so Jesus is the word/wisdom "in the beginning," (John 1:1) with the Father before the world existed (John 17:5). John combines Gen. 1:1 and Prov. 8:22–23.

Church fathers of the second century made use of Jewish allegory and typology to demonstrate that the Old Testament spoke of Christ, and thus that

---

10. P. W. Skehan, "Structures in Poems on Wisdom: Proverbs 8 and Sirach 24," *CBQ* 41 (1979): 375.

Christ (or the Spirit), interpreted as Wisdom, was always *with* God the Father. Almost any incident or phrase in the Old Testament could be made into a predictor of the triune God. The *Dialogue with Trypho* (61.3–5) of Justin Martyr gave Prov. 8:22 a christological interpretation; the apologist Athenagoras in his *Supplication* (10.3; ca. 177) followed Justin.

In the next century, Eusebius of Caesarea (ca. 260–ca. 339) used the same Proverbs text to explore the nature of the substance (Greek *ousia*) of the Son, his exact relationship to the Father, and whether he was begotten out of nothing and before time began (*Praeparatio evangelii* VII.12.5; XI.14.2–10; *Demonstratio evangelii* V.1.8.9). Eusebius, influenced by Origen, interpreted the text in an orthodox fashion but differently than did Justin and Athenagoras in the previous century.

In the fourth century, the same text was used to *deny* the full divinity of Christ.[11] Arius (ca. 260–336), a priest of Alexandria, taught that the primary characteristic of God is to be "unbegotten." Father and Son could not therefore both be unbegotten or else the monotheistic heritage of Judaism would be compromised. Hence, Arianism's catechetical slogan, "There was once when he [the Son] was not." To support the claim that the Son came into existence in time, Arians applied to Christ the Septuagint rendering of Prov. 8:22 ("the Lord *created* me in the beginning of his ways") as well as the New Testament text of Col. 1:15 ("the firstborn of all creation"). The Council of Nicaea (325) rejected the subordinationist view of Christ. Christian orthodoxy thereafter never used the Septuagint of Prov. 8:22 to describe Trinitarian relations, but only the incarnation of the Son.

Excursus II: The Translation of *'āmôn* in v. 30

In v. 30, Wisdom declares "I was beside him [as] an *'āmôn*." The Hebrew word has been interpreted in three principal ways: (1) artisan, (2) trustworthy (friend), and (3) ward, nursling.

The translation "artisan" is first attested in the second-century B.C.E. Septuagint (later followed by the Peshitta and Vulgate), which rendered the Hebrew consonants *'mn* by the feminine participle *harmozousa*, literally, "in harmony with, suitable to; arranger, joiner." On the basis of this translation, some scholars suggest that MT *'āmôn* is wrongly vocalized and should be vocalized *'ommān*, like the word that occurs in Cant. 7:2 in the meaning of "artisan."

---

11. M. Simonetti, "Sull'interpretazione patristica di Proverbi 8, 22," in *Studi sull'Arianesimo* (Rome: Editrice Studium, 1965), 9–87; M. van Parys, "Prov. 8,22 chez les Pères cappadociens," *Irenikon* 43 (1970): 362–79; R. P. C. Hanson, "Biblical Exegesis in the Early Church," *The Cambridge History of the Bible*, ed. P. R. Ackroyd and P. R. Evans (Cambridge: Cambridge University Press, 1970), 414–16, 440–42.

'Ommān in Cant. 7:2 is generally recognized as a loanword from Akkadian *ummānu*.[12] One objection to this interpretation is that Wisdom cannot be an artisan because Proverbs 8 does not give her an active role in creating.[13] The objection is not valid, however, for Wisdom is not an artisan here but a sage or culture bringer (see Introduction §5). Unfortunately, the Mesopotamian mythological context that would have preserved the meaning "sage" for *'mn* fell into oblivion and scholars resorted to etymological speculation in order to discover the meaning of the now-unknown word.

The second interpretation, "trustworthy [friend]," is also ancient, being found in the ancient Greek translators Symmachus and Theodotion as well as in T. The translation seems, however, to be an etymological deduction from the triliteral root *'mn* (its root meaning is something like "firm") rather than an attested meaning. Further, "trustworthy" does not shed much light on Wisdom's role.

The third interpretation, "ward, nursling," takes *'āmôn* as the passive participle (*'āmûn*) of the verb *'mn*. "Nursling" has been the Jewish interpretation into modern times and is the majority scholarly view today. It is held, for example, by McKane, Plöger, Meinhold, JPSV ("confidant"), and REB ("darling and delight"). The translation seems at first glance to be supported by the verbs of giving birth in vv. 23–25.

There are serious problems with the rendering "nursling," however. First, *'āmôn* is a masculine form, not the feminine form one would expect for Woman Wisdom, and no epicene noun form is attested. More important, "nursling" does not suit the context. The birth of Woman Wisdom in vv. 23–25 is intended to show the priority of her origin; it does not imply that she always remained an infant. If Wisdom were a child, the analogy that is drawn between her relationship to God and her relationship to human beings (vv. 30b–31) would not make sense. She has an adult relationship to God and an adult relationship to human beings. Moreover, like the second interpretation, "nursling" seems to be an etymological deduction from the triliteral root by interpreters ignorant of the mythological background.[14]

The most satisfactory interpretation is that *'āmôn* in 8:30 is a loanword from

---

12. *HALAT* 60. The MT vocalization *'ommān* presupposes a quttal noun form and is compatible with a late derivation from Akkadian *ummānu*.

13. M. V. Fox, "*'Amon* Again," *JBL* 115 (1996), "The problem with explaining *'mwn* as 'artisan' is that nowhere in Proverbs 8 is Wisdom assigned an active role in creation" (p. 10). C. L. Rogers suggests that *'āmôn* means "artisan" and that it refers to Yahweh rather than Wisdom ("The Meaning and Significance of the Hebrew Word *'mwn* in Proverbs 8,30," *ZAW* 109 [1997]: 208–21). Rogers's proposal runs into at least two difficulties: (1) "artisan" is too weak a term for God after constructing the entire universe; (2) it renders otiose *'eslô*, "beside him."

14. Fox, "*'Amon* Again," proposes that *'mwn* is an infinitive absolute meaning "being raised," "growing up," serving as an adverbial complement to the main verb. Fox explains: "Lady Wisdom is declaring that while God was busy creating the world, she was nearby, growing up like a child in his care" (p. 702). The suggestion, while grammatically possible, seems semantically odd—"I was at his side growing up."

Akkadian *ummānu,* "scribe, sage; heavenly sage," and vocalized *'ommān* in Hebrew. An *ummānu* is a divine or semidivine bringer of culture and skill to the human race. The figure is attested in Mesopotamian mythology and was known to Levantine scribes (see Introduction §5). The word was correctly rendered by the Greek recension but wrongly vocalized by the Masoretes.

Like the Akkadian *ummānu,* Wisdom lives with God and in her role as sage brings to human beings the wisdom and culture they need to live rightly and serve God. Proverbs combines traditions of the heavenly mediator of wisdom with its own literary personification of Wisdom as foil to the forbidden woman.

Proverbs 9

Wisdom Poem III: The Two Women Invite Passersby to Their Banquets (Part 1)

9:1   Wisdom has built her house,
          has set up[a] her seven pillars.
2   She has prepared her meat, mixed her wine;
          she has set her table.
3   She has sent forth her maidservants,
          announcing in the upper city:
4   "Let the simple enter here."
      To anyone lacking wisdom, she says:
5   "Come, eat my food,
          and drink the wine I have mixed.
6   Leave simpleness behind and live,
          walk in the path of discernment,
11[b] for through me your days will be many,
          and years will be added to your life."

Sayings

7   Who corrects a scoffer incurs dishonor,
          and who reproves a malefactor becomes blemished.
8   Do not correct a scoffer, for he will become your enemy;
          correct a wise person and he will become your friend.
9   Teach a wise person and he becomes wiser;
          instruct a righteous person and he will gain insight.
10   Revering Yahweh is the beginning of wisdom;
          obeying the Holy One is understanding,
12   If you are wise, you are wise to your own gain,
          but if you are a scoffer you alone bear the consequences.[c]

Wisdom Poem III: The Two Women Invite Passersby to Their Banquets (Part 2)

13 The foolish woman is restless,
   she is ignorant, and knows nothing.
14 She sits at the doorway of her house,
   on a chair, at the height of the city,
15 calling to those who pass by the street,
   those going on their way:
16 "Let the simple enter here."
   To anyone lacking wisdom, she says:
17 "Stolen water tastes sweet;
   bread eaten in secret gives pleasure."
18 But he does not know the Rephaim are there,
   that her guests are in the depths of Sheol.[d]

a. For MT *ḥṣb* (= *ḥāṣab*, "to hew"), G, followed by S and T, read *hiṣṣibāh* in the causative conjugation of the verb *nāṣab,* which in the niphal and causative conjugations means "to set up." G preserves the superior reading, for *bānāh,* "to build," and the causative conjugation of *nāṣab* occur within the same semantic field in Josh. 6:26 and 1 Kings 16:34. It is thus reasonable to suppose that the two verbs are related here. The confusion of *h* and *ḥ* was easy in the Herodian book-hand.

b. We transfer v. 11 to after v. 6. The pronoun in the phrase "through me" in v. 11 has no antecedent in its present placement. A similar scene in Ugaritic (*KTU* 1.17.VI.26–29) also associates eating at the goddess's banquet with living additional years. Anat promises life to the youth Aqhat: "I will cause you to count years with Baal, / with the sons of El you will count months."

c. G, followed by S, has three verses not in MT: "Who relies on falsehoods will shepherd the winds / and will chase a flying bird; / for he has abandoned the paths of his own vineyard / and strayed from the tracks of his own tilled land; / and he goes through a waterless desert / and a land consigned to droughts, / and gathers barrenness with his hands."

d. G, followed by S, has four verses not in MT: "But turn away, do not remain in the place / nor cast your eye toward her. / For thus you will cross alien water / and go over an alien river. / Abstain from alien water / and do not drink from an alien well, / so that you may live a long time, / and years of life be added to you."

The chapter contains Woman Wisdom's invitation to her banquet (vv. 1–6 + 11), a counterinvitation by Woman Folly (vv. 13–18), and five independent sayings (vv. 7–10, 12). Wisdom and her rival have made appeals before but never in direct opposition. The sayings echo sentiments found in chap. 1: "The beginning of knowledge is revering Yahweh" (v. 7) and "How long, O simple ones, will you choose ignorance, / will you turn away at my reproof?" (v. 22–23a). Besides glancing backwards, the sayings also point forward toward the next part of the book (10:1–22:16) by contrasting of the wise and the righteous.

Of the three sections in chap. 9, the sections on Woman Wisdom and Woman Folly are obviously contrasted. Verses 7–10, 12 are less clear and their originality here is widely questioned. Meinhold is one of the few commentators who defend their direct relevance to chap. 9. In his view, vv. 7–9 and 12 form a frame—scoffer and wise in vv. 7–9 and wise and scoffer in v. 12—heightening the inner statement in vv. 10–11 on the beginning and the fruit of wisdom. Most recent scholars, however, rightly regard the verses as early additions to the chapter. G, it should be noted, made its own subsequent additions to the chapter— three verses after v. 12 and three after v. 18 (reprinted in the textual notes).

The invitations of the two women are not perfectly symmetrical (which is no argument against their originality). They have only one verse in common, " 'Let the simple enter here.' / To anyone lacking wisdom, she says: . . ." (vv. 4 and 16). Woman Wisdom acts but is not characterized personally. She has built her house, prepared a dedicatory feast for it, and commissioned messengers to invite guests (vv. 1–3). Woman Folly does very little; she has not built a house or sent out maids. She is, however, strongly characterized in a negative way ("restless, ignorant, knows nothing"). She calls out to passersby from her chair. Both women offer food to their guests (meat and wine, water and bread). Significantly, Wisdom makes a demand that Folly does not—that her guests leave "simpleness" and live (v. 6). The texts says that life is the result of responding to Wisdom (v. 11) and death is the result of responding to Folly (v. 18).

A number of questions are raised by chap. 9. What is Wisdom's house? What does the banquet symbolize? What do the bread (or food) and wine (or water) represent? What is Folly's counteroffer? Comparable passages suggest that Wisdom has just completed her palace and is inviting guests to her dedicatory feast. Solomon invited Israelites to an enormous feast after building the house of Yahweh in 1 Kings 8:1–5. In the most illuminating parallel, a Ugaritic text from the Baal-Mot cycle (*KTU* 1.4.VI; *ANET,* 134), the storm-god Baal invites the gods to his newly built palace. Cognate words occurring in Proverbs 9 are italicized in the following translations and paraphrase. Baal declares, "My *house* I have *built* of silver, / My palace of gold" (lines 36–38). In preparing his feast, Baal *slays* oxen and other animals. "He calls his brothers into his *house* . . . he supplies the gods with rams and *wine*. . . . while the gods *eat* and *drink* . . . " (*KTU* 1.4.VII.44–59). Since Baal no longer needs to live in El's palace, his house symbolizes his authority. Wisdom's house, one can assume, symbolizes her great authority and dignity, which was stated so strongly in chap. 8, especially in vv. 22–31. Those who come to her banquet acknowledge her authority and rejoice in her company.[1]

---

1. For a general review of such invitations to banquets, see M. Lichtenstein, "The Banquet Motifs in Keret and in Proverbs 9," *Journal of the Ancient Near Eastern Society of Columbia University* 1 (1968): 19–31.

Another Ugaritic text casts light on Woman Folly's invitation and, indirectly, on the counteroffer of Wisdom (*KTU* 1.17.VI.2–45; *ANET,* 151). The goddess Anat gives a feast to which she invites the young man Aqhat. She then asks him to give her his "bow" (a sexual reference). In return, she offers him gold and silver. When he refuses, she raises the offer to eternal life with the gods (cognate words occurring in Prov. 9:1–6, 11 are italicized): "*Eat of food,* ho! / *Drink* of the liquor of *wine,* ho!" . . . Ask for *life* and I will give it to you, / not-dying and I will grant it to you. / I will cause you to count *years* with Baal, / with the children of El you will count months."[2] Aqhat spurns even this offer, declaring that Anat's offer is deceptive in that she has no power to grant eternal life to mortals such as he. Anat's response is in deed rather than word. She tracks him down and kills him.

Woman Wisdom's invitation in Prov. 9:5 draws on the same conventions of Anat's deceitful invitation, even borrowing the Ugaritic fixed pair *lḥm* ("to eat") // *šty* ("to drink").[3] Proverbs makes Woman Wisdom the antithesis to the deceiving goddess, for her offer of life is genuine (v. 11). The switch in speakers may well be the contribution of the biblical author, who wishes to make of Woman Wisdom a contrasting figure.

Wisdom invites "the simple," those who have not yet accepted wisdom, not only to eat and drink but to give up their "simpleness" and live. To live one must give up simpleness, or life without wisdom. Giving up evil conduct before eating food in a sacred precinct is also required by a remarkably similar passage in Isaiah: "Ho, all who are thirsty . . . come buy food and eat. . . . Why do you spend money for what is not bread, your earnings for what does not satisfy? Heed me and you will eat choice food and enjoy the richest viands" (55:1–5). The text urges readers to stop seeking the food that does not satisfy for the food that does satisfy! Isa. 55:6–7 makes the point a second time with even greater clarity: "Seek Yahweh while he may be found. . . . Let the wicked *leave behind* his way, the evildoer, his plans."[4] "Live!" in Prov. 9:6a means avoiding the premature death and sickness of the impious and enjoying the blessings of wealth, protection, honor, children.

Wisdom's antithesis, Woman Folly, is depicted with traits of the adulterous woman in 2:16–19; chap. 5; 6:20–35; chap. 7. She is restless (cf. 7:11), her path leads to the Rephaim and to Sheol (2:18; 5:5; 7:27), and she is ignorant (5:6).

---

2. The text is broken but can be restored with certainty. See R. Clifford, "Proverbs IX: A Suggested Ugaritic Parallel," *VT* 25 (1975): 298–306.

3. The word pair is found only here and 4:17; the more common biblical Hebrew fixed pair is *'ākal,* "to eat" // *šātāh,* "to drink."

4. For detailed examination of the requirement to leave behind profane conduct before eating a sacral meal, see R. Clifford, "Isaiah 55: Invitation to a Feast," in *The Word of the Lord Shall Go Forth* (D. N. Freedman volume), ed. C. L. Meyers and M. O'Connor (Philadelphia: American Schools of Oriental Research, 1983), 27–35.

In the final scene of the drama, she appears in single combat with her nemesis, Wisdom. Though the two women's invitations begin with identical language, they differ profoundly. One demands that her guests leave behind their ignorance, whereas the other trades on their ignorance. Folly promises only clandestine pleasure ("stolen water," "food eaten in secret"), but it ends in death. Wisdom offers food and discipline that enable her guests to live.

The chapter brings the first major part of Proverbs to a close. It draws on the sketches of the seductive woman in earlier instructions for its counterportrait to Woman Wisdom. In the two portraits of chap. 9, life and death are set off starkly against each other, evoking the life and death choice of Deut. 30:15–20. The additions, vv. 7–10, 12, allude to chap. 1, thus forming an inclusio that closes the section chaps. 1–9. The concluding poem in the book, the praise of the wife who creates a great household (31:10–31), may allude to this house of Wisdom.

This memorable portrayal of Wisdom has influenced other texts: "She will feed him with the bread of knowledge, and give him the water of wisdom to drink" (Sir. 15:3); "Those who eat me will hunger for more, and those who drink me will thirst for more" (Sir. 24:21). In the Gospel of John (6:35–40), Jesus extends an invitation: "I am the bread of life; whoever comes to me will never hunger and whoever believes in me will never thirst" (NAB). Especially in early Eastern Christianity, the text was given a eucharistic and christological interpretation. In the Byzantine liturgy it is read at the Holy Thursday celebration of the Lord's Supper. Hippolytus of Rome took personified Wisdom building a house for herself as an image of the incarnation—the divine Word builds a body for himself. Proverbs 9:1–5 served as a reading for feasts of the Virgin Mary and, later, in the dedication ceremony for a new church.[5]

[9:1] The seven-pillared house has stirred much discussion. Archaeologists have not found any seven-pillared houses that might have served as models for it. Noting the lack of evidence, J. Greenfield suggests that "seven" refers not to a house but to the seven sages known in Semitic and Greek sources; emending the text (see textual notes), he translates "The Seven have set its foundations." The seven apkallus were pre-Flood sages in Mesopotamian lore, who in some texts were associated with seven ancient cities and credited with laying their foundations.[6] They are mentioned in Prov. 26:16: "A sluggard is wiser in his own eyes / than the Seven who give wise answers." Greenfield's interpretation is linguistically possible but requires additional confirmation before it can be adopted.

5. For the influence of Proverbs 9:1–5, see K.-G. Sanderlin, *Wisdom as Nourisher: A Study of an Old Testament Theme: Its Development within Early Judaism and Its Impact on Early Christianity* (Acta Academiae Aboensis, ser. A, vol. 64, nr. 3; Åbo: Akademi, 1986).

6. "The Seven Pillars of Wisdom (Prov. 9.1), a Mistranslation," *Jewish Quarterly Review* 76 (1985): 13–20.

With our present knowledge, the best course is to interpret the seven pillars not as decorative columns but as supports on which the palace ("house") rested, like the pillars in Judg. 16:25, 26, 29. "Seven" connotes completeness and perhaps grandeur in the Bible (e.g., "Balak said to Balaam, 'Build me seven altars'" [Num. 23:1]) and in Ugaritic, ("seven chambers, eight enclosures" [*KTU* 1.3.V.34–35]). "Seven pillars" thus is metonymy for a grand house, befitting the exalted status of Wisdom.

[2–3] The feast celebrates the completion of Wisdom's house or palace. Like the Ugaritic text in which Baal states, "*I* have built my house of silver," the text attributes to her alone the construction of the house and giving of the feast. She mixes her wine with spices, a festal touch (Cant. 8:2). The servants issue the invitation in the upper city, which is the site of palaces and the place where she customarily meets her disciples (Prov. 1:20–21 and 8:1–2).

[4–6, 11] The message is directed to "the simple" and "anyone lacking wisdom." The invitees are the same group that Woman Wisdom addressed in chap. 8 — the common crowd likely to be found in the high areas or public spaces of the city. Verse 11 uses the fixed pair "days" and "years," which is common in Ugaritic literature and in the Bible (e.g., Deut. 32:7; Job 10:5; Prov. 3:2; 10:27).

[7–10, 12] The five self-contained sayings repeat words and themes from chap. 1 to form an inclusio. Since they obscure the juxtaposition of the two women's invitations, it is likely that they were added at an early stage and, in the process, displaced v. 11. The Greek recension has three sayings not in MT after v. 12, and four after v. 18. A translation of these verses is contained in the textual notes.

[7] Proverbs 22:10 also associates dishonor with the scoffer who is too contemptuous to learn from others: "Expel the scoffer and out goes quarreling; / strife and dishonor end." According to this saying, all attempts to teach such cynics are doomed; the disgrace that attaches to them will end up on their would-be teacher. The sounds reinforce the sense: *yōsēr lēṣ lōqēaḥ lô qālôn* in colon A; the consonant combination *l-q* is reversed in *q-l* and the vowel combination *ō-ē* is reversed in *ē-ō*.

[8] Verse 7b is restated in the form of an admonition with a reason: attempting to reprove scoffers will turn them into enemies. The wise are shown to be wise by their openness and love of wisdom. So eager are they to learn that they regard those who correct them as their friends.

[9] An expansion of v. 8 and an echo of 1:5 ("a wise person, hearing them, will gain more wisdom, / and a prudent person will grow in skill"), the verse states that a sage is always a student, ever eager to learn. The wise pursue wisdom and are always open to receiving it as a gift (as in chap. 2).

[10] The verse echoes 1:7a: "The beginning of knowledge is revering Yahweh." In this verse, some translators make the phrase "the beginning of wisdom" the subject (JPSV, REB, Alonso Schökel), whereas others make it the predicate (NRSV, McKane). It is difficult to decide the proper subject and pred-

icate, but a decision either way does not greatly affect the meaning. The phrase *da'at qĕdōšîm* can mean "knowledge of holy ones (= angelic figures)" or "the Holy One (= God)." The translation "Holy One" is suggested by the parallel "Yahweh"; the word designates God in 30:3 and Hos. 12:1. "Knowledge" is used as in Hos. 4:1; 6:6; and Prov. 2:5 in the sense of "devotion, obedience." "Revering Yahweh" (traditional "fear of the Lord") does not mean a general religious attitude but devotion to a particular god entailing obedience and proper ritual (see under 1:7). Here it involves Yahweh, Israel's God, who is the guarantor of the way of wisdom. The verse puts the quest for wisdom in explicitly religious terms. Verse 11 was displaced from its original place after v. 6. For its meaning, see under vv. 4–6, 11.

[12] This is a difficult verse, which appears to state the obvious—one is wise or scoffing to one's own account. Perhaps the verse means to shift the customary focus on the effect upon *others* to the effect upon the *doer*. People must bear the consequences of their conduct.

[13–18] The wise person (*ḥākām*) and the fool (*kĕsîl*) are often contrasted in Proverbs, so it is not surprising to find them contrasted here. The grammatical forms of each are rare, however. *Kĕsîlût*, "foolish," occurs only here in the Bible; the ending *-ût* can express the abstract meaning of triliteral roots (J-M §88j). The adjective describing the foolish woman is a feminine singular participle (*hōmîyāh*), which can mean "tumultuous" when applied to cities and lands, "roaring" when applied to waves and the sea, "growling" or "barking" when applied to bears and dogs. In the Song of Songs, the word describes the stirring of the affections (Cant. 5:4). Applied to the foolish woman, the probable meaning is "restless" or "bustling," the opposite of the peace and poise of wisdom. Colon B has a second word for Folly, "ignorant" (*pĕtayyût*), which is derived from the substantive *pĕtî* ("simple, naive") plus the *-ût* ending. Portraits of the dangerous woman in earlier descriptions emphasized her deceit (2:16–19; 5:3–6; 6:24; 7:21) rather than her ignorance (though cf. 5:6).

Both women invite passersby to come into their house for a meal. Unlike Wisdom, Folly has no palace to dedicate and no maidservants to send and she mimics Wisdom's invitation. "Stolen water" in v. 17 seems to refer on a literal level to adultery, the stealing of sexuality belonging to another's household. "Water" refers to the sexuality of the wife in 5:15–17: "Drink the water of your own cistern, / the flow from your own well. / Should your springs flow into the street, / streams of water into the squares? / Let your fountain be for you alone, / not for outsiders to share with you." At the same time, the metaphor extends beyond sexuality to a way of life: the way of life opposite to that of wisdom can appear alluring. "Secret" evokes the furtive meeting of the wife and the youth in chap. 7. The Rephaim in v. 18 are the inhabitants of the underworld. As in 2:18; 5:5–6; 7:24–27, and the invitations to the heroes by the goddesses in *Gilgamesh, Aqhat,* and the *Odyssey* (see Introduction), the woman's guests are invited to an erotic encounter, but they end up in the underworld.

Proverbs 10

Chapter 10 begins the second, and longest, section of the book: the 375 two-line sayings of 10:1–22:16. Like the titles in 1:1 and 25:1, its title, "The Proverbs of Solomon," attributes the material to Solomon. The numerical values of the Hebrew consonants of "Solomon," *šlmh* (š = 300; l = 30; m = 40; h = 5) add up to 375, which is the number of verses in 10:1–22:17.[1] Some commentators argue that not only the number but the arrangement of the sayings in chaps. 10–22 is artful and semantically significant.[2] It is true that many of the sayings have been arranged by catchword and theme; there are many arresting associations of verses worthy of a commentator's attention. At the same time, one must remember that aphorisms are by definition concise and self-contained. Each must be allowed to have its own say.

Some generalizations about content can safely be made about 10:1–22:16. It is widely acknowledged that two groups of sayings can be discerned—chaps. 10–15 and 16:1–22:16. Chapters 10–15 consist almost entirely of antithetic proverbs in which the second line (colon B) restates the first line (colon A) in an antithetical way. The second section persistently contrasts the righteous and the unrighteous and emphasizes the relation of act to consequence, or, in other terms, of character to consequence. The section states the way things generally are or the way they ought to be. There are far fewer antitheses between righteous and wicked, and many more exceptions to the rule. The noun "righteous person" appears thirty-nine times in the first section but only nine times in the second.

Several themes run throughout 10:1–22:16: "house" (in the broad sense of household), giving surety for another's debt, and wealth and poverty. Founding or maintaining a household is a constant metaphor throughout the entire book. Founding a house (and the related theme of finding a spouse) was the great task of the young in Proverbs's society. Founding (or governing) a house becomes a basic metaphor for any reader of Proverbs, young or old, male or female. Everyone is charged with the task of building a "house" in the sense of a personal and

---

1. In the title of the book, "The Proverbs of Solomon, son of David, king of Israel" (1:1), the numerical values of the consonants of "Solomon," "David," and "Israel" add up to 930, just short of the 934 lines of MT. P. W. Skehan argues from this fact for a single editor in "A Single Editor for the Whole Book of Proverbs," *CBQ* 10 (1948): 115–30 (reprinted in *Studies in Israelite Poetry and Wisdom* (*CBQ* Monograph Series 1 [Washington D.C.: Catholic Biblical Association, 1971]), 15–26. Though the numerical value of Hebrew consonants is attested only from the second century B.C.E., it could be much earlier. Generally, numerology played an important role in literature up to the recent past. It is difficult to judge what *semantic* significance the numerology had.

2. See the commentaries of Meinhold and Alonso Schökel and T. Hildebrandt, "Proverbial Pairs: Compositional Units in Proverbs 10–29," *JBL* 107 (1988): 207–24.

communal life. Each person can draw an analogy for his or her own life. The chapters contain over fifty references to the father, mother, son, house, wife, and servant; only chap. 16 is without a reference.[3] The themes of giving surety, and of wealth and poverty, are pervasive but do not provide structure in the same sense.

10:1   **The Proverbs of Solomon**

A wise son makes his father rejoice,
  but a foolish son is his mother's heartache.

2   Ill-gotten treasure is of no avail,
        but righteousness saves from death.

3   Yahweh will not let the throat of the righteous go hungry,
        but rebuffs the craving of the wicked.

4   A slack hand makes a pauper,
        but the hand of the diligent brings riches.

5   Who gathers in summer is a wise son,
        but who slumbers at harvest is a despicable son.

6   Blessings come upon the head of the righteous,
        but violence fills the mouth of the wicked.[a]

7   The fame of a righteous person becomes a blessing,
        but the name of the wicked rots away.

8   A wise heart accepts instructions,
        but foolish lips are rejected.

9   Who walks straight ahead walks secure,
        but who walks a crooked path will be found out.

10   Who winks his eye brings trouble,
        but who reproves brings peace.[b]

11   The mouth of the righteous is a fountain of life,
        but violence fills the mouth of the wicked.[c]

12   Hate stirs up quarrels,
        but love covers all offenses.

13   Wisdom is found on the lips of the intelligent,
        but a rod is for the back of those lacking sense.

14   The wise treasure up knowledge,
        but the mouth of the fool is impending ruin.

3. Father: 10:1; 13:1; 15:5, 20; 17:6, 21, 25; 19:13, 14, 26; 20:20. Mother: 10:1; 15:20; 19:26; 20:20. Daughter: none (only in 30:15, 16). Son: 10:1, 5; 13:1, 22, 24; 14:26; 15:11, 20; 17:2, 6, 25; 19:13, 18, 26, 27; 20:7. House: 11:29; 12:7; 14:1, 11; 15:6, 25, 27; 17:1, 13; 19:14; 21:9, 12. Wife, woman: 11:16, 22; 12:4; 14:1; 18:22; 19:13, 14; 21:9, 19. Servant (occurrences relevant to family or household): 11:29; 17:2; 19:10.

15 A rich person's wealth is a fortified city for him,
       their poverty is the ruin of the poor.
16 The income of the righteous is life,
       the wages of the wicked is want.
17 Who follows discipline is on the path to life,
       but who rejects correction leads astray.
18 Who conceals hatred has lying lips;
       who reveals a slander is a fool.
19 When words are many, there is no shortage of offense,
       but who curbs his lips is a wise person.
20 The tongue of the righteous person is choice silver;
       the heart of the wicked is worth nothing.
21 The lips of a righteous person feed many,
       but the foolish die of lack of sense.
22 It is the blessing of Yahweh that gives riches;
       toil cannot add to it.
23 As a fool delights in lewdness,
       so a prudent person delights in wisdom.
24 What a wicked person dreads will come upon him,
       but the desire of the righteous will be granted.
25 When the storm has passed, a wicked person is no more,
       but a righteous person has a lasting foundation.
26 Like vinegar to the teeth,
       like smoke to the eyes,
       is a sluggard to those who employ him.
27 Revering Yahweh gives an increase of days,
       but the years of the wicked are cut short.
28 The hope of the righteous is joy,
       but the expectation of the wicked is destroyed.
29 The way of Yahweh is a stronghold for the blameless,
       but destruction to those who do evil.
30 The righteous person will never be moved,
       but the wicked will not dwell in the land.
31 The mouth of a righteous person yields wisdom,
       but the tongue of the treacherous will be cut off.
32 The lips of a righteous person know favor,
       but the mouth of the wicked will be distorted.

a. Verses 6b and 11b are identical (as are vv. 8b and 10b). Was one of the verses corrupt or missing and a nearby colon borrowed to remedy the damage as is the case in 13:8 and Isa. 41:1b (which borrowed 40:31a)? Or was the author deliberately using the second colon twice? At any rate, colon B makes sense in both verses. See textual note c.

b. Colon B in MT is identical to v. 8b in MT. Evidently, colon B was corrupt or missing and a scribe borrowed v. 8b for sense. G, followed by S, has, "Who rebukes with boldness makes peace," which reflects the Hebrew *ûmôkîaḥ ya'ăśeh šālôm*. G preserves a superior reading, for it has antithetic parallelism and gives a syllable count closer to colon A than the borrowed Hebrew colon.

c. Verse 11b is identical to v. 6b. The Hebrew can be read in two ways: "the mouth conceals violence" (G, T, V), which is the more natural reading, or "violence covers (= fills) the mouth" (S).

Some structural unity is discernible in chap. 10 (and also in chaps. 25–26). Fourteen of the sayings mention organs of perception (heart, eyes, ["head," v. 6]), organs of expression (tongue, mouth, lips), or organs of activity (hand). Antithetic parallelism of the righteous (usually *ṣaddîq*) and wicked (usually *rāšā'*) occurs fourteen times; the righteous/wicked contrast *and* the organs are both mentioned in the same verse in vv. 20–21 and 31–32. With vv. 20–21, the pairing of bicola (vv. 2–3, 4–5, 6–7, etc.) ends, and with vv. 31–32, a distinct section ends. After vv. 20–21, several verses refer back to the first section. For example, v. 22 refers back to vv. 3–6 and v. 24 refers back to v. 3. As in chaps. 25–26, the structure is subtle and has gone unnoticed by generations of readers. The structure may well be a system of "builder's marks" devised by editors rather than a system meant to communicate to readers.

[10:1] The topic is how parents are affected by their son's wisdom and folly. Wisdom is not theoretical knowledge but the ability to live life successfully, with success being measured in the blessings of health, reputation, spouse and children, and wealth. The saying has a triple antithesis: father and mother, wise and foolish, joy and grief.

Adult children represented the family to the community and their parents lived on in them. Their behavior, good or bad, thus elicited in their parents a deeply emotional response. The verb "to rejoice" includes outward expression as well as inner feeling.

This opening saying in the collection is programmatic in the structure of the book. "Son," "father," and "mother" refer back to the opening line of the first instruction (1:8): "My *son,* hear the instruction of your *father,* do not disdain the teaching of your *mother*." And the son is the object of parental exhortation in chaps. 1–9. Founding or maintaining a house is a major theme in those chapters. The saying points forward thematically within this collection, for it is the first of many sentences on domestic happiness (or unhappiness) in family relationships—between parents and son (15:20; 17:21, 25; 19:13, 26; 23:22–26) or husband and wife (12:4; 14:1; 18:22; 19:14; 21:9, 19). Like a red thread through the collection, the domestic sayings keep before the reader the theme of building or founding a household. Metaphorically, founding a house and choosing and being faithful to a life partner is the project of any serious seeker after wisdom. This verse, and the next two, introduce the reader to the full dimensions of wisdom, which are, in Alonso Schökel's phraseology, the sapiential (v. 1), the ethical (v. 2), and the religious (v. 3).

[2] This verse is an expression of the ethical side of wisdom. Which is more effective in preserving life—treasure (improperly gained) or righteousness? The phrase "is of no avail" in all but two of its biblical usages appears in a negation or in a question implying a negative answer. This saying affirms the traditional connection between righteous conduct and long life. Contrasts make the statement lively: "treasures" (plural in Hebrew) and "righteousness" (singular); the fixed pair "of no avail" and "saves" (also in 11:4 and 1 Sam. 12:21). The final word, "death," introduces the special perspective of the saying. Wealth, which is usually acquired to ward off future misfortune, actually makes matters worse if improperly gained, for it invites retribution. Righteousness, on the other hand, assures God's blessing and protection from the premature death resulting from wickedness (3:2, 16; 9:11; 28:16). In Proverbs, wealth offers security (as in v. 15) only if it is honestly gained. The first colon is united by four /ō/ sounds, and the second, by three /ā/ sounds.

The Hebrew idiom "to save from death" (eleven occurrences in the Bible) has the nuance of staying alive in adverse situations, as in Josh. 2:13, where Rahab asks "that you will spare my father and mother, my brothers and sisters, and all their kin, and save us from death [in the coming invasion]." See also Ps. 33:18–19: "See, the eyes of Yahweh are on those who fear him, / on those who wait for his gracious help, / to save their souls from death, / and keep them alive in times of famine." Jeremiah. 49:4–5 is an example of illusory trust during a crisis: "Why do you glory in your strength? . . . You trusted in your *treasure,* saying, 'Who can attack me?' I am going to bring terror upon you, says Yahweh, the God of hosts."

Proverbs 15:16 and 21:6 are also about the uselessness of ill-gotten treasure, the former saying that few possessions with piety are better than tainted treasure, and the latter (like our verse) stating such possessions will not endure.

[3] This last of the three introductory sayings on wisdom underscores its religious aspect by mentioning Yahweh. Yahweh will never allow the righteous to starve and will keep the appetite of the unrighteous from being fulfilled. One appetite—hunger—is singled out but it stands metaphorically for other desires. See also Ps. 37:19, 25.

[4] Verses 4–5 associate laziness with poverty and diligence with wealth, a common association in Proverbs (6:6–11; 12:24, 27; 13:4; 15:19). The basic antitheses of the saying are rich and poor, lazy and diligent, palm (*kap*) and hand (*yād* = fingertip to elbow). When first read, colon A says, "A pauper acts with a slack hand." Colon B, however, forces a rereading of the first colon. A diagram may help to show the ambivalence:[4]

---

4. Oral communication from Prof. Choon-Leong Seow.

Colon A: Pauper   makes   slack hand
Colon B: hand of diligent   brings riches.

As the Hebrew sentence unfolds, "pauper" turns out to be the object rather than the subject of the verb. "A slack hand" makes something—a pauper!

[5] In the precarious economy of the ancient Near East, harvesttime demanded everyone's energies to bring the crops in on time. To lounge in bed at such a time was foolish and wicked. Sound reinforces sense: in colon A *baqqayiṣ*, "in summer," is matched in colon B by *baqqāṣîr*, "at harvest"; *bēn maśkîl*, "wise son," is matched by *bēn mēbîš*, "despicable son."

[6] The saying plays on the range of meanings in the verb "to cover," which occurs frequently in Proverbs. Colon A and B are related chiastically (ABC/CBA) in the Hebrew: (A) blessings (B) upon (C) the head of the righteous // (C) the mouth of the wicked (B) covers (A) violence. The verb "to cover" (*kissēh*) has two virtually opposite senses—concealing (as in Job 16:18 and Prov. 10:18), and filling (as in Isa. 60:2; Ezek. 30:18; Hab. 2:17; Jer. 3:25). S, T, and V prefer the first sense, "the mouth of the wicked *conceals* violence," as does NRSV. But the second sense is also possible, "violence *fills* the mouth (= head) of the wicked." The first is the more natural reading of the Hebrew; it describes the *characteristic behavior* of the wicked. The second meaning is less obvious; it describes the *result* of wicked behavior—violence comes upon the head of the wicked (so JPSV). The ambiguity is intentional. The proverb can be read both ways.

[7] The verse is linked to v. 6 by the word "blessing" and the righteous/wicked contrast. The topic is the manner in which the righteous and the wicked live on in the memory of their children and the community. The memory of one type remains alive in blessings such as "May you be as blessed as X!" whereas the memory of the other rots away like their bodies. "Rot" is in the final position and springs the surprise. "Fame" and "name" are a fixed pair in the Bible. The consonants *r-k* (or *q*) recur in reversed order: *zkr*, "name," in colon A appears in *brkh*, "blessing," and *yrqb*, "rot."

[8] The antitheses are wise and foolish, the verbs "to accept" and "to reject," "heart" (inside, reception) and "lips" (outside, expression) as in 16:21, 23; 22:11; 24:2. Fools speak rather than listen to the counsels of wiser heads. Unwilling to receive, they are rejected; "rejected" is probably a divine passive. "Instruction" (*miṣwāh*) occurs ten times in Proverbs and means teaching, often of a sage or parent.

[9] Colon A declares that right living, literally, walking straight ahead (using the metaphors of straight and deviant) is the basis for confidence. Straightforward behavior wins divine protection. Colon B hints that even if one makes one's way twisted, that is, hard to track, one will be found out. The alliteration

(*l-k*, *t* or *ṭ*) and assonance (/ō/ and /ē/) of colon A is remarkable: *hôlēk battōm yēlek beṭṭah*.

[10] Some proverbs assume that character can be read from certain physical gestures. Winking (or compressing) the eye or mouth indicates a bad character (see 6:13; 16:30), as do shuffling one's feet and pointing with one's finger (6:13). Precisely what physical gestures are meant we do not know. They are either signs of a restless schemer or signals of something over and above the plain meaning of the speaker's words, hence deceitful. Direct communication through honest speech in "reproving," on the other hand, brings wisdom, which is the basis of peace.

[11] Four things are said to be a fountain of life in Proverbs: the teaching of the wise (13:14), revering Yahweh (14:27), wisdom (16:22), and here, the mouth (= word) of a righteous person. The righteous bring life to anyone who heeds their teaching.

The verb *kissēh* in colon B has two senses as noted under v. 6. The verb has a different sense depending on whether colon B is read backwards or forwards: the mouth of the wicked *covers* (= conceals) violence within (so G, T, V) or violence *covers* (= fills) the mouth of the wicked (so S). The proverb produces ambiguity and each sense offers an interesting contrast to colon A. Colon B in v. 6 is identical.

[12] This is another saying (like vv. 6, 11, and 18) that plays on the multiple senses of "to cover." "Love" and "hate" are here acts rather than attitudes. Love covers sins, either in the sense of disregarding faults (cf. 11:13; 17:9) or in the sense of forgiving sins (with the preposition '*al*) as in Neh. 3:37 (4:5E) and Deut. 13:9. In Prov. 29:22, anger (= hatred expressed) *stirs up* quarrels. The basic antithesis in our saying is thus between pacifying and provoking.

[13] Job 28:12 asks, "Where is wisdom to be found?" This saying answers that it is found on the lips (= words) of the wise. In the educational psychology of Proverbs, the words one hears are memorized or stored in the heart (= mind). Those who lack sense (lit., "lack heart") do not heed the words of the wise. They are fated to pay a price for their obtuseness—feeling the rod on their back. The pairing of "lips" and "back" occurs only here and is possibly meant humorously.

[14] "Knowledge" here refers to what one knows and stores in one's heart. The wise feel no need to express all their knowledge in words. They treasure it up (Josh. 2:4; Prov. 2:1; 7:1). Fools do not, squandering it thoughtlessly.

[15] Though Proverbs blames poverty on laziness (as in v. 4), it does not blame the poor. On the contrary, the book urges almsgiving as a religious duty and records the plight of the poor in a compassionate manner, as in this verse. Using metaphors from warfare, the verse contrasts the relative security of rich and poor folk. Wealth protects a rich person like a fortified city, whereas its absence, poverty, destroys the poor. The word "ruin" describes a ruined city in

Ps. 89:41. By means of a chiasm (ABC // CBA), colon B mirrors colon A: wealth, wise person, strong city // ruin, the poor, their poverty.

[16] The verse is perfectly symmetrical. "Life" in colon A is enhanced life, which includes health, children, and reputation, whereas "want" is their absence. Wages become a metaphor for reward and punishment in a larger sense. The meaning of Hebrew *ḥaṭṭā't* in colon B is not "sin" (despite many translators) but "want," "falling short" as occasionally in wisdom literature (e.g., 21:4 and Job 14:16). Romans 6:21 expresses a similar sentiment: "But what profit did you get then from the things of which you are now ashamed? For the end of those things is death."

[17] The main antithesis is following and rejecting discipline. The verbs are a fixed pair in 2 Chron. 13:11; Ps. 119:8; and Jonah 2:9 [8E]. The second verb in colon B, "to lead astray," has caused discussion. It is the participle of the verb *tā'āh,* "to wander," which, in the causative conjugation, means, "to cause to wander, to lead astray." Gemser and NRSV, however, take it as an internal hiphil with the sense "go astray," but Isa. 63:17, cited in evidence, is not truly parallel. The point here is that anyone heeding instruction embodies wisdom and becomes a path to life. Those who reject correction not only do not show the way, they mislead others.

[18] The verse is the first of four on the topic of words and represents another occurrence of wordplay of the verb *kisseh,* "to cover" (cf. vv. 6, 11, and 12). The phrase "who conceals hatred" is antithetic to "who reveals a slander." Diametrically opposite actions (concealing and revealing) can both be evil.

Translators differ on the subject of the nominal sentence in colon A. NRSV and REB take "lying lips" as the subject, whereas McKane, Alonso Schökel, and JPSV take "who conceals hatred" as the subject. The latter reading is preferable, for it makes possible an antithetic parallelism. Gemser, Scott, and Whybray take the saying as a single sentence ("Both the one who conceals hatred with lying lips and the one who utters slander are fools"), but such a rendering is flat and destroys the contrast of concealing and revealing. Sibilants (*mksh ṣn'h ṣpty ṣqr*) link the words of the first colon; the similarity of the opening and closing words of the saying, *mksh* and *ksyl,* unifies the entire sentence.

[19] The contrast is between abundance and scarcity. Ordinarily, abundance is good (as in vv. 4, 14, 21, 27) and scarcity is bad (as in vv. 15, 21). But with regard to words the opposite is true. Words should be few and well chosen (17:27; 23:8). In colon A, the consonants *b-r* are repeated in *běrōb děbārîm,* and colon B repeats *ṣ* three times.

[20] Heart and tongue stand, respectively, for knowledge and its verbal expression. Together, tongue and heart symbolize the person as a communicating being. The nouns are parallel also in 16:1 and 17:20. The arrangement is chiastic: (A) silver, (B) tongue of the righteous // (B) heart of the wicked,

(A) worthless. If the source of words is wicked, so also will be the words themselves.

[21] This verse concludes the four sayings on speech. The righteous nourish many people by their words (lit., "lips"), whereas foolish people die from a want of sense (lit., "heart"). Like the fixed pair "tongue" and "heart" in v. 20, "lips" and "heart" mean, respectively, what one says and what one knows. The saying implies that the foolish have not listened to the righteous, for they "lack heart," the organ of receiving and storing words of others. In Hebrew idiom, teaching can be expressed by the metaphor of shepherding (see Qoh. 12:11; Ezek. 34:2: "Should not shepherds [kings] *feed* the sheep?").

[22] Yahweh's blessing is the sole cause of wealth (colon A) and human striving can add nothing to the divine gift (colon B). The subject of the masculine singular verb in colon B syntactically can be either "Yahweh" or "toil." Toy, NRSV, and REB take Yahweh as the subject, "and [Yahweh] adds no sorrow with it," but most commentators rightly take "toil" as the subject. "It" in colon B in Hebrew is a feminine singular suffixal pronoun whose antecedent is "blessing" (feminine singular) in colon A. The point is not that human effort is useless but rather that human effort cannot make an addition to the blessing of God. Proverbs elsewhere says that effort brings riches (v. 4).

[23] Two kinds of pleasures are compared. "Lewdness," literally, "committing a (forbidden) sexual act," occurs in Judg. 20:6; Ezek. 16:43; 23:48. The noun *zimmāh* can refer to fornication and incest. A discerning person finds pleasure and delight in wisdom. What gives pleasure is a good indication of character.

[24] Fear and desire are fundamental but antithetical emotions. They are here predicated of two basic human types in Proverbs, the wicked and the righteous. "Dread" and "desire" are used in an objective rather than subjective sense, designating the object eliciting the emotion rather than the emotion elicited. The two other occurrences of "dread" (*mĕgûrāh*, Ps. 34:5 and Isa. 66:4), are similarly objective, the thing that causes dread. The idea that what each type dreads or desires will come upon him or her is in accord with poetic justice.

JPSV interprets "dread" as the dreadful act that the wicked are planning ("What the wicked man *plots* overtakes him"), but the interpretation destroys the parallel between fear and desire. In colon A, the verb *yittēn*, "he will give," is to be repointed to *yuttan*, "it will be given," a qal passive that was not recognized by the Masoretes.

[25] The verse describes the fates of the wicked and the righteous in a storm, which in the Bible can represent divine judgment (e.g., 1:27, Isa. 21:2; 29:6; 66:15; Ps. 83:16). Both wicked and righteous experience such a storm, but the righteous live through it.

In 12:7 the family line of the righteous survives the storm. Matt. 7:24–27 is also about the ability of the wise and foolish to survive a storm:

> Everyone who listens to these words of mine and acts on them will be like a wise man who built his house on rock. The rain fell, the floods came, and the winds blew and buffeted the house. But it did not collapse; it had been set solidly on rock. And everyone who listens to these words of mine but does not act on them will be like a fool who built his house on sand. The rain fell, the floods came, and the winds blew and buffeted the house. And it collapsed and was completely ruined" (NAB)

[26] The verse is the only tricolon in the chapter. The sluggard is a type in Proverbs and usually the object of scorn or humor. Anyone who sends a sluggard on an errand is in for an unpleasant surprise. "To send" can mean simply to entrust with a task, so NRSV, "employers." A sluggard is as sure to cause distress to an employer as vinegar and smoke are sure to pain the nerve endings of teeth and eyes. Parallelism is heightened through the repetition of Hebrew *k . . . l* ("like . . . to . . . ") and *kēn . . . l* ("thus . . . so").

[27] The verse presents another antithesis between the righteous and the wicked, though "the righteous" is implied (cf. "revering Yahweh") rather than stated. The active verb in colon A is balanced by a passive verb in colon B, a "divine passive," which is an indirect way of expressing divine activity or the way the world works. Long life is one of the blessings of revering Yahweh. Impiety diminishes life and brings about a premature end.

[28] The saying is highly condensed. The "joy" in colon A comes from fulfillment of one's hopes and plans, which the righteous can count on. An example of such joy is the Song of Hannah, "My heart exults . . . yes, I rejoice in your delivering me" (1 Sam. 2:1). JPSV renders colon A freely but accurately: "The righteous can look forward to joy." The opposite emotion in colon B is not, as we might expect, sadness or disappointment but dreams not fulfilled ("destroyed").

[29] "The way of Yahweh" can mean either Yahweh's way of acting or the path Yahweh invites human beings to walk on. In the first meaning, God's way of acting means protection for the righteous and punishment for evildoers. In the second meaning, the righteous find protection but the wicked find destruction in that the latter incur guilt by disobedience. Hosea 14:9 states both meanings: "For the ways of Yahweh are straight. / The righteous walk in them, / but the wicked stumble in them."

[30] The result of right conduct is standing firm forever, and the result of wicked behavior is not dwelling in the land. The description of the righteous person who "will never be moved" is common in Psalms and Proverbs (e.g., Pss. 10:6; 62:3, 7; 112:6; Prov. 12:3). In Ps. 112:6 the phrase refers to

the security that comes from fidelity. Similarly, "dwelling in the land" is a mark of the blessed life in Ps. 37:3, 29 and Prov. 2:20–22. It may refer to dwelling in the promised land of Israel but it need not, since dwelling on any arable land fulfills the basic human aspiration. There are two contrasts: righteous and wicked; being stable (not moving) and being unstable (not possessing land).

[31–32] These verses like vv. 20–21 and vv. 6–7, put in parallel within the same verse two pairs: two bodily organs, the wicked and righteous. As noted above, paired verses mark the boundaries of sections (though matters are less clear for vv. 6–7). This last pair of verses ends the first segment of individual proverbs.

[31] "Mouth" and "tongue" are a fixed pair in 15:2; 21:23; 26:28; 31:26. The closest parallel is Ps. 92:13–15 (words identical to our passage are italicized): "*A righteous person* will flourish like a palm tree. . . , *yielding* fruit even in old age." In Proverbs the mouth of the righteous person yields the fruit of wisdom, whereas the lying tongue is cut off. The verb "to cut off" (*kārat*) has two uses relevant to this saying: to cut off a tongue as in Ps. 12:4 ("May Yahweh . . . cut off the tongue of the one speaking arrogance!") and to cut down a tree as in Job 14:7 (which keeps the agricultural metaphor). The words of a righteous person are fruitful but those of a treacherous person are fruitless, lacking long-term effect and even posing a danger to the speaker.

Verses 31–32 go together. "Mouth" and "tongue" in v. 31 are matched in v. 32 by "lips" and "mouth," and "cut off" in v. 31 is matched by "distorted" in v. 32. J. Greenfield has shown that the background of both sayings is legal. With poetic justice, the organ that has deceived suffers the evil consequences: one's tongue is cut off, one's mouth is disfigured.[5]

[32] Wise words are gracious and win the favor (*rāṣôn*) of God or the king. The Hebrew word occurs fourteen times in Proverbs, always of acceptance by a higher authority—by Yahweh (ten times) or by the king (four times) but never of acceptance by peers. The ordinary idiom for winning the favor of fellow human beings is "finding favor" (*māṣā' ḥēn*). *Rāṣôn* in the following verse (11:1) also means divine acceptance. The phrase in colon A, "know favor" occurs only here and puzzled the ancient translators. The meaning of the phrase is clarified by 16:13: "truthful lips win the favor of the king." Words from a righteous person create a climate of acceptance, whereas wicked words are perverted, that is, crooked, with the implication that they will not win acceptance from God or the king. The mouth of the wicked suffers harm; it will be distorted or disfigured. This proverb is closely related to the previous one, as is suggested in the commentary under v. 31. The sounds /ṣ/ and /d/ unify colon A.

---

5. "The Background and Parallel to a Proverb of Ahiqar," in *Hommages à Dupont-Sommer* (Paris: Librairie d'Amérique et d'Orient Adrien-Maisonneuve, 1971), 58.

Proverbs 11

11:1   Rigged scales are an abomination to Yahweh,
        but a true weight is pleasing to him.

2   When arrogance arrives dishonor arrives,
        but wisdom is with the modest.

3   The honesty of the upright provides guidance to them,
        but the duplicity of the treacherous leads them to ruin.[a]

4   Wealth is of no avail on a day of wrath,
        but righteousness saves from death.

5   The righteousness of an honest person makes his path straight,
        but through his iniquity a wicked person falls.

6   The righteousness of the upright rescues them,
        but deceivers are trapped by their greed.

7   When a person dies, hope is destroyed;[b]
        expectation pinned on wealth is destroyed.

8   A righteous person is rescued from a dangerous place
        and a wicked person enters in his stead.

9   By a word a scoundrel destroys his neighbor;
        by their knowledge the righteous are rescued.

10   When the righteous prosper, the city rejoices,
        but when the wicked perish, there is a shout of joy.

11   By the blessing of the upright, the city is built up,
        but by the mouth of the wicked it is torn down.

12   Who belittles his neighbor lacks sense,
        but a person of discernment keeps silent.

13   Who reveals a secret traffics in slander,
        but one who conceals a matter is stable in spirit.

14   When there is no strategy an army falls,
        but victory comes with much planning.

15   Trouble will befall one giving surety for another,
        but one rejecting bond is secure.

16   A charming woman gets renown,[c]
        and ruthless men get wealth.

17   A kindly person benefits himself,
        but a cruel person torments his own flesh.

18   A wicked person makes illusory wages,
        but who sows justice has a lasting reward.

19   Righteousness leads[d] to life,
        but who pursues evil heads toward his death.

20   A perverted mind is an abomination to Yahweh;
       acceptable to him are those straight in their way.
21   Assuredly, a wicked person shall not be acquitted,
       but even the children of the righteous will go free.
22   A ring of gold in a pig's snout —
       a beautiful woman lacking sense.
23   The desire of the righteous leads only to good;
       the expectation of the wicked, to wrath.
24   One person gives freely and ends up with more,
       another holds back what is due and grows poorer.
25   A generous soul will have food aplenty,
       and one who gives drink will be given drink.
26   Who holds back grain the people damn,
       but blessing is on the head of one who sells it.
27   Who strives for good seeks acceptance,
       but who pursues evil will have it come back upon him.
28   Who trusts in his wealth will fall,
       but the righteous will flourish like green foliage.
29   Who disturbs his house will inherit the wind,
       and a fool will become a slave to a wise person.
30   The fruit of a righteous person becomes a tree of life,
       and one who takes lives is a sage.
31   If the righteous get their due on the earth,
       how much more the scoundrel and the sinner.

a. We read the qere *yĕšāddēm*, "leads them to ruin," which is supported by G, T, and V. For the verb form, see GKC §67n.

b. MT is banal: "When a wicked person (*'ādām rāšā'*) dies, hope is destroyed, / and the expectation of potency is destroyed." The phrase *'ādām rāšā'* is strange for "wicked man/person"; one expects simply *rāšā'*. The simplest explanation for the redundancy is to assume that a scribe, troubled by the apparent statement that hope is destroyed at death, added the adjective "wicked" to make it clear that only a wicked person has no hope. G was similarly troubled but resolved the problem in its own way — by creating an antithesis: "When a *just* man dies, hope is *not* lost, / but the boast of impious people is destroyed." The removal of "wicked" makes the syllable count of both cola even.

c. G, followed by S, interprets colon A: "A gracious woman gets honor *for her husband*" and supplies its own B colon to 16a ("a seat of shame is a woman who hates justice") and its own A colon to 16b: "The lazy are in want of wealth." T seems influenced by S though it keeps to MT: "A righteous woman gives honor [to her husband]." These versions presume the woman is a wife on the assumption that *'ēšet ḥēn* is like *'ēšet ḥayil* in 12:4 and 31:10, but *'ēšet ḥēn* is unique and not necessarily parallel.

d. We adopt the emendation of Ehrlich: [*ti*]*kkōn*, the original *tāw* being lost through haplography. The niphal conjugation of *kûn* in Proverbs can imply a permanent state.

[11:1] The saying applies the terminology of ritual ("abomination" and "acceptable, pleasing [to God]," as in Ex. 8:22 (26E); Deut. 7:25) to weights used in commerce. In a sense, standard measures are a language, a means of communicating through signs. Proverbs 12:22 speaks of lying words in the way that this verse speaks of false weights. This saying memorably states the divine will behind ancient Near Eastern common law.

Most balances were two metal trays suspended from a handheld beam. The Hebrew word for the basic unit of currency in the Bible, the shekel, is derived from the verb *šāqal*, "to weigh." Weights and measures were fixed by royal administrators as indicated by the phrase "the king's weight" (2 Sam. 14:26). The phrases "rigged scales" and "true weight" (20:23; Hos. 12:8; Amos 8:5) show that shaving weights was a common practice. English "to chisel" is derived from the practice of shaving weights. Altered weights have been found in excavations in Palestine. For similar strictures against false weights, see Deut. 25:13–16.

[2] Arrogance and dishonor are personified as companions. One travels in the company of the other. Dishonor, however, is the very opposite of what the arrogant believe is due them. The assonance in colon A is notable: *bā' zādôn wayyābō' qālôn*. In colon B we should probably understand the verb *bō'*, "to come, arrive," (Alonso Schökel), that is, wisdom accompanies the modest, whereas dishonor accompanies the arrogant. The word for "humble" (*şĕnûa'*) occurs only here in the Hebrew Bible. In Sir. 34:22 and 42:8 and in postbiblical Hebrew it means "restrained, modest." Paradoxically, modest people will be given the honor they do not demand.

[3–6] Verses 3–6 form a subsection within the chapter, linked by the recurring Hebrew triliteral roots: *yšr*, "upright," in vv. 3a, 5a, 6a; *tmm*, "honesty, innocence," in vv. 3a, 5a; *nşl*, "save," in vv. 4b, 6a; *bgd*, "deceive," in vv. 3b, 6b; *şdq*, "righteous," in vv. 4b, 5a, 6a. In vv. 3a, 4b, 5a, 6a, the abstract quality stands for the concrete instance, that is, the quality stands for the person possessing the quality. The virtues of the righteous protect or guide them, whereas the vices of the wicked destroy them. Verses 3 and 6 are interlocked by their subjects (the upright and deceivers). Verses 3 and 5 state that the integrity of the righteous guides those journeying on life's course, and in vv. 4 and 6 righteousness saves in a particular moment of disaster. All share the common background of commerce, which was begun in v. 1.

[3] The saying is related to v. 5, which is also concerned with honesty or innocence and employs the metaphor of path for the course of one's life. "Innocence" is what Job claims (2:3, 9; 27:5; 31:6), which is not human perfection in a general sense but guiltlessness regarding a particular sin. The word is always used of a human being in relation to God. The opposite of innocence in the saying is *selep*, "duplicity," which elsewhere in Proverbs (15:4) refers to words. The context seems to be commercial. In business transactions, where it is all too easy to cheat, the saying affirms the value of honest dealing.

[4] Continuing the theme of commerce from v. 3, the saying declares the uselessness of wealth in a life-or-death crisis. "Day of wrath" is a general expression for any life-threatening disaster, as in Job 21:30; Ezek. 7:19; and Zeph. 1:15. In Prov. 10:2 it is only ill-gotten gains that were useless; here it is wealth of any kind. In mortal danger, riches are of no avail, but only that which assures ultimate protection—righteousness.

[5] The righteousness of the honest makes their path straight and free of obstacles, like the roads that are made straight and clear in Isa. 40:3 and 45:2. Straight and crooked are metaphors for morally good and bad. The path of the wicked is not smooth; their malice creates hindrances and "pits." Probably we are to assume that the wicked fall into the pits they dug to trap the righteous.

[6] The final statement in the series picks up the words from previous statements: "righteousness," "rescues," and "deceivers." *Hawwat* in colon B means "greed" as it does in 10:3. In the competitive world of trade as well as in the world of human relations, it is righteousness that keeps the upright out of harm's way, whereas deceivers are ensnared by their desires.

[7] As explained in the textual notes, a scribe glossed MT: "When a *wicked* person dies, hope is destroyed." What is the meaning of the original text? Two of the three parallels in the verse are clear: "hope" and "expectation" (cf. 10:28); "destroyed" and "destroyed." The latter is an instance of parallelism of the same verb, one occurrence in the perfect tense and the other in the imperfect tense.[1] That leaves only the difficult third parallel: *'ādām,* "person, man," and *'ônîm,* which can be either of two nouns: "trouble, sorrow; wickedness" or "vigor; wealth." The latter word has a broad range: In the economic sphere it means "riches," in the sphere of physical health, "vigor," and in the sexual sphere, "virility." Given the economic context established by v. 1 and elaborated in vv. 3–6, *'ônîm* here probably refers to wealth. The statement is similar to v. 4: In the face of death all hopes based on one's own resources are wiped away. Similar sentiments are expressed in Ps. 49:13: "A person for all his wealth does not abide; he perishes like any animal." This aphorism is the climax to the preceding six verses: Money has no ultimate power; it cannot be preferred to uprightness, righteousness, and honesty, which can save one from premature death (v. 4).

[8] The verbs describe a typical incident, which is a parable of the way the world works: A righteous person is rescued from a dangerous situation and a wicked person gets involved in the situation instead. Possibly the verse is a variant of the familiar theme of the wicked falling into the pit they have dug to trap others (Ps. 7:16; Prov. 26:27; 28:10). Alliteration (*ṣaddîq miṣṣārāh neḥĕlāṣ*) unites colon A.

---

1. M. Held, "The *YQTL-QTL (QTL-YQTL)* Sequence of Identical Verbs in Biblical Hebrew and in Ugaritic," in *Studies and Essays in honor of A. A. Neuman,* ed. M. Ben-Horin et al. (Leiden: Brill, 1962), 281–90.

[9–12] The verses are related in theme (the relation of the righteous and the wicked to the community) and in vocabulary ("mouth" ["words"] as source of words in vv. 9 and 11, and "his neighbor" in vv. 9 and 12). Every colon except the last (v. 12b) begins with the Hebrew letter *bêt*.

[9] The verse contains a subtle contrast. Colon A: what is expressed by corrupt people harms others; colon B: what is not expressed (*da'at,* specific "knowledge") by the righteous assures their own protection. What the wicked *say* harms others; what the righteous *know* leads to their protection.

[10] The verb *'ālaṣ,* "to rejoice," is a link to *ḥālaṣ* in the niphal conjugation ("to be delivered"), used in the two previous verses. The verb "to rejoice" implies both outward manifestation of joy and the inner feeling, nicely paralleling the final noun of colon B, "a shout of joy." There is a certain humor in the contrasts: The prosperity of the righteous and the destruction of the wicked elicit the same emotional reaction in the citizenry—joyous expressions. The final noun, *rinnāh,* means "ringing cry," usually in joy and praise. One of the blessings of righteousness is a good name, which is dramatically represented by the civic rejoicing. Popular hatred is fueled by injustice, as in v. 26.

[11] The meaning is close to v. 10: As the fates of the righteous and wicked affect the city (v. 10) so does what they say (v. 11) affects the city. Good words, like the blessings spoken by Isaac (Genesis 27), Jacob (Genesis 49), and Moses (Deuteronomy 32), benefit a community, which is here symbolized by the "city," that is, the world beyond the family. As the words of the righteous lift the city up, so the words of the wicked bring it down.

[12] In the final of the four sayings on human types and their effect on the community, the types of the wicked and the righteous shades into that of the foolish and the wise. Verse 12 is a bridge between vv. 9–11 and the following verse, harking back to v. 9 with "his neighbor" and with the topic of refraining from harming one's neighbor. It points forward to the following verse in its topic of community. Hebrew "to belittle" implies verbal expressions of contempt as in 30:17; 2 Kings 19:21 (= Isa. 37:22). The opposite of using contemptuous language is keeping silent, which in Proverbs is often the sign of a shrewd person.

[13] The antithesis between revealing and concealing is common in Proverbs (see under 10:18). This saying adds another antithesis—going about (*hōlēk*) and standing still (*ne'ĕman*). The Hebrew word behind "slander" is *rākal,* "to traffic, trade, sell," which came to mean "to slander" because merchants traded in gossip. "Stable in spirit" is a unique phrase, possibly coined in opposition to the movement expressed in colon A. In Isa. 22:23, 25, *māqôm ne'ĕmān* means "firm place."

[14] Hebrew *'am,* "people," can mean "army" in a military context, and "fall" can refer to a military defeat, as in Ps. 20:9. The antithesis is between *no* plan with defeat and *many* counselors with victory (cf. Prov. 24:6). This verse offers a metaphor from waging war applicable to daily life.

[15] Proverbs is consistently opposed to providing surety for another's loan (see under 6:1) and expresses the view frequently and bluntly. The danger looming over the debtor will come upon the guarantor; the way to financial security for oneself is to spurn all such appeals (see 22:26–27). In this saying, the financial harm the debtor is protected from will come upon the guarantor (colon A); one's own financial security and peace of mind are compromised by providing security to someone else (colon B). The alliteration and reversal of the consonants *r* and ' is memorable in colon A: *ra' yērôa' kî 'ārab zār.*

[16] Certain behaviors get different results. Wealth and honor are good things in Proverbs; they are given by Wisdom (3:16; 8:18). Here, however, the means for acquiring them are flawed, as pointed out by Ehrlich. Renown attained through charm is as fleeting as the physical beauty that acquired it (cf. "charm is deceptive" in 31:30). Wealth got by aggressive and brutal action lasts only as long as one has physical strength. Despite the multiple contrasts (singular/plural; male/female; seductive/brutal), the same type of unwise behavior is described, which is shown by the same verb in both cola, *tāmak,* "to get."

Some suggest that the meaning is that gentle methods, such as charm, acquire renown, which is more valuable than the wealth acquired by ruthless methods. Hence, charm accomplishes more than its opposite in the saying — ruthlessness. The parallel syntax of each colon, however, makes the statements parallel as well. Some commentators, such as Gemser, Ringgren, and Alonso Schökel, regard the longer Greek text as original (words beyond MT are italicized): "A gracious woman gets honor *for her husband / a woman who hates justice is a throne of shame. / The lazy are in want of wealth /,* but the diligent support themselves with wealth." The Greek text, however, must be judged a verbose attempt to explain a subtle saying.

[17] This is the first of three sayings on actions and their consequences. We normally think of kindness and cruelty as primarily affecting others, but the saying calls attention to the effect they have upon the one who does them. Being kind to others is being kind to oneself; cruelty inflicts suffering on the heartless person.

[18] Hebrew *pě'ullāh* can mean "work" or "wages" earned by work. Obviously, the two senses are related as act and consequence. Colon A is therefore slightly ambiguous on first reading: Does it mean illusory acts or illusory wages? The ambiguity is only resolved in colon B, which makes clear that the acts of the wicked are deceptive in that the wicked deceive themselves. They lose their wages. Colon A is united by the repetition of the letters *rēš, šîn* or *śîn,* and *'ayin.*

[19] The first step in interpreting this elliptical statement is to note the unproblematic parallelisms: righteousness // evil; life // death. The third parallelism, however, is impossible, for the adverb "so" in MT (*kēn*) in no way parallels the participle "one who pursues." The emendation *tikkōn* (niphal of *kûn*), "to be firm, established" (see textual notes), makes possible a subtle antithesis to colon B—stable support versus frantic pursuit. Righteousness leads to a long and happy life whereas frantic pursuit of evil brings death closer.

[20] The saying applies the terminology of ritual (acceptable and unacceptable sacrifice) to human conduct as in v. 1. "Twisted" (*'iqqēš*), "straight" (*yāšār*), and "whole" (*tāmîm*) are frequent metaphors in Proverbs for the course of life. "Heart" (internal plan) and "way" (external conduct) are a merism expressing the whole of human life. The whole of human life comes under divine judgment, not just liturgical sacrifices.

[21] "Assuredly" is tentative for the mysterious Hebrew phrase "hand to hand" (also in 16:5b). In colon B (lit., "but the seed of the righteous will escape"), "seed" is offspring. In Job 18:19 Bildad says the wicked have no offspring, whereas Job in 21:7–8 asserts that they do in fact have children. Colon B in extremely condensed fashion states that not only the righteous but even their children are safe. Sound complements sense in that the final word of colon A, *ra'*, "wicked," is linked to the initial word of colon A, *zar'*, "seed, children," in its original monosyllabic form.

[22] Ear and nose rings were common adornments of women. The point is the priority of wisdom over beauty in assessing a woman, perhaps a future wife. The comparison to a pig seems to have been made on the basis of sound as well as humorous incongruity, for the consonant *z* predominates in colon A: *nezem zāhāb bĕ'ap ḥăzîr*, "a ring of gold in the snout of a pig."

[23] The righteous and the wicked are contrasted in what they desire and in the outcome of their desire. The word *tā'ăwāh* "desire," can mean both the act of desiring and the thing desired, that is, it can be subjective or objective. In both senses, "the desire of the righteous" is wholly good. But the hope of the wicked in the objective sense is contrary to what they expect. It is (divine) wrath, which has been provoked by their evil behavior.

[24] Two types of giving to others are compared. The paradox is that generosity to the poor leads to more wealth, and stinting on giving makes one poorer. "Gives freely" is used in the positive sense as in Ps. 112:9: "He gave freely, he gave to the poor." Similar openhandedness is espoused in Deut. 15:1–11 and Sir. 29:1–13. The paradox is also found in New Testament statements such as "to anyone who has, more will be given and he will grow rich; from anyone who has not, even what he has will be taken away" (Mark 4:25; Matt. 13:12; Luke 19:26).

[25] This saying, in synthetic parallelism, develops the topic of generosity from v. 24 through the example of food and drink. Those who feed others will themselves be fed. Colon A is more vivid than an English translation might suggest. "Soul" (*nepeš*) is the throat area, the core of the body or self. A literal translation is "the throat of blessing will grow fat." One who gives food and drink to others will be given food and drink and will thrive. See Luke 6:38:

"Give, and gifts will be given to you." The consonant sequence that begins colon A, *n-š* in *npš*, "soul," is reversed in the last word to *š-n* in *tdšn*, "grow fat."

[26] This verse is another statement on openhandedness in the context of marketing grain. The reference is to holding back grain to drive up prices. S and T add "in famine," but unnecessarily. Withholding grain for private gain earns the manipulator curses from the populace. The saying presupposes major traders rather than small farmers. The consonants of the second word in colon A, *br*, "grain," are repeated in colon B in *brkh*, "blessing," and *mšbyr*, "distributes."

[27] The saying is about seeking one thing and finding another. Earnestly striving for what is good is implicitly to seek divine favor, and perhaps human favor as well. On "acceptance" as divine acceptance in Proverbs, see under 10:32. Pursuing after evil (*rāʿāh*), on the other hand, means only that trouble (*rāʿāh*) will follow. The same Hebrew word can mean both moral evil and the trouble that comes with it.

[28] The participle "one who trusts" is important in Proverbs, occurring seven times, twice with the negative meaning of foolish complacency (14:16 and 28:26) but elsewhere of peaceful confidence in God (in 31:11, of confidence in one's wife). Wealth cannot substitute for God as a refuge from ultimate danger (see 11:4). The righteous are by definition "right with God" and need rely on nothing other than God for protection. "Fall" is used several times in Proverbs of the wicked person's fall into a pit (e.g., 22:14; 26:27; 28:10). In contrast, the righteous are compared to a leaf that not only does not fall but blooms, like the righteous in Ps. 1:3 "whose leaves do not fail."

[29] This proverb on running one's household is one of many in Proverbs (see under 10:1). The meaning of *ʿākar* is "to disturb the peace, (unnecessarily) create trouble or danger." Saul disturbed his army by an imprudent command in 1 Samuel 14, and Achan disturbed Israel by violating the ban in Joshua 6–7. To disturb one's family and household destroys one's future; one inherits empty air. Continuing the metaphor of the household, colon B sketches the breakdown of the family by declaring that the troubler of his family is a fool, who will inevitably become the slave of a wise person, that is, someone who has safeguarded family and household.

[30] In colon A, "fruit" is a metaphor for the consequence of one's action. Such fruit grows into a tree of life, a source to others of food and medicine, nourishment and healing. Colon B is problematic. It is, literally, "the wise person takes lives/souls." "To take a life (*lāqaḥ nepeš*)" is a Hebrew idiom for "to kill" (as it is in English). But how can a wise person kill? The versions have different answers. G, followed by S, uses a partial metathesis of the consonants of *ḥākām*, "wise person," to produce a new word *ḥāmās*, "violence, wrong; violent person": "but a violent person takes away lives." T, and possibly V, in-

terpret "taker of souls" in a benign sense—"and wisdom is the winner of souls," which is followed by JPSV, "a wise man captivates people."

Our solution is contextual. A clue is the Hebrew word order, literally, "one taking souls is a wise person." The identity of the subject of the participle is revealed only in the very last word. The Hebrew reader would have to revise the idiom: The one who takes souls is not the violent but the wise person. The meaning of this strange statement is that the wise have power over life. The surprising reversal of the idiom is dictated by colon A. In short, a wise person promotes life.

[31] The Hebrew syntax, "if . . . how much more . . ." (*hēn . . . 'ap kî . . .*), is found in Deut. 31:27, 1 Sam. 23:3, Job 15:15–16 and 25:5–6. In Prov. 19:7 it occurs without the opening "if." The Hebrew verb in colon A translated as "get their due" connotes full correlation between a deed and its consequence as in Jer. 18:20 and Prov. 13:13. The phrase in colon A does not mean "on earth," for that would imply life after death, but "on the earth," that is, in the present world. The judgment exercised on human actions, even the best, should strike terror into the hearts of habitual wrongdoers. G and S omit "on earth," translating instead, "If the just person *barely* survives. . ." and it is this rendering that 1 Peter 4:18 follows: "And if the righteous one is barely saved, / where will the godless and the sinner appear?"

Proverbs 12

12:1 Who loves discipline loves knowledge,
   but who hates reproof is brutish.

2 A good person finds acceptance from Yahweh,
   but a schemer he condemns.

3 No one is established through wickedness,
   but the root of the righteous is not shaken.

4 A capable wife is the crown of her husband,
   but a disgraceful one is like rot in his bones.

5 The plans of the righteous are justice,
   but the intentions of the wicked are deceit.

6 The words of the wicked are a deadly ambush,
   but the mouth of the upright will deliver them.

7 Overthrow the wicked and they are no more,
   but the house of the righteous will stand.

8 A man is praised according to his intelligence,
   but a perverse mind is held up to contempt.

9 Better to be ignored and own a slave
   than to put on airs and have no food.

10   A righteous person knows the health of his animal,
        but the compassion of the wicked is cruel.
11   Who tills his field has food in plenty,
        but who pursues vanity has a lack of sense.
12   A wicked person desires the catch of evil people,
        but the root of the righteous will bear fruit.
13   Sinful lips ensnare a wicked person,
        but a righteous person escapes from trouble.[a]
14   From the fruit of one's mouth one is filled,
        from what one's hands have done one is paid.
15   The path of a fool is straight in his own eyes,
        but a wise person listens to advice.
16   A fool reveals[b] his annoyance at once,
        but a wise person conceals an insult.
17   Who speaks honestly testifies truly,
        but a deceiver makes a lying witness.
18   Rash words are like the blows of a sword,
        but the tongue of the wise brings healing.
19   Truthful lips abide forever,
        but a lying tongue lasts only for a moment.
20   Deceit is in the minds of those who devise evil,
        but for those planning peace there is joy.
21   No evil will come near a just person,
        but the wicked are filled with trouble.
22   Lying lips are an abomination to Yahweh,
        but those who act truthfully please him.
23   An intelligent person conceals knowledge,
        but the minds of fools broadcast their folly.
24   The hand of the diligent will exercise rule,
        but an idle hand will be put to forced labor.
25   Anxiety in the heart weighs it down,[c]
        but a good word makes it rejoice.
26   A righteous person gives his neighbor directions,
        but the way of the wicked leads them astray.
27   A lazy person hasn't even a bird to roast,[d]
        but the diligent possess great wealth.
28   On the path of righteousness is life,
        but the way of malice leads to death.[e]

   a. After v. 13 G has a verse not in MT: "Whose looks are gentle will win mercy, /
but he that contends in the gate will oppress souls."

b. The versions correctly interpret Hebrew *ywd'* as the causative, written defectively. MT points the word as niphal (*yiwwāda'*).

c. The syntax of the verse is unusual. (1) In colon A the subject ("anxiety") is grammatically feminine though the verb is grammatically masculine. (2) In the same colon, *lēb*, "heart," grammatically masculine, is the referent of the feminine suffixes of the verbs in both cola. The solution to the first problem is that the gender of the verb was influenced by the masculine word *'îš*, "man, person," which occurs immediately before the verb (GKC 145u). The solution to the second problem is that the Masoretes probably mispointed the final *hē* as the feminine suffix; in early Hebrew the consonant *hē* could represent *ō*, "his," as well as *ā*, "her."[1]

d. The verb in colon A, *yaḥărōk*, "to roast," occurs only here. The versions take it as "to encounter," that is, the deceitful person will not encounter game. We take the verb *ḥārak* as "to singe" on the basis of Aramaic, Syriac, and postbiblical Hebrew.

e. The second word of colon B, *nětîb*, "path," is corrupt. No ancient version reads it. G has "but the ways of those who bear grudges (*mnēsikakōn*) are toward death," and is followed by S and T. G's *Vorlage* cannot be reconstructed. V has "perverted way." In our view, the Masoretes, faced with a corrupt word, assumed the parallelism was synonymous and pointed colon B to mean "along its [righteousness's] path, there is no death." The phrase, "no death" (*'al māwet*) is unique in the Bible; it is odd, if not impossible, Hebrew. The consonants are more naturally read *'el māwet*, "to death," as in 2:18, and this reading is adopted by many (Toy, Plöger, REB). A Ugaritic text, however, has a similar phrase *bl mwt*, "not dying," which is in parallel to *ḥym*, "life" (*KTU* 1.17.VI.27). For the meaning "no death" in Hebrew, one normally expects *'ên māwet*, *bĕlî māwet*, or *lō' māwet*.

[12:1] Knowledge is not simply information but what one needs to live wisely. Such knowledge is gained dialectically through conversation with others and by reproof. One must give up one's preconceived ideas and undergo discipline in order to gain wisdom. The antithesis of such knowledge is brutishness. To reject correction is to choose an animal level of consciousness. The one who wills the end (wisdom), wills the means (discipline).

[2] The antithesis appears to be between the good person who, by virtue of goodness, already has divine acceptance and the person whose ceaseless striving ("schemer") gains only condemnation. The Hebrew word "schemer" is literally "person of hidden, private thinking," which can easily pick up the connotation of destructive planning.[2] The sound /ō/ predominates in colon A; /i/ in colon B.

[3] "Established" // "not be shaken" is a fixed pair (Pss. 93:1; 96:10; 1 Chron. 16:30). A human being may be described as "enduring, established"

---

1. F. M. Cross and D. N. Freedman, *Early Hebrew Orthography: A Study of the Epigraphic Evidence* (New Haven, Conn.: American Oriental Society, 1952), 57.
2. M. Fox, "Words for Wisdom," *ZAH* 6 (1993): 159.

(Job 21:8; Pss. 101:7; 102:29; 140:12). "Root" is used as in Isa. 5:24; Mal. 3:19; Job 8:17; 18:16—what endures to succeeding generations. One must hear the saying to get its point fully. A person cannot be *established* by *wickedness* (*yikkôn . . . rešaʻ*) but *the root* of the righteous *is not shaken* (*šoreš . . . yimmôṭ*). The consonants of Hebrew *rš*ʻ, "wickedness" are reversed by *šrš*, "root."

[4] In Proverbs several things are called a crown: riches (14:24), gray hair (= long life, 16:31), grandchildren (17:6), and, in this verse, a good wife. A good wife attests to her husband's shrewd judgment and is a sign to the community that God's blessing is upon his household.

The verse may allude to the crowns worn by the bride and groom in the wedding ceremony. Song of Songs 3:11 suggests that a crown was placed on the bridegroom's head. According to the Babylonian Talmud, the custom was only abandoned in the time of the war with Rome in 70 C.E. as a sign of mourning (*b. Soṭ*. 49a). It is not known when the custom arose. A rabbinic saying makes the groom a king: "a bridegroom resembles a king" (*Pirqe R. El.,* chap. 16). If the custom is relevant to the saying, the point would be that the truly beautiful crown of the husband is not the one he wears in the ceremony but the wife that he is marrying.

The antitheses in the two cola are between not only a competent and foolish wife but also between the public ("crown") and the private spheres ("rot in the bones"). An incompetent spouse causes anguish to the other. The capable wife is the theme of the concluding poem of the book (31:10–31).

[5] The antitheses are unusually regular. The saying is not concerned with thoughts (despite NRSV) but with plans and intentions (so rightly JPSV). The opposite of "justice" (*mišpāṭ*) is not injustice in this case but "deceit" (*mirmāh*). The wicked will be deceived in their planning, that is, their plan will not succeed.

[6] Words are a favorite theme in Proverbs. The words of the wicked deal death to others, whereas the words of the wise enable them to escape the deadly trap. Repeated sounds reinforce the meaning. In colon A, the consonants of the phrase "the words of the wicked" (*dibrê rĕšāʻîm*) are arranged in a new combination, "in a deadly ambush" (*ʼĕrāb dām*). The sounds of "the wicked" (*rĕšāʻîm*) in colon A reappear in "the upright" (*yĕšārîm*) in colon B.

[7] The verb "to overthrow" has wicked people as its object also in Amos 4:11 and Job 34:25. As in Prov. 10:25 ("When the storm has passed, a wicked person is no more, / but a righteous person has a lasting foundation"), the point is the ability of the two types to survive a disaster. The wicked person disappears but the property and progeny ("house") of the righteous endure (cf. Matt. 7:25).

[8] The mind (lit., "heart") is the seat of intelligence in Hebrew psychology. When the mind is twisted, its perversity will eventually show itself in words and in conduct. What is hidden (in the mind) will eventually come out—and merit praise or blame.

[9] This verse is a "better . . . than . . . " saying. Others in this collection are

15:16, 17; 16:8, 19; 17:1; 19:1. To be valid, the opinion of others must have a foundation in reality. Substance without recognition by others is preferable to recognition by others without substance.

[10] The phrase "to know the health (lit., "soul")" occurs also in Ex. 23:9, where it means to know how it feels to be a sojourner. Here the phrase does not mean to know what an animal feels like (despite Delitzsch) but, more generally, to be sympathetically aware of an animal's condition, especially whether it has enough to eat. The righteous are concerned with the physical needs of their domestic animals, both because the animals can feel pain and because they provide their owners with food and clothing (cf. 27:23–27). The careless attitude of the wicked is branded as cruel. Deuteronomy 25:4 also provides for the humane care of animals: "Do not muzzle a treading ox."

[11] Steady working of the soil brings an *abundance* of food whereas frenetic pursuit of vanity brings a *want* of wisdom. The observation has a metaphorical meaning—careful and steady work is better than frantically chasing rainbows. Proverbs 28:19 is identical except for the last two words of colon B: "has want in plenty."

[12] Colon A is generally judged to be corrupt, but MT effectively plays on the sounds *m-d* and *r-ʿ*: ḥmd rš' mṣwd r'ym, "A wicked person desires the catch of evil people." And the versions, though confused, appear to have read the consonants of MT. In the absence of convincing emendations, we retain MT. The antithesis seems to be between the desire of the wicked for the hunting net (= its contents, the prey) of evil people and the firm root of the righteous, which produces fruit. We presume the Hebrew word "to give" (*nātan*) in colon B is elliptical for the full idiom "to produce fruit" (*nātan pĕrî*, Lev. 26:4, 20; Zech. 8:12; Ps. 1:3). Elsewhere in Proverbs (1:22; 6:25), ḥāmad, "to desire," has a negative connotation, implying unhealthy zeal to realize one's plans. The wicked desire what the malevolent have captured or killed. All their great efforts will go for naught, for their actions invite punishment. The righteous, on the other hand, will bear fruit.

[13] The antithesis is between the offensive words of the wicked that entrap them, and the ability of the righteous to get out of such traps.

[14] The ketib reading *yāšûb*, "will return," gives better sense than the qere, *yāšîb*, "will give back," though the latter was read by the versions. One cannot escape the consequences of one's words and actions. They may be primarily addressed to others but they inevitably come back on oneself. "Fruit" is used metaphorically of the consequences of an action as in 1:31; 31:16, 31. Proverbs 13:2a and 18:20a are variants of colon A.

[15] "Straight" and "crooked" in Hebrew as in English, are metaphors for true and false. Fools are know-it-alls, certain their path is straight and their decisions are correct. The wise, on the other hand, learn from others because they accept their correction.

[16] The antithesis is between revealing and concealing, which is frequent in Proverbs (e.g., 10:18 and 17:9). Fools reveal their anger, that is, they take instant offense at events or words, but the wise conceal or ignore offenses that cause arguments. The wise refuse to lower themselves to the level of their attackers.

[17] Verses 17–19 are about the effect of good and evil speech. The verb *yāpîaḥ* in colon A means "to testify in court" in all of its six instances in Proverbs (in those instance with "lies" as direct object). How can one evaluate courtroom testimony? Is there a reliable way to determine which witness is telling the truth? The phrase *yāpîaḥ 'ĕmûnāh* in colon A can mean testifying accurately (as in JPSV, "He who testifies faithfully"), but more likely it refers to a person's normal manner of speaking. In other words, one should examine how the witness speaks outside of court and look to the character of the witness.

[18] Colon A is, literally, "there is a rash talker like the blows of a sword." The syntax of colon A, *yēš* + participle, occurs also in 11:24; 13:7, 23; and 18:24, and connotes a type who does such and such. The metaphor of words as sword blows occurs also in Ps. 64:4, "those who sharpen their tongue like a sword." Rash words cause serious wounds. The carefully chosen words of the wise, on the other hand, bring healing and edification.

[19] The saying seems to have a double meaning: (1) lies are quickly found out, whereas truthful statements endure; (2) truth-tellers, being favored by God, live long, whereas liars will not live or prosper. By metonymy the source is named for the effect—"lips" and "tongue" for words.

[20] The antitheses are between deceit and joy, trouble and peace. Those who, through their counsel, bring about treachery and security are affected by them even as they promote them. Deceit is already in the hearts of the planners of evil in that they do not realize their evil will come back on them. Joy, which is an aspect of *šālôm,* comes to those who counsel peace and wholeness.

[21] Hebrew words for evil can sometimes express both the act and its effect. For example, *'āwen* means "evil" in colon A and *rāʿ* in colon B means "trouble." Colon B plays on the duality: the wicked are full of evil and full of trouble. The saying should be spoken aloud in Hebrew. The first two words in the five-word colon A are echoed in the final two words: *lō' yĕ'unneh . . . kol 'āwen,* "comes near . . . no evil." The verb of colon A, *yĕ'unneh,* "to come near, to befall," is used as in Ps. 91:10 (words identical to our saying are italicized), "*no* evil *shall come near* you, no affliction approach your tent."

[22] The phrase "an abomination to Yahweh" occurs only in Deuteronomy (eight times) and in Proverbs (eleven times). In Proverbs it is sometimes contrasted with "pleases him" (11:1, 20; 15:8 and here). Deuteronomy uses "abomination" for violations of the Mosaic law, whereas Proverbs uses it more generally, for things perverted from their right purpose. Like scales and sacrifice, speech can be perverted from its proper function. "To do faithfulness" (*'ōśê 'ĕmûnāh*) probably means telling the truth, to judge from the parallel and from the meaning of *'ĕmûnāh* in v. 17. "To do the truth" evokes John 3:21: "Whoever does the truth comes to the light."

[23] Proverbs frequently notes the paradoxes connected with concealing and revealing. The intelligent are aware that their knowledge must fit the occasion; part of wisdom is knowing when and where not to speak. Thus a wise person inevitably "conceals" knowledge. "Knowledge" here is that which one knows "in one's heart (mind)," that is, specific knowledge rather than knowledge in general. Fools have no sense of time and place, and lack self-control. Cf. Qoh. 10:3: "Yes, even when travelling a fool's mind is deficient: he states to all he is a fool."

[24] In 10:4, the hand of the diligent provides riches, but a slack hand makes one poor. Here the results of diligence and laziness are, respectively, dominion and forced labor. The irony is that the diligent person becomes a king who no longer needs to labor, whereas those who refuse to work end up laboring.

[25] JPSV meticulously renders the odd syntax ("If there is an anxiety in a man's heart, let him quash it"), but the translation destroys the antithesis and unduly stretches the meaning of the verb *šāḥâ,* "to depress." The antithesis is, rather, between internal worry that depresses within and a word from outside that lifts one's spirits like the "good words" that the elders urge upon Rehoboam in 1 Kings 12:7: "If you respond to them with *good words* they will be your servants forever." A sure cure for depression is good news.

[26] Colon A (especially the verb *yātēr*) is unclear, possibly corrupt. Each version understands the word differently. Alonso Schökel summarizes the possible translations: (1) "a righteous person is better than his neighbor"; (2) "a righteous person searches for his pastures" (cf. the remarkably similar Job 39:8: *yātûr hārîm mir'ēhû,* "he searches the hills for his pasture"); (3) "a righteous person departs from evil" (emending MT to *yāsur mērā'āh,* cf., e.g., Prov. 3:7; 13:19). The best parallel to colon B is the second translation. The righteous can guide their flocks to the good pastures (cf. v. 10), whereas the wicked cannot, for the way they are walking leads them astray.

[27] Though the meaning of the verb in colon A and the word order in colon B are in doubt, the basic contrast—sloth and diligence—is clear enough (cf. 10:4; 12:24). Concretely, the contrast seems to be between a bird, which is the food of the poor, and vast wealth. Does the verb in colon A mean "to encounter" (so the versions) or "to singe, char" (its meaning in postbiblical Hebrew)? Better sense is given by "to singe; to roast." Also unclear is colon B, literally, "the wealth of a man is precious, a diligent person." The saying is obscure, apart from the basic contrast of sloth and diligence.

[28] The phrase in colon B, "the way of . . ." is corrupt and the colon was restored by the Masoretes on the assumption that it was synonymous parallelism (see textual notes). Two of the three parallels are clear and provide a clue to the general meaning if not to the precise nuance: path and way, life and death. That leaves only one uncertain parallelism, "righteousness" and the corrupt word in colon B. The Masoretes read it *nĕtîb*, "path," and interpreted the colon as "along its [righteousness's] path there is no death" (*'al mawet*). "No death" is unlikely syntactically and ideologically in Proverbs. Resurrection is first recorded in the Bible in Dan. 12:1–3 (ca. 164 B.C.E.), much later than Proverbs. The best solution is to read the Hebrew consonants as *'el mawet*, "to death," as in 2:18. Several scholars adopt this reading (Toy, Plöger, REB). It should be noted that some translations accept MT (NRSV and JPSV) and that some scholars, among them Delitzsch, M. Dahood, and V. Cottoni, take the verse as referring to the afterlife.[3]

Proverbs 13

13:1   A wise son displays the instruction of his father,
          but a scoffer does not listen to rebuke.
2   From the fruit of his mouth a person enjoys good,
          but from the throat of the treacherous comes violence.
3   Who guards his mouth safeguards himself;
          who opens wide his lips will suffer ruin.
4   The throat of a sluggard hungers but has nothing,
          but the maw of the diligent is filled with good food.
5   The just person hates a lying word,
          but the wicked are odious and shameful.
6   Righteousness protects the one whose way is right,
          but wickedness overturns a sinner.
7   One person acts rich but has nothing;
          another acts poor but has great wealth.
8   His wealth is the ransom of a rich person,
          but a poor person does not listen to rebuke.
9   The light of the righteous shines,[a]
          but the lamp of the wicked is extinguished.[b]
10   Arrogance produces strife,[c]
          but wisdom is with those who take advice.
11   Treasure got in haste[d] ebbs away,
          but what is slowly gathered increases.

3. Cottoni, *La vita futura nel Libro dei Proverbi: Contributo alla storia dell'esegesi* (Studii Biblici Franciscani analecta 20; Jerusalem: Franciscan Printing Press, 1984), 65.

12   A hope deferred makes the heart sick,
       but a desire come true is a tree of life.
13   Who scorns a precept is in debt to it,
       but who respects a command is unencumbered.ᵉ
14   The teaching of a wise person is a fountain of life,
       turning people from deadly snares.
15   Prudence wins praise,
       but the way of deceivers vanishes.
16   Every wise person acts according to wisdom,
       but fools display their folly.
17   An evil messenger stumbles into trouble,
       but a trustworthy envoy delivers healing.
18   Poverty and disgrace come to one letting go of discipline,
       but who holds on to correction will be honored.
19   A desire realized is sweet to the soul,
       but turning from evil is abhorrent to fools.
20   Who walks with the wise becomes wise,
       but who consorts with fools gets into trouble.
21   Misfortune pursues sinners,
       but the righteous are repaid with prosperity.
22   A good person leaves a legacy to grandchildren;
       but a sinner's wealth is stored up for a righteous person.
23   The tillage of the poor yields food aplenty,
       but assets are swept away for lack of justice.
24   Who spares the rod hates his son,
       but who loves him disciplines him early.
25   The righteous person eats and satisfies his appetite,
       but the belly of the wicked is empty.

a. The Hebrew verb in colon A, *śāmaḥ*, "to rejoice," here means "to shine," which is made certain by its context. The triliteral root *śmḥ* in Proto-Northwest Semitic must have included the meanings "to grow," "to shine," and "to rejoice." Other Semitic languages contain words with the same range of meanings. In the case of the Proto-Northwest Semitic verb *śmḥ*, two dialectical offshoots, Ugaritic and Hebrew, preserved the meanings "to shine" and "to rejoice" for the verb, though in Hebrew "to shine" is rare.[1]

b. G has a saying not in MT: "Deceiving souls wander in sins, just men show pity and are merciful."

c. Colon A in Hebrew is literally, "Only by arrogance he gives a quarrel," or "By arrogance he gives only a quarrel." We omit *raq bĕ* (with Aquila, Symmachus, Theodotion, and V) as a corrupt repetition of *d'k* from v. 9 (so Toy); there has been confusion of the graphically similar letters *r* and *d*, and the ligature of *'k*. We take MT *ytn* as *yutan*, passive of the qal conjugation.

d. MT *mēhebel*, "than vanity," should be read *mĕbōhal*, "hastily acquired" (participle, pual conjugation), like *bāhal* in Prov. 20:21 and 28:22. All three passages are about hastily acquired wealth that slips away. G *epispoudazomenē* here and in 20:21 reflects *bhl*. In colon B we point MT *qōbēṣ* as *qubbaṣ,* passive in the qal conjugation, "what is gathered" (see J-M §58), to match colon A.

e. G, followed by S, has a couplet not in MT: "A devious son will have nothing good, / but a wise servant's affairs will be free from trouble, / and his way will be directed aright."

[13:1] This is another in the series of proverbs on adult children and their parents, which began in 10:1. Every wise son advertises to the community the training his father gave him. Children become wise only by obeying their parents and accepting correction; knowledge comes through a dialectical process. Scoffers scorn the process and end up fools, advertising to the world their parents' inability to educate them.

[2] One's mouth normally eats food that comes from outside but, metaphorically, things are reversed: one eats from the fruit of one's mouth (= words). One experiences blessings according to the quality of one's words. The throat of the treacherous, on the other hand, is filled with violence. The saying implies that the "fruit" of their ways will come upon them. Proverbs 12:14a is nearly identical to colon A. "Mouth" and "soul" (lit., "throat") figure in vv. 2–4.

[3] Those who guard their mouth guard their throat (= life). Words are important. If one speaks with truth and justice, by that fact one will protect one's life. Colon B, however, makes a noteworthy antithesis with a touch of sardonic humor. The antithesis to guarding one's mouth is opening one's lips wide, that is, removing all restraints from the organ of speech. Unrestrained talk brings ruin.

[4] The appetites of the lazy go unfulfilled whereas the diligent enjoy their fill of food. The literal reference is to food, but appetite is a metaphor for desires in a broader sense, just as in Ps. 42:2 ("As the deer longs for streams of water, so my soul longs for you, O God") and Ps. 63:2 ("O God, you are my God—for you I long! For you my body yearns; for you my soul thirsts"). The lazy live frustrated lives. The Hebrew words in colon A, "hungers but has nothing" are linked by sound: *mit'awwāh wā'ayin.*

[5] The antithesis is between the deceit that the righteous "hate," that is, keep far from them, and the shameful vileness that is part and parcel of the character of the wicked. The verbs in colon B were pointed by the Masoretes in the causative conjugation and can be translated "to make odious and shameful" but, more probably, they are intransitive (GKC §53g) and should be translated, "act shamefully."

---

1. See J. Greenfield, "Lexicographical Notes II," *Hebrew Union College Annual* 30 (1959): 144; G. Anderson, *A Time to Dance, A Time to Mourn: The Expression of Grief and Joy in Israelite Religion* (University Park, Pa.: Pennsylvania State University Press, 1991), 51–53.

[6] The sentiment is the same as 11:5, but stated in the figure of abstract for concrete. "Integrity of way" (as in Job 4:6) and "sin" stand for "one whose way is right" and "sinner." The way of life one chooses ultimately guides one's course.

[7] Verses 7–8 both concern riches and poverty. Proverbs does not draw the same kind of antithesis between the rich and poor that it does between the wise and the fool. Instead, it prefers to make observations such as this one and 10:15. The observations often serve to relativize riches and poverty as in this verse. Money or its lack does not define a person, and often provides little insight about the quality of a person.

[8] Colon B was corrupt by the time of G (second century B.C.E.).[2] A scribe borrowed 13:1b and inserted it in place of the corrupt or missing colon B of our verse. The borrowing of 10:10b from 10:8b is similar. As it stands, the verse now states that the wealthy can ransom their own lives but those without wealth are so because of their failure to heed rebuke, that is, to accept correction and become wise. The sentiment is similar to 13:1; 17:10; and especially Qoh. 7:5. This meaning cannot have been the original meaning, however, for colon B is not antithetic to colon A; it is rather an explanation of why some people are poor.

Some scholars believe MT is sound. Delitzsch and Alonso Schökel, for example, suggest that the poor are too insignificant to hear the shouted threats of kidnappers who would demand ransom from them. Delitzsch takes *ga'ărāh* as "shouted threat" as he interprets Isa. 30:17, resulting in the following translation for our verse: "A ransom for a man's life are his riches; / But the poor hear no shouted threat." His suggestion is ingenious but forces the meaning. Colon B is not recoverable.

[9] A statement of the fate of the righteous and the wicked. The same vocabulary is employed by Bildad in Job 18:5–6 as he responds to Job (the words in Job identical to our saying are italicized): "Yes, the *light* of the wicked *is extinguished,* / the flame of his fire does not shine. / The *light* becomes dark in his tent / and his *lamp* above him is *extinguished.*" The extinguishing of a lamp thus signifies the end of a person (Prov. 24:20; Job 21:17) or a household (2 Sam. 21:17). At the same time, a sign of a prosperous household is the lamp that never goes out, as in Prov. 31:18: "[The capable wife] enjoys the profit from her trading; / her lamp is not extinguished at night." Where righteousness rules, there life and joy are to be found.

[10] The Hebrew of colon A is uncertain (see textual notes). Arrogance produces strife; in contrast, wisdom, the antithesis of superiority and presumption, is found with those who do not have antisocial and contemptuous attitudes of arrogance. They can engage in the give-and-take of conversation and "reproving."

[11] The Masoretic pointing of the Hebrew text requires emending in two

---

2. G reads MT but partially metathesizes MT *šm'*, "to hear," to *'md,* "to stand, stand up to."

words (see textual notes). Wealth hastily acquired grows less, but what is gradually acquired increases. The saying assumes that lasting riches come from hard work and prudence. For the thought see 20:21 and 28:22.

[12] Verses 12 and 14 mention "tree of life" and "fountain of life" and verses 13–14 are concerned with the value of a command. Verse 12 is concerned with the effect of expectations upon the emotions. When hopes do not come true, one's heart (mind) is sickened and weakened, whereas fulfillment is a source of life. "Tree of life" occurs in the Hebrew Bible in Genesis 2–3, Prov. 3:18; 11:30; 13:12; 15:4, and in the New Testament in Rev. 2:7; 22:2, 14, 19. Proverbs 10:28 is also about the fulfillment of hopes.

[13] The versions, except V, took the verb in colon A as *ḥābal* III, "to act corruptly," and most translations follow suit (e.g., JPSV): "He who disdains a precept will be injured thereby; / He who respects a command will be rewarded." The saying has more sharpness, however, if the verb is taken as *ḥābal* II, "to impound, to seize something as a pledge," as in Ex. 22:25 (words identical to our saying are italicized): "If you *seize as a pledge* the garment of your neighbor, when the sun goes down you shall return it to him." The legitimate precept that one refuses to obey exercises the same power as a pledge. Suppose X borrows a plow from Y and a third party (Z) allows his plow to be used as a pledge to Y until X returns the plow. Z's plow is liable to seizure until the plow is returned to Y. Similarly, one remains bound to a legitimate command in the way that Z in the example remains bound. The only way to get free of the obligation is to carry out the command. Once carried out, it no longer hangs over one's head; one is free.

[14] The wise speak words of wisdom, which protect them from the danger arising from wicked behavior. Earlier, the simple are exhorted to keep the teaching of parents and teachers (1:8; 7:2) in order to avoid those waiting to kill them (7:25–27). In 10:11 the mouth of the righteous is a fountain of life because it shows how to avoid premature death. Colon A is balanced through sound: *tôrat ḥākām mĕqôr ḥayyîm*. Proverbs 14:27 is identical except that "revering Yahweh" replaces "the teaching of a wise person."

[15] Colon B in MT, literally, "the way of deceivers is everlasting," is senseless and corrupt. No emendation has proved convincing. The versions read *'ābad*, "to perish, vanish," for MT *'êtān*, "everlasting." We follow the versions' sense of "to vanish," in particular of the vanishing of memory or name as in Job 18:17, Pss. 9:7 and 41:6. As the behavior of the wise wins favor, so the conduct (lit., "way") of the treacherous destroys their reputation and makes them unwanted outcasts. Some retain MT and interpret it as saying that the wise can advance through winning favor of others, but deceivers are fated to stay where they are: "Good sense wins favor; / The way of treacherous men is unchanging" (JPSV).

[16] The wise conceal their knowledge while fools shout it out. In this saying,

the wise reveal their wisdom in their actions, whereas fools reveal their folly. Like vendors with their wares, they spread it out for all to see. "Display" in colon B is used of merchants displaying their merchandise. For the thought, see 15:2 and 12:23.

[17] In a predominantly oral culture, untrustworthy messengers are a hazard. According to the axiom, the trouble they create by their negligence or malice will come upon their own heads. Perhaps there is wordplay in "stumbles into trouble" (lit., "falls into trouble"). The phrase evokes the common idiom for getting into trouble, "to fall into a pit" (22:14; 28:10, 18). Evil messengers will run into trouble on the road. Accurate and trustworthy messengers, on the other hand, not only avoid such trouble for themselves but bring benefit to others.

[18] The verb "to let go" in colon A connotes irresponsible and self-willed behavior such as is described in Ex. 32:25: "Aaron let the people go wild." Those who keep hold of discipline, on the other hand, will gain the honor that is customarily given to the wise. Wisdom means accepting the tradition and embracing instruction.

[19] Fools do not experience the fulfillment that gives delight. "Desire" in colon A is literally "appetite," and "soul" is literally "throat." Metaphorically, the words refer to the hunger and thirst for the fulfillment of one's deep longings. Fools cannot experience such satisfaction, for they will not turn from evil. The Hebrew word for "evil" includes both the evil act and its troublesome effects. By refusing to turn from evil, the wicked experience trouble. And their trouble is the antithesis of the fulfillment and pleasure of the good.

[20] One becomes like those with whom one associates. The point is wittily made by the repetition of similar words: In colon A, to be with "wise people" (*ḥăkāmîm*, makes one "wise" (*yeḥkām*, qere reading); in colon B, "who consorts with (*rōʿeh*) fools gets into trouble" (*yērôaʿ*).

[21] The verb "to pursue" in Hebrew connotes great energy and (usually) hostile intent—hunting down. Following the versions, we emend *yĕšallem*, "he repays," to *yĕšullam*, "it will be repaid," an instance of the divine passive. This verb is often used with the words "good" or "evil" as in Pss. 35:12; 38:21; Jer. 18:20. Genesis 44:4 contains words from both cola (words identical to our passage are italicized): "And Joseph said to his steward, '*Pursue* the men and overtake them. Tell them, "Why have you *repaid evil* [misfortune] for *good* [prosperity]?'" Trouble dogs sinners' footsteps, whereas the righteous are already repaid with prosperity.

[22] In the Hebrew text, the first word in colon A repeats the last word of colon B of the preceding verse, and the last word in colon B repeats the first word of colon A of the preceding verse. Good people not only have enough to leave to their numerous descendants, "their children's children," but become the beneficiaries of the wicked who are wealthy. Ill-gotten goods end up in the hands of the righteous (cf. Job 27:13–17).

[23] The versions are in a state of confusion, but at least V (and Theodotion) read the consonants of MT. We take *yēš* in colon B as "substance, assets, riches," as in 8:21, "endowing those who love me with riches" (cf. Sir. 42:3). The verse, like many other verses on the poor, is an ostensibly neutral observation. The problem that poor people have is not infertile fields as such, for their cultivated fields or tillage produces as much as those of the wealthy. Nature does not discriminate against the poor. Their problem is rather a lack of justice, which puts their harvest at risk. Unjust people take advantage of poor people's helpless position. The absolute equality of rich and poor before God (or the order of the universe) is an axiom: "Rich person meets poor person; / Yahweh made them both" (22:2).

Ehrlich takes another line, revocalizing MT *rāb,* "much, abundance," as the verb *rīb,* "to bring a lawsuit": "Going to law devours the tillage of the poor, / and many die before a legal decision is given." The suggestion is ingenious but it yields a flat and obvious statement.

[24] Successful education is paradoxical. You show your hate by not using the rod on your child, and show your love by disciplining the child early, when change is still possible. The English proverb, "Spare the rod and spoil the child" ("and" expressing the consequence) is derived from this verse. In 1377, William Langland in *Piers Plowman* (B. v. 41) rendered biblical "hate" with "spoil," and that rendering entered the language. Sparing the rod and hating the child are paradoxical and memorable ways of stating the effects of parental indifference to their children. The necessity of parental discipline is a common topic in wisdom literature: Prov. 19:18; 23:13–14; 29:17; Sir. 7:23 and 30:1–13. It goes without saying that this paradoxical language cannot be used as an argument for the corporal punishment of children.

[25] Like vv. 2, 4, 12, and 19, the saying is about the satisfaction of appetites. Doing good is fulfilling; doing evil is frustrating. Three contrasts are presented with subtlety: throat ("appetite") and belly; righteous and wicked, satiety and hunger.

Proverbs 14

14:1   A wise woman builds her house,
         but folly tears it down with her own hands.
2   Who walks a straight path reveres Yahweh,
         but one whose ways are crooked condemns him.
3   In the mouth of a fool is a rod of pride,
         but the lips of the wise protect them.
4   Where there are no cattle the manger is clean,
         but bountiful crops come from the strength of the ox.

5   A trustworthy witness does not lie,
         but a spouter of lies makes a lying witness.
6   A scoffer seeks wisdom but it's not there,
         but knowledge is easy for the wise.
7   Go away from the face of a fool!
         You will not encounter wise lips.
8   The wisdom of a clever person makes him know his way,
         but the folly of fools is deceit.
9   Fools scorn a guilt offering,
         but the upright find acceptance.
10   The heart knows its own bitterness,
         and another cannot share in its joy.
11   The house of the wicked will be destroyed,
         but the tent of the upright will flourish.
12   There is a road that seems straight to a person,
         but its end is the path to death.
13   Even in laughter the heart may be sad,
         and joy may end in sadness.
14   From his own ways a turncoat is sated;
         from his own actions, a loyal person.[a]
15   The simple believe every word,
         but a shrewd person watches his step.
16   A wise person fears and turns from evil,
         but a fool is confident and gets embroiled.
17   A hothead does perverse folly,
         and a schemer is hated.
18   The simple have folly as an adornment,[b]
         but the wise wear knowledge as their crown.
19   The malicious bow down before the good;
         so also the wicked at the gates of the righteous.
20   Even by his peers a poor person is despised,
         but a rich person's friends are many.
21   Who despises a hungry person[c] comes up short,
         but who shows kindness to the poor enjoys prosperity.
22   Surely, those who devise evil lose their way,
         but steadfast love is with those who devise good.
23   In all toil there is profit,
         but from idle talk, only a loss.
24   The crown of the wise is their wealth;
         the garland of fools is their folly.[d]
25   A truthful witness saves lives,
         but a spouter of lies is deceit.

26   Revering Yahweh is a sure stronghold
     and will be a shelter to one's children.
27   Revering Yahweh is a fountain of life,
     turning people from deadly snares.
28   A multitude of people is the ornament of a king,
     but when the people become few, a leader is ruined.
29   Long-suffering results in great wisdom;
     a short temper raises folly high.
30   A tranquil mind gives life to the body,
     but jealousy rots the bones.
31   Who oppresses a poor person affronts his maker,
     but who promotes the needy honors him.
32   When trouble befalls him, a wicked person is swept away,
     but a righteous person finds refuge even in death.ᵉ
33   In the heart of a wise person, wisdom remains silent,
     but in the midst of fools, it makes itself known.
34   Righteousness raises a nation high,
     but sin is a stigma to any people.
35   The king favors a prudent servant,
     but his wrath will fall on an incompetent one.

a. The versions were puzzled by *m'lyw,* "from his actions," in colon B (G: "his thoughts"; S and T: "his reverence"; V: "above him" = the wicked person of colon A). The meaning of it is clear, however, from Hos. 12:3 (words identical to our saying are italicized): "to requite Jacob according to *his ways* (*kidrākāyw*); according to *his actions* (*kĕma‘ălālāyw*) he will repay him." See also Judg. 2:19 and Jer. 17:10.

b. The meaning of the verb *nāḥal* in colon A is uncertain. The Masoretic tradition took it as "to inherit": "The simple inherit folly." The meaning would be that the clever have honor now but the simple will have folly later. "To inherit" does not seem a suitable parallel to "wear a crown," however. A number of scholars (McKane, Alonso Schökel, REB, NRSV) adopt the suggestion of G. R. Driver and take the verb as a denominative from *ḥălî,* "ornament," "to wear as an adornment."[1]

c. The superior reading in colon A is G *rā'ēb,* "to be hungry," which differs in only one consonant from MT *rē'ēhû,* "his neighbor." "His neighbor" is a copyist's error from the preceding v. 20, influenced perhaps by 11:12. "Hungry" and "poor" are parallel in Isa. 58:7 and make better sense here.

d. The parallelism in 4:9, *liywat // 'āṭeret,* supports the emendation of colon B to *liywat kĕsîlîm,* "garland of fools." The emendation of *'ošrām* to *'ormāh,* "cleverness," on the basis of G is unnecessary, for wealth is a gift of wisdom in 3:16.

e. Colon B in MT, literally, "but a righteous person seeks refuge in his death," troubled G, which used the device of metathesis to change *mwtw,* "his death," to *twmw,* "his

1. "Problems in the Hebrew Text of Proverbs," *Biblica* 32 (1951): 181.

integrity." The G translation, however, is insipid: "but the righteous person seeks refuge in his integrity." REB and NRSV follow G. The Qumran scroll 4QProv[b] supports MT.

[**14:1**] The relationship between wisdom and folly to building a house has been a persistent theme, as has the contribution of a wife, good or bad, to the household. Proverbs warns in chaps. 5–7 that the adulterous woman can destroy a household and praises the "house-building woman" in 31:10–31. Colon A characterizes the wise woman as a house builder. As in chap. 9, the foolish woman builds nothing; she is defined only in opposition to wisdom. The verbs "to build" and "to tear down" are a fixed pair, as in Jer. 24:6; 42:10; 45:4. In 1 Cor. 14:4, Paul speaks of building the church. "A wise woman" is actually a superlative in Hebrew, "the wisest of women" (*ḥakmôt nāšîm*), similar to Judg. 5:29 (*ḥakmôt śārôteyhā*, "the wisest of her serving women") and Isa. 19:11 ("the wisest of the counselors of Pharaoh").

[**2**] "To walk" and "path" are metaphors for living and course of life, and straight and crooked are metaphors for good and evil conduct. Revering a god primarily meant obeying the god and performing the appropriate rituals. True piety is walking a straight course (cf. English "to be straightforward," "to be straight with someone" and their antonyms "devious" or "crooked").

[**3**] Fools' words get them into trouble, whereas the speech of the wise protects them. "Mouth" and "lips" are often paired in Proverbs (10:32; 16:10; 18:6, 20; 27:2). "Fool" and "wise" are likewise commonly paired. The third antithesis is not so obvious: "rod of pride" and "protect them." In Isa. 11:1, *ḥōṭer* is "twig, sprout," but in Aramaic the word can be "rod (for punishment)," and thus a weapon. "Rod of pride" is a Semitism for "rod doing prideful acts," like "rod (*šēbeṭ*) of my anger" in Isa. 10:5. A proud tongue does not offer protection, for haughtiness eventually gets one into trouble. The lips (= words) of the wise, on the other hand, protect them.

[**4**] Like 12:10, the saying is about farm animals. If there are no animals, there is no necessity of keeping the crib full, but without farm animals there will be no crops to fill the barn. Benefits have a cost. You don't get something for nothing. Colon A reverses colon B, which is nicely shown by the reversal of the consonants of *bār,* "clean," to *rāb,* "bountiful."

[**5**] How does one know whose legal testimony to believe? Knowing how to assess witnesses in court is a constant question in Proverbs (6:19; 12:17; 19:28; 25:18). The ultimate criterion here is the character of the witness. What does a person normally do? "What's bred in the bone will come out in the flesh." Formally, unity is achieved by the repetition of "witness" in colon B, the occurrence of the triliteral root *kzb* in each colon, and by the repetition of /ēl/, which opens and closes colon A.

[**6**] Scoffers, the habitually cynical, will never attain wisdom, for their scornful attitude keeps them from listening to others. For the astute, on the other

hand, knowledge (in the sense of wisdom) is easy, for there is an affinity between them and what they seek.

[7] This is one of the most difficult sayings in the book. It is possibly corrupt. All the versions read the consonants of MT but interpreted them differently. G, followed by S, was forced to alter the text. V and T added explanations to colon A, respectively, "Go *against* a stupid man and do not let him know lips of prudence," and "Go on another road away from the fool." The Masoretic interpretation remains the most probable and is the basis of JPSV: "Keep your distance from a dullard, / For you will not learn wise speech." REB is similar: "Avoid a stupid person; / you will not hear a word of sense from him." If the text is sound, there may be a wordplay on the *front* of a fool, whose face (lit., "front") and lips are dangerous. Leave the face of a fool, for only folly is there. The Hebrew words for "face" and "front" are parallel in Ps. 44:16.

[8] Wisdom enables the wise to understand their way, that is, whether it is "straight" and leads to life. Folly offers no guidance to fools; it misleads them ("deceit").

[9] The versions found the Hebrew text difficult to understand, though they all seem to have read the MT consonants. G changed the Hebrew consonants in *'wlym*, "fools," and *byn*, "between," to get the parallel "tents" (*'ohālîm*) and "houses" (*bāttîm*), probably under the influence of v. 11. The Masoretes rendered the verse, "Reparations mediate between fools, / Between the upright, good will" (JPSV), that is, fools have to pay money to mend their relationships with others, but the righteous already enjoy goodwill.

Another interpretation is preferable. The Hebrew verb in colon A, *lîṣ,* can mean "to scorn" as well as "to mediate," making possible the translation, "The wicked scorn a guilt offering."[2] The meaning is either that fools scornfully refuse to take any steps to remove their guilt by offerings or that they simply continue in their wicked behavior, whereas the upright by reason of their uprightness already enjoy divine acceptance and favor.

[10] In the psychology of Proverbs, the heart is the place where a person's sense impressions are stored and reflected upon. It stands for the person at a highly personal level. Proverbs ordinarily takes a social view of the human person, seeing the individual in society, but here it looks at the private and incommunicable side of a person. One's sorrows and one's joys—a merism meaning *all* deep emotions—cannot be completely shared with others.

[11] This verse represents a perfect antithetic parallel. "House" and "tent" is a fixed pair in Hebrew poetry. The paradox seems to be that a house can be less secure than a tent if its inhabitant is wicked. Assonance and alliteration link

---

2. The problem of plural subject and singular subject in colon A can be resolved in either of two ways: (1) an original *'awîl-mi* (*mi* enclitic) was interpreted as plural; (2) an original *yālîṣû,* "they scorned," written without vowel letters, could be read as singular or plural.

the human types to the fate of their dwelling: *rĕšā'îm* — *yiššāmēd* ("the wicked" — "will be destroyed") and *yĕšārîm* —*yaprîaḥ* ("the upright" — "will flourish"). In 14:1 wisdom and folly are also linked to the fate of a house.

[12] This well-known saying contrasts the judgments that people make of their paths (course of life) and their actual outcomes. "Path" is a metaphor for human conduct, and "straight" is a metaphor for what is honest and good. The word "end" (*'aḥărît*) in wisdom literature often means the outcome in the light of which the whole is evaluated. Its end indeed shows the rightness of a path, but only God can see the end at the beginning. Human beings judge only what is directly in front of them, but cannot see what is further down the road, the future. Proverbs 16:25 is a duplicate. Cf. 5:5; 7:27; Sir. 21:10 and Matt. 7:13.

[13] The saying repeats *'aḥărîtāh* from the previous verse. Its theme harks back to v. 10, which is also about the emotions. The saying denies that outward demeanor always mirrors inner feeling and attitude. The perspective of colon A differs from that of B. In colon A laughter and sadness coexist, whereas in B one emotion follows the other. People are complex. Outward emotions often are not the whole story. Emotions are fleeting.

[14] Deeds come back upon their doer, the recompense being determined by the character of the one who performed them. A "turncoat" is someone who withdraws from a principled position, a backslider.

[15] The simple are gullible, giving credence to everything said by others. Oblivious of danger, they do not practice discernment. The shrewd, on the other hand, watch their *own* steps rather than swallowing whole what others say. The difference between the two types is nicely highlighted by the placement in the middle of each colon of the similar-sounding verbs *ya'ămîn* and *yābîn* ("believe" and "watches").

[16] Normally, the wise should be confident and unworried, and fools should be fearful because of the retribution that looms over them. But evil or trouble (Hebrew *ra'* means both) turns the ordinary situation upside down. The wise now "fear," that is, exercise caution by removing themselves from the evil, whereas fools, unreflectively confident, get involved. The repetition of *r* in colon A unifies the colon (*ḥākām yārē' wĕsār mērā'*).

[17] The antithesis is between impetuousness and cunning. Acting with no reflection is bad, but so is acting with reflection but maliciously. In the first case, grievous folly results, and in the second, public hatred or ostracism.

Translators and commentators have puzzled over the saying. In order to arrive at antithetic parallelism (the predominant type in chaps. 10–15), REB and others have emended MT *yiśśānē'*, "is hated," to *yinnāśē'*, "to be raised up [in success]," which yields "Impatience runs into folly; / advancement comes by careful thought." The emendation, however, strains the sense of the verb *nāśā'* and is unnecessary, as may be seen by examining the words. "Folly" (*'iwwelet*) is the most serious grade in the Proverbs lexicon for foolishness—folly resulting from moral perversity, "perverse folly."³ The hothead is a less evil type in Proverbs's rogue's gallery. In colon B, the parallel to the hothead in colon A is a "schemer" (*'îš mězimmôt*), literally, "a person of schemes." The Hebrew word *mězimmôt* connotes private, hidden thought, which is never said to be expressed. From hidden thought it is a short step to hostile plan.⁴ Though *mězimmāh* alone can be positive in Proverbs (1:4; 2:11; 3:21; 5:2; 8:12), the phrase "person of *mězimmôt*" is negative (12:2 and 24:8).

[18] It is impossible that the inner quality of a person not be revealed. In this saying the inner quality of the simple and the clever are on display like clothing and jewelry. The righteous wear a crown, which is a good thing in Proverbs. It is a sign of God's blessing as a good wife for her husband (12:4), gray hair for the righteous (16:31), and grandchildren for the elderly (17:6).

[19] "High" and "low" in Hebrew and in English are metaphors for prosperity and misery. In Hannah's Song, God casts down and raises up (1 Sam. 2:7). In this saying the wicked sink down in the presence of the good. Their fall becomes an act of homage. In colon B, *rěšā'îm 'al šě'ārîm*, "the wicked at the gates") reverses the consonants *r* and *š* and repeats /*îm*/ (cf. the parable of the rich man and Lazarus in Luke 16:24–31).

[20] An unsparing observation on the connection between wealth and popularity (cf. 19:4 and Sir. 13:21–23).

[21] The paradox is that those who despise a hungry person will themselves suffer a lack, and anyone showing mercy (by giving alms to the poor) will enjoy prosperity. The verse draws on sentiments such as in Ps. 41:2: "Happy the one concerned for the poor" (cf. Matt. 5:7: "Blessed are the merciful, for they will be shown mercy").

[22] The text is disturbed. The first Hebrew word, *hălô'*, "surely," ("is it not the case . . . ?") is not reflected in any ancient version and the syllable count of MT is uneven. As the text stands, the meaning is that two groups with diametrically opposite plans experience different outcomes. With a nice touch of irony, it affirms that planners (of evil) cannot keep to the road, meaning that their plans will come to nothing. Those who plan good things, on the other hand, end with something far more precious—steadfast love, a gift of God.

[23] The antitheses are between physical labor and idle talk (lit., "a word of the lips"), profit and loss. Proverbs elsewhere puts a high value on good words.

[24] In Proverbs a crown can be a good wife for her husband (12:4), gray hair for the righteous (16:31), or grandchildren for the elderly (17:6). A crown is thus a visible sign that one is blessed by God. Wealth is a sign of God's favor. The foolish behavior of fools is a visible sign of their folly.

[25] The saying exploits a duality in the meaning of truth and lies. "Truth"

---

3. M. Fox, "Words for Folly," *ZAH* 10 (1997): 6–7.
4. M. Fox, "Words for Wisdom," *ZAH* 6 (1993): 159.

can mean accurate reporting and faithfulness (= offering rescue). Lying testimony is deceptive in the dual sense that it is not accurate and offers no hope of freeing a prisoner. The saying is sometimes explained as pertaining to testimony in a capital case, for later rabbinic literature calls capital cases *dyny npšm,* "judgments of lives" (*Tg. Neof.,* Lev. 24:12), but such an interpretation seems too specific for the saying. "Spouter of lies" occurs also in 6:19; 14:5; 19:5, 9. The saying underlines the social aspect of truth and falsehood.

[26] Revering Yahweh protects both oneself and one's children as well. Parents' reverence is a refuge to their children in two ways: (1) God rewards a righteous person's family extending into future generations ("[I, Yahweh] showing steadfast love to the thousandth generation of those who love me and keep my commandments," Ex. 20:6; Deut. 5:9); (2) the parents transmit their religious devotion to their children as a legacy.

[27] The saying is linked to v. 26 by "revering Yahweh." Proverbs 13:14 is the same except that its subject is "the teaching of a wise person." In the ancient Near East, "fear of a god" was less an emotion than an action—obeying and performing the rituals of one's god. Revering Yahweh helps protect one from evil actions that cause premature death.

[28] This is a statement of the relation of the king to his people. In stating that the more numerous the people the more worthy of respect is their king, the saying locates royal glory not in riches or military power but in the people. The saying gives a new perspective: A king's glory depends not on himself but on his people, and he will be ruined if his people become too few.

[29] This saying and the next are concerned with the relation of virtue to wisdom. Spatial punning is employed to link wisdom to patience and folly to impatience. The Hebrew idiom for patience is "long of nostrils," and for impatience, "shortness of spirit [breath]."

[30] In the two nominal clauses, the predicates—life of the body and rot of the bones—are contrasted. "Flesh" and "bones" is a frequent fixed pair in the Bible (e.g., Gen. 2:23; Judg. 9:2; Job 2:5), but in Proverbs is found only here. The heart is the storage place of thoughts and feelings, and the organ of deciding. Its tranquillity or disquiet affects the whole person. Like some Egyptian instructions the saying inculcates tranquility and rejects disordered passion as dangerous to one's health.

[31] The antithesis is between taking from the poor and giving to them. The verb in colon B, "to honor, show favor," is used of giving to the poor in 28:8 and Ps. 109:12. God is the maker of all, rich and poor, and God's honor is bound up with each person, no matter how lowly. A similar sentiment is found in Amenemope chap. 25: "Don't tease a man who is in the hand of a god [i.e., an epileptic or insane person], / Nor be angry with him for his failing. / Man is clay and straw, / The god is his builder." Oppressing the poor "oppresses" God, and honoring the poor honors God. Proverbs 17:5 is similar to colon A, and 19:17

is similar to colon B. The sound pattern CōCēC (C = consonant) in the first and last word unites colon A; the sound /ō/ occurs three times in colon B.

[32] The antitheses are: (1) "a wicked person" and "a righteous person"; (2) "swept away" (passive) and "find refuge" (active); (3) "trouble" and "in death." The general meaning is similar to 10:25: "When the storm has passed, a wicked person is no more, / but a righteous person has a lasting foundation." A righteous person continues to seek refuge in God to the very end, even when close to death or a near-death situation, whereas the wicked are utterly swept away by their misfortune. The verb *ḥāsāh* ("to seek refuge") normally has God as its object (expressed with the preposition *b*).

[33] "In the heart of " (= within) a wise person wisdom "rests" (*tānûaḥ*) as in its natural habitat; it belongs there and can be silent. Not so among fools, because wisdom is not at home there; it must speak out and make itself known. The Hebrew colon B, literally, "in the midst of fools [wisdom] will be made known," puzzled the versions. G and S added "not": "[wisdom] will *not* be made known," which is adopted by NRSV. In the same spirit, T added: "*stupidity* will be made known." But these readings fail to understand the nuance of the verb in colon A, *tānûaḥ*, "to rest, remain silent," which is antithetical to "to be known, recognized." Cf. Qoh. 7:9: "Anger rests in the bosom of fools." Ehrlich points out that *nûaḥ* can mean to remain peacefully in one's place; it is parallel to *šāqaṭ*, "to be silent," in Isa. 14:7 and Job 3:26. The Hebrew prepositions in each colon can mean both "in the heart of, within" (Jer. 31:33) or "in the midst of, amid" (Amos 7:8).

The paradox is that wisdom can remain silent in the heart of or in the midst of the wise, not because it is absent but because it is so thoroughly at home, so connatural. Among fools, however, it must speak out because of the dissonance between fools and wisdom.

[34] Only T interprets colon B of MT correctly, taking *hesed* not as "fidelity, steadfast love" but as the much less common word "shame, reproach." The noun occurs elsewhere in the Bible only in Lev. 20:17, and the verb of the triliteral root occurs in Prov. 25:10. G read *r* for *d* to get *heser*, "lacking, deficient," but G often exploits the graphic similarity of *r* and *d*, and it is unnecessary here.

In evaluating a nation or people, one ordinarily considers its territorial extent, wealth, history, and military might. This verse affirms that the key factors in assessing a people are "righteousness," that is, being in right relationship to God. The reader is meant to be momentarily puzzled in colon B. The word "righteousness" prepares one to understand *hesed* in its customary meaning of "fidelity, steadfast love," but the word "sin" forces a rethinking and, finally, a recognition that the word must be the rarer word, "reproach, stigma." The next saying deals with national life in the person of the king.

[35] The intelligent servant is contrasted with the incompetent. Here, only a wise person knows how to win the king's favor at court (see also 16:13 and Ps. 101:6–8).

Proverbs 15

15:1 A soft response turns back anger,
       but a harsh word stirs up wrath.

2 The tongue of the wise aptly states their thoughts,
       but the mouth of fools pours out folly.

3 In every place, the eyes of Yahweh
       are watching the wicked and the good.

4 A soothing tongue is a tree of life,
       but a devious one shatters the spirit.

5 A fool spurns the discipline of his father,
       but one who attends to reproof grows wise.

6 In the house of the righteous are great possessions,
       but the harvest of the wicked is in peril.

7 The lips of the wise disseminate knowledge,
       but the hearts of fools are not steadfast.

8 The sacrifices of the wicked are an abomination to Yahweh,
       but the prayer of the upright wins his favor.

9 The way of a wicked person is an abomination to Yahweh,
       but he loves anyone who pursues righteousness.

10 Discipline is bad to one who forsakes the way;
       one who hates correction will die.

11 Sheol and the Abyss lie open to Yahweh;
       how much more the hearts of human beings!

12 A scoffer does not like being corrected;
       he never visits the wise.

13 A joyful heart makes the face radiant,
       but a burdened heart makes a despondent spirit.

14 The mind of a wise person seeks knowledge,
       but the mouths of fools feed on folly.

15 All the days of the poor are evil,
       but a good heart is a continual feast.

16 Better a little with the revering of Yahweh
       than great wealth with turmoil.

17 Better a serving of vegetables where love is,
       than a fattened ox where hatred is.

18 An angry person stirs up strife,
       but patience quiets a quarrel.

19 The way of a lazy person seems a hedge of thorns,
       but the path of the upright is a highway.

20 A wise son makes his father rejoice,
       but a fool of a man contemns his mother.

21   Folly is fun to one without sense,
           but a person of discernment walks straight ahead.
22   Plans are foiled for want of counsel,
           but succeed with many advisors.
23   Conversing gives joy to a person.
           How pleasing is a word at the right time!
24   The path of life leads upward for the wise,
           turning them from Sheol below.
25   Yahweh will tear down the house of the haughty
           but will set up the boundary stone of the widow.
26   Evil plans are an abomination to Yahweh,
           but gracious words are accepted.
27   Who takes unjust gain brings trouble to his house,
           but who spurns bribes will live long.ª
28   The heart of a righteous person ponders a response,
           but the mouth of the wicked blurts out malice.
29   Yahweh is far from the wicked
           but hears the prayer of the righteous.ᵇ
30   A welcoming glance makes the heart glad;
           good news puts fat on the bones.
31   One whose ear heeds life-giving reproofs
           finds a home among the wise.
32   Who lets go of discipline rejects his very self,
           but who heeds reproofs gains wisdom.
33   Revering Yahweh is training for wisdom,
           humility comes before honor.

a. G has a couplet not in MT: "By alms and faithful actions sins are taken away, / and by fear of the Lord everyone turns from evil."
b. G has two sayings not in MT. The first (Rahlfs v. 29a) is the same as 16:8: "Better a small share with righteousness / than much fruit with injustice." The second (Rahlfs v. 29b) renders 16:9: "Let the heart of a man think just thoughts, / so that his steps may be made straight by God."

Verses 1–7 are a section, beginning and ending with the topic of words.
    [15:1] The topic is the effect words have upon anger, one of the great enemies of wisdom. Paradoxically, where words are concerned, soft is hard, that is, effective, and hard is soft, that is, ineffective. The Hebrew word for "response" is broader than an answer to a query; it can refer to the give and take of conversation. Colon A is current in English, "A soft answer turns away wrath."
    [2] The wise and the foolish are distinguished by their speech. The wise aim at a careful and apt expression of their thoughts. "Thoughts" (*da'at*) is, literally,

"knowledge" in the sense of what one knows. The word has this meaning also in v. 7 and 12:23a. The verb "to pour out" is also used of fools speaking in 15:28b. In colon A, the common emendation *taṭṭîp*, "drip [honeyed words]" for MT *têṭîb*, "to be or to make beautiful," is unlikely, though it is adopted by *HALAT* and NRSV. In Hebrew, the mouth drips honey, but never the tongue. Further, *taṭṭîp* is not attested as a fixed pair with "pours out" (*nābaʿ*). The verb in colon A (the causative conjugation of *yāṭab*) means "to beautify" in 2 Kings 9:30, where Jezebel "beautifies her head." The meaning here is "beautifies the thought" or "aptly expresses the thought." The wise carefully and eloquently state their thoughts, whereas fools pour them out without reflection.

[3] The saying does not simply say that God is all-seeing, but that in every place — whether frequented or inaccessible, holy or profane — God observes the good and the wicked (Ehrlich). What is good and evil is judged so by God's standards rather than by human standards. The same thought is developed in Psalm 11, Sir. 16:17–23 and especially 23:19.

[4] As in v. 1, the topic is the effect of one's words upon others. Words can bring life and destruction. The phrase "tree of life" appears only in Genesis (2:9; 3:22, 24) and Proverbs (3:18 [see commentary]; 11:30; 13:12 and here). In Ezek. 47:12 waters from the Temple nurture trees whose fruit provides food and whose leaves provide healing. Words can heal and lift up the spirit. A spirit can be shattered (Ps. 51:19). The opposite of a soothing and healing tongue is a treacherous and deceitful one that demoralizes others. Ephesians 4:25 similarly associates truth-telling with support of others: "Therefore, putting aside falsehood, speak the truth, each one to his neighbor, for we are members of one another" (NAB).

[5] The proverb states that a person becomes foolish by rejecting something and becomes wise by keeping something. The "something" in both cases is discipline, the process of education (sometimes painful) that leads to wisdom. Wisdom in Proverbs is not innate, the unfolding of what is seminally present within, but something that comes through a process, often from an authority such as a parent or teacher. Disobedient offspring will never become wise, for they reject the very process that makes them wise. Colon A is framed by /î/ sounds in its first and last words.

[6] The antithesis is between possessions already in the house of a righteous person and the ungathered harvest of the wicked, which is not secure while still in the field. The wicked endanger all they have by the way they live.

[7] "Lips" (or "tongue") and "heart" are a fixed pair (Isa. 29:13; Prov. 10:20); they are, respectively, the expression and the source. The lips of the wise guard the contents of their heart; "knowledge" here means "what one knows," the contents of one's heart, as in v. 2 and 5:2. Fools, on the other hand, are unsound even in the source of words, their heart. In colon B Hebrew *lōʾ kēn*, ("not steadfast") is related to the verb "to be firm" (*kûn*), which is used of the heart (e.g., Pss. 10:17; 78:8, 37; Job 11:13).

[8] The statement, "X is an abomination to Yahweh, but he is pleased with Y," is the language of ritual (see under 11:1). An offering improperly made is declared an abomination to Yahweh. Offerings presented by people whose conduct makes them God's enemies are likewise abominations. Ritual without sincerity is abhorrent to God as in the prophets (e.g., Isa. 1:10–17 and 29:10). The prayer of those loyal to God receives a favorable hearing. Proverbs 21:27 and Sir. 7:9 are similar in thought.

[9] Verse 9 shifts the focus of v. 8 from conduct in the sanctuary (sacrifice) to everyday conduct—one's way of life. Those whose *way* is evil are an *abomination* to Yahweh, but Yahweh loves those who pursue righteousness. The antithesis is expressed by nouns ("abomination" and "way") and verbs ("to pursue" and "to love"). The saying links public worship and daily life.

[10] "Hate" in colon B relates the saying back to v. 9 ("love") and forward to v. 12 ("like"). Discipline, which is a good thing in Proverbs, is bad to those who forsake the right way. "Discipline" is not otherwise called *rā'*, "bad," in Proverbs. The phrase "bad to" (*rā' l*) is equivalent to "bad in the eyes of, distasteful" as in 1 Sam. 29:7. Its parallel is "hates" in colon B. Another parallel in the saying is "forsakes the way" and "will die." To reject discipline invites premature death, for evil conduct puts one in peril. JB, NRSV, and REB, in somewhat different ways, take "discipline" as punishment for abandoning the path. NRSV, for example, translates, "There is severe discipline for one who forsakes the way." *Mûsār* in Proverbs, however (apart from the unclear 7:22), never means punishment. The first and last syllables of the verse begin with *mū*.

[11] Sheol and the Abyss (*'ăbaddôn,* lit, "Destruction") are terms for the place where the spirits of the dead live a shadowy existence. Job 26:6 similarly declares that "Sheol is naked before God, / and Abaddon has no covering," in a hymn celebrating the omnipotence of God. This maxim states that even the most inaccessible and mysterious place in the universe is "before Yahweh." How much more the human heart. For the same sentiment, see Ps. 139:8 and Sir. 42:18.

[12] A scoffer contemns others and their viewpoints. But the only way one becomes wise is through dialogue with others, receiving and giving corrections. Rejecting openness to others and learning from them, the scoffer is doomed to remain a fool.

[13] This is the first of several sayings (vv. 13–17) that are linked by "heart" (in vv. 13–15) and the adjective "good" or "better" (vv. 15–17). This maxim is about the relation of inner thought and outward expression, which is a frequent polarity in Proverbs. The heart is the crucial organ in the psyche; its state is inevitably reflected in one's physical appearance. The adjective "despondent" several times modifies "spirit" (e.g., Ezek. 21:12; Isa. 61:3; Prov. 17:22; 18:14). Similar in thought are 17:22; 18:14; Sir. 13:25–26.

[14] "Heart" and "mouth" are parallel in Proverbs only here and in 15:28.

In 15:28, they symbolize, respectively, reflection and expression. In this verse the heart of a wise person seeks more wisdom, whereas the mouth of fools is content to feed itself on folly.

[15] "Good heart" does not refer to good intentions but to an instructed mind. Being wise makes impoverishment not only bearable, but even joyful, like the joy of feast days. Wisdom keeps one from being defeated by the troubles that come with being poor.

[16] When is a small amount of money better than a large amount? When the large amount of money is accompanied by the trouble that comes from impiety. Hebrew *mĕhûmāh*, "turmoil," baffled the versions. The word can mean the horrific tumult of war (Deut. 7:23; 1 Sam. 5:9), but it is used more generally here (cf. 17:1 and Ps. 37:16).

[17] This is the last of the sayings, begun in v. 13, that are linked by *lēb*, "heart," and *ṭôb*, "good, better." The seemingly ridiculous statement that a meal of vegetables is better than a rich feast underlines the fact that a meal becomes a feast because of the joyous fellowship of the guests rather than because of the food (see v. 15). A similar saying is found in the *Instruction of Amenemope* IX.8–9: "Better is bread with a happy heart / Than wealth with vexation" (*AEL* 2.152).

[18] Angry people incite quarrels because they so readily communicate their anger to others. The cool or patient person, on the other hand, quells strife. It is the function of wisdom to keep passion within bounds. Colon A is identical to 29:22a except for a different word for anger.

[19] Proverbs likes to quote the deluded and self-defeating words of the sluggard: for example, "The sluggard says, 'There's a lion in the street, there's a lion in the square!'" (26:13; cf. 22:13). Here, in the sluggard's imagination (lit., "in the eyes of"), the way "seems" to be hedged in and impassable. The just, on the other hand, are confident that their way is level and smooth, like the well-trod road leading to the city.[1]

[20] Verses 20–23 are linked by a catchword, the triliteral root "joy," in vv. 20, 21, and 23. This saying belongs to the series on the household. G, followed by S and T, inserts "son" in colon B but "fool of a man" is acceptable Hebrew (GKC §128l). Adult children's conduct affects their parents. Wise children advertise their parents' wisdom and foolish children advertise their parents' inability to educate them properly.

[21] To find joy and satisfaction in folly is a sure sign of stupidity, for folly brings disaster in its wake. The wise, who realize the danger, walk the straight and narrow.

[22] One might expect that plans are foiled only by an external agency, as happens in 2 Sam. 15:34; 17:14; Ezra 4:5; and Job 5:12, but here they are foiled

---

1. For the meaning of "highway," see N. L. Tidwell, *VT* 45 (1995): 264–65.

from within—by failure to consult others. In contrast, having many advisors insures that a plan will succeed. The contrast is reinforced by the contrast of singular and plural number: plans (plural) fail for want of counsel (singular) but a plan (singular) succeeds because of advisors (plural).

[23] The topic is the pleasure of conversation, of saying the right thing at the right time. Words not only dispense information but also enable people to communicate on a deep level (cf. 25:11).

[24] In Hebrew, as in English, "up" and "down" are metaphors of success and failure. The route of the wise leads them away from the trouble and premature death that results from evil conduct. Sheol was regarded as below the surface of the earth. Deuteronomy 28:43 is a good commentary on the verse (words identical to our verse are italicized): "The resident alien who is in your midst will go *up above* you higher and higher (*ma'lāh*) and you will go *down lower* and lower (*maṭṭāh*)," that is, the alien will succeed rather than you.

[25] To have a house and land was a great thing in the ancient Near East and in Israel, giving status and ensuring food and clothing. Unfortunately, one could easily lose house and home, especially when there was no male head of the household. Indeed, "the widow and the fatherless" is an age-old description of the poor. Ancient Near Eastern kings boasted in their inscriptions that they protected the rights of such vulnerable people. Here Yahweh takes on that royal role directly as in 23:10–11: "Do not move the boundary stone of a widow, / and do not trespass on the fields of orphans, / for their redeemer is mighty; / he will take up their case against you." In Isa. 5:8, Isaiah inveighs, "Ho! those who add house to house" (that is, those who add the small plots of the poor to their already large estates), Yahweh will knock down those great houses and set up again the boundary stones of the poor. Cf. Deut. 19:14.

[26] The saying uses the abomination formula (see under 11:1) to declare what is and what is not acceptable before God. "Accepted" (lit., "pure") means acceptable for sacrifice, as in the classifications of clean and unclean animals. A further contrast is between "plans" and "words." The actions of daily life are linked to ritual; they too can be acceptable or not to God.

[27] The opening scene of Proverbs (1:8–19) warned that taking unjust gain (1:19) was the wrong way to build a house (1:11–14). Income for one's family must be honestly gained or it can endanger one's house. "Live" means to live long because of divine protection. Cf. Isa. 1:23.

[28] As in v. 23, speech is in response to the speech of others. The saying pairs "heart" (= mind, which rehearses words) and "mouth" (which delivers words). The righteous carefully consider the words they speak to their neighbor, whereas the wicked do not, and spill out their malice on others. Cf. v. 2 and 19:28.

[29] Like vv. 8 and 26, the topic is what is acceptable and not acceptable to God. Distance and closeness are here not a matter of space but of the ability to communicate, to speak and be heard. The wicked have put themselves out of God's range.

[30] As colon B shows, the welcoming glance (lit., the "light of the eyes") is not in one's own eyes but in another's warm and friendly look. A frequent theme in Proverbs is the effect one's words have upon others (e.g., vv. 1, 4, 18, 23), and this saying applies it to nonverbal communication. The next saying continues the theme.

[31] To become wise means hearing and integrating perspectives often contrary to one's own instincts, which is implied by "reproofs." Wisdom does not make one solitary but places one in the number of the wise.

[32] Discipline—ancestral instruction and training—is often at odds with youthful inclinations. Discipline might be considered alienating, but in fact it enlivens one's inmost self. The contrasts are vivid: "to let go of" (often with the suggestion of license and self-indulgence) and "to heed"; "to reject" and "to gain." To reject or accept discipline means ultimately to reject or accept one's very self. All four verbs are participles in the qal conjugation and have an /ō/ + /ē/ pattern.

[33] Just as humility comes before honor and is the road to it, so revering Yahweh is training, a school for wisdom. To act loyally toward Yahweh is a school of wisdom. Colon B continues the logic: To revere Yahweh is an act of radical humility, for it implies that one embraces one's true place in the world as a creature.

Proverbs 16

16:1 Plans are made in the human heart
     but the word of the tongue is from Yahweh.

2 One's ways are pure in one's own eyes,
     but the measurer of motives is Yahweh.

3 Entrust your projects to Yahweh,
     and your plans will be established.

4 God makes everything for a purpose,
     even a sinner for an evil day.

5 Everyone haughty in heart is an abomination to Yahweh;
     assuredly none will go unpunished.

6 By loyalty and faithfulness iniquity is expiated,
     and by revering Yahweh evil is avoided.

7 When Yahweh is pleased with someone's ways,
     he turns his enemies into allies.

8 Better a little with righteousness
     than a large income without justice.[a]

9 A person's heart plans his course,
     but it is Yahweh who assures his steps.

10 Inspired decisions fall from the king's lips;
     his mouth does not err in giving judgment.

11   Scales and balances belong to Yahweh;[b]
       every weight in the sack is his work.
12   Doing evil is an abomination to kings,
       for by righteousness the throne endures.
13   Truthful lips win the favor of the king;
       he loves the one who speaks reliable words.
14   A king's wrath is a herald of death,
       but a wise person can assuage it.
15   A king's smile means life;
       his favor is like the clouds in spring.
16   It is better to acquire wisdom than gold,[c]
       more valuable to acquire insight than silver.
17   The road of the upright leads away from trouble;
       who attends to his way preserves his life.
18   Arrogance goes before a fall,
       and a haughty spirit before a collapse.
19   Better to be humble of spirit among the lowly
       than to share booty with the proud.
20   Who attends to business will find success;
       who trusts in Yahweh will be happy.
21   One wise of heart is deemed intelligent;
       pleasing lips gain a reputation for wisdom.
22   Good sense is a fountain of life for those who have it,
       but folly is the training of fools.
23   The heart of a wise person instructs his mouth,
       and gives discernment to his lips.
24   Pleasing words are a honeycomb,
       sweet to the palate, strengthening the bones.
25   There is a path that seems straight to a person,
       but its end is the path to death.
26   A laborer's appetite labors for him;
       his mouth imposes labor upon him.
27   A scoundrel plots evil,
       which is like a blazing fire on his lips.
28   A deceiver stirs up quarrels,
       and a talebearer alienates friends.
29   A violent person leads his neighbor astray,
       gets him to walk a path that is not good.
30   Who narrows his eyes is planning deceptions,
       who compresses his lips is deciding on evil.
31   Gray hair is a glorious crown;
       it is found in the path of righteousness.

32 Better a patient person than a warrior,
    a ruler of his spirit than a conqueror of a city.
33 Into the bag the lot is cast,
    but from Yahweh comes every decision.

a. In G this verse occurs after 15:29. Proverbs 16:8 in G bears no relation to MT except for the phrase "with righteousness" occurring in both: "Whoever seeks the Lord will find knowledge with righteousness, / and those who seek him in uprightness will find peace."

b. We excise *mišpāṭ* in colon A as a dittography from v. 10b, for (1) one would expect *ṣedeq* for "just" here rather than a repetition of *mišpāṭ* from colon A; (2) its omission makes better parallelism. The original text was *m'znym lyhwh*. The dittography occurred earlier than G.

c. We excise *māh*, "what, how," as dittography. It is not attested in the versions.

Proverbs 15:33–16:9 form a string of sayings on divine governance. In the series, "Yahweh" occurs ten times. G does not have vv. 1, 3–4, 6–9 of MT. The placement of other verses shows much variance.

[16:1] A literal rendering is, "Of man are the arrangements of the heart, but from Yahweh is the response of the tongue." Interpretations of this enigmatic saying range from "Man proposes but God disposes" (Toy) to Delitzsch's view that God's answer comes in the moment of verbal expression. Neither is adequate. An important clue is the customary antithesis of heart and tongue (or mouth or lips) to express the totality of human activity. One dreams of projects, but their realization is not within one's capacity.

[2] One's judgment, even of one's own actions, is not definitive. "Pure," in a moral sense applied to human beings, is found only in Job and Proverbs. In the nearly identical 21:21, "hearts" is found in place of "spirits" here, suggesting that "spirits" means the mind or conscience. The point is not that we assume that all our actions are correct but that God is the ultimate examiner and arbiter of human action. The antithesis is made through sound (*darkê 'îš* // *rûḥôt YHWH*, "all one's ways" // "spirits, Yahweh"). The sounds /rk/ and /rḥ/ are contrasted. Cf. 21:2 and 1 Cor. 4:4: "I am not conscious of anything against me, but I do not thereby stand acquitted; the one who judges me is the Lord" (NAB).

[3] An imperative followed by a hypothetical clause beginning with *wāw*, "and," functions as a conditional sentence—"*If* you entrust your projects . . ." The saying completes v. 1, which said the beginning of a project ("plans") comes from a human being but its completion is from God. Here one may finish a task but must entrust it to Yahweh in order for it to endure. The verse shares vocabulary with the prayer of Ps. 90:17, "Establish (*kônĕnăh*) the work (*ma'ăśēh*) of our hands." Cf. Ps. 37:5 and 1 Pet. 5:7.

[4] Everything has a purpose in the universe, even the wicked. God created even them for punishment on "an evil day," that is, when disaster strikes (cf.

Qoh. 7:17 and Prov. 11:4). This statement (and similar ones such as Ex. 9:16 and Rom. 9:22) should not be read as a metaphysical principle, as if God made some people evil so their perdition might illustrate divine justice and contribute to the divine glory. The saying is simply an interesting way of stating that God deals with evil people. The statement is not deterministic; the wicked and the good are not permanent groups but types of conduct.

[5] Proverbs applies to everyday life the cultic formula of declaring offerings unacceptable to God (see under 11:1). Lifting up one's heart in pride, forgetting one is a fallible human being, is so profound an error that one cannot escape exposure and punishment. "Assuredly" is a guess for the uncertain Hebrew phrase "hand to hand."

[6] Loyalty and faithfulness (*ḥesed we'ĕmet*) is a venerable expression for unstinting devotion. Such conduct cancels the effects of sin. Revering Yahweh alone itself turns one from evil. In G the verse occurs after 15:27.

[7] The theme of divine acceptance continues. God's pleasure at one's way of life blesses not only oneself but creates a surrounding peace that takes away the dangerous hostility of enemies. Interior peace is not enough. Examples of how enemies reconcile as a result of God's favor are Gen. 26:26–31 (Abimelech and Isaac), Genesis 44–45 (Joseph and his brothers), and Solomon's prayer in 1 Kings 8:50: "Forgive your people their sins and all the offenses they have committed against you, and grant them compassion in the sight of their captors, so that they may have compassion on them."

[8] In this "better-than" saying a small amount of money is of greater value than a large amount amassed through evil means (cf. 15:16). The reason is that ill-gotten wealth will not last (see 10:2; 11:4) and is dangerous. Colon B is three syllables longer than colon A, which serves to accentuate the last two words in Hebrew, "without justice."

[9] The heart (= mind) is sometimes contrasted with an organ of expression such as tongue, mouth, lips, or else of locomotion such as feet or, here, stride. The thought is similar to v. 1: human beings may plan, but execution is not in their power. G places MT 16:9 after 15:28.

[10–15] Verses 10–15 are a series of six sayings on the king and his God-given authority. In ancient Near Eastern thought the king was the representative and regent of the gods, ensuring the continuance of the order established at creation. Thus, it is not surprising that the section on the king follows immediately that on Yahweh (15:33–16:9). The sayings about the king are in three pairs: The first two sayings begin with identical noun patterns (*qesem*, "divination; inspired word," and *peles*, "scale"); the next two begin, respectively, with "abomination" and "acceptance" (normally a fixed pair); and the last two are concerned with the effect on others of royal wealth and favor.

[10] Divination, which attempts to foretell the future or discover hidden knowledge by means of omens or supernatural powers, is ordinarily condemned

in the Bible. Here it is a metaphor for the special insight given to the king for the proper performance of his duties, including his judicial role. For examples of the king's judicial role, see 1 Sam. 14:1–24, especially v. 19; and 1 Kings 3:28 (the judgment of Solomon); Ps. 72:2.

The differences in the sequence of verses in G (MT 15:27–16:9) come to an end with this verse. Differences in verse sequence appear again in chaps. 17 and 20.

[11] In the ancient Near East, the belief was widespread that the gods created the universe and determined all its ways. Laws, weights, and measures were part of that determination. The king as regent of the gods was responsible for ensuring that the divinely implanted justice was observed in the conduct of business. Weights and measures were instruments in the administration of divine justice. Cf. Micah 6:11.

[12] "Abomination" ordinarily designates what is not acceptable to God. Verses 10–15 mingle sayings about the king (vv. 10, 12–15) with ones about Yahweh (v. 11), using conventional court rhetoric. The saying implies that it is in the king's interest to get rid of malefactors, for the stability of his throne depends on justice. Psalm 101 is another statement of the king's duty to remove the wicked from royal service. Cf. 25:5.

[13] The saying is linked to v. 12, for the first word of v. 12, "abomination" and the first word of v. 13, "favor," are elsewhere a fixed pair, which are ordinarily used to describe what is acceptable and not acceptable to God. This saying applies that language to the king's acceptance and nonacceptance of officials in the court.

[14] Whereas vv. 12–13 are concerned with what kings detest and oppose, vv. 14–15 are about the effects of royal wrath and favor upon courtiers. Colon A pictures the deadly effects of royal wrath. Only one thing offers protection— wisdom. Biblical examples of wisdom assuaging a king's wrath include Abigail shrewdly dissuading the future king David from killing Nabal (1 Samuel 25) and Daniel assuaging the wrath of Nebuchadnezzar (Daniel 2). The phrase "herald of death" occurs only here in the Bible. In colon A, the repetition of the consonant sequences *m-t* and *m-l* serve to connect "death" and "king's wrath": *ḥămat melek māl'ăkê māwet,* literally, "the wrath of a king angels of death." Cf. 19:2.

[15] The last in the series of six sayings on the king. In the previous verse royal wrath meant death. In this verse royal favor means life, presumably, the avoidance of a death sentence and the bestowal of position and wealth. Significantly, royal favor is compared to a powerful phenomenon not under human control—the clouds preceding the spring rains that water the first crop. It is a moment of joy and relief (Whybray). The sound of *malk,* "king," in its original monosyllabic pronunciation is echoed in *malqôš,* "spring [rain]."

[16] Traditionally, wisdom is declared more precious than gold and silver (see 3:14 and Job 28). Gold and silver can buy much, to be sure, but wisdom

paves the way for *God* to give life, wealth, and honor. Such gifts can only be given; they cannot be bought. Gold and silver thus have less value than wisdom.

[17] In the metaphorical system of the two ways, the way of the righteous is protected. Those who stay on the way save themselves from trouble. One must constantly choose to stay on the path. Colon A declares that the good way avoids trouble and colon B affirms the effort of staying on it. The saying is given unity by sibilants; in colon B, CōCēC CaCCô (C = consonant) occurs twice, giving an aphoristic tone. The verse is the exact midpoint of the book, according to the Masorah.

[18] The saying exploits the metaphor of high in the sense of proud (cf. English "haughty" from the French *haut,* "high"), and low in the sense of abased (cf. English "humble" from Latin *humilis,* "low"). To raise oneself high is the prelude to a fall. The Hebrew word for "arrogance" (*gā'ôn*) can mean "exalted" (when applied to God). This proverb is attested in English as early as 1390 C.E., in John Gower, *Confessio Amantis* I. 3062, "Pride . . . schal down falle."

[19] The phrase "humble of spirit" links the saying to "haughty spirit" in the previous verse. Sharing booty is an act of victory in war, which of itself is not a bad thing. What makes the sharing of booty bad, however, is when the group that shares it attributes the victory entirely to their own prowess. Contrasted with them are the humble, perhaps those defeated and despoiled by the self-centered victors. The proud will eventually lose their gains, whereas those who are humble win God's favor.

[20] The meaning of the saying hinges upon the interpretation of the word *dābār,* "word; affair; business," in colon A. Is it the word of God in a scriptural sense (so Delitzsch and Ehrlich) or simply an affair or business of human beings? It is preferable to take it as a person's own word, or better "affair, business." The phrase "attends to" is comparable to Ps. 41:2: "Happy the one *concerned with* the poor." The point seems to be that success and happiness depend on both God and our own efforts. Neither can be neglected. The saying simply states this truth, without exploring philosophical and theological questions arising from it. REB takes the saying as antithetical: "He who is shrewd in business will prosper, / but happy is he who puts his trust in the Lord," but the antithesis between shrewdness in business and happiness is found nowhere else.

[21] The phrase *yōsîp leqaḥ* in colon B, literally, "to increase wisdom" (see 1:5 and 9:9), has the sense of gaining wisdom or a rightful reputation for wisdom. In the fixed pair "heart" and "lips," "heart" is the organ of memory and reflection, and "lips" is the organ of verbal expression. There is strict parallelism between the cola: "wise of heart" // "pleasant of lips"; "deemed" // "gain a reputation"; "intelligent" // "wisdom." To win a reputation for wisdom, one must be both discerning and eloquent. Cf. Sir. 6:5.

[22] Intelligence benefits the one who has it (13:14). It is a fountain of life, a source of the blessings of long and healthy life, wealth, and repute. Other "fountains of life" in Proverbs are the words of the wise (10:11; 13:14) and the fear of the Lord (14:27). The second colon is difficult. Syntactically, it could mean "to educate fools is folly" (so McKane), but that translation seems too simple. Most commentators take *mûsār* not in its usual sense of "discipline, training" but of "punishment" (on the basis of 13:24 and 22:15). JPSV, for example, renders, "and folly is the punishment of fools." The ordinary meaning of *mûsār* makes sense, however. As long as perverse folly is the discipline of fools, they will remain fools and eventually bring retribution on their heads. Such faulty training is the very antithesis of "fountain of life."

[23] The verse is linked to the three preceding verses by the triliteral root *śkl,* "wise," in vv. 20 and 22. Elsewhere in the same chapter, "heart," "lips," "tongue," and "mouth" occur in proximity (vv. 1, 9–10, 21, 26–27). It is the source of the sage's powers of persuasion. Wise words come from a wise heart. Cf. Matt. 7:17: "Every good tree bears good fruit."

[24] Well chosen words are compared to sweet and delightful food. The Hebrew word conventionally translated "soul" is more literally "throat, palate." For other metaphorical uses of honey, see Ps. 19:10 and Ezek. 3:3.

[25] Identical to 14:12. See the commentary there.

[26] The subtle adage puzzled ancient versions and modern commentators. One hint of its meaning is the fixed pair *nepeš,* "gullet, throat; hunger; soul," and *peh,* "mouth," which also occurs in 13:2; 21:23; Job 7:11; and Qoh. 6:7. Qoheleth 6:7 is especially relevant (triliteral roots identical to our saying are italicized): "All the *labor* of a person is for his *mouth* (peh), but his *gullet* (soul, self; *nepeš*) is not filled," that is, one works to satisfy the basic necessities ("mouth"), but this does not satisfy the whole person. Our proverb paradoxically asserts that a person does not toil to fill the gullet but that the gullet itself "toils" in the sense that appetite forces one to work. As often in Proverbs, the source organ stands for the faculty or drive. With all the versions we omit *kî,* "for," in colon B; it is a later explanation that destroys the parallel.

[27–30] These are three sayings on three types of wicked people and their speech. Each begins with Hebrew *'îš,* "man, individual." Colon B of each states the particular damage the villain's words inflict on others. The final saying (v. 30) mentions facial mannerisms common to the malefactors. There may be progression in the three portrayals of wickedness, from thought (v. 27) to speech (v. 28) to actions harming others (v. 29). Verse 30 is linked to vv. 27–29 by reprise of words: "deceptions" from v. 28a; "lips" from v. 27b; "evil" from v. 27a. This little section is remarkably like 6:12–15 in its concern with intent, words, and facial gestures; 6:15 differs in speaking about their fate.

[27] A scoundrel conjures up evil against others, and it hangs on his lips like dangerous fire. Colon A, "to dig evil," is a unique phrase in the Bible. It may be a shortened form of the idiom "to dig a pit [so that another may fall into it]," which is found in Pss. 7:16; 57:7; 119:85; Prov. 26:27; Jer. 18:20, 22. One normally digs *something*—a well, cistern, ditch, or grave—but never evil. If the text is sound, the meaning is to plan evil (so S and T). When anyone's intent is

malicious, his words are a destructive fire. There is a play on *'îš bĕlîyaʻal,* "scoundrel," and *'ēš,* "fire."

[28] The second type of malicious person is the backbiter. Such people destroy human relationships, which are founded on affection and trust. A gossip's words are filled with insinuations that destroy trust and respect.

[29] Here "violence" (*ḥāmās*) means wronging one's neighbor. A good example of such violence is 1:8–19, where the wicked invite the young person leaving home to join them in their predatory schemes. Another biblical example is Cain, who caused Abel to walk on a way that was not good in order to kill him: "Let us *go* out to the field" (Gen. 4:8, according to the versions).

[30] The saying probably rounds off the series that began in v. 27. Proverbs constantly stresses the intimate relationship between thought and expression, heart and tongue. External behavior gives a clue to intent. Such is the point of these physiological observations. The precise nature of the facial gestures unfortunately escapes us. Cf. 6:13 and 10:10.

[31] Nature, as it were, bestows a glorious crown—the gray hair of a senior or elderly person. "Glorious crown" (*'ăṭeret tip'eret*) rhymes in Hebrew. Gray hair is a synecdoche for old age (Lev. 19:32): "You shall rise before gray hair and honor the visage of an elder." Colon B explains where the glory comes from—not from a long life as such but from a long *righteous* life. Cf. 24:5–6.

[32] Conquest of self is better than conquest of others. Self-possession is the sign of wisdom.

[33] Casting lots was a common way of making important decisions. Dice were given meanings "yes" or "no" and then cast for their answer. The designated die or dice "comes out" (*yāṣā'*) with the decision. The first king of Israel, Saul, was chosen by lot (1 Sam. 10:17–27) and the land was divided after the conquest through casting lots (Num. 26:55; Josh. 14:2). The word "lot" (*gôrāl*) can also mean destiny (Isa. 17:14; Jer. 13:25; Dan. 12:13), and at Qumran the word comes close to meaning "fate." Hebrew *ḥêq,* "fold in the garment; bosom," here is the fold of a garment or purse in which the lots were cast. Exodus 28:15–30 describes such a purse, which is traditionally translated "breastpiece of judgment" (*ḥōšen mišpāṭ*). The word rendered "judgment" (*mišpāṭ*) is the same as "decision" in our saying. The issue is similar to 16:1: We can plan something, but it is not in our power to bring it to consummation. Cf. 18:18 and 1 Sam. 14:41–42.

Proverbs 17

17:1   Better a dry crust with peace,
          than a house filled with feasting and strife.

2   A shrewd servant will rule an unworthy son,
          and will share an inheritance with the brothers.

3   A crucible proves silver and a furnace proves gold,
       and the assayer of the heart is Yahweh.

4   An evildoer heeds wicked lips;
       a liar hearkens to a destructive tongue.

5   Who ridicules a poor person contemns his Maker;
       who gloats over a wretch will not go unpunished.

6   The crown of seniors is grandchildren,
       and the glory of children is their parents.[a]

7   Fine words do not fit a knave,
       still less do lying words fit a noble.

8   A bribe seems like magic to one who holds it;
       he succeeds at every turn.

9   Who seeks friendship conceals an offense,
       but who reveals a story alienates a friend.

10   A rebuke touches a person of discernment
       more than a hundred blows touch a fool.

11   An evil person pursues rebellion
       and a ruthless envoy is sent against him.

12   Sooner meet a she-bear missing a cub
       than a fool with his folly.

13   Who returns evil for good—
       evil will not depart from his house.

14   To start a quarrel is to let water go free;
       before it breaks out let go of the dispute.

15   One who acquits the guilty and one who convicts the innocent—
       both are an abomination to Yahweh.

16   Why is this money in the hand of a fool
       to purchase wisdom when he has no mind?[b]

17   A friend is a friend at all times;
       a brother is born for a time of distress.

18   A person without sense gives his hand
       and goes surety on behalf of his neighbor.

19   Who loves an offense loves a fight;
       who makes his doorway high is asking for a collapse.

20   One twisted in heart will come to no good;
       the double-tongued will fall into trouble.

21   Who begets a fool gets grief for himself;
       no father can rejoice in a villain.

22   A joyful heart makes a happy face,
       but an anxious spirit dries up the bones.

23   From his bosom a guilty person takes out a bribe
       to pervert the course of justice.

24 On the countenance of a discerning person is wisdom,
      but the eyes of a fool are on the ends of the earth.
25 A foolish son is a vexation to his father,
      and bitterness to her who bore him.
26 To fine an innocent person is not right,
      nor to flog nobles for their justice.
27 Who knows his mind makes his words few;
      one who knows is cool in spirit.
28 Even a fool keeping silence is deemed wise;
      one shutting his mouth, intelligent.

a. G has another couplet: "The whole world of wealth belongs to the faithful person, / but not even a small coin to the faithless."

b. In G two lines, which are the same as MT 19b and 20b, immediately follow: "Who makes his house high is asking for a collapse; / who neglects instruction will fall into troubles."

[17:1] This "better-than" saying states the circumstances when a dry crust is better than a banquet. It is peace and fellowship that make a true feast, not the food. For a similar sentiment, see 15:16–17 and 16:8.

[2] Virtuous and shrewd behavior opens doors, even providing access to the privileges and wealth customarily reserved for family members. Probably presupposed in the saying is the *famulus* system, where a young man entered the household of a great house as private secretary and worked his way up. If the master's son were a scoundrel, he could lose out to a wise servant. Wisdom can transcend natural boundaries and expectations.

[3] A crucible is a container used for refining metal by separating out impurities or for testing whether there is impurity in precious metal. The process provides an analogy to God's testing human hearts as in Pss. 26:2; 66:10; Jer. 9:6. The verb *bāḥan,* "to assay," can refer to proving metal, as in Zech. 13:9 (identical roots to the saying are italicized): "I will *refine* (*ṣārap,* the root appears in "crucible") them as one refines *silver,* and I will *test* (*bāḥan*) them as one assays *gold.*" Proverbs 27:21a is identical to colon A. See also Job 23:10 and 1 Pet. 1:7.

[4] A common theme in Proverbs is that fools' words are destructive. This saying shifts the perspective: those who take in evil words themselves become evil. Using the figure of abstract for concrete, Hebrew *šeqer,* "lie," is "liar," as in 12:27, "sloth" for "slothful person."

[5] The dignity of each human being comes from being created by God. Contempt toward anyone insults the person's maker. The example of a poor person, the type perhaps least likely to gain respect, is used to dramatize the point. Every human being, irrespective of wealth, is worthy of respect. Cf. 14:31.

[6] Prov. 16:31 declares a corona of gray hair to be a glorious crown (*'ăṭeret* *tip'eret*). The stereotyped phrase "glorious crown" is broken up in this saying. The crown (*'ăṭeret*) of elders is their offspring, children and grandchildren. Colon B reverses the sentiment—the glory (*tip'eret*) of children is their parents. This is one in the series of sayings on household and family.

[7] Heart (= mind) and lips (or tongue or mouth) are related as source and verbal expression. Noble words cannot have as their source a foolish heart, nor can foolish words issue from a noble heart. Cf. Matt. 7:17: "Every good tree bears good fruit, and a bad tree bears bad fruit" (see also Matt. 12:33 and Luke 6:43–44). The sounds of *l-n* are prominent: *l' n'wh lnbl . . . lndyb,* "not fitting to a knave . . . to a noble."

[8] This verse offers an observation on the attitude of a bribe-giver. A bribe gives its user a feeling of power. Biblical law forbade bribery in certain cases, but gift-giving to curry favor was and still is in many places an accepted means of dealing with government. The phrase *'eben ḥēn,* literally, "stone of favor," is unique in the Bible. Ehrlich believes the verse is about the *receiver* of the bribe (so also T), but most commentators rightly take it as referring to the giver of the bribe. Like other observations on money, this one is ostensibly neutral. It suggests, however, that proffering a bribe makes one feel important (the Hebrew in colon A is, literally, "in the eyes of its possessor") and that the inflated feeling is a delusion. Cf. 18:16.

[9] In this memorable paradox on love and friendship, one finds love by losing and loses love by finding or revealing. Love has a price—bearing with the other person. The nuance of the verb in colon B, literally, "to repeat by (or with) a word (or story)," is unclear. Antithetic parallelism suggests the meaning "to reveal," that is, repeating a word better left unsaid. One loses by uncovering something. In 10:12 love also "covers" a multitude of offenses.

[10] The wise learn from mere hints, whereas fools do not learn even from many blows. G and S, and some modern translations, are troubled by the initial verb *tēḥat,* which is best parsed as third-person singular qal of *nāḥēt,* "to go down, descend, fall." A relevant usage is Ps. 38:3b: "your hand has fallen upon me." Ehrlich suggests there was a confusion between the consonants *'aleph* and *tāw.* The original reading was *'aḥat,* "one" (= one rebuke versus one hundred blows). Nowhere else in the Bible, however, are "one" and "one hundred" paired in this way. Comparison is expressed elliptically here as in Job 28:18; Ps. 4:8; Qoh. 4:17; 9:17.

[11] The Hebrew verb in colon A, "to pursue," connotes great energy (usually with evil as its object). The Hebrew intensive adverb *'ak* underscores the energy. Ironically, those engaged in such a pursuit will attain what they so vehemently chase after—in the form of an unrelenting emissary sent to them. The passive verb is an indirect way of expressing divine activity or "the way things happen." The occurrence of the vowel /ī/ in the middle of each colon underscores the parallelism.

[12] Hyperbole is used here for humorous effect. Bears were regarded as exceedingly dangerous and as instruments of Yahweh's wrath (e.g., 2 Kings 2:23–24, where bears attack and kill the children ridiculing Elisha). A dangerous animal in a state of rage poses less danger than a fool.

[13] Returning evil for good ensures that the evil will remain within one's own house. The paradox is that inflicting evil upon another does not get rid of it but ensures it will stay with the perpetrator.

[14] The breaking out of a quarrel is compared to opening a sluice. The water rushes forth, following its own course, unable to go back. There is a remedy—keep the sluice closed, abandon the quarrel before it breaks out. The metaphor of water may be grounded in the disputes about water that must have been common in arid Palestine.

[15] The language is that of the law court and the perspective is theocentric. The malice is the violation of divine order rather than a particular injustice done to plaintiff or defendant. For "abomination" see 11:1. Sound unifies colon A: *maṣdîq rāšā' ûmaršîa' ṣaddîq*.

[16] To acquire (*qānāh*) wisdom is a common exhortation in Proverbs (4:5 and elsewhere). The verb *qānāh* can also mean "to purchase." Fools misunderstand the metaphorical exhortation, taking it literally of buying it with money. The very misunderstanding shows they have no "heart" (= mind). Without a mind, they have no place to store what they have bought.

[17] Constancy and loyalty are the marks of both friend and kin. Conceivably, colon B could be antithetical to colon A, but it is more likely synonymous, for the phrase "at all times" (= continually) is a nice contrast to a particular point—the time of adversity. The saying does not identify true love with family relationships as such but, more generally, with constancy in difficult times. Cf. 18:24 and Sir. 37:5.

[18] One of a series of sayings on the folly of providing surety. Proverbs is unequivocally opposed to the practice, stating its opposition in plain language. The obligation undermines the personal freedom that Proverbs prizes. Cf. 6:1–5 and 22:26–27.

[19] The consequences of two actions are compared, "loving an offense" and "raising the height of one's doorway." The Hebrew verb *'ōhēb*, "one who loves," in colon A means "cling to," probably in the sense of harping on. The noun *peša'*, "transgression," in colon A has the same meaning it has in v. 9, "offense" rather than "sin." To paraphrase, whoever dwells on an offense is asking for the quarrel that inevitably follows an unforgiven slight.

What does the metaphor of building found in colon B contribute to the saying? Isaiah 30:13 gives a hint (roots identical to those in our saying are italicized): "This iniquity shall be in you like a spreading breach in a *high* wall; all of a sudden its *collapse* will come." The point of the saying is that harping on a fault risks an eruption like that from a poorly constructed wall.

[20] The fixed pair "heart" and "tongue" stands, by metonymy, for someone reflecting and speaking. Crooked or twisted means perverted, not straightforward. If one does not go straight ahead, one will never attain a good goal.

[21] The stress is on the private grief of the father of a foolish son.

[22] Proverbs has many maxims on the relation of the inner life (often symbolized by heart or spirit) to the exterior self (e.g., 14:10, 13, 30; 15:13, 30; 16:24; 18:14). In colon A the word "face" (*gēhāh*) is uncertain, though parallelism with "bone" suggests it is a part of the body. S and T take it as "body," which is probably correct, though too general. Cf. 12:25 and 15:13.

[23] This verse makes an observation on a use of wealth — bribery (see also v. 8). There is a dramatic contrast between the sly withdrawing of the bribe money from the garment of the guilty person and the abrupt statement of the intent in colon B, "to pervert the course of justice." Gift-giving itself is not condemned, for in many societies it is a form of politeness. It is only evil when it perverts justice. Cf. 21:14.

[24] In this contrast of two parts of the body (face and eyes) and of two types (a wise and a foolish person), wisdom is visible in the countenance, that is, the mouth, lips, and tongue (= word) of the wise person. Wise words come from a wise heart. Fools have no such source of wisdom close at hand. Their distance from the source of wisdom is nicely captured by their eye gazing on the distant horizon. This may be a reference to wisdom that is thought to be distant and inaccessible but is actually close at hand, as in Deut. 30:11–15: "This commandment that I am commanding you today is not too difficult for you, nor is it too far away. . . . No, the word is very near to you; it is in your mouth and in your heart for you to observe." The polarities are boldly emphasized by sound patterns: *pěnê* // *ênê,* ("countenance" // "eyes"), *mēbîn* // *kěsîl* ("discerning person" // "fool").

[25] This verse is one in the series on the household. Here the focus is on the anguish caused to parents by adult children. As in other sayings on foolish offspring (the nearest being v. 21), the emphasis is on the suffering borne by the parents. For similar sentiments, see 10:1; 19:13; 29:15; Sir. 16:1–3.

[26] The maxim is uncertain. Consonantal MT is supported by the ancient versions. The parallels in the Hebrew text are "to fine" // "to flog", and "innocent person" // "noble persons." One expects the third parallel to be "not right" and the unclear phrase *'al yōšer,* "against uprightness (?)." Ehrlich suggests an *a fortiori* argument: Even to fine an innocent person is not right, so how much more to beat nobles. The Hebrew also permits the translations, "to flog a noble in his integrity," or "to flog those generous to the poor." It is best to assume the saying is about the legal system, and it has the same sense as 17:15: It is wrong to inflict any punishment on an innocent person, and even more wrong to flog such a one.

[27] Modern translations differ on identifying subject and predicate. NRSV: "[subject] One who spares words [predicate] is knowledgeable; // [subject] one who is cool in spirit [predicate] has understanding." JPSV has the opposite: "A knowledgeable man is sparing with his words; / A man of understanding is reticent." In colon A, "Who knows his mind" (lit., "one who knows the knowledge"), "knowledge" is not general but the contents of the mind of the knower. Colon A means that those who know their own mind use few words; what is in their heart is clear and does not require a flood of words. In the synonymous parallelism of colon B, "one who knows" (lit., "a person of learning") again refers to specific rather than general knowledge—what is on one's mind. "Cool in spirit" is unique in the Hebrew Bible but the metaphor "cool" in Egyptian instructions means "restrained." One who uses few words shows clarity of mind. Garrulousness shows one does not know what is in one's mind. Cf. 10:19 and Sir. 20:6–8.

[**28**] If few words betoken a wise person (v. 27), total silence can make even a fool appear wise. Words reveal the heart. By their silence, fools can at least temporarily delay the discovery of their perverted heart. In 15:2 fools are said to pour out words.

Proverbs 18

18:1   An estranged person seeks his own will,ᵃ
           rails against wisdom.
2   A fool takes no delight in learning,
           but only in broadcasting his views.
3   When wickedness comes, contempt comes too,
           and with ignominy, reproach.
4   The words of a person's mouth are deep waters,
           a flowing brook, a fountain of wisdom.
5   Lifting the face of a guilty person is not right;
           nor is depriving an innocent person of justice.
6   The lips of a fool walk into a fight,
           and his mouth invites blows.
7   The mouth of a fool is his own destruction,
           and his lips are a trap to himself.
8   The words of a slanderer are like delicious morsels;ᵇ
           they go down to the pit of the stomach.
9   One slack in his work
           is kin to a vandal.
10   The name of Yahweh is a strong tower:
           a righteous person runs to it and is safe.
11   A rich person's wealth is a fortified city for him,
           like a high wall in his estimate.

12   Before a fall, one's heart is haughty;
          before glory, lowliness.
13   Who gives an answer before hearing
          is a fool incurring disgrace.
14   One's spirit sustains one when ill,
          but when the spirit is broken who can raise it?
15   The heart of a sage acquires knowledge,
          the ears of the wise seek knowledge.
16   A person's gift makes room for him;
          it leads him before the great.
17   The first speaker in a trial seems in the right;
          then his opponent comes and cross-examines him.
18   The lot puts an end to quarrels,
          and keeps powerful adversaries apart.
19   A brother offended[c] is more unyielding than a fortified city;
          such quarrels are more daunting than castle gates.
20   With the fruit of one's mouth one's belly is filled;
          with the produce of one's lips one is sated.
21   Death and life are in the power of the tongue;
          those who choose one shall eat its fruit.
22   Who finds a wife finds a great thing,
          and enjoys the favor of Yahweh.[d]
23   A poor person must say "please,"
          but a wealthy person can be rude.
24   There are[e] friends who spend time with you,
          and there is a friend who is closer than a brother.

a. G and V read *tō'ănāh*, "pretext," for MT *ta'ăwāh*, "desire," evidently following *biqqēš tō'ănāh*, "to seek a pretext," in Judg. 14:4: "the estranged person seeks a pretext." Despite some uncertainties, MT makes reasonable sense.

b. Each of the versions interpret in a different way the rare word in colon A, *mtlh-mym*, "delicious morsels," which occurs only here and in the identical 26:22. T and V take the word as "insidious," and S, as "slothful." In colon B, "stomach" is taken as "Sheol" by T and S. G does not render MT, having in its place a version of 19:15: "Fear overthrows the effeminate man, / and the soul of the sluggard goes hungry."

c. G, followed by S, V, and T, seems to have read not MT *npš'* but *nwš'* ("to be helped, saved"): *'ah nwš' kqr't 'z wmrwm* [d/r confusion in *mdwnym*]: "A brother helped by a brother is like a city strong and high." G is unlikely, however, as is shown by the need to supply "by a brother" and the resulting unsatisfactory parallel with colon B. We read MT as simply as possible, only emending *miqqiryat* to *kĕqiryat*.

d. G has a couplet not in MT: "Who sends away a good wife, sends away goods; / but who keeps an adulteress is stupid and impious."

e. S and T read *yēš*, "there is/are," for MT *'îš*, "man, person," which gives excellent sense. The same confusion is found in 2 Sam. 14:19 and Micah 6:10 (Toy).

[18:1] The aphorism is uncertain because of the uncertainty of the words here translated "estranged" and "rails against." Those who follow their own will (*t'wh*) rail against wisdom (*twšyh*). The Hebrew wordplay is partially caught by English "<u>wi</u>ll" and "<u>wi</u>sdom." Hebrew *tûšîyāh*, "wisdom," according to M. Fox, "denotes clear, proficient thinking in the exercise of power and practical operations, as distinct from thinking as an intellectual act."[1] The point is that excessive devotion to one's own ideas is an obstacle to prudent decision making. The parallelism is synonymous. Colon A: Extreme devotion to one's own ideas characterizes an antisocial person; colon B: such people contemn the clear thinking that leads to wise action. One cannot become wise by isolating oneself.

[2] The verbs in vv. 1b and 2b sound alike (*yitgallā'*, "rails at" and *hitgallôt*, "broadcasting"), and the verses may have been juxtaposed for that reason. Fools take no pleasure in the wisdom of others but only in telling others their own "wisdom." As in v. 1, fools are smug and self-centered, not open to others. Two /ō/ sounds open and close the saying.

[3] The first attitude named in each colon has an inevitable but unwelcome companion—disrespect. The parallel nouns *bûz*, "contempt," and *ḥerpāh*, "reproach," are also parallel in Ps. 119:22. Evil conduct leads to loss of reputation. Such a loss would be especially painful in ancient Mediterranean culture, which placed a high value on honor.

[4] The best explanation of this enigmatic saying is 20:5: "A plan in the human heart is deep waters, / but an intelligent person draws it up." Deep waters lie hidden until revealed by words. Colon A of our verse describes the deep thought that has been expressed in words. Colon B is more problematic. It has two phrases, "a flowing brook," and "a fountain of wisdom." Some interpreters make it a nominal sentence, "but the source of wisdom is a flowing stream" (NRSV, Whybray), but this does not go well with colon A. With Toy, McKane, and JPSV, we take the two phrases of colon B to be in apposition to "deep waters" in colon A, that is, words express a person's thoughts, bringing them to the surface. Those words in turn become a source of wisdom to others.

[5] The saying assesses the acts of judges in court cases. Lifting the suppliant's bowed head is a gesture of pardon; thrusting an accused person away is a gesture of rejection or finding guilty. To perform these gestures inappropriately, that is, to declare the innocent guilty or the guilty innocent, is a profound violation of good order. It is "not good," a phrase used seven times in Proverbs to characterize such profound breaches of order. See 17:15, 26.

[6] The bold personification of lips and mouth recalls Ps. 73:9: "[The wicked] set their mouth against heaven, and their tongue strides through the earth." There are antecedents in the Ugaritic texts of ca. 1400 B.C.E.: "one lip

1. "Words for Wisdom," *ZAH* 6 (1993): 167.

against the earth, one lip against the heavens, the tongue against the stars" (*KTU* 1.5.II.2–3 and cf. 1.23.61–62). Words, especially provocative words, are so powerful that they can lead a person into trouble, almost as if one's lips had a life of their own. Similarly concrete is the modern maxim, "Don't let your lips get you into a place where your feet can't get you out."

[7] Verse 7 is linked to v. 6 by its use (in reversed order) of the fixed pair "mouth" and "lips." Normally, Proverbs is concerned with the damage that foolish words do to others, but in vv. 6–7 the accent is on the damage done to the speaker.

[8] Slanderous gossip is likened to delicious food, which is anticipated with pleasure and devoured with gusto, and goes down to the innermost stomach. Slander is eagerly heard and printed indelibly in the memory. The word for "delicious morsels" is attested only here and in the identical 26:22; its meaning is derived from context and from an Arabic cognate, "to devour greedily."

[9] Failure to work with care and commitment is judged equivalent to destroying. In one sense, it matters little whether a task or product is destroyed by enemies from without or ruined by the carelessness of its maker. The saying probably belongs to the series on the sluggard. Colon A is united by two three-syllable words beginning in /m/. Colon B has /ḥ/ in the opening and closing syllables.

[10] This and the next saying are about strength and security, which can be true (v. 10) or false (v. 11). The adjective '*ōz*, "strong," and verb *niśgab*, "to be safe, raised on high," occur in both verses. This is the only occurrence of the phrase "name of Yahweh" in Proverbs, which occurs frequently elsewhere in the Bible. For Yahweh as a tower of strength, see Ps. 61:4. An illustration of the adage is Judg. 9:51 (words identical to our saying are italicized): "But there was *a strong tower* in the city, and all the men and women fled to it."

[11] The juxtaposition of v. 10 implies that "the strong citadel" here is much less secure than "the strong tower" of v. 10. Colon B, though textually uncertain, suggests that the wealthy person is deluded in the confidence placed in the fortress ("in his estimate"). Proverbs 10:15a is identical to colon A but occurs in a quite different context.

[12] The metaphors of high and low are used for pride and humility in both Hebrew and English. What is high can fall and what is low can be raised up. "Before" is temporal but with a causal nuance. "Lowliness" implies loyal and difficult service, as in Ps. 132:1: "Remember, O Yahweh, to David's credit his lowly service." Exalting oneself is a prelude to humiliation, whereas being low (humble) is a prelude to being raised up. Honor is given, not taken. One can, however, prepare to receive it by humility, probably in the sense of self-effacing service. Colon A has a variant in 16:18a, and colon B is identical to 15:33b.

[13] Much of Proverbs' teaching on words presumes they are uttered in dialogue with another person. To cut off dialogue by a premature reply is to show

oneself a fool and bring shame on oneself (see 10:14 and Sir. 11:8). The sounds in colon A provide unity: *m-š* in the first word is reversed in the last word *š-m,* and the consonantal sequence *b-r* recurs in the two middle words.

[14] Hebrew *rûaḥ,* basically "air [in motion]," has a range of meanings: life-breath (and by metonymy its source within the body), wind, and spirit (of God or of human beings). The aphorism seems to be a paradox. Colon A states that a stream of air—invisible and slight—is nonetheless strong enough to defend against life-threatening illness. But if that thin column of air, which carries life through the body, is broken, nothing can replace it. Human life hangs by a thread.

[15] Ehrlich and REB take the verse as antithetical: Some people have an innate gift for knowing, whereas others have to seek out knowledge from their peers. There is no antithesis, however. The wise store knowledge in their hearts without lessening their desire to acquire more. Proverbs views the heart as the storehouse of observations (from ear and eyes) and the organ of decision.

[16] In this observation, the money is probably not a bribe as in 17:23 but simply a gift, which in ancient Near Eastern culture was given to render others appreciative and benevolent. Such generous (and shrewd) behavior makes one successful in life. The verse may imply that such access, purchased by a discreet gift, is worth less than access gained by virtue or talent.

[17] Hearers enthralled by a good speech in court can easily forget that they have heard only one side of the argument. More information is needed before a verdict can be reached. When the other party speaks in refutation, people realize they have heard only one side. The experience at court offers a lesson to all who make judgments about others. Truth appears gradually; one must listen to all sides. The old Latin axiom is relevant: *audiatur et altera pars,* "Let the other side be heard too." Protagoras in the fifth century B.C.E. said, "There are two sides to every question."[2]

[18] One throw of a tiny die has the power to keep violence at bay. As in v. 16 with a gift, a seemingly insignificant thing—in this verse, dice—is more effective than great force. Perhaps the implication is that human wrath is not of enormous significance if it can be allayed by the cast of dice. "Apart" in colon B is used as in 2 Kings 2:11, "to keep two people apart," in this case two potential combatants. Another intriguing observation on the power of the lot is 16:33.

[19] Fraternal and familial love and loyalty is a precious thing, but such love, once offended, can be the cause of bitter and undying enmity. An offended relative is compared to the fortified upper city, which was its most impregnable part. Family feuds are the bitterest conflicts and civil wars are the bloodiest wars. G, followed more or less by the versions, has a diametrically opposite reading (the additions of G are italicized): "A brother *helped by a brother* is like

---

2. Diogenes Laertius, *Lives of Eminent Philosophers,* Book 9, section 51.

a strong and *lofty* city; it is strong like a well-founded palace." See the textual notes for the argument that MT is superior.

[20] Colon A plays on the idiom "to eat from (or be sated with) the fruit of a tree," as in Gen. 3:2 and Ps. 104:13. Here the fruit is metaphorical—one's words. Speaking is the most expressive human activity. Fruit from the ground provides sustenance to the body, but the "fruit of one's lips" (words) also affects one's well-being. If one's words are right, then one is blessed, one's belly is filled. If one's words are wicked, one will eat the fruit of those and suffer the evil consequences. The phrase "fruit of one's mouth" also occurs in 12:14a and 13:2a. The theme continues in the following verse.

[21] The meaning, but not the translation, is disputed. Both NRSV and JPSV, for example, translate similarly: "Death and life are in the power of the tongue; / those who love it will eat its fruit." Interpretations vary widely: those who are judicious in speech will reap the reward of their wisdom (McKane); "those who love the tongue" (= those who rattle on) must face the consequences of their loquacity (Whybray). Any solution must first resolve the syntactical difficulty in MT colon B, literally, "those who love *her* (feminine singular suffix) *he* (masculine singular) will eat *her* fruit." The plural subject of a singular verb is best explained as a distributive: "(each) will eat." The real problem is the antecedent of the object suffixes (feminine singular *hā*, "her"). Strict syntax suggests that "tongue" is the antecedent, for it is the only feminine singular noun in colon A. Ehrlich takes it that whoever "loves" the tongue, in the sense of making good use of it, will experience the results of using it. So also REB: "Make friends with it and enjoy its fruits." Meinhold too takes "tongue" as the object ("Life and death are in the power of the tongue, / and all who love it—each eats its fruit.").

But is "tongue" the object of "love"? In Proverbs, one does not love the tongue (= words), but rather wisdom or discipline. The best solution is to take "to love" (*'ahab*) in colon A in its meaning "to choose" as in 12:1; 20:13; 29:3. In Deut. 4:37; 10:15; and Isa. 41:8 the verb *'ahab* is semantically parallel to *bāḥar*, "to choose." Elsewhere, "to love" can be in antithetic parallelism to *śānā'*, "to hate = reject." In this interpretation, the feminine suffixes in colon B have as their antecedents in colon A not "tongue" but rather "death" (masculine) and "life" (abstract plural). A feminine suffix is versatile; it can refer to the verbal idea in a preceding sentence ("it"), or to the plural of things (e.g., 2 Kings 13:2, 6, 11; 10:26; see GKC §135p). Here the suffix refers to both—"death" and "life."

Death and life face the human person, as in the sermon of Deut. 30:15–20: "See, I set before you this day life and prosperity, death and adversity. . . . Therefore choose life." The meaning is that death and life are in the power of the tongue in the sense that people will experience one or the other depending on the quality of their words. Words are the most expressive human product (cf. 12:14; 13:2; 18:20). Colon B is in synthetic parallelism to colon A: You will eat the fruit of your choice.

[22] "To find a good" is an idiom for prospering or being lucky as in 16:20; 17:20; and 19:8. To find a spouse is a great thing in a person's life and it is also a gift of God. The human and the divine work stand side by side, and the author does not attempt to relate or explain them. Colon A repeats the verb, creating a refrain *māṣā' 'iššāh māṣā' ṭôb*.

[23] Like other observations about poverty (10:15; 13:8, 23; 14:20; 19:4, 7; 28:15), the verse simply states the situation of the poor, their powerlessness and their need to ingratiate themselves with others. The wealthy, in contrast, speak as they please. The Hebrew consonant *'ayin* begins all three words in colon B.

[24] Like many other observations, this verse simply records a fact—many friends (plural) are quite happy to socialize. How different is their company from the love of the friend (singular) who does not walk away in adversity. The sixfold repeated /ē/ sound unites the whole.

Proverbs 19

19:1   Better a poor person walking in his integrity
       than one walking on a crooked way though he is rich.[a]

2   Without wisdom the appetite is misguided,
       rushing feet never reach their goal.

3   A person's folly ruins his life,
       but his heart rages against Yahweh.

4   Wealth adds many friends,
       but a poor person loses his last friend.

5   A lying witness will not be acquitted,
       and a spouter of lies will not go free.

6   Many seek the favor of a prince,
       and everybody is a friend to a gift-giver.

7   All the kin of a poor person spurn him;
       even more do his friends keep their distance.[b]
       [Whoever pursues words—they are not these.][c]

8   Whoever acquires wisdom benefits himself;
       whoever safeguards insight enjoys prosperity.

9   A lying witness will not be acquitted;
       a spouter of lies will perish.

10   Luxury is unseemly for a fool;
       even more a servant ruling princes.

11   A person's shrewdness curbs his anger,
       and his honor makes him overlook an offense.

12   The wrath of a king is like the growling of a lion,
       but his favor is like dew on the grass.

13   A foolish son is a disaster to his father,
        and a quarrelsome wife is unending dripping of water.

14   House and wealth are inherited from parents,
        but a capable wife is from Yahweh.

15   Laziness brings on deep sleep,
        and an indolent person goes hungry.

16   Who keeps a command keeps his own soul,
        but who disregards his ways will lose his life.

17   Who shows favor to the poor lends to Yahweh
        who will pay back his gift in full.

18   Correct your son while there is hope;
        do not be intent on killing him.

19   An angry person carries around punishment;
        if you effect one rescue, you'll need to again.

20   Listen to advice and take in instruction
        that you may be wise in later life.

21   Many are the plans of the human heart,
        but the intent of Yahweh will come to pass.

22   What is desired of a person is his fidelity;
        better to be poor than perjure oneself.

23   Revering Yahweh leads to life:
        one sleeps in contentment, free from danger.[d]

24   A sluggard buries his hand in a bowl,
        not lifting it to his mouth.

25   Beat a scoffer and the untutored learn a lesson;
        reprove a sage and he understands.

26   One who plunders a father and evicts a mother
        is a son acting dishonorably and causing disgrace.

27   My son, stop attending to correction;
        start straying from wise words.

28   A malicious witness mocks justice,
        the mouth of the wicked gulps down evil.

29   Punishments are readied for scoffers;
        blows for the backs of fools.

a. MT colon B, literally, "than one of perverted lips though he is a fool," is unsatisfactory. It abandons the metaphor of path that was introduced in colon A, shifts the antithesis from poor and rich to poor and foolish, and is banal in declaring a person of integrity better than a fool. A clue to the original meaning is 28:6, which is identical except that it has "though he is rich" rather than "though he is a fool." MT of 19:1 is supported only by V. S and T have "way" and S also has "rich person." There is ample basis for emendation.

b. In G two sayings immediately follow: "A good understanding will draw near to those who know it, / and a wise man will find it. One who does many evil deeds brings evil to fulfillment, / and who uses words to provoke will not escape."

c. A corrupt half-verse, which the Masoretes left incomplete, though they pointed it.

d. G colon B: "but the person without fear [of the Lord] will spend the night in places where knowledge (*dēaʻ* for Hebrew *rāʻ*, from d/r confusion) is not observed." We take *śābēʻ yālîn* as the concrete illustration of "life" in colon A. The second line seems overloaded; *yālîn* is probably an ancient variant for *śābēʻ*.

[**19:1**] This is a "better-than" saying on rich and poor people. As emended (see textual notes), the familiar biblical metaphors of life as a path and straight and crooked as moral terms are employed to state that a poor person of integrity is better than a wealthy reprobate. Wealth is not a criterion for judging moral worth.

[**2**] The antithesis is between the "soul" (lit., "throat"), which is, by metonymy, "appetite," and feet, which are, by metonymy, physical movement. Throat (soul) and feet evidently represent the inner and the outer side (or the thinking and acting side) of a human being. Without wisdom, neither plan nor action attain their goal.

[**3**] One's own perverse folly destroys one's life. It is a mark of that perversity that one blames Yahweh rather than oneself.

[**4**] In this observation on the effects of poverty and wealth on friendship the contrasts are dramatic: adding and losing, many friends and one friend, rich and poor. The repetition of /ō/ and /ī/ unites colon A, and the repetition of /ē/ unites colon B.

[**5**] The law court is a frequent topic in Proverbs. Some phrases are frequent: "spouter of lies" occurs in 6:19; 14:5, 25; 19:9̇ and here; "will not go free" in 6:29; 11:21; 16:5; 17:5; 19:9; 28:20. The legal process, which the wicked subvert by their lying testimony, will itself convict them, in accord with poetic justice. The verbs of both cola can have a legal meaning. The verb in colon B has a legal nuance in Job 22:30.

[**6**] Like v. 4, this is an observation on wealth and its effects. People make much of the rich and famous. The saying implies that the attention given to the wealthy comes from self-interest. It is thus a critique of wealth.

[**7**] The third observation of the chapter (the others are vv. 4 and 6), not without sympathy, on the poor. If even the blood relatives of the poor avoid them, no wonder that a friend (singular!) keeps away.

[**8**] Wisdom is the great means to happiness and prosperity. One should acquire it in preference to silver and gold (2:2–4). The acquisition of wisdom is the greatest benefit one can obtain for oneself. It is true self-interest, for with wisdom come all other gifts (3:13–20). To preserve and guard that wisdom is prosperity, literally "to find good," as in 16:20; 17:20; 18:22. For an explanation of *limṣōʼ* in colon B as an infinitive construct, see GKC §114i.

[**9**] A variant of v. 5. See under that verse for related sayings. Perjurers who

try to convict others will themselves be convicted, and those who seek to destroy others by legal means will be destroyed by the same means. The justice system will recoil upon those who abuse it.

[10] Fools do not deserve great prosperity, for such luxury is properly the fruit of wisdom and wise behavior. Even more unfitting is when servants give orders to rulers. It is abhorrent that slaves should rule a household. Cf. 30:21–23.

[11] Proverbs commonly recommends patience and the avoidance of quarrels. It is contrary to self-interest to lose one's temper, for quarrels lead to loss. Colon B suggests, paradoxically, that one gains glory by giving up a common means of protecting it—argument.

[12] This is an observation on royal power. A lion growling evokes fear for one's life and so does the king's anger. Equally powerful is the king's favor. As Whybray points out, dew is a gift of God that can be withheld or given (Deut. 33:28; 1 Kings 17:1; Hos. 14:9; Hag. 1:10; Zech. 8:12). Both images suggest that royal attitudes and judgments are beyond the control of the king's subjects. Be forewarned! Colon A is a variant of 20:2a and colon B is a variant of 16:15b.

[13] One in the series of sayings about family happiness, here from the male point of view. The reader might expect in colon B a parallel phrase such as "a pain to his mother," but instead there is mentioned the other main source of potential domestic misery for a man, an unsuitable wife. Domestic unhappiness is aptly and humorously expressed by that most discomforting occurrence—a steadily dripping roof on a dark and rainy day. A positive view of the wife follows immediately in v. 14, perhaps to balance this negative comment.

[14] Juxtaposed to the preceding maxim on a contentious wife, the saying affirms that a capable wife is a gift of God. Parents can give their house and their wealth to their children. Far greater than these is a capable spouse, who is a gift of God.

[15] Sleep characterizes the lazy (6:4–11; 10:5; 20:13; 24:33–34). The Hebrew word *tardēmāh* usually refers to the "deep sleep" that comes through the agency of God (Gen. 2:21; 15:12; Job 4:13; 33:15; 1 Sam. 26:12). The usage may be mock-heroic. By a paradox, laziness, and not industry, brings deep sleep. Laziness means no crops (20:4; cf. 10:4).

[16] A play on the aspects of *šāmar*, "to keep," in the sense of obeying and of safeguarding or preserving. Keeping the command of a legitimate authority benefits the doer, and inattention to one's behavior hurts a person. Whybray suggests that the commands are those of the teacher in chaps. 1–9 as in 4:4 and 7:2. Obeying legitimate commands is a good thing (10:8a and 13:13). Colon B is antithetical, though "but" (*w*) has fallen out of MT through haplography as the versions show. JPSV catches the antithesis: "He who has regard for his life pays regard to commandments; / He who is heedless of his ways will die." Respect for legitimate authority benefits oneself.

[17] Like 14:31 and 17:5, the saying shows warm sympathy for the poor, to whom God is committed. Gifts given to the poor are considered as a loan to Yahweh, who will repay them in full.

[18] The first of three sayings (vv. 18–20) on youthful receptivity to the wisdom of elders. In colon A the word *kî* can be understood as causal ("because") or temporal ("while"). As in 23:13–14, the pain involved in disciplining the young is slight compared to the fatal danger of not disciplining them. The chief motive for correcting the young is their potential for change. Revenge and punishment are thus excluded as motives for correcting them.

[19] The saying is somewhat obscure, in particular the relation of the two cola to each other and the meaning of the particles introducing colon B. Colon A states that the *persistently* angry person (such is the nuance of *gĕdāl ḥēmāh,* the qere reading) "carries a penalty," a unique phrase that may suggest that someone is a "walking invitation" for punishment. There is no way to protect someone dominated by anger. Efforts to help such people out of their self-created difficulties generally do not succeed. No matter how often aid is provided, the person will get into a fresh scrape.

[20] This is the last of the three verses (vv. 18–20) on respect for traditional wisdom. Like v. 18, it is an admonition. Acting wisely presumes extensive listening. For *'aḥărît* as a stage of human life, Delitzsch adduces Job 8:7: "and though your early days were insignificant, your *latter days* will be very great." Cf. 23:22–23: "Obey your father who begot you; do not despise your mother when she grows old. / Buy truth and do not barter away / wisdom, discipline, and intelligence!" The way to a wise old age is to be a receptive and open youth. Be receptive in youth and be a teacher in old age.

[21] Human beings may make plans, but God's intent will prevail. The point is made by antitheses: Yahweh versus human beings, many human plans versus a single divine intent, a nominal sentence in colon A versus a verb plus emphatic pronoun in colon B. For similar sentiments, see 16:1.

[22] The consonantal Hebrew text seems sound (though G reflects some alteration). The proverb has been read in two quite different ways. (1) "Desire (= greed) is a shame to a person." This interpretation takes *ḥesed* not as the common word for "kindness, loyalty," but as the rare word found only in Lev. 20:17 and Prov. 14:34: "shame, reproach." (2) "What is desired in a person is fidelity (or kindness), / and a poor person is better than a liar" (so Rashi and Kimchi). The second interpretation is preferable. *Ḥesed* is used in its covenantal and contractual sense of "fidelity, loyalty." "Liars" in colon B means perjurers, as often in Proverbs (6:19; 14:5, 25; 19:9; 21:28), that is, those who violate an oath sworn before God, presumably for a bribe. There is a play on the word "desire." One's desire should not be money but fidelity in fulfilling one's responsibility. Better to forego money than to perjure oneself in court.

[23] Revering Yahweh is a source of life (see 14:27a). Colon B expresses this concretely as having enough food and sleeping soundly because the dangers of the night have been taken away. Cf. 6:22.

[24] A humorous description of a type that Proverbs laughs at—the lazy person. Lifting one's hand to one's mouth is an idiom for eating. See Judg. 7:6 and 1 Sam. 14:26, though the Hebrew verbs are different. Sluggards barely have the energy to feed themselves. Nearly identical is 26:15.

[25] The contrasts are striking—to beat and to rebuke; the inability of the scoffer to learn even from a beating and the ability of the intelligent person to learn from the slightest gesture. The latter point is wittily and subtly made in colon A: even a naive onlooker learns the lesson a scoffer being beaten does not.

[26] The subject of the two participles in colon A is not named until colon B. One would expect the author of such a heinous crime to be a stranger to the family—a tax agent or robber. But it is someone within the family! A son who disgraces his family equivalently plunders his father's wealth and expels his mother from the home. The parents and their house are ruined. Some commentators suggest a specific setting: a son evicting parents unable to keep up the ancestral property. Such specificity misses the point of the metaphor, however. Children's shameful conduct ruins the house, personified in the parents. The saying belongs in the series about the household and the dangers to it. Delitzsch proposes that this verse begins the fourth part of the Solomonic collection.

[27] Ancient and modern translations are troubled by the verse. G reflects *šāmar,* "to guard," instead of MT *šāmaʻ,* "to hear," but this is an instance of G altering a difficult word by changing the triliteral root. The other versions read the consonants of MT, though V has a different interpretation. S and T take the first verb absolutely and add a negative in colon B: "Abstain, and listen . . . *do not* wander . . . ," but this interpretation does not explain what one is to abstain from, nor on what basis "not" was inserted. JPSV strains the syntax: "My son, cease to stray from words of knowledge / and receive discipline"; it makes "receive discipline" independent of "cease." The solution that is most respectful of the syntax is to interpret the verse as ironic advice as in 22:6. In addition to the irony, there is wordplay: to stop (listening) is to go (wandering). In Judg. 5:6, the verb *ḥādal* has exactly that meaning, "to stop."

[28] Verses 5 and 9 state the penalty for lying, in memorable fashion. This saying goes further and asks why people lie. The answer cannot be understood apart from the sounds of the Hebrew: *ʻēd bĕlîyaʻal yālîṣ mišpāṭ ûpî rĕšāʻîm yĕballaʻ ʼāwen,* literally, "A witness malicious mocks justice and the mouth of the wicked swallow evil." The sounds of *bĕlîyaʻal,* "malicious," repeat in *yālîṣ,* "mocks," and in *yĕballaʻ,* "swallows." The sounds relate malice and mocking the judicial system, implying that the motive of a lying witness is the witness's ingesting of evil, that is, active collusion with evil (see 4:17). Two triliteral roots from this saying, *lwṣ* and *špṭ,* occur in the next saying.

[29] Completing the thought of v. 28 on the scoffers who contemn the judicial process, v. 29 asserts that their punishment is as inevitable as that of fools. Just as their mouths took in injustice (v. 28) so will their backs take blows. Scoffers deny that God acts purposefully or with justice. Punishment awaits them (divine passive).

Proverbs 20

20:1   Wine is a scoffer, beer a roisterer;
     none who stagger from them will ever be wise.

2   A king's wrath[a] is like a lion's roar;
     who rouses it endangers his life.

3   Honor is won by avoiding quarrels,
     but every fool gets embroiled.

4   A sluggard does not plow in season;
     at harvesttime he seeks but there's nothing.

5   A plan in the human heart is deep waters,
     but an intelligent person draws it up.

6   Many are called loyal,[b]
     but who can find a person of trust?

7   Who walks in integrity as a righteous person—
     his children will come after him.

8   A king sitting upon a throne of justice
     scatters evil by a mere glance.

9   Who can claim, "I have made my heart pure;
     I am free from my sin?"

10   Two weights, two measures:
     both are an abomination to Yahweh.

11   In his actions even a boy can playact,
     though his deed be blameless and right.

12   The ear that hears and the eyes that see—
     Yahweh created them both.

13   Do not love sleep lest you fall into poverty.
     Open your eyes and you will have plenty of food.[c]

14   "Bad! Bad!" says the buyer,
     then goes away and boasts.

15   One can put on gold and abundant jewels,
     but wise lips are the most precious adornment.

16   Take his garment, for he went surety for another—
     on behalf of strangers, take his pledge!

17   Bread gained by deceit is sweet,
     but afterwards one's mouth is full of gravel.

18 Plans are realized[d] through counsel,
    and by strategy war is waged.
19 One who traffics in slander reveals secrets.
    Do not associate with anyone with reckless lips.
20 Who curses his father and his mother—
    his lamp will go out in dead of night.
21 An inheritance greedily[e] guarded in the beginning
    will not be blessed in the end.
22 Do not say, "I will requite an evil."
    Wait for Yahweh! Let him deliver you.
23 False weights are an abomination to Yahweh;
    a lying balance is not right.
24 From Yahweh are the steps of a man.
    How can a human being know his way?
25 It is a trap to make a vow
    and only later count the cost.
26 A wise king winnows out the guilty,
    and rolls the threshing wheel over them.
27 The lifebreath of a mortal is the lamp of Yahweh,
    searching through all the chambers of the stomach.
28 Loyalty and fidelity guard the king,
    and he makes his throne firm by loyalty.
29 The boast of young men is their strength
    and the glory of old men is their gray hair.
30 Blows and wounds come upon[f] the wicked,
    beatings, into their inmost being.

a. MT *'êmat melek,* "the terror of a king," does not suit the context nor match the variant in 19:12. G has *apeilē,* "threat," and S *rawgnā,* "anger," which reflects the more suitable Hebrew *ḥămat,* "anger." In colon B, Hebrew *mit'abbĕrû,* a denominative verb from the noun *'ebrâ,* "overflow, fury," should presumably be intransitive, "the one who is angry." The desired meaning, "who angers [rouses] him," is difficult syntactically. Delitzsch interprets it as a reflexive of the causative or niphal conjugation (GKC §54f).

b. S, T, and V take MT *yqr'* as the niphal conjugation *yiqqārē',* "is called, calls oneself," and *ḥsd* as *ḥāsîd:* "Many men are called loyal but a faithful man who can find?" We read *ḥesed* for MT *ḥasdô,* the error occurring through dittography of *wāw.*

c. G does not render vv. 14–20 of the Hebrew.

d. With S, T, and V, we read *tē'āśeh,* the imperfect of the niphal conjugation of *'āśâ,* "to do, make," in place of MT *'āśēh,* the imperative, which arose through haplography of *t* (so also Ehrlich and others).

e. In colon A, the verb is unclear. The ketib is *mĕbuḥelet* and the qere is *mĕbōhelet,* "hastily acquired (?)." The meaning of the ketib is obscure. No light is shed by the other instance of *bḥl* in the Bible (Zech. 11:8, "to loathe") nor by *bḥl* in rabbinic Hebrew ("to ripen"). In the absence of good parallels, we draw on the Arabic verb *baḥila,* "to be avaricious, be niggardly, refuse someone something." The qere preserves an early Hebrew variant resulting from the graphic similarity of the consonants *hē* and *ḥēt* in some Hebrew scripts. G and all the versions follow the qere. The ketib, nonetheless, makes better sense and, in addition, provides alliteration of the consonants *ḥl* in *naḥălâ*, "inheritance," and *mĕbōḥelet*.

f. MT is obscure because in colon A the words *tamrîq* (ketib) and *tamrûq* (qere) are unknown. G, followed by T and S, takes *tamrîq* as "meet [in a hostile sense], attack" (*qr'* for *tmrq?*). V derives *tamrîq* from *māraq*, "to purify." The meaning is beyond recovery.

[20:1] Wine and strong drink are personified according to their effects on human beings. So powerful is alcohol in inducing disrespect toward others that it can be called a scoffer. In Proverbs wine is not only a sign of prosperity and symbol of feasting (3:10; 9:2, 5) but also a threat to wisdom (21:17; 23:29–35; 31:4). The saying plays on straying from the path in a literal sense (Ezek. 34:6) and in a figurative sense (1 Sam. 26:21 and Job 19:4). Drink causes one to stagger and to stray from the right path (Isa. 28:7).

[2] A king may be awe-inspiring but he can also be dangerous. A lion was a common royal symbol in the ancient Near East. The symbol shows all too clearly a king's majesty and danger to ordinary mortals.

[3] Nowhere is the difference between the foolish and the wise as clear as in disputes. The wise keep away from them, whereas fools get embroiled (e.g., 13:10; 15:18; 18:6; 22:10). Paradoxically, the honor one might gain from winning a fight comes without fighting to the person who does not get involved. Honor will never be given to the fool who plunges intemperately into quarrels.

[4] Laziness is often mentioned in the context of crops, food, and eating (e.g., 12:27; 13:4; 19:24; 24:30–34; 26:15). "In season" is literally "in winter" (= October to March), which is the time for planting in the Palestinian agricultural year. In colon A, the sounds of *ḥōrēp*, "season," are repeated in *yaḥărōš*, "plow."

[5] In Isa. 29:15, "deep plan" means concealed plan: "Ho, those who would hide their plans deep from Yahweh." "Deep" is what is unexpressed in words and thus unknown to others. But a wise person knows how to bring up those deep waters and express them in appropriate words. Deep waters have the same meaning in 18:4.

[6] The adjectives in colon A and colon B, "loyal" and "of trust" have virtually the same meaning, for they often occur as a fixed pair. The antithesis is not, therefore, between being loyal and being trustworthy but between having a reputation for a virtue and actually practicing it, between untested and tested friendship. Friendship is proved when trouble comes. For the construction "many . . . but . . . " see 31:29: "Many women have done well but you surpass them all." The same idea is found in 14:20; 17:17; 18:24; 19:4, 6, 7.

[7] MT as it stands is flat: "Who walks in his integrity as a righteous person—blessed are his children after him." The versions with only slight variation follow MT. A slight emendation of MT *'ašrê*, "happy," to the verb *'iššĕrû*, "they

walk," supplies the missing depth in the form of a double meaning: The children of the righteous will come after them, that is, the righteous will be blessed with children, and the children will imitate ("walk after") their righteousness.[1]

[8] A king's throne is established in justice (16:12; 20:28; 25:5; 29:14), and the king is the agent of that justice. A king effects God's intent by putting down the wicked and upholding the righteous. Justice is not merely a personal virtue of a particular king but belongs to the office. The king sits to give judgment. The Hebrew verb "to scatter" can mean "to winnow" and may refer to winnowing in a metaphorical sense—separating the good from the bad. In the Ugaritic story of Aqhat, King Danil judges at a threshing floor (*KTU* 1.17.V.7). For the coherence of vv. 8–12, see Whybray.

[9] As if in response to the exalted claim made for the king in v. 8, this saying denies that any human being can claim to be without fault before God. Only God can forgive sins. Colon A is united by four /ī/ sounds and the entire verse has three /t/ and two /ṭ/ sounds.

[10] The Hebrew is, literally, "a stone and a stone, an ephah and an ephah," in the sense that each is of a different weight or (dry) measure. Different weights are signs of a dishonest trader. Deuteronomy 25:13 makes the same condemnation: "You shall not have in your sack a stone and a stone, [one] large and [the other] small." The "stone" is a weight of indeterminate heaviness. An ephah is a dry measure equal to one-tenth of a homer or kor, estimated to be 1.5 or 2.5 pecks, three-eighths or two-thirds of a U.S. bushel. It was the most common dry measure. Altering weights is an abomination to Yahweh, who is the guarantor of the just order of the world (see under 11:1). See also 20:23. G places Hebrew vv. 20–22 here.

[11] The text of MT is supported by all the versions but it is interpreted in different ways. The verb *yitnakker* in colon A can be either of two different triliteral roots: (1) to make oneself known; (2) to play another person, feign (in this sense, it is a denominative verb from *nokrî*, "foreigner," as in Gen. 42:7 and 1 Kings 14:5, 6). The first triliteral root yields, "Even a boy *reveals himself* by his deeds," but the verb is not a suitable parallel to colon B, "whether his deed is pure and upright."[2] The second triliteral root yields, "even a boy may *playact* in his deeds," and is a better parallel to B. The meaning is that if a child can fake

---

1. It would be easy for ancient scribes to confuse the two forms; the only difference is *yôd* and *wāw*, which were often confused because of their graphic similarity. In Ugaritic texts, the triliteral root *'šr* is parallel to *hlk*, "to walk" (*KTU* 1.14.II.39–42; 1.14.IV.17–20). In Prov. 4:14 the D stem of the verb is in parallel to *tābō'*, "go." Ehrlich makes a similar suggestion. MT colon A has "*his* integrity" and G and S have "integrity"; both are attested.

2. One might be tempted to emend colon B, "whether his deed is pure *or wicked*" (*rāšā'* instead of MT *yāsār*), but such an emendation has no versional support, and *zāk* and *rāšā'* are not elsewhere parallel. The emphatic particle *gam,* sometimes rendered "also," in colon A can modify either the first or last word.

virtuous actions, an adult can do so even more. How difficult it is to get at inner motivation from outward actions! Character is not always revealed by actions.

[12] In the psychology of Proverbs, the ear and the eye take in data for the heart to store, ponder, and decide. What the heart decides, the mouth, the hands, and the feet will effect. The saying can mean either that God intends people to use their senses to become wise (God created them), or, what is far more likely, that if human beings can see and hear, how much more can God. Psalm 94:9 is relevant: "The one who planted the ear, does he not hear? The one who formed the eye, does he not see?" The argument is a fortiori, "how much more."

[13] Sleep, laziness, and poverty are closely linked as in 19:15. The abrupt imperative of colon B is a humorous contrast to colon A: "Open your eyes and eat!" The reader perhaps expects the idiomatic phrase "Open your eyes and see!" The latter is a common idiom (e.g., Gen. 21:19; 2 Kings 6:20; Isa. 37:17).

[14] Shopping by bartering invites playacting and masking one's true judgments (see also 14:13 and 20:11). Words are to be judged by their context. This humorous sketch of an Eastern marketplace stands for other situations where people do not say what they really mean.

[15] In 3:14; 8:10, 19; and 16:16 wisdom is declared to be preferable to gold, which is the universal measure of value. Colon B makes it clear that the gold and jewels of the saying are jewelry for the face. The word for "adornment" (*kĕlî*) is often used of jewelry (Gen. 24:53; Ex. 3:22; Isa. 61:10). Wise lips are a more precious adornment than the finest jewelry, for they display the wisdom of the heart. Wisdom is more beautiful than gold or silver.

[16] Proverbs regards giving surety for another as a foolish risk to one's own security. The saying makes its point by a fictive command to seize the very clothing (symbolizing the person) of the one who has given surety for another. See also 6:1–4; 11:15; 17:18; 22:26–27; 27:13. The last verse is a duplicate except for "unfamiliar woman" in colon B, which we render simply as "stranger" there. The triliteral root '*rb* is a connecting word in vv. 16, 17, and 19.

[17] "Bread [food] of lies" (*leḥem kĕzābîm*) means food obtained through fraud (so JPSV, REB, NRSV). The Hebrew phrase has a different meaning in 23:3—"food that deceives." Eating it does not satisfy the appetite but leaves the bad taste of disappointment. The saying plays on the two senses of *kĕzābîm*, "lies." Food obtained through deceptive behavior provides deceptive nourishment.

[18] It is a long step from a plan to its realization. The means to realization is taking counsel from others; so also in war. Though popularly thought to be a matter of weaponry and armies, it is carried on by counsel or strategy. A similar prizing of wisdom over military might is 24:5: "A wise person is more powerful than a mighty one, / a learned person, more than one endowed with strength: / for by strategy war is waged, / and by many counsellors victory is achieved."

[19] Colon A is not tautologous as it might appear at first reading, for it implies that one who traffics in slander[3] will reveal *your* secret. Colon B draws out the implication. To protect your private thoughts and judgments, stay away from gossips. The statement (colon A) is couched in the repetitive sound-pattern of the participle in the qal conjugation (*gôlēh sôd // hôlēk rākîl*), which is followed by an imperative in colon B. The syntax (nominal sentence plus imperative verb) is unusual, but the preceding verse in MT is similar. Also unusual is the negative particle *lō'*, "not," for the more usual *'al*, and the verb in the qal conjugation *gôlēh* instead of the expected piel (as in 11:13). These innovations may have been used because their /ō/ sounds contribute to the aphoristic effect.

[20] In the law codes, those who curse their parents incur the death penalty (Ex. 21:17; Lev. 20:9; Deut. 27:16). Something more than punishment is meant here. The extinguishing of a lamp is a metaphor for death (Job 18:5, 6; 21:17; Prov. 13:9; 24:20; Isa. 43:17). Commandment and instruction are called a light and a lamp in Prov. 6:23. One who despises parents quenches a great source of instruction and discipline.

[21] On purely text critical grounds, the ketib reading "greedily [guarded]" is to be preferred to the qere reading "hastily [acquired]," despite the preference of most scholars for the latter (see textual notes). An inheritance is by definition a gift from one's parents (19:14), not acquired by one's own efforts. If, when first received ("in the beginning"), one follows the natural inclination to keep others away, the result, paradoxically, will be that it will ultimately not "be given." An inheritance in an agricultural society such as Israel typically was not money but farmland, which was believed to require God's blessing to be productive. The qere reading remains possible, however: One ought not to take one's inheritance hastily, perhaps in the sense of taking it with undue haste from elderly parents.

[22] Instead of resolving to retaliate for an evil inflicted on one, one should turn trustfully to God, who in response to that trust will bring one out of the evil. This is not a long step from the counsel to abandon thoughts of revenge on enemies as in 24:17–18 and 25:21–22. The advice does not come from indifference to evil but from a conviction that only God can deal adequately with serious evil.

[23] Two stones of different weight (lit., "a weight and a weight") and deceptive scales to trick the buyer are an abomination to God. Fair trading comes under divine justice. True weights are part of honest communication among human beings. The saying is a variant of v. 10 and 11:1.

[24] If it is Yahweh who directs one's steps, how can a human being claim to known their sum total, their course? "Way" is a metaphor for the course of life.

---

3. For the meaning see 11:13 and especially Lev. 19:16.

[25] Like Qoh. 5:3–4, Proverbs is against precipitous vows. One is bound by one's words (Lev. 27:28). One should reflect on the cost and consequences before vowing rather than after. The great biblical example of a reckless vow is Judg. 11:29–40: Jephthah vowed to offer up as a holocaust "whatever comes out of the doors of my house to meet me when I return in triumph from the Ammonites" and ended up sacrificing his only daughter. See also the oath of Saul (1 Samuel 14) and of Herod (Matt. 14:1–12). What is said of vows applies also to human promises generally.

[26] The king is a judge who rights unjust situations. Solomon in 1 Kings 3:16–28 upholds the right of the natural mother and denies the unjust claimant. In this saying, the royal duty of giving judgment is portrayed in two agricultural images—exposing grain to a current of air so that the chaff is blown away, and rolling a wheel or drum over a cereal to break the husk. Ehrlich and *BHS* propose *'ônām*, "their guilt," for *'ôpān*, "wheel," but the imagery is consistent as Isa. 28:27 shows: "nor is the wheel of a threshing sledge rolled over cumin." "Wheel" is found in all the versions except V, which does not understand the image.

[27] Lifebreath is the special gift of God that turns a body into a living and breathing human being. Genesis 2:7b and Ezek. 37:9–10 distinguish the making of the body from its animation through God breathing breath or spirit into the nostrils. Lifebreath is an apt symbol for the divine spark in a human being, for it is powerful, invisible, and disappears at death. The saying uses this sign of life to express divine dominion and scrutiny of human life. The divinely given breath flowing through the inner part of the body ("the chambers of the stomach") functions like a claim. There is no part of a human being that is beyond divine scrutiny. Zephaniah 1:12 speaks of a lamp that is used in searching (words identical to our passage are italicized): "And in that day I will *search through* (*'ăhapēś*) *Jerusalem with lamps* (*nērôt*), and I will punish the people who . . . " For the theme of God viewing human actions, see 15:3; 16:2; 21:2.

[28] God's loyalty and fidelity guard the king. The king is the agent of God and so God protects him as he exercises his important function. The venerable word pair "loyalty and fidelity" are personified as soldiers who protect the throne, but the king also has his role to play. His own conduct also stabilizes the throne. The saying affirms the importance of divine protection and human virtue, without trying to explore the relation between them.

[29] "Boast" and "glory" express what one takes pride in. Elsewhere in Proverbs, wisdom is preferred to strength (21:22; 24:5–6), but this epigram simply states two boasts of the two groups, leaving the reader to draw conclusions. Is the meaning that physical vigor and wisdom are never found in one and the same person? "If youth but knew and age but could."

[30] The verb in colon A is unknown, making the entire saying uncertain. The words for "blows" and "wounds" occur together in Isa. 1:6. The meaning may be that outer blows destroy the inner person.

Proverbs 21

21:1 A king's heart is like channeled water controlled by Yahweh:
    he directs it where he pleases.

2 A person's ways seem right in his own eyes,
    but it is Yahweh who probes the heart.

3 Doing what is righteous and just
    is more acceptable to Yahweh than sacrifices.

4 Haughty eyes and a proud heart—
    the lamp of the wicked will fail.

5 The plans of the diligent end in profit,
    but those of the hasty end in loss.

6 Treasures acquired by a lying tongue
    are a fleeting breath and a deadly snare.[a]

7 The violence of the wicked drags them away,
    for they refuse to act justly.

8 A person's path may zigzag and be strange,
    but his actions are blameless and right.

9 Better to live on a corner of the roof
    than in a noisy house with an angry wife.

10 The appetite of a wicked person desires evil;
    his neighbor does not please him.

11 When a scoffer is punished, a simple person learns a lesson;
    when a wise person prospers,[b] he gains insight.

12 The Righteous One observes the house of a wicked person,
    turning the wicked toward trouble.[c]

13 Who blocks his ears from the cry of the poor
    will call out but go unheard.

14 A hidden gift allays[d] hostility,
    a bribe in the pouch, towering wrath.

15 Justice done is joy to the righteous,
    but ruin to evildoers.

16 Who strays from the path of wisdom
    will end his journey in the assembly of the Rephaim.

17 Who loves festivity will be in want;
    who loves wine and oil will never be rich.

18 A scoundrel is ransom for a righteous person;
    a deceiver takes the place of the upright.

19 Better to live in a wilderness
    than with an angry and peevish wife.

20 Fine wines and oil are in the shed of a sage,

but a fool drinks them down.

21 Who pursues righteousness and kindness
   will find life and honor.[e]

22 A wise man went up against a city of warriors
   and brought down its mighty stronghold.

23 Whoever guards his mouth and his tongue,
   guards himself from dangers.

24 A haughty braggart, scoffer is his name,
   ever acting in insolent wrath.

25 The appetite of the sluggard will kill him,
   for his hands refuse to do anything.

26 Some spend their days in craving,
   but a righteous person gives without stint.

27 The sacrifice of the wicked is an abomination;
   how much more when one offers it with calculation.

28 A lying witness perishes,
   but an accurate one will testify again.

29 A wicked person puts on a brazen face,
   but an upright person examines his course.

30 There is no wisdom, there is no discernment,
   there is no knowledge that prevails against Yahweh.

31 The horse is readied for the day of battle,
   but the victory belongs to Yahweh.

a. The Hebrew of colon B is uncertain. No version reads the Hebrew as the Masoretes pointed it. We read "snares (*mwqšy*) of death" (for the anomalous MT *mbqšy*) with G and V. "Snares of death" occurs in 2 Sam. 22:6; Prov. 13:14; 14:27.

b. In colon B, *lāmed* before *haśkîl* arose from haplography.

c. All the versions read MT, though G (followed by S) reflects *lbwt*, "hearts," in place of MT *lbyt*, "houses," which looks like an attempt to wrest sense from the difficult Hebrew. MT may be corrupt.

d. The verb in colon A, *yikpeh*, occurs only here in the Bible. In later Hebrew it means "to turn upside down, to bring down, to force"; in Aramaic "to overturn"; and in Syriac, "to bend." Symmachus, V, and T, read *ykbh*, "to quench," which has as its object *nēr*, "lamp," in 1 Sam. 3:3 and Prov. 31:18.

e. With G we omit "righteousness" in colon B on the grounds that it arose through dittography.

[21:1] "Channeled waters" occurs in Isa. 32:2 and Prov. 5:16 in a positive sense—waters that fertilize arid areas. So also the similar phrase in Isa. 30:25. It takes great skill and power to direct water, whether it is confining the cosmic waters at creation to their proper spheres or bringing water to fertilize arid land. Water by its nature is "chaotic"—powerful and elusive. It also takes great skill to direct the heart of a king, for the king's mind is inscrutable and beyond human control. Yet God controls waters and the royal heart with ease. Wisdom is compared to water in 18:4 and 20:5. Water is associated with the Mesopotamian god of wisdom, Ea (Enki). "Heart" points to the next saying.

[2] Human beings may make judgments about the rightness of their actions, whether their "ways" have been "straight." But Yahweh can scrutinize the heart and judge truly. Human judgment is partial and incomplete, but God's is full and definitive. There is a contrast between "eyes" and "heart," as in v. 4. This saying points to the next verse, which is also about Yahweh the judge of human actions. Variants of colon A are 16:2, 25; 30:12. For a variant of colon B see 24:12.

[3] The fixed pair "righteous" and "just" is common in the Bible, appearing in 18:19 and Ps. 33:5 and, in reverse order, in Isa. 56:1; Job 37:23, and 2 Sam. 8:15. The two qualities are the heart of biblical religion, summing up the proper attitude toward God. To live in accord with them is to make of one's own life an offering pleasing to God; there is a sacred dimension to just action. This axiom is like other adaptations of liturgical language, such as the use of "abomination" and "acceptable" to characterize profane acts. Cf. Ps. 51:18–19 and Hos. 6:6.

[4] Eyes and heart depict, respectively, the outer and inner person. "Haughty eyes" peer out from a "proud heart." The same phrase occurs in Ps. 101:5. Hebrew *nēr,* "lamp" (so all the versions) can also be read *nîr,* "tillage, cultivated land" (Hos. 10:12; Jer. 4:3; Prov. 13:23) and is so taken by JPSV. Both meanings make sense here. In colon B, *haṭṭā't* means "failure, missing the mark" (as in Prov. 10:16 and elsewhere) rather than "sin." Colon A describes an arrogant person and colon B declares the lamp of the house (cf. 31:18) or perhaps the tillage of such a person will fail. Arrogance cannot be the basis of anything enduring.

[5] The antithesis is diligence and impetuousness. The results of the activity of each type are stated in metaphors of commerce—profit and loss (cf. 11:24; 14:23). In commerce, one might be tempted to equate bustle with profit. Activity itself is not determinative, however. The diligent will end up with earnings, for they take time to plan and reflect. Frenetic activity leads to waste.

[6] Treasures acquired by deceitful words are not only ephemeral ("a fleeting breath"), but are dangerous ("deadly snares") to those who possess them. Ill-gotten goods cry out to heaven for retribution.

[7] Injustice in the form of violent acts comes back on the head of the doer. The statement is made indirectly: If one refuses to act justly, then another agency will come into operation (i.e., the violence will explode on the head of the violent). Hebrew *šōd,* "violence," is a strong word, often found in juxtaposition with *šeber,* "destruction," and *ḥāmās,* "violence, lawlessness." Colon A is interlocked by alliteration of *š* and the assonance of /ō/ and /î/ (*šōd rĕšā'îm yĕgōrîm*).

[8] Most translations make a simple opposition between wicked and good behavior. Plöger, for example, renders, "Twisted is the way of a guilty man, but

the pure—upright is his action." NRSV is similar. But the words describing the path in colon A are morally neutral—"to zigzag" and "to be strange (= unfamiliar)." The adjectives of colon B, "blameless" and "right" (lit., "straight"), are found also in 20:11b, which likewise denies that inner intentions can always be gauged from external actions. The point: unfamiliar does not mean bad.

[9] The two great obstacles to domestic happiness are perverse offspring and a contentious spouse. Both cause profound pain. It is preferable to live on top of the house (on the exposed roof) than inside with a noisy and nagging spouse. Verse 19 states the same thought, except that "wilderness" is in place of "corner of a roof." The nagging wife is also mentioned in 19:13 and 27:15. The phrase (*bêt ḥāber*) is usually translated "a house *shared with*," derived from Hebrew *ḥeber*, "association." It is preferable, however, to relate the word to the Akkadian noun *ḫubūru*, "noise," and *ḫabāru*, "to make noise," and translate "house of noise."[1] Proverbs 25:24 is a duplicate.

[10] The maxim is about the effect of appetite on a person. Colon A: the wicked (*rāšāʿ*) are so obsessed by their desire for evil (*rāʿ*) that (colon B) they totally neglect their neighbor (*rēʿēhû*). In other words, the wicked are so absorbed by *rāʿ* that they forget *rēʿ*. Absorption with evil kills one's humanity. The meaning is underscored by alliteration of /r/ and the guttural consonants.

[11] How do the uninstructed (or the young) learn about the consequences of good and bad behavior? The answer to the question is not entirely clear because the subject of the second verb in colon B is uncertain. The subject of colon B has been taken in two ways by commentators. A majority believe "the wise person" of colon B is the subject throughout, making the antithesis of the entire saying "a simple person" (who learns from the punishment of a scoffer) and "a wise person" (who learns from wise words). So JPSV: "When a scoffer is punished, the simple man is edified; / When a wise man is taught,[2] he gains insight." It is preferable, however, to take "a simple person" as the subject of both cola, and to take *haśkîl* not in its sense of "to learn; to teach," but "to succeed, prosper," as in 17:8. "Scoffer" and "wise person" are contrasted also in 9:8; 13:1; 15:12, and *haśkîl* in the latter sense makes a better antithesis to *ʿănāš* ("to punish") than *haśkîl* in the former sense. The point of the proverb is that ordinary people learn about the blessings of wisdom from its concrete results. Cf. 19:25.

[12] This difficult verse has found no single satisfactory solution. Two antitheses are certain: "righteous one" and "the wicked," the participles "understands" and "overturns." The third antithesis is unclear: "[to the] house of a wicked person" and "toward trouble." The text may be disturbed but there is insufficient evidence for emending it.

---

1. Cohen, 139–40.
2. JPSV takes *haśkîl* as "to learn" rather than "to succeed."

Another problem is identifying the subject of the verbs. Does *ṣaddîq*, "righteous [one]," in colon A refer to a human being ("a righteous person," RSV) or to God ("the Righteous One," so Rashi, JPSV, NRSV, REB)? The arguments for "righteous [one]" as a human being are that all the ancient versions assumed a human subject, and "Righteous One" is used elsewhere as a title for God only in Isa. 24:16. The argument for identifying "righteous one" as Yahweh is that in other wicked-righteous contrasts in Proverbs the righteous never do anything to the wicked. Rather it is God who punishes them. Further, the subject of the verb *sillēp*, "turning," in Proverbs is always Yahweh (13:6; 19:3).

Several interpretations have been proposed: "The Righteous One instructs the family of wicked people, when he overturns a wicked person into trouble" (Meinhold), but the alleged contrast on which this translation is based—the family versus its individual member—is contradicted by the Hebrew grammatical number (singular in colon A and plural in colon B). "A righteous person observes the house of a wicked person, how it [the house] overturns the wicked into trouble," (one of several suggestions of Alonso Schökel) that is, the righteous learn from others' fate (as in v. 11), but this strains the syntax. The most satisfactory translation is to understand "righteous one" as God. The identity of the subject is revealed only gradually, being definitively recognized only in colon B with the participle form (used often in hymns) of the verb "to subvert, turn." Statement follows form: the wicked are inevitably, if not immediately, overthrown by God.

[13] It would be hard to imagine a more concise and challenging statement of the importance of the poor in God's sight. One must hear the cry of the poor in order to be heard by God. Neglect them and you will be cut off from God. See also 14:31; 17:5; 19:17; 22:22–23; Ps. 41:2.

[14] Fools act from anger and the wise know the means for taming it: a soft answer (15:1; 29:8) or patience (15:18) or a bribe as here. The strategies of the wise for quieting angry people, especially bribes, imply a certain disdain for the passion of anger, for towering rage can be quickly assuaged by a shrewd gift. An example of wise words allaying wrath is 2 Kings 5:11–14, where Naaman's anger is calmed by his servants' shrewdness. Cf. 17:23.

[15] Proverbs' point is not psychological, that is, the joy of a good conscience. The outlook is more objective and utilitarian (Ehrlich): When justice is done, prosperity ("joy") comes to the righteous, and ruin comes to the wicked. "Joy," as in 10:28 and 21:17, means outward rejoicing, and suggests prosperity. Proverbs 10:29b is a duplicate of colon B.

[16] According to Proverbs, there are ultimately only two ways open to human beings. To leave one is inevitably to walk on the other. Leaving the way of wisdom puts one on the way of the wicked, which has its own goal—death. The Rephaim are the shadowy inhabitants of Sheol (Ps. 88:11; Prov. 2:18;

9:18). The association of "way" and "path" with death is frequently made in Proverbs (5:5; 7:27; 12:28; 14:12; 16:25). The Hebrew verb in colon B, *yānûah*, can have the nuance of finally coming to rest or ending a journey (cf. Gen. 8:4; Ex. 10:14; Josh. 3:13).

[17] The obvious meaning is that those who enjoy riches now will remain in want. Wealth does not come to the idle and pleasure-loving but to the diligent (cf. 6:6–11; 10:4; 12:24, 27). "Joy" in colon A denotes festivity as in Qoh. 2:1, 2; 8:15; 9:7. Wine and oil belong to the vocabulary of banqueting, as in Judg. 9:9, 13; Qoh. 9:7–8. Wine is a sign of joy and feasting in Zech. 10:7 and Ps. 104:15. The meaning is more subtle than mere praise of diligence, however: Those who *seek* primarily the enjoyment of wealth instead of the practice of virtue will not attain the first. Wealth is a gift of God given only to those who practice virtue.

[18] The righteous are rescued from danger and the wicked are placed there instead. In a bold metaphor the wicked become ransom for the deliverance of the righteous. They end up as objects of divine wrath from which the righteous have been preserved. Proverbs 11:8 and 13:8 express similar sentiments.

[19] The fear of domestic unhappiness arising from foolish offspring or a quarrelsome spouse haunts the book of Proverbs. Living in an utterly deserted place is preferable to living in a house spoiled by an angry spouse. The saying belongs to the chain of sayings about the household. Verse 9 states the same sentiment but with "corner of a roof" instead of "wilderness."

[20] Those who set their hearts exclusively on rich feasting (wine and olive oil) rather than on the virtue by which they are acquired will never enjoy them (cf. v. 17). The phrase in colon A, literally, "precious treasures," means cellared fine wine, as in 1 Chron. 27:27. "Wine and oil" occur together in v. 17 and elsewhere (e.g., Jer. 40:10; Hag. 2:12; 1 Chron. 9:29). The antithesis is in the way the wise and the foolish handle wealth. One preserves it and the other consumes it.

[21] The Hebrew verb "to pursue" is strong, conveying energy and determination, at times having the sense "to hunt down." In this saying, the intense pursuit comes upon something other than the original object of the pursuit—long and vigorous life and honor. Life and honor come from the pursuit of virtue. First pursue virtue and other things will be given. "First seek the kingdom of God and its justice and all these things will be given to you" (Matt. 8:33).

[22] To make the point that wisdom is more powerful than military might, this mininarrative describes a typical act using the metaphors of height and depth. "To go *up*" is a Hebrew idiom for mounting a military assault and "to bring *down*" is an idiom for defeating an enemy. This is one of several maxims in wisdom literature about the superiority of wisdom to strength in war. Cf. Qoh. 9:13–16; Prov. 16:32; 24:5.

[23] If you guard your tongue you guard your *nepeš*, literally, "your throat," the moist and breathing center of the body, which, by metonymy, is "life, self." In other words, in order to guard your "throat" (= self), you must guard your tongue. Speech, for Proverbs, is the quintessential human activity, so the meaning is broader than speech: acting rightly is the best way to protect yourself. The sound unifies and underlines meaning: each colon begins with /šō/ *and ends with* /ō/.

[24] The saying seems at first reading to be tautologous—a proud person acts with pride. The saying aims at intensification of experience. It defines the scoffer ("his name") and describes a scoffer's typical activity. Similar intense portraits are found in 6:12–19.

[25] "Appetite" (*ta'ăwāh*) is implanted in all animals to drive them to consume the food and drink necessary for survival. What keeps normal people alive kills sluggards, for they cannot lift their hands to their mouths to feed themselves (cf. 19:24). Alonso Schökel suggests a psychological interpretation: unfulfilled desires exhaust a person (cf. 13:12). The lazy are divided between desires they cannot control and hands that do not respond. REB takes vv. 25–26 as a single four-colon saying: "The sluggard's cravings will be the death of him, / because his hands refuse to work; / all day long his cravings go unsatisfied, / while the righteous give without stint." JPSV is similar. Each couplet, however, makes sense on its own, and linking them obscures the proper statement of each.

[26] The Hebrew text is supported by the versions (though G interprets heavily). MT (and REB) seems to take the verse as a continuation of the preceding: "All day long [the sluggard] is filled with craving." "Sluggard," however, is nowhere else antithetical to "righteous person." Further, the point is not laziness but selfish craving for oneself versus unselfish giving to others. Verses 25 and 26 are thus totally different. In v. 26 "their days" of colon A is contrasted with "without stint" of colon B; both express a habitual attitude (Ehrlich).

[27] The wicked in Proverbs deliberately choose the state of rebellion against God's will; their offerings are by that fact unacceptable. The word *zimmāh*, "calculation," in colon B suggests that the insincere sacrificer perverts the very means of being reconciled to God—a liturgical offering. Cf. 15:8.

[28] Lying witnesses are a preoccupation of Proverbs (see under 19:9). Colon A is clear and has been stated before (6:19; 12:17; 14:5; 19:5, 9, 28). Alliteration underscores this point (*'ēd* . . . *yō'bēd*, "witness . . . perish"). How are the two cola related? One possible antithesis is that between a lying and an accurate witness. The latter testifies accurately to what has been heard (so NRSV and JPSV). Another interpretation imagines a court scene in which a false accuser is heard out by the accused who then offers an effective rebuttal; the one who listens will offer the last word.

Perhaps the simplest solution is to suppose that a lying witness quickly loses all credibility as a witness for the future. Accurate (lit., "hearing") witnesses, on the other hand, will be called again and again because of their credibility. Their truthfulness brings a good reputation that endures, whereas a lie is only for the moment (12:19). Colon A is identical to 19:9b.

[29] This is another contrast of the behavior of the wicked and the upright. The Masoretic tradition preserved two readings of the Hebrew verb in colon B: (1) ketib, *yākîn*, "to establish, direct aright," meaning in this context, "maintains a faithful course" (cf. 2 Chron. 27:6); (2) qere, *yābîn*, "to understand, to discern," meaning in this context, "knows his way," that is, where his course is heading. G reflects the second and S, T, and V reflect the first.

The possible meanings are two: (1) A wicked person is defiant (lit., "makes his face hard"), but an upright person considers his ways, that is, is willing to consider the counsel of others; (2) An evil person goes off in his own direction, but an upright person maintains a faithful course.

[30] The positive statement that Yahweh is the source of all wisdom is made by negative statements. The negative substantive *'ên*, "there is no . . . ," is repeated three times. There is no wisdom apart from God.

[31] Yahweh alone determines the victor in every battle. The horse was the most powerful and majestic weapon of war at the time, but even it cannot be credited with victory. Human beings do not command the power to bring their projects to consummation. Cf. 16:1.

Proverbs 22:1–16

22:1   A good reputation is preferable to great wealth;
     esteem is better than silver and gold.

2   Rich person meets poor person—
     Yahweh made them both.

3   A shrewd person spots trouble and withdraws,
     but the simple walk on and pay the penalty.

4   The consequence of a humbling is the revering of Yahweh—
     wealth, honor, and life.

5   Thorns and traps are on the path of a perverse person,
     but who guards his soul keeps far from them.

6   Train a boy according to his own way;
     even when old he will not depart from it.

7   A rich person rules over the poor,
     and a borrower is slave to a lender.

8   Who sows injustice reaps trouble;
     his angry flail is useless.

9   A generous person receives blessings,
      for he gave his food to the poor.^a

10 Expel the scoffer and out goes quarreling;
      strife and dishonor end.

11 The king^b is a friend to the pure-hearted;
      one gracious of lips is his companion.

12 The eyes of Yahweh guard knowledge,
      but he undermines the words of a deceiver.

13 A sluggard says, "There's a lion out there;
      in the square I'll get killed."

14 The mouth of a forbidden woman is a deep pit,
      anyone incurring Yahweh's wrath falls into it.

15 Folly is bound to the heart of a boy;
      the rod of discipline will remove it from him.

16 Who extorts from the poor increases his wealth;
      who gives to the rich suffers loss.

a. G has three variant renderings on giving generously (Rahlfs 8a, 9, 9a)—8a: "God blesses a cheerful and generous man"; 9a: "Whoever gives gifts wins victory and honor for himself, / and takes away the life of those who possess them." The first line of each renders colon A of the Hebrew text more or less literally. Verse 8a is cited by 2 Cor. 9:7: "God loves a cheerful giver."

b. The Hebrew text is disturbed and no emendation has gained general support. All the versions except V follow G in placing "Lord" in colon A ("The Lord loves the pure-hearted"), but G probably inserted it for sense. The subject of both cola is most likely the same—the king. The simplest solution is to assume that the word *melek,* "king," was inadvertently moved by a copyist from its original position at the beginning of colon A to its present position in MT at the end of colon B. The emendation gives a balanced syllable count—six/seven. Alonso Schökel notes the possibility but does not adopt it.

[22:1] Two similar sounding monosyllabic nouns, *šēm,* "name, repute," and *ḥēn,* "favor, grace, esteem," are declared to be worth more than great wealth. Human beings are inherently social and find their happiness in society. Without the acceptance by others that is founded on esteem and trust, one becomes an unfulfilled outsider. Riches, though more immediately alluring, are less essential to the human spirit than that which enables someone to live happily with others—a good name.

[2] Rich and poor come into contact in a variety of ways. Their relationship to a large extent is determined by considerations of wealth. The saying relativizes such distinctions by naming Yahweh the creator and sustainer of every human being. That basic relationship comes before all others. The verse continues the theme of wealth from v. 1. The threefold repetition of the sound /š/ unifies colon A; the first two words *'āšîr wārāš* reverse consonants (*š-r* becomes *r-š*). The first word of each colon begins with the guttural consonant *'ayin.*

[3] The saying is a mininarrative of a typical scene. The shrewd are circumspect looking around so as not to stumble into danger. The simple, on the other hand, heedlessly go on their way. "Simple" here denotes inexperienced and naive people. The alliteration of the guttural consonants in colon A (*'ārûm rā'āh rā'āh,* "a shrewd person spots trouble") is impressive. 27:12 is identical except for the conjugation of the verb in colon A.

[4] In Proverbs, revering Yahweh brings life (10:27; 14:27; 19:23) and honor (15:33), but "humility" (the usual translation of *'ănānāh*) does not. Some modern versions translate "the result of humility and revering Yahweh is . . . ," but no ancient version read it so. The word *'ănānāh* should rather be translated "humbling" in the sense of reduction to a lowly state. Of the seven occurrences of the word in the Bible, the most relevant instances are 15:33 and 18:12, which suggest the word means "humiliation, low estate." In modern English, "humble" can mean a state (lowliness) as well as the virtue (humility).

Humiliation can lead one to know one's place in God's world, which is one definition of "fear of the Lord." And fear of the Lord, or revering Yahweh, brings the blessings of wealth, honor, and long life. The axiom probably is meant to counter the view that humiliation is an unqualified evil. On the contrary, a humbling can help one recognize one's place and foster an earnest search for God who is the source of all blessings.

[5] According to this saying, the best way to travel safely on life's path is not to watch the road but to watch one's "throat" (*nepeš*), the source of one's words. Proverbs regards speaking as the most characteristic human activity. In this saying, it stands for human activity as such. The message: to keep safe, speak rightly. See 21:23 for a similar idea.

[6] One of the few exhortations in this collection. Some others are 14:7; 16:3; 19:18, 20. The Hebrew word for "to train" elsewhere in the Bible means "to dedicate [something]," such as a temple (1 Kings 8:63 and 2 Chron. 7:5) or a house (Deut. 20:5). The meaning in this verse is nearer to rabbinic Hebrew usage, "to accustom, train" (*b. Nazir* 29a: "in order to train him [*lḥnkw*] to carry out his religious duties").

The phrase in colon A, *'al-pî darkô,* literally, "according to his way," has been taken by commentators in three ways: (1) the "way" is the morally right way ("according to the way he ought to go" [McKane]) such as a way of life (6:23) or the good way (2:20); (2) personal aptitude, that is, the manner of life for which one is destined, as "the way of Egypt" is the manner characteristic of Egypt (Isa. 10:24), so Saadia, Delitzsch, and Toy; (3) Hebrew *na'ar,* "boy," can mean status, for example, a highborn squire, so that the saying is about initiating him into his official responsibilities.[1] None of the explanations is satisfactory. The first

---

1. T. Hildebrandt, "Proverbs 22:6: Train Up a Child?" *Grace Theological Journal* 9 (1988): 3–19, reprinted in *Learning from the Sages: Studies on the Book of Proverbs,* ed. R. Zuck (Grand Rapids: Baker Book House, 1995), 277–92.

solution leaves the suffixal pronoun "his" unexplained; the second presupposes the boy is being trained for a special purpose, but the proverb is general; the third suggestion neglects the young/old distinction of the saying and is banal.

The interpretation that best explains the phrase "according to his way" is to take the command as ironic (like the ironic command in 19:27). Let a boy do what he wants and he will become a self-willed adult incapable of change! (So also the fourteenth-century French Jewish commentator Ralbag [Gersonides].) Proverbs 19:18 deals with the same issue: "Correct your son while there is hope." Colon A opens and closes with an /a-ō/ sequence.

[7] In this observation on money and power a borrower ends up in the same situation as a poor person—a slave controlled by a wealthy master. The primary intent is not to criticize the wealthy but to point out the folly of those who borrow. Alliteration of /š/ gives an aphoristic tone to colon A, *'āšîr běrāšîm yimšôl.*

[8] The saying uses agricultural metaphors to state the danger and uselessness of acting maliciously. In colon A, bad actions are seeds that yield trouble. In colon B, a rod used in anger is useless. "Rod" is a flail for threshing grain as in Isa. 28:27, "dill is beaten out with a rod." A flail is a hand thresher consisting of a wooden handle on which hangs a stouter and shorter stick that swings freely.

Planting and harvesting deal with elemental forces beyond human control. The results of wicked conduct are likewise beyond human control. Its ineluctable outcome is trouble and frustration. For sowing and reaping in a similar metaphorical sense, see Job 4:8.

[9] "Generous," literally, "good of eye," means viewing others with kindness. Its antithesis, "evil of eye," means stingy in 23:6. By metonymy, eye stands for its operation, in this case a welcoming look or expression. To be gracious to the poor by giving them goods is to lend to God (cf. 19:17). The passive in colon A is the divine passive. "To give" and "to bless" are parallel in Gen. 24:35; 26:3; Deut. 28:12. A similar thought is found in 11:25.

[10] G may be correct in assuming the context is a public assembly. If one expels a scornful person from a meeting, hateful and unproductive attitudes are gotten rid of also. Wherever scoffers, who are contemptuous of others (21:24), set the tone there will be no harmony.

The sounds of colon A, *gārēš lēṣ wěyēṣē' mādôn* (/ē/ four times and /ēṣ/ two times), establish an aphoristic tone. The sounds link the first three words and make the fourth word, *mādôn* ("quarreling"), stand out by its different sounds. The final word of each colon, *mādôn,* and *qālôn,* "dishonor," have the same sound pattern (*ā-ô*).

[11] The parallel "heart" and "lips" (the sources of memory/reflection and verbal expression) occurs also in Ps. 21:3; Job 33:3; Prov. 10:8; 16:21; 24:2. Further, "friend" and "companion, neighbor" are associated in Pss. 38:12; 88:19; Prov. 17:17; Lam. 1:2. "Pure-hearted" and "gracious" are paired only here.

The route to power is through wisdom, which the saying defines as speaking gracious words from a true heart. The implicit corollary of the axiom is that it is dangerous to worm one's way into the king's confidence by dishonorable means. As God's chosen, the king will see through such tricks and vent his wrath upon those who try them. Cf. 14:35; 16:13; 20:2.

[12] The common interpretation (JPSV, NRSV) that "knowledge" (*da'at*) is "a wise person" (abstract quality for concrete instance) is unlikely for three reasons: (1) *bōgēd*, "deceiver," in Proverbs is ordinarily paired with ethical terms such as "upright" and "wicked" rather than with sapiential terms such as "wise person"; (2) the antithesis is not wise person and deceiver but "knowledge" (cf. 10:14 and 11:9) and "words" (cf. 15:2; 14); (3) the statement that God protects the wise and subverts deceivers is banal.

The axiom states that Yahweh scrutinizes and safeguards the knowledge that comes to expression in words. If one's words do not express faithfully what one knows, Yahweh will subvert those deceptive words. In Ex. 23:8 and Deut. 16:19, a bribe "undermines the words" (*sillēp dĕbārîm*) of the innocent person in a legal trial. REB assumes a legal context: "The Lord keeps watch over every claim at law, / and upsets the perjurer's case." God watches the plans of the human heart and subverts lying words.

[13] With sardonic humor the observation cites the imagined words of a lazy person, exposing the delusions such a person lives by. The sluggard always has a reason not to act, no matter how ridiculous. The sounds of "lion" (*'ărî*) repeat in the verb in colon B (*'ērāṣēaḥ*), "I'll get killed." Similarly humorous depictions of the sluggard are 19:24 and 26:13–15.

[14] "Pit" stands for "trap," as in the saying, "Who digs a pit will fall into it" (26:27). In this saying the pit is the mouth of a "foreign" or forbidden woman, the source of the deceptive words that lead the unwary to their death. Colon B declares that anyone taken in by her words must be an enemy of God, for it is inconceivable that a friend of God would be allowed to fall under her spell. Repetition of /u/ links the two cola, *šûḥāh*, "pit," *'ammuqqāh*, "deep," and *zĕ'ûm YHWH*, "the one under the wrath of Yahweh."

[15] The idea that children are not inherently wise but require discipline is common in the book. Folly is attached to the heart of a youngster in the way that the outer membranous covering (the husk or hull) is attached to a seed. The agricultural metaphor is maintained in colon B, where "rod" (*šēbeṭ*) means both a rod that is applied to the back of the recalcitrant (13:24; 23:13–14) and a "flail" (see 22:8b). "Discipline" (*mûsār*) may be an early addition, for it lengthens the second line unduly and makes the statement too obvious.

[16] One of the many observations in the book on rich and poor people, there is no consensus on this verse's interpretation, although the three antitheses are very clear: extorting/giving, poor/rich, profit/loss. One interpretation can be ruled out as overly ingenious: To oppress the poor makes them cry out to God who will enrich them; to give to the wealthy makes them indolent and, eventually, poor. Several translations assume colon B explicates colon A: "To profit by withhold-

ing what is due to the poor / is like making gifts to the rich—pure loss" (JPSV, in a similar vein NRSV and Meinhold). Whybray sees no real parallelism of sense and suggests the two lines were "originally unconnected fragments which have been erroneously set side by side because of their formal parallelism."

We take the verse as a typical dispassionate observation on the rich and the poor. Colon A observes that one can enrich oneself by taking from the poor, a fairly obvious conclusion in view of the defenselessness of the poor against tax farmers, debt collectors, and bandits. Colon B makes precisely the opposite statement, which seems at first reading to be ridiculous: giving to the wealthy makes one poor. Who in their right mind would give to the wealthy? On reflection, however, colon B makes sense. Many people try to bribe the wealthy or ingratiate themselves with them by means of presents. The rich may accept the money and presents but are sufficiently cunning not to be fooled or coerced. The rich will always do what they want. Those who curry favor with them end up the poorer. The seemingly absurd antithesis memorably expresses the great gulf between the poor and the rich.

Proverbs 22:17–24:22

The Words of the Wise

The Words of the Wise consists of an introduction and thirty brief "chapters," most of them admonitions but including a few exhortations, observations, and aphorisms. The Words of the Wise is distinctive in Proverbs, not only by its forms but by its content. The first part seems to be addressed to young people ambitioning a career (22:22–23:11); the second part deals with the concerns of youth (23:12–35); the third part characterizes the destinies of the good and the wicked (24:1–22). The whole is a kind of professional ethical guidebook. Its aim is to help its readers avoid trouble and advance their careers by living according to wisdom. It advises against bad companions on the very practical grounds that over time one will take on their qualities: Do not offer surety because of its dangers to yourself; do not use strategies to advance yourself, but rely on the benefits wisdom gives; avoid abusing sex and alcohol, for they can only harm you. Being a sage is held up almost as if wisdom were a vocation (especially in 22:29–23:9). The advice not to envy and imitate the wicked, repeated three times (23:14; 24:1, 19) is another means of inculcating confidence in the way of wisdom.

In 1923 the *Instructions of Amenemope* (ca. 1100 B.C.E.) was published. Its close relationship to Proverbs 22–24 was recognized immediately—its thirty chapters (cf. XXVII.6 and Prov. 22:20 emended), its preface (cf. III.8–IV.1 and Prov. 22:17–21), the match between its first two admonitions and the first two of Proverbs (cf. IV.4–19 and Prov. 22:22–25). Specific references are noted under individual verses below.

A few scholars have argued for dependence of *Amenemope* upon Proverbs, but the discovery of a fragment of *Amenemope* from the twelfth century B.C.E. has settled the argument in favor of the priority of *Amenemope*. Some scholars, such as A. Alt and I. Grumbach[1] have argued that both works derive from a now lost Egyptian source, but they have found few followers. Proverbs' use of the Egyptian work is neither slavish nor predictable; *Amenemope*'s influence is traceable only in 22:17–23:11 and even there the borrowing is free. Proverbs imposes on these verses its characteristic mechanisms for engaging the reader— wit and wordplay, irony, and paradox (see under 22:26–27; 23:1–3).

More important than individual verses is the importation into Proverbs of the spirit of the Egyptian work. *Amenemope* represents a stage in the development of the Egyptian genre of instruction. It displays a new inwardness and a quest for serenity. Though *Amenemope* still presumes that worldly success attends the practice of virtue, it no longer emphasizes action and achievement but inner calm and the expectation that correct behavior will triumph, if not in this life then in the next. The ideal is not achievement but contemplation, modesty, compassion, and serenity.[2]

Relevant sections of *Amenemope* are reprinted in the textual notes and commentary. Proverbs' thirty paragraphs are noted in brackets. Many scholars, it should be noted, do not believe that thirty sections can be marked off in this way. Readers will have to judge for themselves the persuasiveness of the following divisions in the commentary below.

22:17   **The Words of the Wise**

> Incline your ear and listen to my words,
>   let your mind attend to my teaching.[a]
18 How good it is when you store them within
>   so they can be constantly on your lips!
19 I am teaching you today, yes indeed, you,
>   that your trust might be in Yahweh.
20 See, I have written for you thirty sayings[b]
>   containing counsel and knowledge,
21 to teach you truth and reliable words,
>   so you can speak to those who employ you.[c]

---

1. A. Alt, "Zur literarischen Analyse der Weisheit Amenemope," in *Wisdom in Israel and in the Ancient Near East* (*VT* Supplement 3), ed. M. Noth and D. W. Thomas (Leiden: Brill, 1955), 16–25, and I. Grumbach, *Untersuchungen zur Lebenslehre des Amenemope* (Münchener Ägyptologische Studien 23; Munich: Deutscher Kunstverlag, 1973).

2. M. Lichtheim, *AEL* 2.146.

22[1] Do not rob a poor person because he is poor;
          do not crush a needy person in the gate,
23   for Yahweh will take up their case,
          and despoil their despoilers of life.
24[2] Do not associate with an angry person,
          do not accompany a hothead,
25   lest you learn his ways,
          and spring a trap upon yourself.
26[3] Do not be among those giving their hand to another,
          those pledging themselves as surety.
27   If you cannot make good,
          your very bed will be taken[d] from under you!
28[4] Do not move an ancient boundary stone,
          one that your ancestors set up.
29[5] Do you see a man skilled in his craft?
          He will enter the service of kings;
          he will never enter the service of the obscure.[e]
23:1[6] When you sit down to dine with a ruler,
          consider carefully what is before you.
2   Stick the knife in your gullet
          if you have a big appetite.
3   Do not crave his viands,
          for it is food that deceives.
4[7]   Do not wear yourself out to acquire wealth;
          use your intelligence, hold back.[f]
5   No sooner do your eyes fly to it than it disappears,
          for it makes wings for itself,
          flying away like an eagle to the sky.
6[8]   Do not eat dinner with an unwilling host,
          and do not crave his viands;
7   for they will become inedible in the throat.[g]
          "Eat and drink," he tells you,
          but his heart is not with you.
8   Take only a bite and you will vomit it up
          and ruin your choice words.
9[9]   Do not speak in the ear of a fool,
          for he will despise your wise words.
10[10] Do not move the boundary stone of a widow,[h]
          and do not trespass on the fields of orphans,
11   for their redeemer is mighty;
          he will take up their case against you.
12[11] Apply your mind to discipline,
          and your ears to discerning speech.

13[12] Do not withhold discipline from a youth.
  If you strike him with a rod he will not die.
14 Strike him with a rod
  and you will save his soul from Sheol.
15[13] My son, if your heart becomes wise,
  my heart too will rejoice.
16 My innards will rejoice,
  if your lips speak what is right.
17[14] Do not let your heart emulate sinners,
  but rather those who revere Yahweh at all times,
18 for then you will have a future,
  and your hope will not be cut off.
19[15] Listen, my son, and become wise,
  walk on the path your own heart chooses.
20 Do not be one of those who quaff wine,
  one of those who devour meat.
21 For quaffers and devourers will come to poverty,
  and sleeping late will put you in rags.
22[16] Obey your father who begot you;
  do not despise your mother when she grows old.
23 Buy truth and do not barter away
  wisdom, discipline, and intelligence!
24[17] The father of a righteous person surely exults;
  he who begets a wise son rejoices over him.
25 Give your father and mother cause to rejoice over you,
  and make her who bore you exult!
26[18] My son, direct your heart to me,
  let your eyes observe my ways:
27 A foreign woman[i] is a deep pit,
  a forbidden woman is a narrow well.
28 Yes, like a robber[j] she lies in wait,
  she destroys the faithless among the human race.
29[19] Who has woe? Who has trouble?
  Who has fights? Who has shouts?
  Who has unexplained wounds?
  Who has bleary eyes?
30 Who stays up late over wine,
  who goes around quaffing liquor.
31[20] Do not gaze at wine when it shimmers red,
  when it sparkles in the cup!
  It goes down smoothly,
32 then it bites like a snake,

stings like a viper.

33 Your eyes see strange sights,
    your mind speaks absurdities.

34 You will be like someone asleep on the high seas,
    asleep on the top of the mast.

35 "They beat me up but I'm not hurt,
    they clubbed me but I didn't feel it.
When can I get up,
    when can I go out and shop for more?"

24:1[21] Do not envy wicked people,
    and do not yearn to be with them,

2 for their hearts contemplate havoc,
    and their lips speak mischief.

3[22] By wisdom a house is built,
    by prudence is it established;

4 by knowledge are its rooms filled
    with every precious and beautiful possession.

5[23] A wise person is more powerful[k] than a mighty one,
    a learned person, more than one endowed with strength:

6 for by strategy war is waged,
    by many counsellors victory is achieved.

7[24] Wise words[l] are beyond a fool's reach,
    in the assembly he does not open his mouth;

8 as he calculates how to do evil
    people brand him a troublemaker.

9 A fool's plan gains no acceptance,
    a scoffer is an abomination to the community.

10[25] Did you fail in a day of trouble,
    did your strength fall short?[m]

11 Did you refrain from rescuing those in danger of death,[n]
    those tottering, near slaughter,

12 because you said, "We didn't know about it?"
Surely the Searcher of hearts understands,
    the Watcher of souls knows,
    and will recompense each according to his actions.

13[26] My son, eat honey for it is good,
    the honeycomb is sweet to your lips.

14 Reflect: so wisdom is to your soul.
If you attain it, you will have a future,
    and your hope will not be cut short.

15[27] Do not lie in wait[o] at the house of a righteous person,
    do not lay siege to his dwelling.

16   For though a righteous person fall seven times he will get up,
       but the wicked collapse from just one mishap.
17[28] When your enemy falls, do not celebrate,
       when he collapses, do not let your heart rejoice,
18   lest Yahweh see it and be displeased
       and turn his wrath from him.
19[29] Do not be upset by malefactors,
       do not look enviously at the wicked,
20   for an evil person has no future,
       the lamp of the wicked will go out.
21[30] Fear Yahweh and the king, my son,
       with those of a different view have nothing to do.
22   For disaster will issue suddenly from the two,
       and calamity from both—who knows when.ᵖ

a. The parallelism in MT is awkward, literally, "Extend your ear and listen to the words of the wise and place your heart to my teaching." One expects "my words" in colon A as a match to "my teaching" in colon B. S, T, and V all read MT (T prefaces "my son"). G, despite its running the final words of v. 17 into v. 18, preserves the superior reading: *logois sophōn paraballe son ous kai akoue emon logon*, "To the words of the wise direct your ear and hear my word." One may conjecture (with Alonso Schökel) that the original Hebrew, *dibrê ḥăkāmîm*, was copied on the manuscript line below its proper one, where the phrase became confused with *dbry* in the original *ht 'znk wšmʻ dbry* (= *děbāray*, "my words"). "The Words of the Wise" is the original title. The emended title is confirmed by 24:23, "These *Also* Are of the Wise," and by the fact that the other sections of Proverbs all have titles except 31:10–31, where the acrostic form suffices to set it apart.
   b. We read *šělōšîm*, "thirty," for MT *šilšôm*, "three days ago."
   c. The Hebrew is corrupt. No version reads it in the way that MT does. We take the following as original: *lhwdy'k qst 'mry 'mt lhšyb 'mrym lšlhyk.'mt* came into colon B through dittography. MT *'mrym 'mt* is not idiomatic Hebrew.
   d. MT *yiqqaḥ*, "he takes," should be repointed to the passive, *yuqqaḥ* (as G).
   e. The final Hebrew word, *ḥăššukîm*, is uncertain, though the context suggests it means a state opposite to royalty. The Targum elsewhere translates Hebrew *dal* and *'ebyôn* by Aramaic *ḥăšîk* (Jer. 39:10; 2 Kings 24:14 and 25:12). Colon C is odd since triplets are rare in Proverbs; it woodenly repeats *yityaṣṣēb* ("enters the service of"). Perhaps it is an addition.
   f. The phrase "from your intelligence" occurs also in Job 39:26 with the same meaning. The verb *ḥādal* used absolutely can reverse a preceding verb, as in Judg. 5:6–7 and 1 Sam. 2:5, hence "cease [from wearing yourself out]." Verse 5c has a qere reading (*hătā'îp*, "have you caused [your eyes] to fly," i.e., "cast [your eyes]") and a ketib reading (*hătā'ûp*, "do your eyes flutter/hover upon it?"). The ketib seems more natural; the qere may have arisen from a desire to preserve normal agreement between verb and subject. Feminine plural "eyes" can be the subject of a masculine singular verb especially if the verb precedes.
   g. All the versions except T read MT, but understand it differently. The Masoretes

pointed the Hebrew to read, "like someone who has [already] calculated in his mind, so is he," evidently interpreting Hebrew *šʿr* by Mishnaic Hebrew *šěʿar*, "to calculate, measure." G, followed by S, took the word as *šěʿār*, "hair": "for in the manner that someone might swallow a hair so he eats and drinks," i.e., sparingly. T reads *trʿʾ*, "gate": "for as a gate is high so is he haughty in his soul." V renders MT freely: "because like a soothsayer and riddler he evaluates what he does not know: 'Eat and drink . . . ' "

　　We retain MT (changing only *npšw* to *npš*) and interpret (with Rashi) *šʿr* as *šōʿār*, "inedible, indigestible (?)," from Jer. 29:17 *wěnātattî ʾôtām kattěʾēnîm haššōʿārîm ʾăšer lōʾ těʾākalnāh mērōaʿ*, "and I will make you *rotten* figs so bad they cannot be eaten." See *HALAT* 1490 for references to philological opinions on *šʿr*.

　　h. Though there is no ancient textual warrant for doing so, we emend with many commentators MT *ʿôlām*, "ancient," to *ʾalmānāh*, "widow," for (1) *ʿôlām* seems to have been borrowed from 22:28; (2) "widow and orphan" is a common phrase in the ancient Near East and in the Bible; (3) "widow" occurs in *Amenemope*, chap. 6 (VII. 15; see commentary on 22:28), which has demonstrably influenced our saying; (4) the graphic similarity of *ʿwlm* and *ʾlmn* satisfactorily explains the scribal error.

　　i. We emend MT *zônāh*, "prostitute," to *zārāh*, "foreign woman, prostitute," on the grounds that the usual fixed pair in Proverbs is *zārāh//nokrîyāh* and that G has *allotrios*.

　　j. Hebrew *ḥetep* in colon A (lit., "seizing") is abstract for concrete, "one who seizes" (GKC §83c). It is tempting (with Ehrlich) to relate the word to the rare verb *ḥātap*, "to seize, snatch away," and *ḥāṭap*, "to catch, seize." The latter verb is used in Judg. 21:21 for seizing women for the sake of marriage and in Ps. 10:9 is used twice with "to lie in wait."

　　Colon B, literally, "and the faithless among human beings she will increase," does not make sense. Gemser repoints "faithless" as a passive participle, "those who have been deceived." G. R. Driver takes the word as a collective noun, "treachery," rendering "she repeats treachery toward human beings."[3] The translation of JPSV offers perhaps the best parallel to colon A: "[she] destroys (*tāsēp*) the unfaithful among men." The verb is the hiphil conjugation of the verb *sûp*, which in Zeph. 1:2, 3 refers to the destruction of the human race.

　　k. G, followed by S and T, correctly interpreted Hebrew *gbr* (MT *geber*, "man") as the verb *gābar*, "be strong, mighty; be more powerful than" (with *min* as in 2 Sam. 1:23 and Ps. 65:4). G therefore read in v. 5a *mēʾāz* rather than *beʿôz*. Most commentators rightly adopt G's readings. In v. 6, G and S do not reflect *kî*, which is again the superior reading. With S and T we interpret MT *tʿśh* as niphal *těʾāśeh*, "is done," and reject *lk* of MT as secondary. The typifying use of the second person singular in v. 6, which is frequent in English, is rare in Hebrew.

　　l. *Rāʾmôt* occurs in Job 28:18 and Ezek. 27:16 with the meaning of something precious or imported, prompting some to suggest "a luxury to fools is wisdom," but this proposal is farfetched. *Rāʾmôt* is the qal conjugation feminine plural participle of *rûm*, "to be high," which here, as sometimes with hollow verbs, is written *plene* with *aleph*, like *lāʾt* in 2 Sam. 9:5 (mispointed *lāʾaṭ*) and *rāʾš* in Prov. 10:4 (mispointed *rēʾš*; so G. Bergsträsser, *Hebräische Grammatik* [Hildesheim: Olms, 1962, reprint of 1918 edition], 2.28g).

---

3. "Problems in the Hebrew Text of Proverbs," *Biblica* 32 (1951): 196.

m. Verse 10b seems too short and may be corrupt. We follow Alonso Schökel, who regards colon B as semantically parallel to colon A ("did your strength falter?").

n. *Haṣṣēl* is the hiphil conjugation infinitive absolute dependent on *taḥśôk,* "cease." The meaning of *hitrappîtā* is assured by 18:9, "to be slack, careless."

o. With several commentators we excise *rāšā'* in colon A as a gloss ("Do not, O wicked person, lie in wait . . . "), though all the versions have it.

p. G has five sayings not in MT that develop the theme of obedience to the king in 24:21–22. The translation follows Rahlfs's numbering.

> ²²ᵃA son obeying a commandment will avoid destruction,
>   for such a one has fully received it.
> ²²ᵇLet nothing false be spoken by the tongue of the king;
>   let nothing false go forth from his tongue.
> ²²ᶜThe tongue of a king is a sword and not flesh;
>   who is delivered up [to it] will be destroyed.
> ²²ᵈFor if his wrath is aroused,
>   he will kill human beings with bowstrings
> ²²ᵉand devour the bones of human beings,
>   and he will burn (them) as a fire
>   so nothing edible is left for the young of eagles.

[22:17–21] The prologue draws on the prologue in *Amenemope,* chap. 1. Like that chapter (part of which appears below), Proverbs issues an invitation to listen to the words of the wise and store them in the heart (memorize them), whence they can be called up and provide guidance.

> Give your ears, hear the sayings, / Give your heart to understand them; / It profits to put them in your heart; / Woe to him who neglects them! / Let them rest in the casket of your belly; / May they be bolted in your heart. / When there rises a whirlwind of words, / They'll be a mooring post for your tongue. / If you make your life with these in your heart, / You will find it a success; / You will find my words a storehouse for life; / Your being will prosper upon earth. (III.9–IV.2)

Proverbs presumes the same process of hearing, memorizing, reflecting, and speaking (vv. 17–18, from ear to mind to lips). Differently from *Amenemope,* the God (Yahweh) is named explicitly. In fact, "Yahweh" in v. 19 is in the center, the eighteenth of thirty-six words. As in the instruction to Proverbs in 1:7 ("revering Yahweh is the beginning of wisdom"), placing one's trust in Yahweh is the goal of the teaching.

The old controversy about the meaning of MT *šlšwn* in v. 20 (ketib *šilšôm,* "three days ago," ordinarily preceded by *těmôl,* or qere *šālîšîm,* "threefold,") has been resolved by a like phrase in the final lines of *Amenemope.*

> Look to these *thirty* chapters. / They inform, they educate; / They are the foremost of all books, / They make the ignorant wise. / If they are read to the ignorant, / He is cleansed through them. / Be filled with them, put them in your heart,

/ and become a man who expounds them, // One who expounds them, / One who expounds as a teacher. / The scribe who is skilled in his office. / He is found worthy to be a courtier. (XXVII.6–17)

The title "Words of the Wise" was damaged in MT but can be reconstructed from G (see textual notes). "The *Words* of . . . " rather than, say, "The *Proverbs* of . . . " (as in 1:1 and 10:1) is also the title of 30:1–4 ("The Words of Agur") and of 31:1–9 ("The Words of Lemuel"). The latter sections came from non-Israelite sources.

[22:22–23] The Words of the Wise follows the topical order of *Amenemope*, chap. 2 (IV.4–5), which immediately comes after the prologue. It warns against robbing the poor: "Beware of robbing a wretch, / of attacking a cripple." A similar sentiment is expressed in chap. 20 (XX.21–XXI.8):

> Do not confound a man in the law court, / In order to brush aside one who is right. / Do not incline to the well-dressed man, / and rebuff the one in rags. / Don't accept the gift of a powerful man, and deprive the weak for his sake. / Maat is a great gift of god, / He gives it to whom he wishes. / The might of him who resembles him, / It saves the poor from his tormentor.

In the entire section (only partially quoted above) the motives given to act justly in court are reverence for the overriding power of *maat* on the side of the poor and the dangers that come upon evildoers. In other words, one should not go against the (divinely implanted) system. Proverbs argues in a similar way. The poor, by not having human protectors, have Yahweh as their protector. Paradoxically, their poverty gives them a more powerful protector than the rich could afford. The "gate," or space inside the city gate, was a meeting place and site of legal trials (e.g., Deut. 21:19; Amos 5:12; Prov. 24:7). "Case" (*rîb*) is a legal term, as in Ex. 23:2, 3, 6; Deut. 21:5. "Life" is emphatic by its final position. Cf. Isa. 1:17.

[22:24–25] *Amenemope*, chap. 3 (V.10–19), is about "the hot-mouthed man." Proverbs drew also on chap. 9 (XI.13–XIII.9):

> Do not befriend the heated man, / Nor approach him for conversation. / Keep your tongue from answering your superior, / And take care not to insult him. . . . / He is the ferryman of snaring words. / He goes and comes with quarrels.

Hotheads bring trouble upon themselves and everyone around them. Proverbs has a similar view; from such people one learns angry behavior, which provokes evil consequences, which, metaphorically, are a snare. Hebrew *môqēš* ("snare") is literally the trigger of trap, by metonymy the trap itself.

[22:26–27] In biblical law, the seizure of a pledged person or debtor could be prevented by someone providing bail or surety. Whoever intervened assumed responsibility for the debt. Proverbs consistently inveighs against providing such surety for others (e.g., 6:1–5; 11:15; 20:16; 27:13) on the grounds that it poses a danger to the guarantor. Proverbs's prohibition is not universally shared, however; Sir. 29:14–20, for example, is more open to the practice.

Grasping the hand of another was the legal gesture of agreeing to a contract (6:1; 17:18). There may be sardonic humor in the argument against the practice. Debtors themselves were protected by law from having their cloaks kept from them at night (Ex. 22:25–26 [26–27E]; Deut. 24:12–13; and the Yabneh Yam ostracon[4]) on the grounds that for the poor their cloak was their sleeping garment. Guarantors had no such legal protection and could lose their very bed.

[22:28] *Amenemope,* chap. 6, forbids moving a boundary marker to enlarge one's own holdings:

> Do not move the markers on the borders of fields, / Nor shift the position of the measuring cord. / Do not be greedy for a cubit of land, / Nor encroach on the boundaries of widows. / The trodden furrow worn down by time, / He who disguises it in the fields, / When he has snared [it] by false oaths, / He will be caught by the might of the Moon [= the disk of the god Thot]. (VII.12–19)

The next twenty-eight lines of *Amenemope* develop the idea that unjustly acquired property will disappear. Proverbs states the motive briefly: to move a boundary stone is to trample on the work of one's ancestors. Deuteronomy 19:14 also speaks of land markers (words identical to our passage are italicized): "You *shall not move* the *boundary marker* of your neighbor, which the ancestors established in your inherited land, which you will inherit in the land that Yahweh your God is giving you to possess." The boundaries the ancestors drew remain authoritative. This verse repeated in a variant form in 23:10, which demarcates the material between the two verses as a unified section.

[22:29] This observation ends the opening series of prohibitions and points forward to the series of admonitions on a sage's career (23:1–9). For a similar use of the hypothetical perfect "Have you seen . . . ?" see 26:12 and 29:20. "Skilled" (*māhîr*) can refer to composing or interpreting literature; the word is used in that meaning in Ps. 45:2; Ezra 7:6; and *Ahiqar* 1:1 (Aramaic, *spr ḥkym wmhyr,* "a wise and skillful scribe"). The meaning here seems more general, however. The observation seems to draw on the final observation in *Amenemope:* "The scribe who is skilled in his office, he is found worthy to be a courtier" (XXVII.16–17). Proverbs' observation points forward to 23:1–9, which warns about traps for an ambitious young sage—misusing social occasions as opportunities for advancement (vv. 1–3, 6–8), greed (vv. 4–5), and self-importance. The section is marked off by 22:28 and 23:10, admonitions on boundary stones.

[23:1–3] Dining etiquette is found in the Old Kingdom instructions of *Kagemni* and *Ptahhotep,* as well as in chaps. 23 and 26 of *Amenemope.* Luxurious meals apparently were rare enough to be occasions of intemperance and

4. For a recent translation and discussion, see K. A. D. Smelik, *Writings from Ancient Israel* (Louisville, Ky.: Westminster John Knox Press, 1991), 93–100.

of later regret for young and ambitious courtiers. *Kagemni* advises restraint at table and *Ptahhotep* exhorts one to be content with one's serving:

> When you are a guest / at the table of one who is greater than you / then take what he gives you, as they serve it before you. / Do not look at what lies before *him*, but always look only at what lies before *you*. [5]

Amenemope, chap. 26 (XXIV.2–XXX.15), warns against using a repast to curry favor with one's social betters: "Do not sit down in the beer house / in order to join one greater than you." Chapter 23 is especially relevant to our passage:

> Do not eat in the presence of an official / And then set your mouth before <him>; / If you are sated pretend to chew, / Content yourself with your saliva. / Look at the bowl that is before you, / And let it serve your needs. An official is great in his office, / As a well is rich in drawings of water. (XXIII.13–20)

Proverbs is equally vivid. Important is the double meaning of "set before you," which refers both to the food and the host: Consider carefully the food/host before you and put your knife not to your food to satisfy your hunger but to your gullet to restrain your hunger. Unless you do, you will obtain neither food nor favor. The versions missed the play in Hebrew *lĕpāneykā,* "before you," which can refer both to food set before one (e.g., Gen. 18:8; 24:33; 1 Sam. 9:24) and to a human being standing before one (e.g., Gen. 18:22; Deut. 10:11; Judg. 9:39). The versions (which all read MT) take it only of food and end up in considerable confusion.

The usual scholarly interpretation—a sage should show modesty and restraint at the meals of the powerful—does not fully explain the Hebrew. First, the Hebrew idiom (used only here) in v. 1b, "understand completely, consider carefully," is inappropriate for food alone. Second, the folly of putting one's table knife in oneself rather than in one's food at the moment of greatest hunger shows that the entire business of currying favor is useless. The NRSV translation, "Put a knife to your throat," (lit., "stick the knife in your jaw") is misleading because in English the phrase is an idiom for threatening someone with death. Hebrew *śakkîn* is a table knife, not a dagger. Though occurring only here in the Bible, in Aramaic and in Mishnaic Hebrew it is a knife for cutting meat and vegetables. Third, "food that deceives" in v. 3b is best read on the two levels already established: the meal that cannot be eaten because of the need to restrain oneself and the meal that cannot further one's career. The phrase does not mean, despite Toy, food offered with deceitful intent but as in 21:28, that which deceives. Cf. Sir. 31:12–21.

---

5. My translation of H. Brunner, *Die Weisheitsbücher der Ägypter,* 2d ed. (Zurich: Artemis, 1991), 114; his italics.

[23:4–5] *Amenemope,* chap. 7 (IX.10–X.15), warns against setting one's heart on wealth, for destiny (personal) and fate (from outside) are beyond one's control; ill-gotten good disappear into primordial nothingness (Egyptian *dat*) and "make wings for themselves like geese and fly away to the sky":

> Do not set your heart on wealth, / There is no ignoring Fate and Destiny; / Do not let your heart go straying, / Every man comes to his hour. / Do not strain to seek increase, / What you have, let it suffice you. / If riches come to you by theft, / They will not stay the night with you. / Comes day they are not in your house, / Their place is seen but they're not there; / Earth opened its mouth, leveled them, swallowed them, / and made them sink into *dat.* / They made a hole as big as their size, / And sank into the netherworld; / They made themselves wings like geese, / And flew away to the sky. / Do not rejoice in wealth from theft, / Nor complain of being poor. / If the leading archer presses forward, / His company abandons him; / The boat of the greedy is left in the mud / While the bark of the silent sails with the wind. / You shall pray to the Aten when he rises, / Saying: "Grant me well-being and health"; / He will give you needs for this life, / And you will be safe from fear. (x. 4–5)

Proverbs develops the imagery in *Amenemope*—fleeting birds and wealth—by imagining covetous intent itself as a flight of the eyes. Just as *Amenemope* speaks of the heart straying, so Proverbs speaks of the eyes flying away. On the topic of avarice, see 28:22 and 1 Tim. 6:9.

[23:6–8] The versions follow G's translation of *ra' 'ayin* (lit., "evil of eye") as "envious," but the meaning is more subtle. Translations such as "Do not eat of a stingy man's food" (JPSV, similarly NRSV, REB, and nearly all commentators) leave major questions unanswered: Why would anyone go to a known miser's in the first place? Why does the host say one thing and mean another? Why does the guest vomit up the food? Moreover, in this reading v. 7 is puzzling.

The best solution is to assume that Proverbs combines in an original manner two traditional elements from Egyptian instructions: warnings against going to banquets uninvited such as are found in *Cheti* (= *Satire of the Trades*), a passage from *Amenemope,* (chap. 11 (XIV.5–XV.7), and *Any* X.10–13:

> Attend to your position, / Be it low or high; / It is not good to press forward, / Step according to rank. / Do not intrude on a man in his house, / Enter when you have been called; / He may say "Welcome" with his mouth, / Yet deride you in his thoughts. / One gives food to one who is hated, / Supplies to one who enters uninvited.

Cheti IX.7–9 is similar. Hence we render "evil of eye" by "unwilling host." In 28:22 and Sir. 14:10 the phrase means "stingy." Its opposite, "good of eye," in 22:9 describes a person who shares his food with the poor. As Römheld points out, the uninvited and unwanted guest forces the host, who is bound by oriental custom to utter gracious words (v. 7b), into a negative attitude (v. 7c).[6] A passage from *Amenemope* is relevant:

> Do not covet a poor man's goods, / Nor hunger for his bread; / A poor man's goods are a block in the throat, / It makes the gullet vomit. / He who makes gain by lying oaths, / His heart is misled by his belly; / Where there is fraud success is feeble, / The bad spoils the good. / You will be guilty before your superior, / And confused in your account; / Your pleas will be answered by a curse, / Your prostrations by a beating. / The big mouthful of bread—you swallow, you vomit it, / And you are emptied of your gain. (XIV.5–18)

Proverbs takes only the food imagery from *Amenemope:* line 6 ("Nor hunger for his bread"), lines 7–8 ("a block in the throat"; "It makes the gullet vomit"; "you vomit it up"), line 10 ("His heart is misled by his belly"), line 17 ("The big mouthful of bread—you swallow, you vomit it"). To the author of Proverbs, uninvited banqueters are thieves who will suffer the same consequences as those who rob the poor in *Amenemope*, chap. 11. They cannot keep their unjust gain. Since the setting is a banquet, they vomit up their ill-gotten gains. Like the previous two admonitions, this one warns against strategies to advance one's career by any means other than fidelity to wisdom and to the vocation of sage.

[23:9] A fourth error of young sages is to assume that everyone will be impressed with their learning. They will not. The sage should have a sense of the audience.

[23:10–11] The admonition reprises 22:28 and draws on 22:22–23 to affirm the paradox that the poor, *because* they have no one to call upon, are powerful since Yahweh directly takes up their case. Standard weights and measures (see under 11:1) and fixed boundaries, which are an important protection to the lowest strata of society, are guaranteed by Yahweh. *Amenemope*, chap. 6, bases its exhortation on pragmatic grounds: one puts oneself in danger from the Moon's (the god Thot's) judgment and puts one's own property at risk.

[23:12] A new section (23:12–35) begins here, in which positive commands and an affectionate parental tone replace the admonitions of 22:22–23:11 (in which there were seven occurrences of the negative particle *'al*). Allusions to *Amenemope* cease with this verse. The concern from now on is with issues associated with young people: finding role models (v. 17–18), restraining high sexual energy (vv. 26–27), and the dangers of alcohol (vv. 19–21 and 29–35). Though beginning a new section, this verse manages to sum up the immediately preceding verses: Avoid shabby self-promotion and self-importance; devote yourself purely to wisdom.

---

6. *Wege der Weisheit: Die Lehren Amenemopes und Proverbien 22:17–24:22* (BZAW 184; Berlin: de Gruyter, 1989), 7.

Verse 12 urges the submission of one's entire self (ear and heart [mind] = hearing and reflection) to discipline and wise sayings. No individual, especially when young, can become wise without accepting tradition, which is often at odds with untutored instinct. The fixed pair *mûsār* ("discipline") // *'imrê da'at* ("discerning speech") occurs also in 19:27. "Ear" // "heart" occurs in Deut. 29:3; Ps. 10:17; Prov. 18:15 and 22:17.

[**23:13–14**] This counsel assumes young people find it difficult to accept the traditions of their elders. *Ahiqar,* lines 81–82 are similar:

Spare not your son from the rod; otherwise, can you save him [from wickedness]?

> If I beat you, my son,
> you will not die;
> but if I leave you alone,
> [you will not live].
>
> A blow for a serving-boy,
> a rebuke for a slave-girl,
> and for all your servants, discipline![7]

Ahiqar and Proverbs play with a certain grim humor on death: A young person will not die from instructional blows but from their absence, for (premature) death results from uncorrected folly. The humor and wordplay show the verse cannot be used as a justification for corporal punishment. The very next verse, in fact, is full of affection for the child. There is notable Hebrew alliteration in v. 13a, *timna' minna'ar mûsār.* Cf. 13:24; 19:18; 22:15. Sirach 30:1–13 develops the topic of training a child.

[**23:15–16**] As if to counterbalance the harshness of vv. 13–14, this statement expresses the intense joy and pride of parents and teachers when a child or student acts wisely in mind and speech. The repetition of "heart" and the /ī/ sound in Hebrew in v. 15 (three times) underline the bond of feeling between parent and offspring.

[**23:17–18**] Peer groups exercise a strong influence on young people. The sage warns against becoming a member of the wicked, who, as a doomed group, will have no descendants (cf. 1:8–19). Rather, one should learn to admire those who revere Yahweh, a group that has a future. The advice not to envy or emulate the wicked was common (Ps. 37:1; Prov. 3:31; 24:1, 19). In Psalm 37 (esp. v. 1) the temptation to envy sinners is answered, as it is here, by assuring a blessed future to the righteous. The warning against envying the wicked is repeated within the section in 24:1–2, 19–20.

---

7. Translation of J. M. Lindenberger, *The Old Testament Pseudepigrapha,* ed. J. H. Charlesworth (New York: Doubleday, 1985), 2.498.

[23:19–21] The idiom *'aššēr bĕderek* in 4:14 and 9:6 means simply "to walk in the way" (= "to conduct oneself"). Our saying means to walk according to one's own (instructed) mind. To listen to one's own mind (lit., "heart") rather than to evil companions is difficult, especially for young people.

There are serious obstacles to acting out of one's own convictions; two of these are alcohol and luxurious living. Excessive consumption of alcohol (and meat) symbolizes here a decadent style of living. In Deut. 21:18–21 the verbs "to quaff" and "to devour" describe a son who refuses to listen to his father and mother; he is judged deserving of death. There may be an allusion to that ancient law here, except that here not listening to father or teacher leads to poverty rather than death. Anyone trying to play at being rich by conspicuous consumption will end up poor.

[23:22–23] Most commentators regard vv. 22–25 as one unit, but we see two. Plöger, for example, suggests that, logically, v. 24 should follow immediately v. 22 (he regards v. 23 as a possible insertion from 7:7, for it is missing in G; so also Ehrlich). Plöger further notes inconsistencies in vv. 24–25. Such difficulties disappear if one takes vv. 22–23 and 24–25 as two distinct sayings. Verses 22–23 play on parallel positive and negative imperatives: listen to // do not despise, acquire // do not barter away, as if truth and wisdom were the parents of a wise child.

[23:24–25] Verses 24–25 differ from vv. 22–23. They develop an exhortation ("make your parents joyful") from the familiar observation that wise children make their parents happy (see under 10:1). The phrase "to get wisdom (or intelligence)" is found in 4:5; 16:16; 17:16 and the phrase "to despise wisdom (or insight)" is found in 1:7 and 23:9.

[23:26–28] The saying is a condensed version of chap. 7 with its emotional call to "my son" to beware of the foreign woman (7:1–5), her traps (7:21–23), and her intent to add the youth to her list of victims (7:24–27). As in 23:15, 19, 22, a trustful and affectionate relationship between father and son (teacher and student) is the basis of education: accept *my* counsel! "Give me your heart (= mind)," is, despite the impression given by a literal English translation, a request for obedience rather than love. The danger of the prostitute is expressed by the metaphor of a deep pit and narrow opening, which in 22:14 and elsewhere may have a sexual connotation.

[23:29–30] These verses present a riddle in six questions. Each riddling question begins with the Hebrew consonants *lm*. Verse 30a, seventh in the series, likewise begins with *lm,* leading the reader to expect one more riddling question. But it turns out to be the answer to the riddle. The humorous tone mocks the drunken brawler.

23:31–35 Humor at the expense of the drunkard continues. As in the portrait of the naive youth (7:6–23), v. 31 catches the fascination with imagined pleasures. The pleasure turns out to be like a snakebite, with hallucinations, vertigo, and blackout. Such physical horrors teach fools nothing (v. 35cd), for by definition they cannot learn from rebuke. The description begins with the visual and tactile sensations that the wine produces and develops the effects of the drink in images: the bite of a snake, the sway of the sea, and the nausea of a sailor. The author cites the foolish thinking of the drunkard. Isaiah 5:11 paints a similar picture: "Ho, you who rise early in the morning to pursue liquor, who tarry in the evening, inflamed by wine."

The New Kingdom Egyptian *Instruction of Any* (4.7–10) relies on exhortation rather than satire to make the same point.

> Don't indulge in drinking beer, / Lest you utter evil speech / And don't know what you're saying. / If you fall and hurt your body, / None holds out a hand to you: / Your companions in the drinking / Stand up saying: "Out with the drunk!" / If one comes to seek you and talk with you, / One finds you lying on the ground, / As if you were a little child.

For further thoughts on the topic of drunkenness, see Sir. 31:25–31.

[24:1–2] A new section (24:1–14)—on the different destinies of the wicked (or foolish) and the wise—begins with a warning. This admonition occurs three times in the thirty sayings (23:17–18, here, and 24:19–20). Common to all the admonitions is the verb *qannē'*, "to be jealous, zealous, envious," which also occurs in 1:15–19 and 3:31. The motive stated in the first and the third occurrence—the wicked have no future—is expressed indirectly here. Their malicious planning and speaking invites retribution. Verses 7–9 and 10–12 detail their self-destruction.

[24:3–4] This saying and the next (vv. 5–6) asserts that one should not rely on the wicked to establish a household or defend oneself. Wisdom suffices. "House" here includes both building and household. The verbs "to build, establish" and "to fill" are used elsewhere of houses (e.g., 2 Sam. 7:13; Deut. 6:11). Yahweh built the universe by wisdom (3:19–20 and 8:22–31). Proverbs 3:13–20 assured those courting wisdom that they would have wealth. This saying (and the similar 14:1) point forward to 31:10–31, the concluding portrait of the household built by wisdom.

[24:5–6] The paradox that the wise are mightier than warriors is proven true in war. Though usually regarded as a showcase of physical strength, war is in fact won by brains not brawn.

[24:7–9] Most scholars judge vv. 7–9 to be two or even three discrete sayings. If the couplets are taken singly, however, they are banal. In our view, the verses make a single statement as part of the section 24:1–14. Verses 3–6 here state the advantage of wisdom: it assures one of a house and strength. Verses 7–9 assert the disadvantage of folly: it alienates one from the community (v. 7), for fools' notoriety becomes known (v. 8), dooming their plans to failure and themselves to ostracism (v. 9). Verses 8 and 9 are linked by their use of the triliteral root *zmm,* translated here as "troublemaker" and "plan." Verses 7 and 9 also share a triliteral root *'wl,* translated here as "fool." Ehrlich understands "the gate [of the city]" in v. 7b to refer to markets as in 2 Kings 7:1, 17, that is, the fool is too stupid to participate in trading, but more likely the reference is to public assemblies where speakers must have credibility in order to be effective.

According to v. 7 fools can neither grasp nor express wisdom. As often in Proverbs, folly includes malice (v. 8a). People soon recognize the character of a fool (v. 8b); their notoriety ruins their plans (v. 9a) and isolates them from society (v. 9b). The Hebrew word *ḥaṭā't* in v. 9a, usually translated "sin," here simply means a missing of the mark, as frequently in wisdom literature.

[24:10–12] Excuses for not coming to the aid of the neighbor in distress do not suffice before the God who sees through self-serving excuses. The context escapes us. Is this about the judicial process (Plöger) or more generally about the necessity of every person to stand up for justice in serious cases?

[24:13–14] According to Ps. 119:103 God's word (or law) is sweeter than honey on the palate (see also Ps. 19:11; Prov. 16:24 and Ezek. 3:3). Here wisdom is sweet. There is a wordplay on the Hebrew word *nepeš* in v. 14, "throat" and "soul" (the moist breathing center of the body = life): as honey is welcome and life-giving so is wisdom. A similar thought is found in Sir. 24:19–20: "Come to me, you who desire me, / and eat your fill of my fruits. For the memory of me is sweeter than honey, and the possession of me sweeter than the honeycomb."

[24:15–16] The words for "house"—*nāweh,* "pasture, dwelling," and *rēbeṣ,* "resting place"—are a fixed pair in Isa. 35:7 and 65:10. In this saying, the ambusher rather than the ambushed is the one actually in danger, for the righteous person always ("seven times") makes a comeback. The wicked person, however, is tripped up by only one fall—perhaps the very act of ambushing. The proverb can be extended to ethics generally, where it is a sign of a righteous person to be able to rise up after a fall (Alonso Schökel).

[24:17–18] The saying is linked to the preceding verse by the recurrence of the fixed pair "to fall" and "to collapse." From motives of reverence, one should leave in God's hands the punishment of evil. Premature public celebration (the verbs of rejoicing imply *public* display of joy) preempts the hidden and often lengthy process of divine righting of human wrongdoing. Similarly, *Amenemope,* chap. 2 (V.3–6), counsels against exacting vengeance from enemies on the grounds that the gods will not ultimately let the enemy attain "the shore" (eternal life): "Lift him [the wicked] up; give him your hand, / leave <him> in the hand of the god; / fill his belly with bread of your own, / that he be sated and weep." Cf. 25:21–22. Romans 12:14–21 develops the idea.

[24:19–20] At the close of the thirty teachings the teacher seeks one last time to counter the corrosive example of the prosperous wicked by affirming evil has no staying power (as in 23:17–18 and 24:1–2). See the similar exhortations in 3:31; 23:17; 24:1–2; and Ps. 37:1.

[24:21–22] The conclusion echoes the pervading sentiment of Egyptian wisdom literature: accept reality, do not change it. Stay away from dissidents who will suffer royal and divine wrath. What takes place "suddenly" or "who knows when" is by definition abnormal and perhaps of divine origin. Human beings must accept boundaries in their lives. The juxtaposing of God and king is unusual in biblical literature (see 1 Kings 21:10 in the accusation against Naboth).

Proverbs 24:23–34

Further Words
of the Wise

This little collection lies between the thirty sayings of 22:17–24:22 and the large Hezekiah collection of chaps. 25–29. Its title in Hebrew, "These also (*gam 'ēlleh*) are of the Wise," indicate that an editor reckoned it as an appendix to the Words of the Wise (22:17–24:22). At this point G begins to arrange sections in a different order from MT. It places 30:1–14 immediately after 24:22 (and has several verses not in MT) after which it places MT 24:23–34.

As recognized by Meinhold, an editor has cleverly arranged the originally separate sayings into two parallel groups of three each. Two basic themes—law and labor—form a framework for the acts of speech and thought. There are additional indications of design: In numbers 1 and 6, a word in the first line— respectively *ṭôb*, "right" (lit., "good") and *'îš*, "lazy man,"—is repeated in the last line to form an *inclusio;* "field" in number 3 occurs again in number 6. The outline is schematized by Meinhold.

The law court	1.	Judges	4.	Witnesses
Speaking and thinking	2.	Helpful speech	5.	Harmful speech
Labor	3.	Positive	6.	Negative

24:23   **These Also Are from the Wise**

[1] It is not right to be partial to parties in a legal case.
24   The one who says to a guilty party, "You are innocent,"
        the nations will curse,
        the peoples will scorn,
25   but those who conduct fair hearings will fare well,
        rich blessings will come upon them.
26[2] He kisses the lips
        who gives straightforward responses.
27[3] Arrange your affairs outside,
        prepare them in the field;
        then you can build your house.

28[4] Do not be a witness against your neighbor without evidence;
    do not use your lips to deceive!
29[5] Do not say,
    "As he has done to me, I will do to him;
    I will repay each individual as his deed deserves!"
30[6] I passed by the field of a sluggard,
    by the vineyard of a person lacking sense.
31 Thorns were growing everywhere,
    nettles covered its surface;
    its stone fence was thrown down.
32 I looked and I reflected,
    I saw and I drew a lesson:
33 A bit more sleep, a bit more slumber,
    a bit more folding of the arms in repose,
34 and the poverty of a vagabond will come upon you,
    the destitution of a beggar.

[24:23–25] Section [1] matches section [4]. The style of these sayings and admonitions differs from those so far seen. These admonitions concern judges and the fourth section concerns witnesses. The idiom "to recognize faces" (*hakkēr pānîm*) in v. 23 occurs also in Deut. 1:17; 16:19; and Prov. 28:21 in the sense of being partial in judgment. The motive proffered for judges to be even-handed in the courtroom is the universal abhorrence they will incur if they let off the guilty. On the other hand, happiness and blessings will be theirs if they judge justly. The participle in v. 25, *môkîḥîm,* occurs often in Proverbs in the meaning "one who reproves, corrects," but here the context is legal, making it likely that the verb means "to conduct a [fair] hearing" (cf. Job 9:33). The law court is in a certain sense a sacred place. Blessings or curses come upon those who perform their duties well or ill. For v. 23, cf. 28:21.

[26] Section [2] matches section [5]. The verse is not about legal testimony, for the phrase "to give straightforward answers" elsewhere means simply to tell the truth or give an accurate report. According to the scheme of section 2 = section 5, the contrast is between answering accurately and lying. Kissing on the lips is an act of lovers (Cant. 1:2; 7:9; *KTU* 1.22:49–50, 55) and of friends. If one followed the logic strictly, the meaning would be that truth telling is as precious as a lover's kiss. A broader meaning seems more likely, however: the kiss is a gesture of respect and affection. The greatest sign of affection and respect for another is to tell that person the truth.

[27] Section [3] matches section [6]. Building a house is not simply a matter of constructing a dwelling. Before one builds, one must prepare the soil, that is, make sure the ground is productive and can support a household. The Hebrew word for "outside, external" normally means the street outside the house.

In Lev. 14:53, however, "outside" and "field" are juxtaposed and designate an area outside the city. That may be the meaning here, though "outside" may simply be anyplace external to the house. According to 1 Chron. 27:26 the phrase "the work of the field" means tilling the soil, as opposed to working vineyards and herding in the verses following (vv. 27–29). In this collection the placement of the verse opposite the sixth saying means that neglect of one's field is a sign that one is not building a house properly. The literal meaning is about preparing fields before building a house. The saying has a metaphorical level: Laying the groundwork is necessary before embarking on any great project.

[28] Section [4] matches section [1]. The condemnation of corrupt judges in vv. 23–25 is matched by this warning against being a false witness. Lying witnesses use their lips to deceive, which is a dishonorable thing. In the long run, a false witness will suffer loss of reputation by practicing deceit. Cf. Ex. 20:16; Deut. 5:20.

[29] Section [5] matches section [2]. The relationship between the two sections is not so direct as the other polarities in the chapter. The admonition warns against exacting vengeance on one's enemies. As often in the Bible, intention is expressed by citing a person's words. The admonition forbids using the principle, "I will treat others as they have treated me." Though the principle may seem reasonable at first hearing, it comes perilously close to playing God, for the statement "I will repay each individual as his deed deserves" is a quote of the divine speech in 24:12d, where it is *God* who repays each person. Proverbs here and in 24:17–18 warns against interfering with the divine process of retribution, which has its own dynamic. Relationships between people cannot be ruled by human beings taking vengeance into their own hands. Cf. 20:22.

[30–34] Section [6] matches section [3]. Neglect of one's fields through laziness is the prelude to poverty. It is a teaching story, like those in Prov. 6:9–11, chap. 7, and Ps. 37:35–36. Psalm 37 has similar vocabulary (identical words italicized): "*I saw* a ruthless scoundrel, / strong as flourishing cedars. / When *I passed by* (G, S, V) again, they were gone (*hinnēh,* as in Prov. 24:31a), / though I searched, they could not be found." The narrative is artful: first the description of the field (vv. 30–31), then the viewer's reflection (v. 32), and finally the viewer's conclusion. The description of the field begins with the observation that its owner is a sluggard, a Proverbs type (6:16–11; 26:13–16). The field is full of thorns, nettles, and its wall is thrown down—all signs of the owner's neglect. The field (and its owner) lie idle. Verse 32 provides a glimpse of the learning process in Proverbs: one sees, stores what one sees in one's heart, and draws a conclusion. Verses 33–34 tell us that the sluggard's failure to act has led to the ruin of the source of life—field and vineyard. Sluggards lose not only their health and household, which v. 27 declares depends on the field, but also their reputation insofar as their impoverishment leads to beggary and dishonor. On the translation "vagabond" and "beggar," see under 6:11.

Proverbs 25

Further Proverbs of Solomon,
Collected by the Servants of King Hezekiah (Chaps. 25–29)

Chapters 25–29 comprise the fifth collection in the Hebrew recension. Proverbs 25:1 provides one of the few clues to the date of the book by its reference to "the servants of Hezekiah" collecting proverbs. Hezekiah, king of Judah from 715 to 687 B.C.E., initiated religious and political reforms in the wake of the destruction of the Northern Kingdom in 722 B.C.E. (2 Kings 18–20; 2 Chronicles 29–32). Such reforms would have included copying and editing sacred literature. We may suppose that this Hezekiah-sponsored collection was added to an existing Solomonic collection (cf. "these *also*" of 25:1 with 1:1 and 10:1). The Solomonic collection to which the Hezekiah collection was added was possibly all or part of chaps. 10–22.

The verb describing what the men of Hezekiah did is *'ātaq* in the causative conjugation, "to move, to transfer from." G, followed by S and T, interpreted it as "write down." On the basis of the biblical parallels we take the basic meaning as moving something from one place to another, hence collecting. It is quite possible that the verb connotes more than collecting, for example, arranging and composing.

Some scholars suggest that the collection is arranged in a meaningful structure. R. Van Leeuwen proposes a complex and subtle arrangement in chaps. 25 and 26. The chart below schematizes some of Van Leeuwen's findings.[1] In the scheme, S = saying, A = admonition, + = positive, and − = negative. Using these categories, one can see a careful balance in chap. 25 between positive and negative statements, and between admonitions and sayings.

Introduction   S: + (vv. 2–5)
Body   I   A: − (vv. 6–10)
            S: + (vv. 11–15; except v. 14 which is S:−)
      IIa   A: − (vv. 16–17)
            S: − (vv. 18–20)
      IIb   A: + (vv. 21–22)
            S: − (vv. 23–27; except v. 25 which is S:+)

---

1. For a detailed discussion, see R. Van Leeuwen, *Context and Meaning in Proverbs 25–27* (SBLDS 96; Atlanta: Scholars Press, 1988).

Van Leeuwen also points out three chiastic structures, which impart unity to the sayings.

1. v. 2   "glory"   "search"   (+)
   v. 5   "scoundrel"   "righteousness (+)
   v. 26   "righteous"   "scoundrel"   (−)
   v. 27b   "search"   "glory"   (−)

2. v. 16   "honey"   "to eat"   (+/−)
   v. 27a   "to eat"   "honey"   (−)

3. vv. 16–17   "to eat"   "reject you"   (−)
   vv. 21   "your enemy"   "to eat"   (+)

Van Leeuwen argues that these structures and chiasms (and other features not given here) serve to highlight two themes: 1) social hierarchy, rank, or position, and (2) social conflict and its resolution.

Chapter 26 also has been carefully arranged in relational topics. In chap. 27, however, no arrangement is discernible; the ordering of proverbs is random. Does this mean that chaps. 25–26 were collected *and arranged* by the servants of Hezekiah and that the more random chaps. 27–29 were later appended to form the present section, chaps. 25–29?

What does the arrangement contribute to the reader? Are they merely "builders' marks" guiding the arranger or do they communicate to the reader, even though subliminally? The question is difficult to answer. The arrangement undoubtedly guides the reader by repeating themes and relational terms and by creating a semantic field. On the other hand, an aphorism is by its nature self-contained, making its statement through its own resources.

**25:1   These Also Are Proverbs of Solomon,
Which the Servants of King Hezekiah of Judah Collected**

2   It is the glory of God to conceal a matter;
        and the glory of a king to search out a matter.
3   Like the heavens in their height and the earth in its depth,
        the mind of a king cannot be searched out.
4   Remove the dross from silver,
        and an object emerges[a] ready for the smith.
5   Remove the scoundrel from the king's circle,
        and his throne is stable in righteousness.
6   Do not claim honor before the king;
        do not stand in the place reserved for the great,
7   for it is better to be told, "Come up here,"
        than have to lower yourself before a noble.
     What your eyes have seen
8   do not hastily make into a legal case.[b]

What will you do at its conclusion
  when your opponent brings dishonor on you?
9 Carry on your dispute with your neighbor,
  but do not reveal the affairs of anyone else,
10 lest he hear and denigrate you,
  and the scandal about you never go away.ᶜ
11 Golden apples on a silver tray—
  such is a word spoken at the right moment.
12 A ring of gold, jewelry of fine gold—
  such is a wise person's reproof to a receptive ear.
13 Like the coolness of snow on a day in harvest
  is a reliable messenger to those who send him:
  he refreshes the soul of his master.
14 Clouds and winds but no rain—
  such is one who promises a gift and does not give it.
15 By patience a commander is persuaded;
  a gentle tongue breaks bones.
16 If you come upon honey eat only what you need,
  lest you become sated and vomit it up.
17 Ration your steps in the house of your neighbor,
  lest he become sated and reject you.
18 A mace and a sword and a sharpened arrow—
  such is one who testifies falsely against his neighbor.
19 A loose tooth and an unsteady leg—
  such is a support that fails in a day of trouble.
20 It's like pouring vinegar on sodaᵈ
  to sing songs to a troubled heart.
21 If your enemy is hungry give him food to eat,
  if he is thirsty give him water to drink,
22 for you will scoop fiery coals upon his head,
  and Yahweh will reward you.
23 The north wind generates rain,
  and a whispering tongue generates angry looks.
24 Better to live on a corner of the roof
  than in a noisy house with an angry wife.
25 Cold water on a parched throat—
  such is good news from a distant land.
26 A trampled fountain, a ruined spring—
  such is a righteous person fallen before a scoundrel.
27 To eat much honey is not good;
  neither is it honorable to search out honor.ᵉ
28 A city breached, without a wall
  is a person without a restraint on his spirit.

a. Verse 4b in MT (lit., "[and] a vessel emerged for the smith") can, with a slight change of vowels (MT *wayyēṣē'* to *wĕyēṣē'*), be made more parallel to the verb in v. 4b, "and there will emerge." In Judg. 17:4 the mother took silver shekels to a smith who made a molten image from them. See R. C. Van Leeuwen, "A Technical-Metallurgical Usage of [*yṣ'*], *Zeitschrift für Alttestamentliche Wissenschaft* 98 (1986): 112–13.

b. We repoint MT *tēṣē'* as *tōṣē'*. The noun *rīb* is written defectively. Hebrew *pen*, "lest," has been inserted secondarily under the influence of v. 10 and should be deleted, though the versions read it. Symmachus's *plēthos* reflects Hebrew *lārōb*, "Do not bring *to a multitude*"; it is accepted by REB. A legal context, however, makes better sense and links the saying to the next verse.

c. G has a proverb between v. 10 and v. 11: "Favor and friendship set one free; / keep them for yourself lest you become an object of reproach; / but guard your ways peaceably."

d. We excise MT v. 20a, "One who strips off (?) a garment on a cold day" (*m'dh bgd bywm qrh*) as a corrupt dittography of v. 19 (*mw'dt . . . bwgd bywm ṣrh*). It is not in G. The rest of v. 20 is probably corrupt also but, in the absence of a certain translation, we give the traditional rendering.

e. Colon B is corrupt, literally, "but (and?) the fathoming of their honor is honor." G uses partial metathesis (MT *kbdm* to *dbrm*) and the exchange of similar consonants (*r* for *k*) to make sense: "but it is good to honor (*hôqēr* for *ḥēqer*) noble words." G influenced S and T. The verb in colon B, *ḥāqar*, however, means "to explore, search out" not "to seek after." Hebrew copyists may have borrowed from v. 2, where two of the three words also occur, to make sense of a missing or unreadable verse.

[25:2–3] God and king were closely related in the ancient Near East and in the Bible. In some creation accounts the king was created to organize the human race to serve the gods. To fulfill his tasks, he was endowed with wisdom, which was the ability to govern the people (*ars gubernandi*, "the art of governing"). King Solomon, to whom most of Proverbs is ascribed, is such a royal paragon of wisdom. In 1 Kings 3:16–28 Solomon renders a wise legal decision about which of two women is the real mother of a child, a judgment that leads Israel to recognize "the wisdom of God was in him to effect justice" (1 Kings 3:28). God's world is full of conundrums and puzzles beyond the capacity of ordinary people, but the king is there to unravel them and lead people to serve the gods. In this saying, the close affinity between God's wisdom and the king's wisdom is expressed by the repetition of the first and last word of each colon— "glory" and "matter," "God" and "king" (the latter pair rhyme in Hebrew, *'ĕlōhîm* and *mĕlākîm*). "Glory" here means "action worthy of glory." *The Contemporary English Version,* though free, catches the nuance: "God is praised for being mysterious; / rulers are praised for explaining mysteries." Cf. 16:10.

In v. 3 the king is given the capacity to govern (= wisdom) the world God has made. The Hebrew idiom for "world, cosmos" is "heavens and earth," as in Gen. 1:1; 14:9; Isa. 37:16. The king's wisdom is commensurate with the world. Because he is God's deputy, his mind transcends the minds of other human beings. Though it might seem that the king is being exalted to an unquestioned status, the next saying, and others in the book as well, make it clear that the king (like any human being) is bound to practice justice.

[4–5] The vehicle is given first, then the thing meant (tenor). The technique is frequent in the chapter (see vv. 14, 18, 19, 23, 25, 26, and 28). In this case, the first command applies to smelting metal. Only with the second command (v. 5) does the reader realize the first is a metaphor. Each command begins with the same Hebrew verb in the imperative mood (the infinitive absolute functions here as an imperative). The imperative verb functions as a condition: If you remove scum you get pure silver; if you remove scoundrels from the king's court you get a stable dynasty in that a just dynasty assures divine protection. In Psalm 101, especially v. 7, the king expresses similar sentiments: "One who deals deceitfully will not live in my house, one who speaks lies shall not remain before my eyes." "The king's circle" has the meaning it has in 1 Kings 12:8. Cf. 16:12.

[6–7b] Like those in 23:1–8, this is an admonition concerning behavior at court with a motive. Self-promotion runs the risk of humiliation and jealousy if someone else is put first. The shrewd thing to do is have someone else promote one's own cause. Luke 14:7–11 is in the same practical spirit:

> When you are invited by someone to a wedding feast, do not recline at the couch of honor, lest someone more important than you was invited by him and the host say to you, 'Give the place to this man,' and then you would proceed with embarrassment to take lowest place. Rather, when you are invited, go to the lowest place, so that when the host comes he may say to you, 'Friend, go up higher.' Then you will have honor before all who are sitting at table with you. For everyone who exalts himself will be humbled and everyone who humbles himself will be exalted." (NAB)

Colon A of v. 6 opens and closes with a monosyllable in /a/ (originally *'al* and *malk*) and colon B opens and closes with /ō/.

[7c–8] Formally, the verse is an admonition with a motive. Avoid rash recourse to law courts, for your adversary could win and you could be shamed. The phrase "What your eyes have witnessed" has a legal sense as in Deut. 21:7. To go immediately to law only on the basis of what has been immediately observed is unwise. One needs to investigate the circumstances to find out if a crime has been committed and whether the courts are an appropriate remedy. The key question, "What will you do at its end . . . ?" occurs in Jer. 5:31 and with variants in Isa. 10:3 and Hos. 9:5.

Caution about going to court is found in other wisdom literature, which generally aimed at avoiding trouble: *Amenemope,* chap. 8: "Do not shout 'crime' against a man, / when the cause of [his] flight is hidden / Whether you hear something good or bad, / do it outside where it is not heard"; The Babylonian *Counsels of Wisdom,* lines 31–34: "Do not frequent a law court, / Do not loiter where there is a dispute, / For in the dispute they will have you as a *testifier,* /

Then you will be made their witness / And they will bring you to a lawsuit not your own to affirm."[2]

The admonition that follows immediately is related to this one by words and theme.

[9–10] This admonition has a motive, related to the preceding by its theme and its reprise of the words "legal case/dispute," "neighbor" (*rīb*), and "lest." The Hebrew word for "dispute" has a range of meaning, from a simple quarrel to a legal case. The context here suggests a quarrel at a stage when it can be resolved by mediation, short of a formal trial. As in vv. 4–5, the imperative verb functions as a condition: If you must pursue the quarrel, keep it between the two of you; don't involve others. Others will become enemies from the breach of trust.

The situation envisioned resembles Matt. 18:15: "If your brother gives offense, go and tell him his fault between him and you. If he listens to you, you have won over your brother" (*NAB*). Cf. Matt. 5:22–26.

[11–12] Both verses give the figure (or vehicle) in colon A and the thing meant (or tenor) in colon B (see under v. 4 for other examples in the chapter). The delay in revealing the tenor provokes suspense, making the reader active. Wise words are compared to precious metal in 8:19. A word is not recognized as "wise" until it is addressed to an appropriate situation. A word has to have a setting, a reception.

The Hebrew word for "tray" is uncertain. The word means an engraved stone in Lev. 26:1 and in Phoenician inscriptions; in Num. 33:52 it means an image. Context suggests an engraved tray for fruit. Also uncertain is "the right moment" (*'al 'opnāyw*) in v. 11b. Symmachus and Jerome rendered it this way (respectively, *kairos* and *in tempore suo*), a translation that is supported by the cognate Arabic word *'iffān*, "time." Cf. 15:23.

[12] The verse is closely linked to v. 11 by its theme and the delay in identifying the tenor. The theme is familiar—the value of openness to wise teaching—but the expression is novel. "Ring" (*nezem*) by its sound echoes "ear" (*'ōzen*), and the consonants in "jewelry of fine gold" (*ḥǎlî ketem*) echo "wise person's reproof" (*môkîaḥ ḥākām*). A wise word received by a willing listener is compared to a gold earring or jewelry for the ear. Cf. 20:15.

[13] A simile breaks the series of paired sayings in the chapter. It is not clear whether snow from the mountains was actually brought to refresh ordinary harvesters in the heat or only to the wealthy. There may be a reference to ice and snow brought from the mountains in jute packing.[3] Toy, Barucq, and McKane regard the third clause, "he refreshes the soul of his master," as a gloss, but it

---

2. *BWL,* 101. Italics indicate an uncertain reading.

3. For the ancient and modern evidence see B. Lang, "Vorläufer von Speiseeis im Bibel und Orient: Eine Untersuchung von Spr. 25:13," *Mélanges bibliques et orientaux en l'honneur de M. Henri Cazelles* (Alter Orient und Altes Testament 212; Neukirchen-Vluyn: Neukirchener Verlag, 1981), 219–32.

is attested in the versions. Harvesttime in Palestine can designate barley harvest in April-May or wheat harvest four weeks later.

Sound play and reversal of consonants unify colons A and B: *šl-* . . . *qāṣîr*, "sn[ow] . . . harvest" / *ṣîr* . . . *šl-*, "messenger . . . sen[d]". Cf. 25:25.

[14] In this humorous saying, the vehicle is given first and the tenor second. In the ancient Near East, to promise gifts was to proclaim oneself a patron and an important person. To promise gifts to clients and then not give them was to make one a rain cloud without the rain.

Colon A begins with the sound -*śî* and colon B begins with '*îš* /*šî*/; each ends with a monosyllable (originally *gašm*, "cloud," and *šaqr*, "not given").

[15] According to this paradox about wisdom and power, one who does nothing wins over a commander. Context suggests that *qāṣîn* means a military leader here, which is its meaning in Josh. 10:24; Judg. 11:6, 11; Dan. 11:18. A "soft" tongue breaks bones. The verb for "to persuade" is negative ("to deceive, seduce") in its four other occurrences in Proverbs, but it has a positive meaning here and in Hos. 2:16 and Judg. 14:15.

[16–17] Again the vehicle is first and the tenor second. Too much of a good and delightful thing, honey or friendship, can be a bad thing. Restraint safeguards the pleasure.

[18] Three horrific weapons of war are listed, each capable of inflicting a fatal wound upon an enemy. Such is any individual who tells judicial lies that lead to a finding of guilt. The lie need not lead to capital punishment, for a guilty verdict destroys one's place in the community, which is a kind of death sentence. Proverbs often states its abhorrence of perjury (6:19; 12:17; 14:5; 19:5, 9).

[19] This saying is related to the previous one by the word *šēn*, "tooth," which is echoed in *šānûn*, "sharpened," in v. 18a. Three words require discussion. The adjective qualifying "tooth" is uncertain and is translated "loose" from context. "Unsteady," literally, "tottering," requires slight revocalization of MT. "A support that fails" is literally "a deceiving confidence" or, with a slight change in MT, "confidence in (or of) a deceiver."

Teeth and legs are things we rely on without thinking about them and hence we are stunned when they fail. That is what it is like when a friend whose support we took for granted or a thing we relied on implicitly betrays us in a crisis.

[20] With many commentators, we omit the first four words of the verse on the grounds that a scribe inadvertently copied part of v. 19 twice (dittography). The rest of the verse is probably corrupt as well. See the textual notes.

According to the text, a sad heart cannot bear joyous songs. "Song" (*šîr*) is the opposite of lament (*qînāh*) in Amos 8:10. For the picture, see Ps. 137:3. There is no affinity between joyous song and unhappy heart. The mixing is turbulent, like acid on alkali. A Greek copyist added a comment on sadness: "As a moth to a garment and a worm to wood, a person's grief harms the heart."

[21–22] The humanity and moderation this admonition expresses so memorably was not uncommon in ancient wisdom literature: "Steer, we will ferry the wicked, / we do not act like his kind; / Lift him up, give him your hand, / Leave him <in> the hands of the god; / Fill his belly with bread of your own, / that he may be sated and weep" (*Amenemope* V.1–6); "It is better to bless someone than to do harm to one who has insulted you" (Papyrus Insinger 23:6); "Do not return evil to the man who disputes with you; requite with kindness your evil doer" (The Babylonian *Counsels of Wisdom*).[4] Biblical law shows the same attitude: "When you come upon your enemy's ox or donkey wandering, take it back to him" (Ex. 23:4); "You shall not bear hatred toward your brother in your heart. Reprove your kinfolk but incur no guilt on their account. You shall not take vengeance or bear a grudge against your own people. Love your neighbor as yourself: I am Yahweh" (Lev. 19:17–18).

Wisdom and legal texts urge human beings away from the difficult and dangerous business of exacting vengeance, and urge them to leave punishment to God. Within the international "humanistic" tradition cited above, this saying makes its own contribution. First, it does not have in view everyday situations, but the moment when one's enemy is vulnerable (like the case of the lost ox in Ex. 23:4). In this case the situation is extreme hunger and thirst. An enemy's vulnerability is not to be made into an opportunity to settle old scores. Second, the motive is to allow God's justice its proper scope, as in 20:22 and especially 24:17–18: "When your enemy falls, do not celebrate, . . . lest Yahweh see it and be displeased / and *turn his wrath from him.*" The counsel is a paradox: Vengeance is best exercised by leaving it in other hands. Presupposed is the existence of a just God who will reward you (v. 22b). The precise meaning of the gesture of heaping coals of fire on someone's head has not been satisfactorily explained, though the context suggests it means to punish.[5] In Rom. 12:20 Paul cites the Greek version, interpreting it, "Do not be overcome by evil but overcome evil with good."

[23] Again the vehicle is followed by the tenor. The verse was subject to many interpretations in the course of history: The north wind raises up clouds, a shameless face provokes the tongue (G); the north wind is pregnant with rain, like an angry face and a concealed tongue (S and T); the north wind drives away the rains and a glare drives away a disparaging tongue (V and Ibn Ezra); as the north wind chases away the rain, such is soft language for a dejected countenance (Saadia).

One problem is that in Palestine it is the west wind rather than the north (*ṣāpôn*) that brings rain. The word for "north" may have been chosen not for meteorological reasons but because it is a wordplay on *ṣāpan,* "to conceal." Perhaps the meaning is that both the north (etymologically, "concealed") wind and a

4. *BWL,* 101.

5. For a review of opinions, see A. Meinhold, "Der Umgang mit dem Feind nach Spr. 25:21f. als Massstabe für das Menschsein," *Alttestamentlicher Glaube und biblische Theologie* (H. D. Preuss volume), ed. J. Hausmann and H.-J. Zobel (Stuttgart: Kohlhammer, 1992), 244–52.

secret (= concealed) tongue have bad effects. In one case the effect is rain and in the other it is the angry looks of people angered by a slanderous tongue. Or perhaps the northwest is meant, an attempt to preserve the wordplay and be reasonably faithful to Palestinian weather patterns. In any event, slander stirs up anger.

[24] Proverbs 21:9 is identical to our saying and 21:19 is similar in sentiment. See under those verses. This humorous saying is one of several about domestic unhappiness. Better to live outdoors in discomfort than indoors with an angry spouse.

[25] Verses 25 and 26 use water imagery. Both also give the vehicle in the first colon and the tenor in the second colon, which forces the reader to be active. Cool water for a parched throat is a metaphor for good news from a distant place. Verse 13 compares the messenger (not the message as here) to cool water and uses the same word for throat.

[26] "Spring" (*māqôr*) is a common metaphor for source. "Spring of life" in Proverbs can refer to the wise words of the righteous (Prov. 10:11; 13:14), revering Yahweh (14:27), or wisdom (16:22). Springs can be easily fouled and rendered useless (Ezek. 34:18). The defeat of a righteous person removes a source of life for others.

What is the nature of the removal of the righteous person? Does the person yield in cowardice to a scoundrel, "giving way," as NRSV and REB render it? Or is the righteous person simply defeated by a scoundrel (with no necessary reference to moral failing), as is the view of JPSV and Whybray? The latter is more likely. The participle "fallen" in colon B is *māṭ,* the same verb in biblical statements that the righteous shall never be "moved" (*mûṭ,* 10:30; 12:3; Pss. 15:5; 16:8). Such statements imply that a righteous person may be defeated but will finally prevail. In the meantime, the triumph of the wicked over the righteous is not only a scandal but also a loss of the "life" that the righteous person provided to others.

[27] Verses 16–17 used the analogy of eating honey to excess to teach that the sweetness of friendship is best enjoyed in moderation. One would expect that colon B in this saying would counsel moderation in seeking the honor that Proverbs views as a fruit of wise living. Unfortunately, colon B is corrupt beyond recovery (lit., "and the searching out of their honor is honor"). Many translations propose "[nor] to seek honor on top of honor," but the verb *ḥāqar* means to investigate rather than to seek. One can conjecture that the original point is that one ought to be as moderate with regard to honor as with honey, but the precise meaning of colon B is not recoverable with any certainty.

[28] Colon A is the vehicle and colon B is the tenor, which is the structure of several sayings in the chapter (see under v. 4). The vehicle is a city (*'îr*) no longer protected by walls, and the tenor is a person (*'îš*) who does not "wall in" or control his spirit. "Spirit" here is the inner force of a person as in 16:32; 29:11, 23. If one does not rule one's inner force, one exposes oneself to enemies.

Walls protect a city from the danger without and self-control protects a person from the danger within. Egyptian instructions and Proverbs hold up as a model the person who is not dominated by inner passions, who restrains it, who is "cool" in the Egyptian idiom. Sound underscores the parallel: a monosyllabic CîC . . . *'ên* (C = consonant) begins each colon.

Proverbs 26

According to its topics, the chapter falls into three parts, each marked by repetition of key words: vv. 1–12, 13–16, and 17–28. In vv. 1–12, "fool" occurs eleven times, being found in every verse but v. 2. "Sluggard" occurs in every verse of vv. 13–16.

26:1   Like snow in summer and like rain at harvesttime,
          so honor for a fool is out of place.

2   Like a sparrow swooping, like a swallow flitting,
          so a curse without cause never lands.

3   A whip for a horse, a bridle for a donkey,
          and a rod for the back of fools.

4   Do not answer a fool according to his folly,
          lest you become like him yourself.

5   Answer a fool according to his folly,
          lest he seem wise in his own eyes.

6   One cuts off one's feet, drinks down violence,
          who sends messages by a fool.

7   Limp like the legs of a lame person
          is a proverb in the mouth of a fool.

8   One puts a stone in a sling[a]
          who gives honor to a fool.

9   A thorn lands on the hand of a drunkard
          and a proverb lands on the mouth of a fool.

10   An archer who wounds all who pass by:
          such is anyone who hires a fool and drunkard.[b]

11   As a dog returns to its vomit,
          so a fool repeats his folly.[c]

12   Do you see someone wise in his own eyes?
          There's more hope for a fool than for him.

13   The sluggard says, "There's a lion in the street,
          there's a lion in the square!"

14   The door turns on its hinges,
          and the sluggard on his bed!

15   A sluggard buries his hand in a bowl,
         too lazy to lift it to his mouth.
16   A sluggard is wiser in his own eyes
         than the Seven who give wise answers.
17   One who grabs the ears of a passing dog[d] —
         such is one who gets into a quarrel not his own.
18   Like one who recklessly shoots
         firebrands and deadly arrows,
19   so is anyone who deceives his neighbor
         and says, "I was only acting in jest."
20   When there is no wood the fire dies;
         when there is no slanderer the quarrel subsides.
21   Charcoal for embers, wood for a fire,
         and a quarreler for igniting an argument.[e]
22   The words of a slanderer are like delicious morsels;
         they go down to the pit of the stomach.
23   Like glaze[f] applied to earthenware
         are smooth lips and a malicious heart.
24   With his lips an enemy dissembles,
         but within plans treachery;
25   when he adopts a pleasant tone, do not believe him,
         for seven abominations are in his heart.
26   Who conceals[g] hatred in duplicity,
         will have his wickedness revealed in the assembly.
27   Who digs a pit will fall into it;
         who rolls a stone will have it roll back on him.
28   A lying tongue hates those crushed by it,[h]
         and a slick mouth brings destruction.

   a. Only one of the three words in colon A is certain. The first word (*ṣĕrôr*) can be "small stone" (2 Sam. 17:13; Amos 9:9), "bag" (Prov. 7:20a), or "to bind, tie." The second uncertain word, *margēmāh*, occurs only here; it seems to be a maqtil noun pattern from *rāgam*, "to stone; to heap up stones," and could mean a stoning, a slingshot, or a stone heap, or perhaps "to place a stone."
   b. The verse was already corrupt by the time of G. G, partly followed by S and T, probably read the same consonants as MT but used partial metathesis and substitution of graphically similar letters to obtain sense: *rb mḥwll kl bśr ksyl ky tšbr 'brtm*, "All the flesh of fools suffers greatly, / for their fury is brought to nothing."
   We tentatively propose the following: Hebrew *rab* is the participle of the verb *rābāh*, "to shoot [with the bow]," as in Gen. 21:20 and Jer. 50:29; *mĕḥôlēl* is the polel of the triliteral root *ḥll* II, "to pierce (Isa. 51:9; Job 26:13), to wound"; *śōkēr* is to be revocalized to *śikkēr*, "drunkard," with S and T. The final word of colon B, "passersby" is to be moved to the final position in colon A for the sake of better syllable balance (like the

displacement of "king" in 22:11). A scribe may have borrowed from vv. 17–18 in an effort to make sense of the verse.

c. G adds from Sir. 4:21: "There is a shame that leads to sin, and there is a shame that is honor and grace."

d. Delitzsch and translations such as NRSV and REB correctly disregard the verse division of MT and make the participle *'ōbēr*, "passing by," modify "dog." MT's division leads to an unbalanced syllable count in colon B. Toy and Alonso Schökel delete *'ōbēr*, but the participle has an important function: the stray dog symbolizes the irrelevant quarrel. There is no need to emend *mit'abbēr* to *mit'āréb*, despite Gemser and *BHS*.

e. A few scholars propose *mappûaḥ*, "bellows" (Jer. 6:29), for MT *peḥām*, "charcoal," on the basis of G *eschara*. But *eschara* means "grate, hearth," and does not make a good parallel to "wood" in any case. G is not an independent reading but a partial metathesis of MT *pḥm* to *mpḥ*.

f. MT *kesep sîgîm*, "silver dross," assumes that litharge, a fused lead monoxide separated out in the ancient process of producing silver, was used to glaze pottery. Though this is possible, the best solution is to redivide and repoint MT *ksp sygym* as *kĕsapsîgîm*, "like glaze," on the basis of Ugaritic *spsg*, as suggested by H. L. Ginsberg in *Bulletin of the American Schools of Oriental Research* 98 (1945): 21 n. 55, and thereafter by many scholars. The discussion is ably summarized by Cohen (122–23). The word *spsg* occurs twice in Ugaritic, once in a list (*KTU* 4.182.8 restored) and once in the Aqhat epic, "glaze [*spsg*] will be poured on my head, plaster (?) on my pate" (in reference to a funerary rite; *KTU* 1.17.VI.36–37). In colon B, we follow G *leia* in reading *ḥălāqîm*, "smooth [lips]," for MT *dōlĕqîm*, "burning [lips]." "Smooth" qualifies "lips" in Ps. 12:3, 4, and "word," "tongue," or "mouth" in Prov. 2:16; 6:24; 7:5.

g. With all the versions we read the participle in colon A, *mskh*, "one who conceals," for MT *tksh*, "it is concealed."

h. MT *dakkāyw*, "its crushed ones," or "those crushed by it" (JPSV) makes little sense. The versions followed G, which probably interpreted the word on the basis of Aramaic *dakyā'*, "purity, purification."

[26:1] Certain kinds of weather do not fit certain seasons, so also with honor and fools. Palestine has only two seasons, the dry summer (April to September) and the rainy winter (October to March). Rain and snow are virtually unknown in summer. Harvesttime can be barley harvest in April–May, or wheat harvest four weeks later, or the fruit harvest (including olives and grapes) in late summer and early fall as in Isa. 16:9. "Honor" is *given* those who live wisely; one cannot pin a medal on oneself. A fool has no more chance of seeing honor than summer has of seeing rain. The phrase "not fitting/unseemly [for a fool]" occurs also in 17:7 and 19:10.

[2] The syntax is similar to v. 1 ("like . . . like . . . so . . . ") but the content is different. The point is not the unfittingness of things as in v. 1, but the similarity of actions: a hovering bird that never lands, a groundless curse that never "lands." The curse hangs in the air posing no threat to anyone. JPSV prefers the qere reading *lô*, "to him" ("So a gratuitous curse must backfire") rather than the ketib *lō'*, "not." The context, however, does not suggest the curse turns on its utterer but simply that it never lands (so most commentators).

[3] The age-old means for handling horses and donkeys is a whip and bridle, and the means for handling fools is a rod. By implication a fool is a stupid animal. Other biblical passages make the same point: "Do not be like a horse or mule; they do not understand. With bit and bridle their temper is curbed" (Ps. 32:9) According to Prov. 19:25, fools do not learn from what they see or hear but only from the blows inflicted on them. In 10:13 blows come to the back of a fool.

[4–5] The two sayings are obviously meant to be read together. Apart from the initial "not" in v. 4, the first four words of each are identical: "Answer a fool according to his folly lest . . . " Each verse makes sense in its own right, but when the verses are read together they show the problem, even the danger, that fools pose to the wise. Verse 4 advises against conversing with them, literally, "lest you become like them, yes you!" "According to his folly" refers to the fool's malicious and ignorant style. How easy it is to adapt that style through association! Proverbs 23:9 advised, "Do not speak in the ear of a fool, / for he will despise your wise words." Granted the discomfort and even danger of such association, someone has to speak up for wisdom. One cannot simply allow fools to hold forth unreproved. The wise have a duty not to remain silent.

[6] Ancient versions and modern commentators have been puzzled by the meaning of the first verb. Does it mean to *cut off* one's own feet, that is, to harm oneself (most commentators), or does it mean to *wear out* the feet of the many messengers who must be sent to rectify the distorted message of the first messenger (Rashi and JPSV)? "To drink violence" occurs also in 4:17 in the sense of devoting oneself to evil. Here, however, it does not mean to act but to experience evil consequences, as in Ezek. 23:32: "the cup of your sister you shall drink." As in v. 10, the employer must accept the consequences of unwise hiring. With regard to messengers, in a premail, preelectronic age the problem of sending messages must have been acute, as 10:26 and 13:17 attest. To send a fool as an emissary is to harm oneself and bear the consequences of garbled or deliberately misstated messages.

[7] The verse is linked to the preceding verse by "feet" and "legs," and to v. 9 by the repetition of colon B. The tone is harsh: As the legs of a physically handicapped person are useless for movement, so a proverb in the mouth of fools is useless for discernment. A proverb is effective only when applied rightly to a situation (25:11), and fools do not know how to apply it.

[8] Colon A is textually uncertain (see textual notes). The sentiment is clear enough from v. 1: honor is out of place for a fool. Colon A has been translated "like a bag of [precious] stones on a heap of rocks" (JB), but in the only passage where "stones" are "precious stones" (Zech. 3:9), the context makes very clear the stones are precious. Another possibility is "to tie a stone to a sling,"

the point being that a sling that cannot release its stone is an example of what is out of place (NRSV, REB). Another, perhaps more plausible, interpretation of MT is that a bundle of sling stones ("stone" is a collective as in Isa. 8:14) is placed on a sling. When the weapon is shot the stones scatter and never reach their target. The purpose of the sling is thwarted; the purpose of honor is thwarted when it is given to fools.

[9] Proverbs are not simply for quoting but for performance, for applying to a situation. A proverb is "a word spoken at the right moment" (25:11). Fools cite them but cannot apply them aptly. Their proverbs are like thorns that attach themselves to clothing. Fools may notice thorns on their jackets but cannot say how they got there. Some translations (McKane, REB, NRSV) read colon B, "like a thornbush brandished by the hand of a drunkard," but the interpretation strains the meaning of the verb.

[10] The text is corrupt (see textual notes). Our interpretation is a conjecture based on the context of vv. 1–12. Previous proverbs stated that fools could not speak a relevant word (vv. 7, 9) and were unworthy of honor (vv. 1, 8). This verse goes beyond v. 6, which expressed the harm fools do to their employers, by stating the harm they do to everybody else. To hire a fool and drunkard is to shoot arrows at a crowd. "One who hires" (*śōkēr*) and "drunkard" (*śikkēr*) are related by wordplay.

[11] This verse portrays a vivid and earthy comparison. "Dog" is a term of insult in 1 Sam. 17:43 and 2 Kings 8:13. Fools cannot help repeating their actions.

[12] In form the saying resembles 22:29: "Do you see a man skilled in his craft? He will enter the service of kings," and in sense it resembles 29:20: "Do you see someone hasty in his words?" To be wise in one's own eyes is to be worse than a fool because self-satisfaction ensures that one will not grow through learning from others.

[13–16] Like vv. 1–12 which were linked by "fool" (*kĕsîl*) in eleven of twelve verses, vv. 13–16 all contain "sluggard" (*'āṣēl*). Proverbs regards the sluggard with derision, chiefly because the type does not act. The ideal of the book is the self-actualizing person, someone who uses heart, lips, hands, feet. All but v. 16 make use of humor.

[13] One has only to quote sluggards to make their folly clear (cf. 22:13).

[14] As a door swings back and forth, firmly attached to its hinge, so the sluggard turns over in bed, as if attached to it. The sluggard will no more get up to act than a door will leave its hinges and walk.

[15] Sluggards lack the desire even to keep themselves alive. Proverbs 19:24 is a variant, differing slightly in colon B.

[16] Like the series on the fool in vv. 1–12, so the series on the sluggard ends with the phrase "wise in his own eyes." Sluggards are a species of fool, suffering from a similar inability to accept the discipline that might change them.

Our rendering, "the Seven [sages]," differs from nearly all translations, which take "seven" simply as a large number as in v. 25 and 9:1. This verse refers to the seven *apkallu* of Mesopotamian tradition, pre-Flood sages (corresponding to the seven pre-Flood kings in some traditions) who brought culture and learning to the human race. As pointed out under 8:30, Israelite scribes knew of the seven antediluvian sages. The Seven Sages are mentioned in Plato (428–348 B.C.E.), *Protagoras* 343a. The lofty status of these mythical figures, renowned for their divine wisdom, adds to the humor of the adage.

[17] Proverbs warns against fits of anger that get one embroiled in quarrels (15:18; 17:14, 19; 20:3). Even more should one stay out of other people's quarrels. The earthy comparison shows the danger of getting involved in something not of one's own.

[18–19] In v. 17 the doer of the deed suffers harm whereas in v. 18 it is others who suffer. As in v. 17, vv. 18–19 puts in parallel an obviously dangerous act (v. 18) with one that might be considered less dangerous (v. 19) in order to show the malice of the second act. The comparison is made more explicit by the words "like . . . so . . . " as in vv. 1 and 2. The subject of v. 18 is more likely "reckless" than "crazy," though the latter term is preferred by many modern translators.[1]

One who misuses words is like someone who misuses weapons. A misused word can be as powerful as a deadly weapon. There may be a play on the verb in v. 19a, *rimmāh*, "beguile, deceive," which has the same consonants as *rāmāh*, "to shoot [arrows]; to cast" (Jer. 4:29 and Ps. 78:9, so Meinhold).

The excuse in v. 19 (*śāḥaq*) is ambivalent. Is it "I was only having fun" or "I was taking delight"? In 10:23a the wicked take delight in doing evil. In any case, misusing words is a perilous business.

[20–22] The three proverbs have a common theme—the destructive power of slanderous and angry words. Certain words are repeated: "wood" and "fire" in vv. 20a and 21a; "slanderer" in vv. 20b and 22a; "quarrel/quarreler" in vv. 20b and 21b.

[20] A slanderer and a quarrel are compared to fuel and a fire, cause and effect. When the first is not present, neither is the second. The Hebrew word "to subside" elsewhere means the stilling of a great force such as waves in Ps. 107:30 and the sea in Jonah 1:11.

[21] The metaphor of fire for strife is continued but in an affirmation rather than in a negation as in the previous verse. A person of strife supplies fuel for the fire.

---

1. The translation "crazy" is derived from a Syriac cognate, "one who is stupefied, stunned," but no ancient version (including the Syriac) so understood the word, nor is it the meaning of the only other ancient occurrence of the Hebrew word, Sir. 32:15: "One who studies torah masters it, but the reckless (*wmtlhlh*) is caught in its snare." The opposite of "to study, attend to," is "to be reckless, inattentive."

[22] Slander is compared to delicious food that is eagerly swallowed and taken into the deepest part of the stomach. Negative comments about others penetrate deeply and are not forgotten. Proverbs 18:8 is a duplicate.

[23–28] The theme of the section is hatred and how it is hid. "Hater" or "hate" occurs in vv. 24, 26, and 28. The topic was broached in vv. 18–19.

[23] The antithesis is "heart," the organ of storing knowledge and reflecting upon it, and "lips," the organ of expression, the source of words. Glaze was applied to clay pottery to make it smooth and attractive, an apt metaphor for the smooth words coming from a hateful heart. Cf. 15:7.

[24–25] Unlike the other double saying (vv. 18–19), which stated the figure (vehicle) in the first verse and only afterwards the thing meant (tenor), each bicolon here makes a complete statement. The second bicolon contains an admonition. Fine words may mask a treacherous heart. The sound /ō/ at the middle and the end of colon A and at the end of colon B demarcate the sentence and give it a rhythm.

[26] Treachery eventually becomes known, for it inevitably leads to a public act. "In an assembly" may simply mean in the public forum or an assembly convoked to deal out punishment or disgrace as in 5:14.

The consonants of the noun "hatred" (*śin'āh*, *śn'*) are literally "concealed" in the noun "duplicity" (*maśśā'ôn*, *mś'n*).[2] A similar revelation of the palatal consonants *g* and *q* is found in colon B: hatred is "revealed" (*glh*) in the "assembly" (*qlh*).

The Hebrew verbs "to reveal" and "to cover" are also contrasted in Isa. 26:21 and Prov. 11:13. Verses 23–25 show how hatred can be concealed; this verse states it cannot be fully concealed but will eventually out.

[27] The evil that one intends for others will come back on one's own head. The general sentiment takes its context from the previous verse: The words that one uses against others will come back upon oneself. What goes around comes around. The saying is a true proverb in that it had currency among the folk, for it is found in Qoh. 10:8 and Sir. 27:26. Cf. Pss. 7:16 and 9:16 and the fourth-century B.C.E. instruction *Ankhsheshonq* 26:21: "He who digs a pit . . ." (partially preserved). Colon B occurs also in the same Egyptian instruction: "He who shakes a stone will have it fall on his foot" (22:5).

[28] The last word in each colon is obscure, making the entire proverb uncertain. In colon B it is not clear whether it is the speaker or the victim who is ruined. The close connection with v. 27 may mean that the digger of the pit is the one ruined.

---

2. The Hebrew consonants *śîn* and *šîn* can be considered one letter, as is shown in acrostic poems.

Proverbs 27

The verses in the chapter are paired by theme (vv. 1–2, 3–4, 5–7, 8–11, 12–14, 15–16, 17–19) and at the end there is a short instruction on the value of farming (vv. 23–27).

27:1   Do not boast of tomorrow,
      for you do not know what the day will bring forth.

2   Let another praise you, not your own mouth,
      another's lips, not your own.

3   Stone is heavy, sand has weight,
      but heavier than both is vexation from a fool.

4   Wrath is cruel, anger is crushing,
      but who can stand before jealousy?

5   Better a reproof in the open
      than love kept hidden.

6   Trustworthy are the blows of a friend,
      dangerous,[a] the kisses of an enemy.

7   A throat that is sated spurns[b] honey,
      but to a throat that is famished bitter is sweet.

8   Like a bird fleeing from its nest
      is anyone fleeing from his place.

9   Oil and incense gladden the heart;
      a friend's sweetness is better than one's own counsel.

10   Do not give up your friend or your father's friend;
      do not resort to your relative's house when trouble strikes:
      better a neighbor near than kin far away.

11   Become wise, my son, and gladden my heart
      so that I can answer whoever taunts me.

12   The shrewd person sees trouble and withdraws;
      the simple keep going and pay the penalty.

13   Take his garment, for he went surety for another —
      on behalf of a stranger, take what he pledged!

14   Who greets his neighbor in a loud voice early in the morning,
      will have it reckoned to him as a curse.

15   Steady dripping on a rainy day
      and a wife who quarrels — they're the same;

16   those who would hide her are hiding the wind;
      the oil on her hand announces her presence.

17   Iron sharpens iron
      and one person sharpens the edge of another.

18   Who tends a fig tree eats its fruit;
          who serves his lord gets honor.
19   As one face turns to another
          one's heart turns to the other.
20   As Sheol and Abaddon are never sated
          so the eyes of man are never sated.^{c}
21   A crucible proves silver and a furnace proves gold,
          and a man is proved by the mouth of those who praise him.^{d}
22   If you pounded a fool in a mortar,
              with a pestle like grain,
          his folly would still not leave him.

Herds and Fields
Are the Best Wealth

23   Be aware of the condition of your flocks,
          give attention to your herds,
24   for possessions are not enduring,
          treasure^e is not lasting.
25   Grass comes up^f and new growth appears
          and the herbage of the hills is gathered in;
26   lambs will provide your clothing,
          he-goats, the price of a field,
27   enough goat's milk for your food,
          food for your household, sustenance for your handmaidens.

a. "Dangerous" is a guess for *na'tārôt*, which the Masoretes apparently took as the niphal conjugation of the verb *'ātar*, "to plead, supplicate." This meaning is not satisfactory, however. The versions offer no help: G has "voluntary" (from *ndābāh*?) and V has "deceptive," both of which seem to be guesses. Some commentators relate the verb to Akkadian *watāru*, "to be excessive," yielding "but the kisses of an enemy are excessive." No proposal has won wide assent.^{1}

b. The common emendation *tābûz*, "to show contempt, to despise," for MT *tābûs*, "trample down," has no versional support and is unnecessary if one takes MT as metaphorical.

c. G has a couplet not in MT: "Who fixes [his] eye is an abomination to the Lord, / and the untaught do not control their tongue."

d. After its translation of MT, G (followed by S) has "the heart of a lawless person seeks evil, / but the upright heart seeks knowledge."

e. MT *w'im nēzer* in colon B ("and if [or] a crown") is senseless. "Crown" is not found in G, S, and T. Translators try to make "crown" parallel to "hoard," but the interpretation is unlikely. Unlike English usage, "crown" in the Bible is never used as a

1. For further proposals, see N. M. Waldman, "A Note on Excessive Speech and Falsehood," *Jewish Quarterly Review* 67 (1976): 142–45.

metonymy for "kingship." Further, kingship of itself is not a symbol of security in the Hebrew Bible. Tentatively, we insert the only relevant attested parallel to *hōsen,* "[hoarded] treasure," i.e., *'ōṣar,* "treasure." It is found in Isa. 33:6 and Jer. 20:5.

    f. Following Ehrlich, we emend MT *glh,* "to reveal; to remove," to *'ālāh,* "to ascend; to grow, spring up." The latter verb is used of vegetation in Deut. 29:22 (grass); Isa. 55:13 (trees); Amos 7:1 (crops), etc. Though *gāl,* "to reveal; to remove," and *nir'āh,* "to be seen" are a fixed pair in Isa. 47:3; Ezek. 29:29; 1 Sam. 3:21, they have a different sense than here. Indeed, the fact that the two verbs were a fixed pair may have prompted a scribe to insert it.

    Meinhold sees v. 25 as reflecting Palestinian agricultural practice: The first cutting of the grass in March is followed by a period of tender grass in April (colon A); what is left can be used for fodder (colon B). But "grass" and "fresh growth" are synonymous in colon A as they are in Isa. 15:6 and Ps. 37:2. The verbs are synonymous here also, "to grow," and "to appear." Colon A refers to the grass of the fields and colon B refers to fodder that is gathered in.

    [27:1] Human fragility and impotence is a common ancient Near Eastern theme. An example is from the Egyptian instruction *Ptahhotep,* "one plans the morrow but knows not what will be" (*AEL* 1.69). A human being cannot "boast" (*hthll*) in the sense of taking life for granted. Verses 1a and 2a are linked by the double appearance of the triliteral root *hll.*

    [2] The triliteral root *hll* in the qal conjugation means "to praise," and the root contributes to a wordplay: Just as one cannot take tomorrow for granted (*hthll* in v. 1, hithpael conjugation) so one cannot praise oneself (*hll* in v. 2). Honor is granted, not taken.

    [3] Verses 3 and 4 are related by identical syntax in colon A of each—predicate plus subject, predicate plus subject. The same syntax is also found elsewhere (e.g., 6:23a; 20:1a; and 31:30a). Colon A states the literal meaning of the adjective (heavy object), and colon B states its figurative meaning (vexation is hard to bear).

    [4] The syntax of colon A is like that in v. 3a (predicate plus subject, predicate plus subject), but colon B breaks from the syntax, for it is a rhetorical question with the implied answer "no one." Jealousy is worse than anger. In its two other occurrences in Proverbs "jealousy" arouses wrath (6:34) and rots the bones (14:30), whereas wrath is readily assuaged by a soft answer (15:1) or a bribe (21:14). Jealousy cannot be assuaged so easily (cf. 6:34–35).

    [5] Verses 5 and 6 are about true and false friendship. "Better-than" sayings often declare that something normally judged to be less preferable is superior in the light of some other value. For example, in 15:16 a small amount of money with the revering of Yahweh is preferable to a great sum of money when it comes with "confusion" from injustice; in 15:17 vegetables eaten with friends ("love") are better than meat eaten with enemies ("hatred"). Here, "reproof" (which can be discomforting) is better than affectionate words ("love" is abstract for concrete) in view of the fact that a reproof imparts wisdom. True love does not hide the truth that needs to be told. False love keeps silent from fear or indifference.

[6] Though formally not a "better-than" saying (though G, S, and V translate it so), the verse declares a slap is better than a kiss in view of the attitude of the one who slaps or kisses. A friend's correction can be life-giving and an enemy's kiss can be traitorous (cf. the kiss of Judas in Matt. 26:48). The two cola are linked by alliteration of three initial /n/ sounds.

[7] Bitter can be more appetizing than sweet depending on one's appetite. If one is sated then even honey loses its appeal, but to a starving person, everything tastes good. Hunger is the best sauce. The play on throat and self (or soul) is common in Proverbs.

[8] A passage in Job 20:8–9 uses similar language (words identical to our passage are italicized) about the brevity and vulnerability of life: "Like a dream he flies away and cannot be found; / [the wicked person] *flees* like a vision in the night. / Eyes that beheld him no longer do so, / they do not see *his place* anymore." A fleeing bird symbolizes flight before hostile forces in Isa. 10:14; 16:2; and Ps. 11:1. "Place" in the Job passage and elsewhere is a human being's place in God's universe, as in Job 7:10; 8:18; 20:9. People are defined by their "place." It is a tragedy when war, poverty, or illness forces them from it.

[9] Colon B is corrupt, putting the whole proverb in doubt. Colon A declares that anointing and beautiful scents gladden the human heart. As MT stands, colon B declares the counsels of one's neighbor to be spices, sweeter than one's own plans. In 16:21 and 24:13 wisdom is "sweet" to one's lips.

[10] The adage is about friends and kin in a crisis, in the form of two admonitions that are grounded in a maxim (colon C). Hebrew *rēaʻ* means "neighbor" in the sense of someone nearby and also "friend" as in "your father's friend." It is here contrasted with kin. Though some regard the three lines as originally unrelated, there is a clear logic: Cultivate old family friends and neighbors; do not automatically count on kin for help in time of trouble, for neighbors and friends are ready at hand. This tripartite verse ends a subsection in the chapter. Verses 22 and 27 are likewise tripartite and end subsections in the chapter (Meinhold).

[11] This father's command to a son is equivalently a condition: if you are wise I will not be shamed in public. The saying states the sentiments of 10:1 and the other verses on parents and adult children in an interesting way.

[12] See under 22:3, which is a near duplicate of this proverb.

[13] See under 20:16, which is identical except that 20:16 has "strangers" (plural) in colon B.

[14] "To bless" in colon A can mean simply "to greet" as in 1 Sam. 13:10 and 2 Kings 4:29, but "curse" in colon B keeps the sense "to bless" to the fore. The verse can be taken seriously or humorously. In the serious interpretation, "a loud voice" would be an insincere greeting as in v. 6 and 26:23–25, 28; the phrase "early in the morning" would mean "insistently" as in Jer. 7:13 (so S: "Whoever blesses his neighbor *with flattery* in a loud voice is no different from one who curses."). Most commentators take the verse as humorous: "a loud voice early in the morning" is unwelcome and untimely. The humorous interpretation better preserves the wordplay in "to bless" or "to greet" and "curse."

The preposition "to him" is ambivalent. Does it refer to the greeter or to the greeted ("he might as well curse him," REB and Alonso Schökel)? More likely it refers to the greeter, on the grounds that the "evil" deed comes back on the head of the doer.

[15] The domestic image of a roof steadily dripping rain is apt for one spouse suffering from the angry words of the other. Steady dripping occurs also in 19:13 as a metaphor for the misery created by a quarrelsome wife.

[16] The saying is completely obscure and any translation is guesswork. In the view of many commentators the verse continues v. 15; the feminine singular suffix of "those who would hide *her*" refers to the wife in v. 15b. If v. 16 is a continuation of the previous verse, then v. 15 speaks of the effect of the wife *within* the house and v. 16 of the effects *outside*. One can no more hide a quarrelsome wife from one's neighbors than one can hide a storm wind. Meinhold conjectures that in colon B the woman's perfume (oil) on her fingers gives her presence away, another illustration that concealing her is futile.

[17] Iron sharpens the "face" (*pānîm* = surface, edge) of iron and a human being sharpens the "face" (*pānîm* = words) of another human being. *Pānîm* means the "edge" of a sword or an ax in Ezek. 21:21 and Qoh. 10:10. In Prov. 15:13 and in 27:19 *pānîm* means one's "face" in the sense of verbal expression or wit. The verse is a fresh way of saying that one learns by conversing with others. Conversation makes one wise, "sharp." One cannot become wise by oneself.

[18] "To keep" (rendered "tends") and "to guard" (rendered "serves") are a fixed pair in Proverbs (e.g., 2:8; 13:3; 16:17). The fixed pair is used here to make an earthy comparison—caring for a fig tree is like caring for a master. A dutiful farmer eats the fruits of the tree. A dutiful servant can expect to share in the honor and prestige of the master.

[19] MT is, literally, "like water a face to a face, so the heart of a man to a man," forcing translators into paraphrase to make sense. JPSV adds a word (italicized): "As face *answers* to face in water, so does one man's heart to another." The translation presumes that water is a mirror and the medium through which one knows oneself (colon A). A person knows the other through the medium of facial contact, which presumably implies verbal exchange as in v. 17 (colon B). Another possible interpretation of MT is that a person recognizes himself in the donation that another brings (colon A); one sees oneself in the heart of a friend (colon B). So Meinhold.

The above interpretations are founded on a corrupt text. G, followed by S, does not have "like water" (*kammayim*) but "like" (*kĕmô*), which is a superior reading: "as a face to a face." The phrase "face to face" of colon A is found in Deut. 34:10 and Ezek. 20:35 in contexts of speaking directly and intimately to someone (though with the preposition *'el,* "to," rather than *l,* "to," as here). The heart is the faculty of reflection and deciding, and the mouth, lips, tongue, face (see 15:14) give voice to the heart. When two people speak directly, "face to face," they ultimately speak "heart to heart." The heart (the interior of a person) communicates to others through words and looks. Words are the route to the core of a person. Verse 17 is somewhat similar.

[20] Sheol, the underworld where all the dead exist in a shadowy world, is personified as a force that is never satisfied and always wants more. Sheol and death are elsewhere personified, for example, "Therefore Sheol opens wide her throat / and exposes its vast mouth" (Isa. 5:14); "Shall I [God] ransom them from the power of Sheol, / rescue them from Death? / O Death, where are your plagues? / O Sheol, where are your destructions?" (Hos. 13:14). So also are human eyes, which stand by metonymy for desires, e.g., "When the woman *saw* that the tree was good for eating and a delight to the eyes . . ." (Gen. 3:6). The saying is one of several ancient anticipations of modern criticisms of consumerism: Unchecked desire for more and better goods contains the germ of death (Meinhold). Cf. Qoh. 4:8 and 1 John 2:16: "For all that is in the world, sensual lust, enticement for the eyes, and a pretentious life, is not from the Father but is from the world" (NAB). Horace, *Epistles,* is similar: *quanto plura parasti, tanto plura cupis,* "the more you accumulate the more you want" (II.ii.147).

[21] Colon A is also found in 17:3a, where it is followed by "and the assayer of the heart is Yahweh." Here the testing is not done by God but by fellow human beings (Meinhold). The refining of ore was done in a thick-walled smelting oven partially buried in the ground. Small openings in the oven let steam out and oxygen in. The fire was fueled by charcoal (26:21). The smelting process shows whether the ores are precious or worthless, true silver or gold. How does one assess the true worth of a human being? One is known by the quality of one's friends. What kind of people approve of what I do? The phrase "each according to his . . . " is also found in Ex. 12:4; 16:16, 18; Num. 26:54. The translation of REB and NRSV, "so a person *is tested* by being praised," suggests that a good character will not become vain when praised, but such an interpretation obscures the parallelism.

[22] Many commentators believe the verse is overloaded and so excise colon B, but there is no versional support for eliminating it. The other tricola in the chapter (vv. 10 and 27) end subsections, and this tricolon does also. Mortar and pestle were not the means for ridding grain of its useless husk, but were ordinarily used for grinding olives, resins, and spices. The point is that even if you used the extraordinary means of mortar and pestle, you could never rid a fool of perverse folly, so deeply ingrained is it.

[23–27] These verses constitute a five-line poem on the advantages of field and flocks over other forms of wealth. Natural assets are less subject to risk than hoarded treasure because they renew themselves. Vegetation comes up from the earth every year; sheep and goats are transformed into food and clothing. Field and flock produce "enough" (v. 27a) basic foodstuffs, in contrast perhaps to the excess that accumulated treasure can buy. The teaching is traditional but the wit and perspective of this poem are remarkable.

[23–24] "Be aware" and "give attention" have a double meaning: take care of your flocks, attend to the kind of wealth they provide. The antithesis to flocks as a form of wealth is *hōsen* ("hoard, treasure"), which is particularly vulnerable to theft or seizure (Jer. 20:5 and Ezek. 22:25).

[25–27] Unproductive wealth is contrasted with vegetable and animal abundance. Unlike stored-up treasure that is subject to theft or seizure, grassland renews itself and sustains herds. The ecosystem of animals and grassland provides sustenance for human beings. Year after year beast and field provide clothing, money to purchase more pastureland, and food for an entire household.

Proverbs 28

28:1 A wicked person flees[a] though none pursue,
    but the righteous are confident as lions.

2 When a land rebels its rulers are many,
    but with a wise man right order endures.

3 A poor man who extorts from the impoverished
    is a torrential rain that leaves no food.

4 Those who reject instruction give praise to the wicked,
    but those who keep instruction give battle to them.

5 Wicked people do not understand judgment,
    but those who seek Yahweh understand all things.

6 Better a poor person walking in his integrity
    than one walking on a crooked way though he is rich.

7 Who heeds instruction is a prudent son,
    but who consorts with gluttons shames his father.

8 Who increases his wealth by interest and surcharge
    amasses it for another who will give to the poor.

9 Who turns his ear away from hearing instruction
    will have his own prayer become an abomination.

10 Who misleads the upright on a wicked path
    will fall into the pit he dug,
    but the innocent will inherit good things.

11   A rich person thinks he's clever,
          but a shrewd pauper sees through him.
12   When the righteous triumph splendor abounds,
          but when the wicked rise, people hide.
13   Who conceals his offenses does not prosper;
          who confesses and turns from them receives mercy.
14   Happy the person who constantly fears;
          who hardens his heart falls into trouble.
15   A roaring lion, a charging bear—
          a scoundrel ruling an impoverished people.
16   Who[b] abounds in extortions is lacking in sense;
          those renouncing loot increase their days.
17   Anyone burdened with bloodguilt
          will be in flight to the grave.
          Do not touch him![c]
18   Who walks in integrity finds help;
          who walks a crooked way will fall.[d]
19   Who works his land has food in plenty,
          who pursues vanity has want in plenty.
20   A trustworthy person abounds in blessings;
          one rushing toward riches will not escape punishment.
21   To favor one party is not good,
          but a person may transgress for a bit of bread.
22   A miser hurries toward money
          but does not see want coming toward him.
23   One who reproves a person wins more favor[e]
          than one who speaks flattering words.
24   Who robs his father and his mother
          and says, "That's no crime,"
          is companion to a brigand.
25   A voracious maw stirs up strife,
          but one who trusts in Yahweh is well fed.
26   Who trusts in his wit is a fool,
          but who walks by wisdom comes through safely.
27   Who gives to a pauper suffers no want;
          who averts his eyes gets curses in plenty.
28   When the wicked arise people withdraw,
          but when they perish the righteous abound.

a. There is no need to emend *nāsû* to *nās* in colon A, for a verb can be plural when the noun (*rāšā‘*) is collective (GKC §145l).

b. The first word in MT, *nāgîd*, "leader," occurs nowhere else in Proverbs. It overloads the syllable count of one line, and is incompatible with the plural subject of B. We follow Toy in excising it. It may have been added on the mistaken assumption that the verse is about political leaders.

c. MT is in disarray and it is impossible to reconstruct an acceptable Hebrew text from the versions. G has a tricolon not in MT (Rahlfs v. 17a): "Teach [your] son, and he will love you / and he will give honor to your soul; / do not hearken to a lawless nation."

d. We omit *bĕ'ehāt*, "in[to] one." Its presence in the colon makes the syllable count unbalanced (7/11). It developed from the early pointing of "way" as dual: "Who is crooked in two ways (dual number) will fall into one." G does not reflect the phrase and S reflects *bĕšahat*, "in a pit," which seems to have arisen from 26:27a.

e. With S we omit *'ahăray*, "afterward (?)," which arose through dittography (*'dm 'hry hn*). The present text overloads the syllable count in colon A and makes overly obvious the paradox that in the long run reproof earns more favor than flattery.

[28:1] The phrase "flees though none pursue" occurs in Lev. 26:17, 36 in a curse for disobedience to the covenant. In Leviticus the phrase means flight that continues even when the enemy has ceased pursuing; the terror is so profound that one cannot stop running. It is the opposite of the lion-like confidence mentioned in colon B. Wicked behavior sets in motion a chain of ills that leads to a life of fear.

[2] The first colon states the paradox that rebellion, far from doing away with rulers, actually multiplies them by introducing new factions or ensuring a succession of leaders in unstable times (Ehrlich). Unfortunately, colon B is corrupt, literally, "by a wise man knowing thus ("right order"?) will he lengthen [his days]." G does not offer an independent reading.

Psalm 82:7 has the same parallel of *śar*, "officer," and *'ādām*, "man," in a context of ruling. Colon B here may refer to the advantage of a single wise leader over many princes. The meaning of the whole is uncertain, however.

[3] REB and NRSV emend "poor man" (*geber rāš*) in colon A to "ruler" (*geber* alone) or "tyrant" (*rāšā'*), but "poor man" has versional support and makes sense. The verse apparently refers to the ancient practice of tax farming, in which collecting was let out to private bidders who collected taxes and took a commission. The experience of poverty, which might be expected to make one sympathetic to the poor, made tax collectors merciless toward poor farmers. The poor would be pitted against the poor. Similarly, rain, which might be expected to make the earth produce food, in its violent form strips the land of its vegetation and causes famine. Isaiah 30:23 has similar vocabulary (words identical to our passage italicized): "[God] will give *rain* for your seed / with which you sow the ground, / and *food* that the earth brings forth / will be rich and fat."

[4] The word *tôrāh* can mean "law, Mosaic law," as well as "teaching, instruction." Most translators and commentators take it here as the Mosaic law or a form of it, but a minority (Gemser, Meinhold, Whybray, JPSV) rightly take it as the instruction of teachers and parents, which is the meaning of the word in its other occurrences in Proverbs. Heeding the tradition has consequences beyond the individual; it is a political act. To spurn the tradition gives aid and comfort to the wicked and furthers their project. To obey instruction is to battle the wicked.

[5] The phrase "to understand justice" means to be wise or act wisely as in Job 32:9. This verse plays on the phrase: People bent on evil are not wise, they do not know judgment in the sense that they do not see the divine justice that eventually will catch up with them. On the other hand, those seeking Yahweh understand "all things," including Yahweh's rewarding them and punishing the wicked. Cf. 1 Cor. 2:15: "The spiritual person can judge everything but is not subject to judgment by anyone."

[6] This verse is another "better-than" saying. "To walk on a path" is an age-old metaphor for living. Riches and poverty ought not to affect one's judgment of personal behavior, but it very often does. Proverbs 19:1 (as emended) is identical. In this verse the first and last words in each colon have similar sounds, /ō/ in colon A, and '-š and 'š- in colon B.

[7] Two of the three parallels are obvious: "son" // "father"; "prudent" (*mēbîn*) // "shames" (*yaklîm*). The third parallel at first reading is odd, "who heeds instruction" // "who consorts with gluttons (*zôlĕlîm*)." The oddness can be explained by Deuteronomic legislation on rebellious sons (Deut. 21:18–21). A rebellious son is termed a "glutton" (*zôlēl*), who can be disowned by his parents by declaring, "he will not heed our voice." The penalty is stoning. Colon A of our saying uses this vocabulary: A son who heeds his father's instruction is prudent, unlike the disowned son in Deuteronomy. One who consorts with "gluttons" or wastrels disgraces his father. The maxim belongs to the series on family in Proverbs. The eight words of the saying are formed into four pairs by shared sounds, respectively /ō/, /ē/, /ō/, and /î/.

[8] Charging interest on loans to fellow Israelites was forbidden in biblical law (Ex. 22:24 [25E]; Lev. 25:36; Deut. 23:20 [19E]). The law has in view money lent to those in distress and not commercial loans in a modern sense. "Interest" (lit., "bite") and "surcharge" are a fixed pair in several of the above passages but the terms are not explained in the Bible. The point here is that profit gained from gouging those in need will ultimately be redistributed to the needy from whom it was originally taken. The profit will find its way into the hands of a generous person who understands that Israelites are kin and not be exploited. The next two proverbs also begin with participles in the hiphil conjugation, which begin with *m*.

[9] In this example of poetic justice, those who turn a deaf ear to the instruction that ultimately comes from God (mediated through teachers or parents) will find their own words to God rejected. "Abomination" is a word used in rituals for what is not acceptable to God. The alliteration and assonance in colon A is remarkable: *mēsîr 'oznô mišmōa' tôrāh.*

[10] Those who mislead others will themselves suffer the consequences of the evil they led others into. The semantic field of path is maintained throughout— "to mislead," "upright" (lit., "straight"), "path," "to fall," "pit." The third colon is unusual and is banal in its sentiment. If it is an addition it was added early, for it is in the versions. The righteous in colon A will not suffer permanent damage but will inherit good things. "Innocent" is parallel with "just" in 2:21.

[11] According to this observation on the effect of wealth and of poverty on wisdom, the social position of the wealthy can mislead them. To be wise in one's own eyes is a sign of folly (3:7; 26:5, 12). The irony is that a rich person's social inferior is actually superior, for wisdom is more valuable than pearls (8:10–11) and enables one to judge others accurately. The verb *ḥāqar* ("to search out") can mean to find out another's attitude as when Jonathan sounds out his father Saul's attitude to David in 1 Sam. 20:12.

[12] What happens when righteous and unrighteous people triumph and come into power? In the first case, there is great *public* celebration, for "splendor" (*tip'aret*) in 16:31; 19:11; and 20:29 designates a public sign of honor. The consequences of the triumph of the wicked in colon B are not so clear, for the meaning of the verb *yĕḥuppaś* is controverted. Read literally as a verb in the pual conjugation, it means "is tracked down," possibly in the sense that people are hunted down by the wicked. Gemser relies on the nearly identical v. 28a, "when the wicked rise, people *hide*," to support his suggestion that the verb should be corrected to the hithpael conjugation, "to hide oneself." It is simpler, however, to accept MT and suppose the word "to be sought out, tracked down" means here something like "to be scarce, to hide." When the righteous exult in the sense of triumphing over their foes and coming into power, oppression ceases and the city flourishes. But when the wicked rise in triumph, people go into hiding; there is no public celebration. Cf. 29:2.

[13] "To conceal the offenses" of another in the sense of overlooking that person's failings is a good thing in Proverbs (17:9). Covering one's own offenses, however, is not a good thing. Psalm 32:1–5 sheds light here (words identical to our saying are italicized): "Happy the person whose *offense* is taken away, whose sin is *concealed*. . . . As long as I said nothing, my bones wasted away. . . . I made known my sin, my iniquity I did not *conceal*. I resolved, 'I will *confess* my offense* to Yahweh.'" "Does not prosper" means that one's plans will not be realized, as in 1 Kings 22:12, 15; Jer. 5:28.

The saying criticizes people's inclination to keep quiet about their faults. Colon B makes clear that the confession is done to God. Mercy will be shown to such people (divine passive). This is the only verse in Proverbs that refers to God's forgiveness of the penitent sinner (Whybray).

[14] The Hebrew word rendered by "fears" is a different verb than in the common phrase "to fear (or revere) Yahweh." The only other occurrence of the verb in this conjugation is Isa. 51:13, which refers to fear and dread of an oppressor. The meaning "to harden the heart" in colon B is illuminated by Ezek. 3:7: "But the house of Israel is unwilling to listen to me, because the whole house of Israel has a hard forehead and a *hard heart*."

The saying states a paradox. Those who are fearful in the sense of cautious are declared happy, and those who are "bold" in the sense of "tough-hearted" as in Ex. 7:3 will fall into traps they did not foresee or "fear." In short, there is a good fear and a bad fear.

[15] A lion is a common image of a king in the ancient Near East. A king is compared to a lion in Ezek. 32:2; Prov. 19:12; 20:2 and 30:29–31 (though with a different Hebrew word for "lion" than that used here). When "lion" and "bear" occur together (1 Sam. 17:34, 37 and Amos 5:19), they are dangerous to human beings. The point of the saying is that a wicked ruler is a lion, yes, but a lion stalking a helpless prey—his own people. Colon B is notable for its alliteration of /š/, /l/, and /ʿ/ and assonance of /ā/: *mōšēl rāšāʿ ʿal ʿam dāl.*

[16] "Loot" in colon B is unjust gain as in 1:19. The Hebrew word *rab* in the construct state, "abounds," is common in Proverbs (14:29; 28:20, 27; 29:22). The antithesis here is lack and abundance. Where there is lack of intelligence there is abundant violence; where there is lack of unjustly acquired wealth, there is abundant life.

[17] The text of MT is uncertain. As it stands, the topic is the plight of someone burdened with the guilt of having killed someone, even if the killing was accidental. Such people were allowed to flee to asylum cities in order to escape blood vengeance from the deceased's relatives (Deut. 19:1–10; Ex. 21:12–14; Joshua 20). The saying implies that the reality was sometimes different from the ideal. Safety was not assured by fleeing to a city; the person will be in flight to the grave. It is true the law does not allow one to be taken (*tāmak* in the sense of "to capture" as in 5:22), but neither will anyone want to touch him (*tāmak* in the benign sense as in 3:18; 29:23; 31:19). The person is a fugitive forever. See Gen. 4:12.

[18] The metaphors of straight and crooked roads are applied to conduct. One who walks "straight" or blamelessly is the antithesis to one "who walks a crooked way." Such a person will be helped on life's journey, whereas the other will fall into a pit. MT points the noun "way" as a dual rather than as a plural. The sounds of colon B echo those of colon A: *neʿqaš,* "crooked," echoes *yiwwāšēaʿ,* "finds help"; *yippôl,* "fall," echoes *hôlēk,* walks."

[19] The saying is the same as 12:11 except that the last two words in 12:11b are "has a lack of sense." For comment, see 12:11. The antithesis is the same in both sayings. Doing one's duty faithfully means being sated with food (*yiśbaʿ leḥem*), whereas frenetic pursuit of what is insubstantial (*rēqîm*) means being sated with poverty (*yiśbaʿ rîš*).

[20] The righteous receive blessings (including wealth), whereas those who seek to get rich quick end up with trouble rather than wealth. The verb "to has-

ten" (*'ûṣ*) in Proverbs always means to act precipitously (19:2; 21:6; 29:20) and without reflection. The right way to become wealthy is to pursue virtue. G, S, and T add the word "wicked" in colon B to make it clear to their readers that haste to gain riches is not of itself a bad thing. Alliteration links the pairs of words in colon A: Each word in the phrase "a trustworthy person" (*'îš 'ĕmûnôt*) begins with *'āleph;* the phrase "abounds in blessings" (*rab bĕrākôt*) repeats *r* and *b* in reverse order. Cf. Sir. 11:10–28.

[21] The context is the law court and the topic is partiality (as in Prov. 24:23–25). A Hebrew idiom for judicial favoritism is "to recognize a face" (Deut. 1:17; 16:19). Despite the strong prohibition of judicial partiality, the reality is that a judge may sell out for a pittance. The saying expresses contempt for the greed that would pervert the integrity of the court for a piece of bread.

[22] Getting rich quickly is also the topic of v. 20. Hebrew "good of eye" is an expression for "generous" in 22:9, and its opposite, "bad of eye" (here and in 23:6) is an expression for "miserly." Misers hurry toward wealth, not seeing that penury is coming toward them. There may be a play on the expression "bad of eye," for the expression literally means the inability to see something coming.

[23] The paradox is that frank and truthful speech wins more favor than flattery. People learn best through honest dialogue that includes the possibility of reproof and correction. Reproof leads to wisdom that wins favor.

[24] This verse consists of a tricolon like v. 17. Sons and daughters normally lived at home under their parents' authority until they married and moved out; they could also remain in the household after marriage. Presumably, there were many cases where parents grew old and children grew domineering, gradually taking over the house and its wealth. According to this saying, such usurpation is simple theft. The children have no more right to their parents' property while they are living than a brigand from outside the family.

[25] "Voracious maw," literally, "to be wide of throat," is similar in meaning to the verb in the hiphil conjugation, "to open the maw" (*harḥîb nepeš*) in Isa. 5:14 ("Sheol has opened wide its gullet") and Hab. 2:5 ("he has made his maw wide as Sheol"). As the versions recognized, the phrase means "greedy" here.

The paradox is that a wide open throat, by metonymy an unbridled appetite, brings strife, whereas its opposite, calm trust in God's care, attains the very thing that the throat desires—satisfaction of appetite. Elsewhere in Proverbs, anger stirs up quarrels (e.g., 15:18 and 29:22).

[26] The syntax of colon A and B is parallel: participle + the preposition "in" + noun + the emphatic pronoun "he." Only the last word in each colon differs— "fool" in colon A, and "comes through safely" in colon B. The implication is that a fool will remain a fool and not find a way out, whereas the wise come through safely. "To trust in one's heart" in colon A is not (as the English might suggest) to rely on one's intuition but on one's (unaided) judgment, for "heart" is the organ of judgment. Such self-centeredness is dangerous. Genuine wisdom comes as a

gift "from above," that is, from God and mediated by tradition (including parents and teachers). To be virtuous is not to be autonomous but to be obedient and receptive.

[27] One hardly misses a coin given to a beggar, but one must often endure an insult or glare from a supplicant denied. One does not lose ("no want") by giving, but one gets what one does not desire ("curses") by withholding care. Hebrew *'ên*, literally, "there is not" (here translated "suffers no want") and *rab*, "much; in plenty") or *rōb*, "multitude," are a fixed pair in 5:23; 11:14; 14:4; 15:22. What is given to the poor comes back in blessing. What is kept from them gives one no benefit.

[28] The antithesis of wicked and righteous plays itself out in society. This maxim states how the presence and absence of wicked rulers affect society. When the wicked come into power, people hide. "Withdraw" in 22:3 and 27:12 describes the wise hiding from trouble. Wicked rulers mean the disappearance of people in community, probably in the sense of people being afraid of appearing in public and enjoying others' company. It is the end of a flourishing and happy community (Meinhold). When the wicked rulers disappear, presumably as a result of their wickedness (see 10:25), the righteous increase— again the contrast between disappearance and appearance. The rule of the wicked destroys social life. Verse 12 is similar in sentiment.

Proverbs 29

Colon A begins with the first letter of the Hebrew alphabet, *'ālep* and the last verse (v. 27) begins with the final letter, *tāw*. The chapter is thus a section.

29:1 One oft rebuked may stiffen his neck;
         suddenly he is shattered beyond healing.

2 When the righteous prevail the people rejoice;
      when a scoundrel rules the people groan.

3 Who loves wisdom makes his father rejoice,
      but who consorts with prostitutes squanders wealth.

4 By justice a king builds up a land,
      but one who raises taxes tears it down.

5 Who speaks flattery to his neighbor
      casts a net at his feet.

6 A scoundrel's offenses entrap him,
      but a righteous person runs rejoicing.[a]

7 A righteous person knows the rights of the poor,
      but a scoundrel does not understand wisdom.

8 Scoffers inflame a city,

but the wise calm anger.
9 A wise person debates a fool,
but there is no calm, only ranting and railing.
10 Murderers hate a blameless person,
but the upright seek his life.
11 A fool gives his spirit free rein,
but a wise person controls it.
12 A ruler who heeds flattery
will see all his servants grow wicked.
13 A pauper and an oppressor meet;
Yahweh gives light to the eyes of both.
14 A king who judges the poor with fairness
will have his throne secure forever.
15 Rod and rebuke impart wisdom,
but a lad let loose shames his mother.
16 When the wicked increase, offenses increase,
but the righteous will look on their downfall.
17 Discipline your son and he will provide for you;
he will furnish delight for your soul.
18 Where there is no vision the people are discouraged,
but happy the one who heeds instruction.
19 By words alone a servant cannot be taught,
for he understands but does not respond.
20 Have you ever seen someone hasty in his words?
There is more hope for a fool than for him.
21 Whoever as a youth is soft on his servant
will have a hard time[b] later on.
22 An angry person causes disputes,
and a wrathful one, many offenses.
23 A person's pride brings him low,
but one lowly of spirit gets honor.
24 Whoever shares loot with a thief hates himself;
he hears the imprecation and does not tell.
25 Fear of other people sets a trap,
but who trusts in Yahweh is raised to safety.
26 Many seek the face of a ruler,
but justice comes from Yahweh.
27 An evildoer is an abomination to the righteous;
one on the straight path is an abomination to a scoundrel.

a. MT of colon B, "the righteous person sings out (*yārûn*) and rejoices," is not a satisfactory parallel to colon A. We accept Pinsker's emendation (cited by Delitzsch) of *yārûṣ*, "he will run," for MT *yārûn*. Rejoicing and running are paired in Ps. 19:6: "[the sun] rejoices (*yāśîś*) like a hero running (*lārûṣ*) his course."

   b. MT *mānôn* is uncertain. G took the word as "grief" and assumed the entire verse was about *self*-indulgence: "Who lives wantonly from childhood shall be a slave and in the end will grieve over himself." Other ancient renderings include: S and Symmachus, "groan"; T, "driven out" (ms. L) or "cut off" (ms. Z); V, "stubborn."

   [29:1] The first words of colon A are, literally, "a man of rebukes," which can be either a subjective genitive (one who gives rebukes, a teacher) or an objective genitive (one who is the object of rebukes, a dullard). The predicate, "stiffens his neck," immediately shows it is an objective genitive (one who is reproved). The plural "rebukes" suggests the person has been reproved again and again, and "stiffens his neck" suggests that the reproofs have not been heeded. The phrase "stiffen the neck" in Deut. 10:16 and 2 Kings 17:14 occurs in a context of not heeding a word or message. In colon B, the adjective "sudden" and the passive mood of the verb suggest an extraordinary origin of the collapse; it is not a routine misfortune. To stiffen one's neck invites having it broken (cf. 1 Sam. 4:18, though with a different word for "neck"). Colon B is identical to 6:15b.

   [2] People's response to a righteous or a wicked ruler is expressed in sound — shouts of joy or groans of pain. The verb "to rejoice" often refers to the expression of an emotion and not just the inner feeling. The saying is similar to 28:28 two lines previous and to 28:12. An example of civic joy that comes with stable government is Isa. 9:2: "You [God] have multiplied the nation, / you have increased rejoicing" (emended).

   [3] Wise adult children have a profound effect upon their parents (e.g., 10:1; 15:20; 17:21). The danger of prostitutes to gaining wisdom is described in chap. 7. The perspective of this verse is eminently practical; the "wealth" that the licentious son loses is his inheritance as in 19:14. An angry and shamed father will disinherit an irresponsible son. Proverbs 5:10 warned that the strange woman would take the man's wealth. Loving wisdom rather than prostitutes, on the other hand, brings an increase of wealth (3:10, 16).

   [4] The metaphor of high and low for prosperity and decline is employed to differentiate between good and bad governance. The metaphor is the same in English. A just king "causes the land to stand up," that is, makes it prosperous. But one who raises taxes brings down a country. Confiscatory taxation is the antithesis of "justice."

   [5] The full form of the idiom "to make smooth [one's words]" is found in 2:16 and 7:5. "Smooth words" refers to deceitful speech calculated to entrap another person, like the speech of the forbidden woman in 2:16 and 7:5, which kills her hearers. This saying states the lethal effect of seductive words through a striking image: to address seductive words to another's face is to cast a net at the person's feet.

[6] The imagery of trapping links vv. 5 and 6. "Scoundrel" (lit., "man of evil") connotes one devoted to evil. For such people a transgression is literally a snare, catching their feet as they walk on the way. The righteous progress unhindered and in joy. Psalm 119:32 has the same idea: "I will run in the way of your commandments, because you have enlarged my heart." The righteous run along the path joyously, confident they are protected, whereas the wicked are entrapped.

[7] Concern for the poor was part of the ancient Near Eastern educational ideal. "Rights" (*dîn*) is used as in 31:5, 8. "Knows" has the meaning it has in 12:10 where the righteous know the appetite of their farm animals. That empathetic knowledge is here extended to a class of beings who are often treated like animals (Delitzsch). Colon B has a double meaning: The wicked do not understand such knowledge, that is, they have no such concern for the poor, and they have no knowledge (wisdom), that is, they know nothing, they are fools. The alliteration of /d/ in colon A is remarkable (*yōdēaʿ ṣaddîq dîn dallîm*).

[8] Scoffers are contrasted with the wise in 9:8; 15:12; and 21:11, where the distinction between the two types is that the scoffer will not listen. The verb "to inflame, exhale" is illuminated by Ezek. 21:36 (the identical Hebrew word is italicized), "I will pour out upon you my anger, with the fire of my anger I will *inflame* you." Scoffers ignite anger in the city, whereas the wise calm it down or, possibly, turn it back from the city. The verb "to inflame," literally, "to blow, exhale," has "lies" as its object in its six other occurrences in Proverbs—"to breathe out lies." There may thus be a wordplay here: As the scoffers exhale their lies, they are actually fanning the flame of popular anger. Social unrest resulting from wicked leadership is also the theme of v. 3 and 28:12, 28. A similar thought is stated in Sir. 28:14.

[9] One of the few proverbs that describes how "discipline" or "reproof" is actually done and what effect it has on people. The verb "to enter into judgment" does not necessarily mean "to go to law with" (despite NRSV and REB) but simply "to dispute, argue with" as in Jer. 2:35; Ezek. 17:20; 20:35, 36 (with God as subject) and 1 Sam. 12:7 (with Samuel as subject). A fool's response to correction is to rant and ridicule, for the type cannot listen and respond. *Naḥat*, "calm," has the meaning it has in Qoh. 9:17, "the calm (*bĕnaḥat*) words of the wise are heeded more than the shout of a ruler among fools." In this verse, a sage's reproof is uttered quietly; it cannot be heard where there are closed minds and raillery.

[10] The text is sound, but, as Delitzsch notes, syntax and idiom are at war with sense. The problem is that the common idiom "to seek the life of" (only here in Proverbs) in its numerous biblical occurrences is always "to seek to kill." The customary meaning, "to take life," makes no sense here. Several solutions have been proposed. JPSV, REB, and JB interpret "to seek the life of" in a positive sense, something like 11:30 (where the verb is "to take lives"). "To seek" occurs fourteen times in Proverbs, usually in a positive sense (to seek wisdom). NRSV takes *tām wĕyāšār,* "blameless and upright," as a fixed pair (occurring five times in the Bible), and understands "the upright" in colon B as *casus pendens:* "and as for the upright, they seek his life." The syntax is tortured and the meaning is banal, however.

The first solution is preferable: Murderous people hate a blameless person but the upright seek his life in a positive sense. "To seek the life of " is here turned on its head. The first two words of colon A are mirrored in the last two words: *'nšy dmym // yśn' tm.* Cf. the reversal of an idiom in 11:30.

[11] The key to the saying is the double meaning of the phrase in colon A, *yôṣē rûaḥ,* "to let loose the wind/spirit/anger." In the hymnic contexts of Jer. 10:13 (= 51:16) and Ps. 135:7, the phrase means "[God] who brings forth wind from his storehouses." Hebrew *rûaḥ* basically means "air in motion," hence, according to context, either "wind" or "that which breathes quickly in animation or agitation (= temper)." The verb *šābaḥ,* "to calm," can describe Yahweh's taming the sea in cosmogonic battle, "When [Sea's] waves surge, you still them" (Ps. 89:10; cf. Ps. 65:8). The precise meaning of the phrase *bĕ'āḥôr* in colon B ("down"? "back"?) escapes us, but the phrase is reflected in all the versions.

The double meaning of *yôṣē rûaḥ* is employed here for comic effect—to show the pomposity of fools. As always, hotheads are fools and the self-controlled are wise.

[12] When rulers heed bad advice, it affects their court. Wicked administrators rise to the top, while the honest and wise are shut out. Leaders are responsible for the quality of their staff. Psalm 101 is similar in theme. The alliteration of *m* and *š* is striking: *mōšēl maqšîb 'al dĕbar šāqer // kol mĕšārtāyw rĕšā'îm.*

[13] The meaning of the Hebrew phrase *'îš tĕtākîm* in colon A is uncertain.[1] The context suggests it means a state opposite to poverty as in the similar saying 22:2: "Rich person meets poor person—Yahweh made them both."

Society includes poor people and those that exploit them. Both have a common creator who "gives light to the eyes of both" in equal measure. The phrase "to give light to the eyes" means "to allow to live" as in Ps. 13:4: "Give light to my eyes lest I sleep in death." Before God, judgments based on wealth are insignificant. Human judgments, on the other hand, are often made on the basis of power and wealth.

[14] In Ps. 82:3, God condemns judges for failing to do what our saying demands (identical words underlined): "How long will you *judge* unjustly, / showing favor to the wicked? / Judge for the *poor* and orphan." If a king wants to

---

1. The phrase may be related to *tôk* ("violence, oppression"), which occurs in Pss. 10:7 and 55:12. The triliteral root *tkk* in Palmyrene Aramaic means "to menace."

stabilize his throne, his law courts must uphold the right of the poor. One might assume that ruling in favor of the rich and powerful would win their support and provide political stability for the king, but our saying recognizes that ultimate stability comes from the divine patron of the king who looks out for the poor.

[15] "Rod and rebuke" exemplify the stylistic figure of concrete and abstract. "Let loose" is said of animals in Job 39:5 and Isa. 16:2. The verse draws an analogy between animals and children. Domestic animals are trained and controlled by a shepherd's staff (*šēbeṭ* in Lev. 27:32 and Ps. 23:4). Animals allowed to run free will never be domesticated. So also children given total freedom will go wrong. Firmness in raising children is a common theme (13:24; 22:15; 23:14–15; Sir. 30:1). This verse is the only one in Proverbs that mentions the mother alone.

[16] Though some translate "when the wicked are in power" (NRSV, REB), the more literal "grow numerous" (JPSV) is preferable. When a wicked faction becomes numerous, it sows the seeds of its destruction through the increase in offenses against others (the nuance of *pešaʿ* in, e.g., 10:12, 19; 17:9; 19:11). The Hebrew word for "downfall" in colon B can describe the downfall of a king (Ezek. 31:13, 16; 32:10) or a city (Ezek. 26:15, 18; 27:27). The very increase of the wicked class will bring about its downfall, for offenses bring social unrest as well as divine retribution. The Hebrew idiom "to look upon" (*rāʾāh bě*) connotes looking on in triumph.

[17] Proverbs presumes that the greatest service a parent can render a growing child is discipline. To discipline a child is to offer guidance, reproving when necessary, but always in a context of love and of confidence in the child. A good example of loving discipline is 23:15–16. This saying is about the goal of the process—the formation of a loving and responsible adult. The outlook is very pragmatic; it is in the self-interest of a parent to educate a child well, for wise offspring will care for their elderly parents. Children's responsibility toward aging parents was sometimes a theme of law in the ancient Near East.[2]

Colon B is more concrete than is implied by its common translation "delight your soul," for the phrase means to provide food. The literal translation is "gives food to your maw." The Ugaritic cognate of Hebrew *maʿădanîm*, "delights," occurs in parallel to *lḥm*, "bread, food" (*KTU* 1.14.II.84; 1.14.IV.175). Hebrew *nepeš*, "soul," literally is "maw, throat; hunger," as in Hos. 9:4, "food for your hunger."

[18] One of several aphorisms in this chapter about wisdom and justice in society (vv. 2, 4, 8, 12, 13, 14, 16). "Demoralized" (*pāraʿ*) is used of a discouraged people (Ex. 5:4) or even a riotous people (Ex. 32:25). "Vision" and

---

2. J. Greenfield, "Adi balṭu—Care for the Elderly and Its Rewards," *Archiv für Orient-forschung* 19 (1982): 309–16.

"instruction" are parallel in Ezek. 7:26 (and Lam. 2:9) in descriptions of a society that has lost its ordinary means of guidance (identical words italicized): "Then they shall seek *vision* from the prophet in vain; *instruction* shall perish from the priest, and counsel from the elders."

Some have sought to relate *ḥāzôn* ("vision") to peripheral Akkadian *ḥazannu* ("mayor") and to Mishnaic Hebrew *ḥazzān* ("supervisor, sexton"), but the biblical parallels indicate the traditional understanding is correct. Meinhold's proposal that "vision" and "teaching" have only a general meaning in Ezek. 7:26 and Lam. 2:9—simply authoritative guidance for the community—is unlikely. "Vision" elsewhere means prophetic vision, which generally concerns itself with the king and nation.

The basic contrast in the saying is between nation and individual. A people may be demoralized from poor leadership, but an individual can still find happiness by heeding inspired wisdom. One can surmount adversity by wisdom, as in 15:15: "All the days of the poor are evil, but a good heart is a continual feast."

[19] The initial position of "by words" (*bidbārîm*) underlines its importance. Its consonants *d-b* are reversed in the last word of the colon, "servant" (originally *'abd*). The point is that words, which elsewhere in Proverbs are a means to wisdom, do not have that effect upon servants or slaves. Ancient Near Eastern custom dictated their style—silent acquiescence. The give and take of reproving is not possible with them. Wisdom requires honest and free dialogue. The aphorism casts an interesting light on what is meant by discipline—dialogue unhampered by fear or convention.

[20] Like the preceding, this is a saying on the limit or misuse of words. Rashness is criticized (cf. 19:2; 21:5; 28:20). Haste in words sabotages the process of knowing and doing in Proverbs. One becomes a moral agent in Proverbs by taking in data through the eyes and ears, memorizing and reflecting on it in the heart, and then speaking and acting "from the heart" (= mind). Haste impairs this sequence of perception, reflection, and response. Instead, one speaks without reflection, making one liable to commit offenses such as lying and slander. The opening question, "Do you see . . . ?" occurs also in 22:29 and 26:12; the latter is identical except it has "one wise in his own eyes" in colon A. Qoheleth 5:1 has a similar stricture against haste.

[21] The verse is made difficult by the uncertain last word in colon B, *mānôn*, which we translate tentatively as "hard time." Modern other commentators are tentative. JPSV and NRSV, "a slave pampered from youth [childhood] will come to a bad end," is unsatisfactory because it shifts the grammatical subject of colon A, "whoever indulges his slave from youth," from the master to the slave. One would expect the master to be the subject of colon B also. A young person who grows up with a personal slave or servant may be too easy on the slave early on and come to regret it later in life. Given the obscurity of *mānôn*,

we can only guess that it means "hard," yielding something like softness in the beginning means hardship at the end. For a similar sentiment, see 22:6.

[22] The basic meaning is clear enough, though the nuance is uncertain. In 15:18 and 28:25, stirring up wrath is the antithesis of being peaceful and productive. Proverbs 22:24 counsels avoiding a hothead lest one spring a trap on oneself. The meaning here must be that anger gets one nowhere; it only brings quarrelling and offense (*peša'*). The latter term, as Ehrlich correctly notes, is not ethical ("sin") but what offends others and brings opprobrium on oneself. Anger hurts oneself and others.

[23] The word for "pride" in colon A is literally "swelling up, rising." In Ps. 46:4 it refers to the waves of the sea. The word means "majesty" in Deut. 33:29 and "pride" in Pss. 10:2 and 31:19, 24. One's lofty pride will bring one down and one's lowly state will lift one up to glory. "Lowly of spirit" is the opposite of an arrogance (colon A) that seizes honor. The proud do not get what they want, for honor cannot be self-awarded. The lowly, on the other hand, can receive it. The phrase "to get honor" also occurs in 11:16.

[24] Partners in a crime, even accessories after the fact who receive stolen goods, hurt themselves. Leviticus 5:1 explains the specific case referred to in the saying (words identical to our saying are italicized): "If a person does wrong: when he *has heard a* public *imprecation* (*šāma' qôl 'ālāh*) [against withholding testimony]—and although he was a witness, either having seen or known [the facts]—yet does not *testify* (*yaggîd*), then he must bear his punishment."[3] According to J. Milgrom, the phrase "then he must bear his punishment" in the Priestly source "always implies that the punishment will be meted out by God, not by man."[4] After a theft, a public proclamation was made, enforced by a "contingent curse." No one in a town or city could avoid hearing it. The curse hung over the accomplice. By doing nothing, neither directly stealing nor confessing, accomplices put themselves in serious danger.

[25] The Hebrew word translated "fear" means "craven fear." Such fear of others is a trap. A time will come when fear of others will override fear of Yahweh and the counsels of wisdom, leading one to sins that will come back on one's head. Trust in Yahweh, on the other hand, keeps one safe, for there is nothing more powerful than God. The verse has a double antithesis: anxious fear of human beings and trust in God; trap and protection.

[26] The substantive adjective "many" also begins 19:6, 21 and 31:29, where "many" is contrasted with something better in colon B. The idiom "to seek the face of" means to seek the favor of someone more powerful than oneself. God is the object of the verb "to seek" except in this verse and

3. J. Milgrom, *Leviticus 1–16* (AB 3; New York: Doubleday, 1991), 292.
4. Ibid., 295.

1 Kings 10:24 (= 2 Chron. 9:23). Though people flock to human rulers, ultimate decisions are not in their hands but in God's. Human rulers do not have it in their power to rectify every situation. Only God can establish justice definitively.

[27] Both cola of the final verse of the chapter begin with the final letter of the Hebrew alphabet, *tāw,* matching v. 1, which began with the *'ālep,* the first letter of the alphabet. Chapter 27 is evidently a section within the collection of chaps. 25–27.

"Abomination," occurring twenty-two times in Proverbs, is a metaphor from temple rituals; sacrifices are either acceptable ("pleasing") or unacceptable ("abomination") to God. Normally, an object or act is an abomination *to God,* but occasionally an object or act can be an abomination to other entities, for example, to Wisdom in 8:7, to fools in 13:19, to kings in 16:12, to any human being in 24:9. This saying is about the abhorrence the righteous and the wicked have toward each other. They live in two opposing worlds. "Evildoer" (*'îš 'āwel*) is, etymologically, "man of perversity, twistedness." Its antithesis is "one straight (*yāšār*) of path." *Yāšār* means "straight" of roads in Isa. 26:7; Jer. 31:9; Hos. 14:10.

The proverb is not primarily about the feelings of abhorrence one type has for the other but about the "either-or" quality of the moral life. One's conduct makes one a member of a group. The saying is an example of ethical dualism, which is developed at Qumran and which also appears in the New Testament— e.g., "the children of light" (John 12:36) and "Or what fellowship does light have with darkness?" (2 Cor. 6:14).

Proverbs 30

Chapter 30 begins a new section, opening with "The words of Agur, the son of Yaqeh, the man of Massa." Commentators are divided, however, on how many verses can properly be called "the words of Agur." G divides the chapter in two sections, placing vv. 1–14 before and vv. 15–33 after 24:23–34. The two sections are indeed different: The themes of vv. 1–14 are God and the name of God, whereas in vv. 15–33 God is not even mentioned; all the familiar numerical sayings ("three . . . four . . . ") occur in vv. 15–33 (vv. 15b–16, 18–20, 21–23, 24–28, 29–31). There are nonetheless links between the two sections in that vv. 7–14 anticipate the lists of vv. 15–33: vv. 7–8 list *two* things sought in prayer, and vv. 11–14 list *four* types.

Verses 1–10 are the most difficult section in Proverbs from a linguistic point of view. Verse 1 is textually damaged beyond sure recovery and its uncertainty taints the whole passage. What is the relation of v. 4 to v. 5? Were the syntactically similar vv. 6 and 10 originally together? Each seems to function as a conclusion to its section. Was the prayer of vv. 7–9 (the only prayer in Proverbs) originally connected to vv. 1–6? While there are no certain answers, the more likely solutions will be mentioned below.

Redactionally, there can be little doubt that vv. 1–10 are a section: Verses 1–5 and 7–9 can be read as logically coherent, and each is concluded by syntactically similar verses, vv. 6 and 10. Verses 11–14 are also a separate section, linked to v. 10 by the catchword "curse" in v. 11. Each verse in the section begins with the same word, "a sort" (*dôr*), a rhetorical figure called anaphora (lit., "carrying back"). With its listing of four types or sorts, the section may be intended as a bridge to the numbered lists of vv. 15–33. The Greek division of the chapter into two parts (vv. 1–14 and 15–33) is not a strong proof that chap. 30 was originally two units, for the Greek division is secondary.[1]

Given the uncertainty of the text, it is not surprising that scholars have gone in different interpretive directions. Scott believes "that the challenge of the skeptic Agur is answered by an orthodox Jewish believer in vv. 5–6, who then appends in vv. 7–9 a prayer to Yahweh that he himself may never be tempted to such blasphemous denial of God." McKane rejects Scott's proposal of an actual dialogue, proposing instead that vv. 5f. are "subsequent corrective comment whose intention is not so much to disavow vv. 1–4, as to put the matter in a proper perspective, by noting that the hidden God is nevertheless one who has made himself known by his word" (so also Toy). Meinhold takes vv. 1–14 as a coherent summary of "late" (in his view, the fourth century B.C.E.) wisdom-theological thought. It uses questions to gain a knowledge of self and God and doctrine about God (v. 4) and God's word (v. 5). Further, personal piety requires God's help for its realization (vv. 7–9); it must prove itself in one's relationship to others, especially to the poor and needy (vv. 10–14).

A good starting point is the literary structure, which is built on the contrast between human ignorance and divine wisdom. The same contrast is found in varying degrees elsewhere in biblical and other ancient literature; for example, Job 28, Psalms 73 and 90, Isa. 49:1–4, and Bar. 3:29–30. All these passages contrast the wisdom and strength of God with human ignorance and weakness. Even if human beings seem to be wise, they are not unless God gives them understanding. Rhetorical features such as self-deprecation, stark contrasts, and questions were well known in ancient Near Eastern writings. They can be viewed as a strategy in prayer to win divine favor and help. To declare oneself helpless is a way of declaring God all powerful; contrasts add drama; rhetorical questions in which the only answer is "God" are a means of giving praise. God has nothing to fear from such fragile and pitiable creatures, and indeed has positive reasons to

---

1. E. Tov, "Recensional Differences between the Masoretic Text and the Septuagint of Proverbs," *Of Scribes and Scrolls: Studies in the Hebrew Bible, Intertestamental Judaism, and Christian Origins* (J. Strugnell volume), ed. H. W. Attridge, J. J. Collins, and T. H. Tobin (College Theology Resources in Religion 5; Lanham, Md.: University Press of America, 1990), 53–56.

alleviate the distress from *noblesse oblige*. How could God allow such loyal servants to wither away and die? Building upon the traditional rhetorical contrast of divine wisdom or strength and human ignorance or fragility, the passage draws on earlier sacred writings to portray someone who has experienced the limits of human wisdom and strength but now experiences God's reliable word and the protection it bestows.

In its use of earlier sacred literature, the section is an example of *relecture,* "rereading" or reuse of biblical passages. Rereading is a phenomenon of Second Temple Judaism, by which period there existed a collection of sacred scrolls available to be quoted. Psalmic examples of *relecture* include 108, 119, and 144, which cite earlier psalms. Biblical material alluded to in our section seems to include Num. 24:3–9, 15–19 and 2 Sam. 23:1–7; Ps. 18:31 (= 2 Sam. 22:31; cf. Prov. 30:6); Ps. 73:22 (cf. Prov. 30:2a); Deut. 4:2 (cf. Prov. 30:6); 30:11–14 (cf. Prov. 30:4a); and the divine questions beginning with "Who" found in Job 38–41 and Isaiah 40–45 (cf. Prov. 30:4bd).

The passage is remarkable for its juxtaposition of archaic and late features. An archaic element is the vision of a foreign sage (*ně'um haggeber*), which, like Num. 24:3–9, 15–19, begins with the insistence that his word is not his own but God's. *Relecture* is a late feature, as noted above. To account for the early and late features, we suggest that an old oracle has been updated. The ancient sage protested that his message was not his or any human being's but God's alone. In place of that oracle, now lost, an Israelite writer saw in the sage's conventional protestations of ignorance a confession of genuine misery that is answered, like the experience of misery of Psalms 12 and 18, by a word of assurance, "every word of God is true." Continuing in this conjectural vein, we suggest that v. 4 was originally "Who has gone up to heaven and come back down? / What is his name, what is the name of his son?" The three other questions are perhaps secondary developments.

Verses 1–6 are a dramatic narrative like Psalm 73. Agur delivers an oracle (*ně'um*, v. 1), which did not come from his own labors. He is worn out from his efforts, incapable of wisdom, not knowing God (vv. 2–3). In fact, no human being can provide divine wisdom, for no one is capable of going up to heaven and bringing it down (v. 4a). Neither this nor other acts of wisdom and power are possible to human beings (v. 4bcd). As Agur acknowledges his impotence and ignorance, he finds the word of God protecting him as it did the psalmists of Psalms 12 and 18 (v. 5). The reader is warned: do not add to that divine word (v. 6). Agur now prays to speak the truth and to enjoy the basic necessities of life (vv. 7–8) lest he offend the God who has rescued him from exhaustion and ignorance (v. 9). Verse 10 seems to be the conclusion of vv. 1–9, to judge by its syntactic resemblance to v. 6. Though syntactically pointing backward to v. 6, thematically v. 10 points forward with the catchword "curse" to the list of four types.

The Words of Agur

30:1 The words of Agur, son of Yaqeh, the man of Massa.[a]
The oracle of the man: "I am weary, O God,[b]
    I am weary, O God, and I am exhausted,
2 for I am a beast, not a man,
    without the brains of a human being.
3 I have not learned wisdom,[c]
    gained knowledge of the Holy One.
4 Who has gone up to heaven and come back down?
    Who has gathered the wind in his cupped hands?
Who has bagged the waters with his garment?
    Who has established the boundaries of the earth?
What is his name,
    what is the name of his son?[d]
5 Every word of God is true,
    a shield to those who trust in him.
6 Add nothing to his words,
    lest he accuse you and you be seen as a liar.

7 Two things I ask from you,
    do not withhold them from me before I die:
8 Falsehood and lying words
    keep far from me.
Give me neither poverty nor wealth,
    give me only the food I need,
9 lest I become sated and play false
    and declare, "Who is Yahweh?"
lest I turn poor and become a thief,
    and profane the name of my God.
10 Do not slander a slave to his master
    lest he curse you and you incur guilt.

Four Sorts of Scoundrels

11 A sort that curses its father
    and does not bless its mother;
12 A sort that is perfect in its own eyes
    yet is not cleansed of its filth;
13 A sort—how haughty its eyes,
    how high its eyebrows are lifted up;
14 A sort whose teeth are daggers,
    and whose molars are knives

to devour the lowly from the earth,
the poor from the human race.

a. Many scholars suggest with good reason that *hammaśśā'* designates the Arabian tribe of Massa, which appears in Assyrian sources as early as 734 B.C.E. as *Mas'aia*. A similar misunderstanding appears in 31:1.

b. S (partially) and T interpret Hebrew *lĕ'îtî'ēl* and *'ukāl* as proper names, like the proper name Ithiel in Neh. 11:7. JPSV takes this line, rendering "the speech of the man to Ithiel, to Ithiel and Ucah." This interpretation is unsatisfactory, however, for the name of Agur ben Yaqeh has already been given, and it is unlikely that another would be given. Neither does the interpretation accord with the syntax of the phrase *nĕ'um haggeber* ("the oracle of the man") in its other occurrences (Num. 24:3, 15, and 2 Sam. 23:1). The latter texts suggest that the Hebrew of Prov. 30:1 up to *haggeber* ("the man") is sound.

The words *lĕ'îtî'ēl lĕ'îtî'ēl wĕ'ukāl* make the best sense as verbs: *lĕ'îtî'ēl* can be read "I am weary, O God" and *'ukāl* (repointed *wā'ēkel* from MT *kālāh*) can be read, "I am exhausted." Alonso Schökel points out the pairing of the same verbs in Jer. 20:9, *wĕnil'êtî kalkēl wĕlō' 'ûkāl*, ("I am too weary to hold it in and I am exhausted"). Other scholars suggest, "I am not God, I am not God that I should prevail," on the basis of Aramaic *lā' itay 'ēl*, but there are doubts the proposal can bear this meaning (McKane). Another clue that the three words should be read as verbs is the first word of v. 2, the conjunction *kî* ("because"). *Kî* explains why the speaker is exhausted, like the conjunction in Jer. 1:6: *lō' yād'tî dabbēr kî na'ar 'ānōkî* ("I do not know how to speak for I am a boy.").

c. The denial that one can learn wisdom apparently troubled the versions. G reflects metathesis (*lō'* to *'ēl*) to get "God gave me knowledge." Conversely, S, T, and V added "not" to the second colon and took Hebrew *qĕdōšîm* as "holy ones, heavenly beings."

d. We omit MT "do you know" at the end of v. 4 on the basis of its omission in the important Greek manuscripts Vaticanus and Sinaiticus. The phrase apparently found its way into Proverbs from Job 38:5, where it also follows a cosmic question. Its presence here spoils the sense, for Agur, not God, is the questioner. S prefaces the questions with "And [Agur] said."

[30:1] "The words of Agur" are parallel to "the oracle of the man." The Hebrew word *hammaśśā'* means the Massaite, a member of the Arabian tribe of Massa. The tribe is attested in Assyrian sources as early as 734 B.C.E., and may be referred to in Gen. 25:14 and 1 Chron. 1:30. Agur is a non-Israelite sage, though nothing else is known about him. He is one of "the people of the East," proverbial in the Bible for their wisdom. 1 Kings 4:30 praises Solomon for having wisdom surpassing "all the people of the East, and all the wisdom of Egypt." Agur's words are introduced like the oracle of Balaam in Numbers 24 and the last words of David in 2 Sam. 23:1–7. Num. 24:15–17 is worth quoting (words identical to Prov. 30:1–3 are italicized): "The *oracle* of Balaam, son of Peor // and the *oracle* of *the man* whose eye is true. The *oracle* of one who hears the words of *God* (*'ēl* as in Prov. 30:1b), // one who *knows the knowledge* of the Most High." In 2 Sam. 23:1 *dibrê* ("words") is parallel to *nĕ'um* ("oracle"), just as in Prov. 30:1. The author thus draws on traditional language of seers recounting their vision.

It might seem on first reading that the Eastern sage Agur says precisely the opposite of what the sage Balaam says. Indeed, some scholars interpret Agur's words as religious skepticism, but that is not the case. Both sages affirm the power of the God of Israel and their own inability to say anything beyond the divine word given to them.

[2] The speech of Agur begins in v. 1 and ends in v. 5. He confesses he is exhausted, a beast, subhuman, without heavenly wisdom, and unable to attain it because no human being can go to heaven and bring it down. The self-abasement of vv. 1–3 is Semitic hyperbole, like Ps. 73:21–22 (identical words italicized): "When my heart had become bitter, when my innards had been pierced, I was a *beast* and *did not know,* I was a brute beast before you." The psalmist later becomes aware of God's powerful presence (Ps. 73:23–26), however. Another example is Job 25:4–6: "How can a mortal be right with God? . . . how much less a mortal, a maggot, the son of man, a worm!" These are examples of "low anthropology," self-abasement as an expression of reverence.[2]

[3] The "knowledge" that Agur denies having is heavenly knowledge, as is shown by the parallelism. "Holy One" in colon B is most likely God, which is its meaning in 9:10. In Num. 24:15–19 Balaam is said "to know the knowledge of the Most High." The term could also mean "holy ones" or angels as it does in Job 5:1 and 15:5. Like Job, Agur denies he has secret heavenly knowledge.

[4] Verse 4 prepares for the resolution of the self-abasement begun in vv. 1–3 by denying that any being other than God can give wisdom. Verse 4a is another way of stating v. 3: what human being could ever have heavenly knowledge? The same thought is stated in Deut. 30:12–14: "[This commandment] is not in the heavens that you should say, 'Who will go up for us to the heavens and take it for us and teach it to us that we should do it?' . . . No, the word is very near you; it is in your mouth and in your heart so you to observe." Deuteronomy draws a different conclusion.[3]

The second, third, and fourth questions seem awkward here, and they may be an addition. As they stand, they develop the question in v. 4a, showing the

---

2. The Qumran Thanksgiving Hymns (Hodayot) also use a low estimate of human nature to celebrate the gift of knowledge, e.g., "Behold, [I was taken] from dust [and] fashioned [out of clay] as a source of uncleanness and a shameful nakedness, a heap of dust . . . " (xi. 24–25). This low estimate is balanced by appreciation of the gift of knowledge from God, e.g., "I [thank you, O Lord], for you have enlightened me through your truth. In your marvelous mysteries, and in your loving kindness to a man [of vanity, and] in the greatness of your mercy to a perverse heart you have granted me knowledge" (vii. 26–27), in D. J. Harrington, *Wisdom Texts from Qumran* (London: Routledge, 1996), 80.

3. For the mythological background of the verses, see R. C. Van Leeuwen, "The Background to Proverbs 30:4aα," in *Wisdom, You Are My Sister,* ed. M. L. Barré (R. E. Murphy volume; CBQ Monograph Series 28; Washington, D.C.: Catholic Biblical Association, 1997).

utter impossibility of any human imparting heavenly wisdom except God. They are cast in the style of the divine questions in Isa. 40:12–17 and Job 38–42. The answer to all the questions is—no one! What human being could supply such superhuman wisdom?

[5] With slight variation, the verse is found in Ps. 18:31 [30E] (// 2 Sam. 22:31): "God (*hā'ēl*), perfect is his way, the word of Yahweh is true, a shield is he to all who hope in him." The king in Psalm 18, like Agur, classes himself with "the humble (*'onî*) people" (Ps. 18:28 [27E]), and is in dire straits, exhausted and without resources. Psalm 12:7 (6E) expresses trust in similar words: "All the words of Yahweh are pure, silver refined in a furnace on the ground." The reference to "word" in Prov. 30:5 brings the movement full circle from Agur's opening statement of exhaustion and ignorance to the word of God. Agur dramatically states that only God can give him heavenly knowledge, and that knowledge is contained in reliable words from God.

[6] As in Deut. 4:2 (identical words italicized, "you must not *add to the word* that I command"; cf. Deut. 13:1), hearers must not add anything to God's words, lest God rebuke them and they be seen as deceivers, that is, pretending their words are wise independently of God. Syntactically, v. 6 is similar to v. 10 ("Do not . . . lest . . ."), which concludes the next subsection, vv. 7–9.

[7–10] Verses 7–10 constitute the only prayer in the book of Proverbs. Thematically it fits the logic of vv. 1–9, though many scholars believe it has been added. The logic is that Agur has rejected all wisdom except that given by God, for only God's word is reliable and gives protection (v. 5). Having rejected other sources of wisdom, Agur now prays directly to God.

The symmetry of the prayer can be shown schematically (after Meinhold).

Address to God			v. 7
Requests			v. 8
1. Do *not* allow		vain oaths	v. 8a
		lying words	v. 8a
2. Do *not* give	poverty		v. 8c
	riches		v. 8c
3. Give only the necessary food			v. 8d
Reasons			v. 9
1. To prevent danger from	riches (which offend Yahweh)		v. 9ab
	poverty (which offends the name of God)		v. 9cd

The section appropriately concludes with a prayer of the sage to remain completely faithful to God. As the sage vehemently rejected false wisdom in vv. 1–4 so he vehemently rejects false words, especially the kind that lead to infidelity to God. The prayer prays *against* two great dangers to fidelity: unjust conduct in the law court (*šāw'*, "falsehood," can refer to false oaths sworn before Yahweh) and extremes of wealth or poverty that could lead to infidelity. It asks *for* only the necessities of life. The prayer expresses a dread of offending God and a desire to remove all incentives to evil behavior.

[10] In thought, v. 10 seems extraneous to vv. 1–9, but its syntax is like v. 6: *'al*, "not," + imperfect second person singular verb + *pen*, "lest" + imperfect verb. The verb "to slander" is a denominative verb from the noun "tongue," occurring only here and in Ps. 101:5. The verb in Proverbs and Psalms connotes telling lies. The verb "to be punished" (*'āšamtā*), like many other terms for wrongdoing, describes not only the evil act but also its consequent punishment. The usage here can be called "consequential *'āšam*," as in Ps. 34:22 (21E): "Evil slays the wicked, / those who hate the righteous incur punishment (*'āšam*)."[4] The verb "to curse" need not refer to a formal curse but to a cry of righteous anger as in 2 Sam. 16:5, 7. Biblical law protected slaves as in Deut. 15:9, which forbids abusing the year of remission to harm the poor: "lest your neighbor cry to Yahweh against you and you incur punishment for your sin (*ḥēṭ*)." The thought is similar to Prov. 22:22–23.

[11–14] A literary unit is formed by anaphora, the repetition of words at the beginning of successive phrases or sentences. Each line begins with the Hebrew word *dôr*, "circle, generation, breed (so JPSV), sort, type." It is linked to the preceding verses by "curse" in v. 10. Honoring parents is commanded in the Decalogue (Ex. 20:12; Deut. 5:16), and cursing them carries the death penalty (Ex. 21:17; Deut. 27:16) and draws a curse upon the curser (Prov. 20:20). Verse 12 is connected to v. 13 by the repetition of "eyes." Verse 12 is a picture of profound self-delusion: one imagines oneself pure though covered with filth. Proverbs 20:9 denies that anyone can say "*I* am pure." In v. 13 haughty eyes are a symbol of arrogance (Ps. 18:27 = 2 Sam. 22:28; Prov. 6:17). Verse 14 is climactic by its length. Sword and teeth are also in parallel in Ps. 57:5 (4E).

The portrait of vv. 11–14 moves outward from the home (parents) to the public arena (attack on the poor). It is a story of cruel persons, the sort who disdain their parents' advice, overprize their own state (v. 12), display arrogance (v. 13), and treat the lowly with viciousness.

Numerical Sayings

30:15 The leech has two daughters, Give and Give.

Three things are never sated,
    four never say "Enough":
16 The underworld, an unfruitful womb,
    earth that never is sated with water
    and fire that never says "Enough."

---

4. J. Milgrom, *Leviticus 1–16* (AB 3; New York: Doubleday, 1991), 339–40.

17   The eye that mocks a father,
          that scorns the homage[a] due a mother,
      will be plucked out by brook ravens,
          scavenged by vultures.

18   Three things are beyond me,
          four I do not understand:
19   the way of an eagle in the sky,
          the way of a serpent on a rock,
      the way of a ship on the seas,
          and the way of a man with a woman.

20   This is the way of an adulterous woman:
          she eats and wipes her mouth, and says, "I have done nothing
      wrong."

21   At three things the earth trembles,
          at four it cannot bear up;
22   at a slave when he becomes king,
          at a fool when he ends up fulfilled;
23   at a rejected woman when she gets a husband,
          at a maidservant when she ousts her mistress.

24   Four things are the smallest on earth,
          but they are the wisest:
25   ants are a species not strong,
          yet garner their food supply in summer;
26   badgers are a species not mighty,
          yet build their homes on crags;
27   locusts have no king,
          but all march in formation;
28   the lizard you can catch with your hands,
          but is in the palaces of kings.

29   Three things are stately in their stride,
          four are imperious in their gait:
30   the lion, mighty among the animals,
          does not run from any creature;
31   the cock preening itself, the he-goat,[b]
          and a king going before his people.

32   If you have been a fool and exalted yourself,
          if you have laid evil plans—put your hand to your mouth!

33   For the churning of milk yields butter,
        the churning of a nose yields blood,
        the churning of anger yields strife.

a. MT *yiqqăhat,* "homage," occurs elsewhere only in Gen. 49:10, "*the homage* of the people is his," which is parallel to "when tribute is brought to him." G, followed by S and T, translated the unusual Hebrew according to Prov. 23:22, "old age" (*lĕziqnat*), but MT makes sense as it stands.

b. The verse is unreadable; the first two words, *zarzîr motnayim,* "girded(?) of loins," and the next to last word, *'alqûm,* "not stand(?)," are corrupt or unknown. In the absence of solid evidence, we adopt the rendering of the ancient versions for the first word, "cock"; for the second we emend MT *mtnym 'w* to *mitnaśśē',* "exalting oneself" (assuming *śîn* was misread as a *yōd-mēm* ligature); for the third, we simply guess. In Num. 23:24, *mitnaśśē'* is used of a lion. Jerome interpreted *'alqûm* literally as *nec est rex qui resistat ei,* "nor is there a king who could resist it [the animal]." Cf. Job 29:25: "I dwelt like a king among his troops." *Mitnaśśē'* occurs also in v. 32.

[30:15] The leech is a bloodsucking worm (of the hirudinea class) that typically has a sucker at each end. The theme of nonsatiety links this verse to the next verse just as v. 20 is linked to vv. 18–19 by the theme of "way."

[15cd–16] This is the first of five numerical sayings in the chapter. The slight variation in number—three and four (Amos 1–2 has eight instances)—is best explained as parallelism applied to numbers (cf. Job 5:19). Numerical sayings are a feature of Canaanite style.[5] A Ugaritic instance is *KTU* 1.4.III.17–21: "Two kinds of feasts Baal hates, three, the Rider on the Clouds—a feast of shame, a feast of meanness, and a feast where maids behave lewdly." *Ahiqar* 92 states: "There are two things which are good, / and a third which is pleasing to Shamash: / one who drinks wine and shares it, / one who masters wisdom [*and observes it*], / and one who hears a word but tells it not." Cf. Prov. 6:16–19: "Six things Yahweh hates, / seven are an abomination to him: / Haughty eyes, a lying tongue, / hands that shed innocent blood, / a heart that devises malicious plans, / feet eager to run to wickedness, / a false witness who gives lying testimony, / an inciter of quarrels among family members."

In this saying, the underworld (Sheol) is not so much the place where the dead live a shadowy existence but a force that eventually draws all the living into it, which is the meaning it has in 27:20; Isa. 5:14; and Hab. 2:5. The underworld in this sense is always at work. Another example of insatiable power is the unfruitful womb. By metonymy, it stands for a woman unable to bear children. Such a woman will never be fully satisfied as long as she is in that state, like Hannah in 1 Samuel 1 and Rachel in Genesis 29–30. In third and

5. For a recent review and discussion, see S. Paul, *Amos* (Hermeneia; Minneapolis: Fortress Press, 1991), 27 n. 168.

fourth place are mentioned the elements earth and fire. Earth, especially the dry land of Palestine, will always absorb more water. Fire always requires more fuel. The latter two are more developed than the first two. There is also unequal treatment in vv. 29–31, where only the *first* item (v. 30) is developed. The juxtaposition here is striking—death, a woman, land, and fire. Despite their great differences, they are alike in having an insatiable urge.

[17] A nonnumerical saying in which contempt for one's parents is depicted as so unnatural that nature itself carries out the punishment—death at the hands of wild beasts.

[18–19] The authorial "I" speaks as in chap. 7 and 24:30–34. Like vv. 11–14, anaphora (repetition of the initial word) serves to underscore the similarity of the four items. "Way" is road, course, manner. In rabbinic Hebrew it can mean sexual relations, a usage that is anticipated in Jer. 2:23, 33; 3:13 (Ehrlich). The first three examples follow the sequence of sky, earth ("rock" is parallel to earth in Job 18:4), and sea. The sequence of heaven, earth, and sea occurs elsewhere (e.g., Ex. 20:11; Amos 9:6; Hag. 2:6). "Way" in the first three instances retains its literal meaning: the effortless flight of the eagle (or vulture), the legless movement of the serpent, the progress of a ship. The medium of each course is different: air, earth, and water. The metaphorical meaning of *derek,* "way, course," serves as a bridge to the fourth instance.

Human beings, the fourth instance, are mentioned after the tripartite universe as in Pss. 33:6–8 and 69:35–37. "Man" and "woman" are sexual beings. The verse refers to the remarkable fact that a man and a woman are mutually attracted; their course is *toward each other.* The attraction was especially notable in ancient Near Eastern society, where boys and girls were raised separately. At puberty, the young, without knowing the opposite sex very well, were suddenly attracted to each other. Alonso Schökel notes, "The great wonder is man, and God has created him male and female."

[20] The saying is connected to the previous verse by its topic of sexuality and by the word "way," but it speaks of the abuse of sexuality in adultery. The vivid vignette is reminiscent of the seduction scene in chap. 7, except that here the accent falls on the woman's nonchalance rather than her cunning. There is a double meaning. In the Talmud, "to eat" can mean "to sleep with" (*b. Ketub.* 65.13–23), and "mouth" can refer to the vulva (*b. Sanh.* 100a; *b. Menaḥ.* 98a).

[21–23] The third numerical saying is developed through anaphora (*taḥat,* "under," is repeated four times) as in vv. 11–14 and 19. Shaking of the heavens is an aspect of cosmic upheaval in Isa. 14:16; Joel 2:10; Amos 8:8; Job 9:6. In light of the examples here, which are humorous (with the possible exception of the first), the effect is mock-heroic.[6]

---

6. For a detailed treatment, see R. C. Van Leeuwen, "Proverbs 30:21–23," *JBL* 105 (1986): 599–610.

A literal rendering of v. 22b, "a fool when he is sated with food," is misleading. "To be sated with food" (*śāba' leḥem*) in Job 27:14; Prov. 12:11; 20:13 expresses the fulfillment that comes from virtue, not simply feeling sated with food. The translation "rejected woman" (lit., "hated woman") in v. 23, is disputed. Some commentators (Delitzsch, Toy, and Plöger) believe the term refers to an older unmarried woman who, contrary to expectation, finds a husband. Others suggest "hated" is a technical term for divorced woman, but "hated" in the passages cited (Deut. 21:15–17 and Gen. 29:31–33) refers to the less favored wife rather than to a divorcée. Deuteronomy 24:1–4, to be sure, uses "hated" in the sense of rejecting a wife but that does not mean that "hated woman" is a divorcée. All the events are not so much immoral as they are instances of people attaining what they do not deserve. Earth itself rebels against such unfittingness. Cf. 26:1.

[24–28] This third numerical saying in the chapter omits the expected number "three." The examples illustrate the title accurately in that "small" means "insignificant" (as in 1 Sam. 9:21 and Zech. 4:10) and "wise" means knowing to take care of oneself.

Ants are not strong; they can be crushed underfoot. Yet they can amass all the food they need at one period of the year. The rock badger (*procaria syriacus*) lives on rocky heights ranging from the Dead Sea to Mount Hermon in Lebanon. It is herbivorous, about the size of a hare, possessing feet with suckers enabling it to climb on rock surfaces. Though small, its nests are in remote crags, secure from enemies. Verse 27 probably refers to the migratory locust, which has six legs and four wings. It moves in vast swarms, capable of devastating all the plant life it encounters. Though without a king, that is, disorganized and apparently vulnerable, it nonetheless moves in serried ranks, and cannot be diverted from its course. The animal named in v. 28 (*śĕmāmît*) is unclear. Two manuscripts of the Targum (Z and W) have *'qmt'*, "spider," but the word is traditionally translated "lizard." G, followed by S, other mss of T, and V, take the word to be a lizard, a gecko, which is omnipresent in the area. At any rate, the animal cannot be confined and goes anywhere it pleases. The examples exalt wisdom over size and power. By their wisdom, these insignificant animals ensure their own survival, they govern themselves.

[29–31] The fourth numerical saying of three and four is about majestic strides. Textual problems in v. 31 unfortunately detract from the full literary effect. Just as vv. 24–28 instanced four insignificant beings of invincible survival ability, so this saying instances four beings whose imperiousness is visible in their walk. In the poetic logic of the piece, only the lion is described in detail; the reader is expected to transpose the fullness of its description to the other portraits. In Job 39:22, the phrase "not to turn back from" signifies fearlessness. Lion and king are also associated in 19:12 and 20:2. The ancient versions could not resist expanding the lines: The cock strides fearlessly among the hens as does the he-goat in the herd, and the king takes his stand and addresses his people.

[32–33] The two verses are correctly taken together by modern versions. The syntax resembles Prov. 6:1–3: if you have done such and such, then do such and such. The phrase in v. 32b, "hand to mouth," occurs several times in the Bible but here has the meaning it has in Judg. 18:19—"Keep quiet. Put your hand over your mouth"—that is, refrain from carrying out your plan.

A mark of a wise person is to make peace and avoid strife. 15:18 is similar: "An angry person (*'îš ḥēmāh*) stirs up strife, / but patience quiets a quarrel (*rîb*)." To think oneself better than others and promote oneself at their expense stirs up strife, which will harm the one who provoked it. Verse 33 grounds the prohibition by drawing an analogy with making butter. The correct meaning of Hebrew *mûṣ,* "to churn," was long ago pointed out by the medieval Jewish interpreters Saadia Gaon and Ibn Janāḥ as "to churn milk."[7] It is etymologically related to Akkadian *māṣu,* "to churn milk." To churn milk produces *ḥem'āh* (ghee), which plays on *ḥēmāh,* "wrath" (Alonso Schökel). The wordplay continues in the second clause, "to churn the nose (*'ap*) brings blood," for "nose" (*'ap*) can also mean "anger" by metonymy (the noise or snout is seen as the source or the sign of anger). Blood is often the result when anger is aroused. Finally, *'appayim,* "anger," yields strife. *'Appayim* can also mean nose (two nostrils). Churning up the anger of another brings strife, which is dangerous for all concerned. As in vv. 11–14, foolish contempt for parents and wiser heads leads to violence.

Proverbs 31

31:1   The words of Lemuel, king of Massa,[a] with which his mother
        instructed him.

2   What are you doing, my son?[b]
        What are you doing, son of my womb?
        What are you doing, son of my vow?

3   Do not give your vigor to women,
        your drive to those who destroy kings.[c]

4   It is not[d] for kings, O Lemuel,
        it is not for kings to drink wine,
        for rulers to crave[e] strong drink,

5   lest he drink and forget his duty,
        and pervert the rights of all the poor.

---

7. See M. Held, "Marginal Notes to the Biblical Lexicon," in *Biblical and Related Studies Presented to Samuel Iwry,* ed. A. Kort and S. Morschauser (Winona Lake, Ind.: Eisenbrauns, 1985), 97–103.

6   Give strong drink to the miserable,
        and wine to the embittered of soul
7   so he can drink and forget his poverty,
        and no longer mind his toil.
8   Open your mouth for the mute,
        for the cause of all the weak.
9   Open your mouth and judge rightly.
        Champion the lowly and poor.

a. The versions and the Masoretic vowel pointing took Hebrew *mś'* as *maśśā'*, "oracle." But, normally, when a king is introduced the name of his country is given. Hence we read Massa, which is a North Arabian tribe appearing in Assyrian sources as *Mas'aia*. In Gen. 25:14 and 1 Chron. 1:30, Massa is a son of Ishmael.

b. "Son" is Aramaic *bar* instead of the expected Hebrew *bēn*, and is one of several Aramaisms in the piece. *Māh*, literally, "what," is difficult and has provoked many suggestions, one being that *māh* functions like Arabic *ā*, which can be a negative particle in sentences such as, "How could I look at a girl?" (i.e., "I have not looked at a girl!") JPSV and NRSV take it in this way: "No, my son! No, son of my womb!" But the texts sometimes invoked to support this interpretation (1 Kings 12:16; Job 9:2; 16:6; 31:1; Cant. 8:4; Qoh. 6:8) are not quite parallel in that they occur in an extended phrase that includes a verb.

We propose that *māh* functions as a call for attention, after which an admonition is given. Proverbs has several examples of the semantically similar construction, "Hear [my] son . . . do not (verb in imperfect tense) . . . " *Māh* seems to be elliptical for *māh lĕkā*, "what is it with you?" or "what is the matter with you?" The full form occurs in Gen. 21:17 (with relevant words italicized): "And the angel of God called to Hagar from heaven and he said to her, *"What is it with you* (= What troubles you?), Hagar? *Do not fear* because God has heard the cry of the boy." Cf. Isa. 3:15: *"What is it with you* (= How dare you!) that you crush my people . . . ?" There is an implied rebuke in these examples, hence our translation, "What are you doing?"

c. The Masoretes pointed *lamĕhôt* as the feminine plural participle of *māhāh* in the construct state—"those who destroy." The versions, apart from V, are very free. G: "Do not give your wealth to women and your mind and life to regret" (similarly Symmachus); S: " . . . and your ways to the food of kings" (i.e., dissipation); T: " . . . and your ways to the daughters (*'mhwt*?) of kings."

E. Lipiński suggests that *mĕhôt* is from Akkadian *maḫḫūtu/muḫḫūtu*, "prophetess, female ecstatic."[1] At the court at Mari (a late second-millennium city near the present Syria and Iraq border) such prophetesses had a relationship to the king. It is easy to imagine such would-be palace policymakers weakening a king's authority and provoking a warning from the queen mother. Lipiński's proposal is linguistically possible but at present more evidence is required. The *nûn* plural ending is an Aramaism.

---

1. "Emprunts suméro-akkadiens en hébreu biblique," *ZAH* 1 (1988): 68–69.

d. One expects *lō'* rather than *'al* in the phrase "it is not for someone to do such and such," as in 2 Chron. 26:18.

e. The ketib is *'w* = *'ô*, "or," and the qere is *'y* = *'ê*, "where?" Some scholars suggest repointing the word to *'î*, which in Phoenician means "not" and is apparently a negative prefix in Job 22:3, *'î-nāqî*, "not innocent." But an independent use of *'î* is not attested in the Bible and it fits awkwardly in any case, despite JPSV and NRSV. The best solution is to read *'awwō* (so *HALAT*), the piel infinitive of the triliteral root *'wh*, "to desire, thirst for."

Like the instructions of 22:17–24:22 and 30:1–10, the section begins with "the words of . . ." but the words are not spoken *by* the king but *to* him by his mother. A mother and father could be a source of instruction in Proverbs (1:8; 6:20). The mother of a king in the Canaanite world played a major role in the palace. Because of her longevity, knowledge of palace politics, and undoubted loyalty to her son, she was in a good position to offer him reliable counsel.[2] The Aramaisms and the place name show the non-Israelite origin of the piece.

Verses 1–9 are skillfully composed. The first section (vv. 3–5, 26 words) is an admonition against the imprudent use of sex and alcohol ("wine," "strong drink") lest the luxury-loving king *forget* the *poor*. The second section (vv. 6–9, 28 words) is an exhortation to the prudent use of alcohol ("strong drink," "wine") in order that the miserable *poor* can *forget* their poverty. Verses 8–9 are positive as v. 3 is negative; the verses urge the king to open his mouth not to drink but to speak for the voiceless and poor. The underlying subject of the poem is a king's duty to effect justice for the poor. How easy it is for a king to squander the authority God has given him to protect the weak!

"Son of my vow" refers to a vow the mother promised if God were to give her a son. A notable biblical example is Hannah in 1 Sam. 1:11: "O Yahweh of Hosts, if you will only regard the misery of your servant and remember me, and not forget your servant, but will give to your servant a male child, then I will bring him to you as a nazirite until the day of his death." After such a vow, the royal son was born to the queen.

The women in the poem are the women of the harem. It is possible that "destroyers of kings" is an Akkadian loanword, *mahhūtu/muhhūtu*, "prophetess, female ecstatic." Such women prophesied about political matters (see textual notes). If this is true, the king is being alerted to the danger of manipulation or seduction by his staff.

---

2. See, most recently, K. Spanier, "The Queen Mother in the Judaean Royal Court: Maacah — A Case Study," in *A Feminist Companion to the Bible*, ed. A. Brenner (Sheffield: Sheffield Academic Press, 1994), 5.186–95. A good general treatment of the entire passage is J. L. Crenshaw, "A Mother's Instructions to Her Son (Proverbs 31: 1–9)," in *Perspectives on the Hebrew Bible*, ed. J. Crenshaw (Macon, Ga.: Mercer University Press, 1988), 9–22, reprinted in J. L. Crenshaw, *Urgent Advice and Probing Questions* (Macon, Ga.: Mercer University Press, 1995), 383–95.

A biblical example of moral callousness resulting from sexual immorality is David's adultery with Bathsheba and murder of Uriah (2 Samuel 11–12). Nathan's parable of the poor man's lamb confiscated by the wealthy man illustrates how such conduct leads to forgetfulness of the poor. Immoderate consumption of alcohol is also criticized by the mother, for drinking makes one forget one's "duty," literally, "what is decreed," probably the laws that protect the poor. Two examples of immoderate consumption of liquor leading to forgetfulness of the poor are Isa. 28:1: "Ah, the proud crown of the drunkards of Ephraim, / whose glorious beauty is only wilted flowers / on the heads of those sated with rich food, / who are overcome with wine"; and Amos 6:6: "They drink from the wine bowls / and anoint themselves with choice oils, / but they are not concerned with the ruin of Joseph."

A biblical example of a woman's deft counsel to a (future) king is Abigail's warning David against exacting vengeance on Nabal in 1 Sam. 25:24–31: "And when Yahweh carries out for my lord the promise of success he has made concerning you, and appoints you as commander over Israel, you shall not have this qualm or burden on your conscience, my lord, for having shed innocent blood or for having avenged yourself personally" (vv. 30–31 NAB).

The Proverbs passage is a well-crafted exhortation from the queen mother to her royal son. The author transforms traditional warnings to rulers against the abuse of sex and liquor into an exhortation to practice justice. Use the wine for the poor, the queen mother urges, and use your mouth to speak for those who cannot speak for themselves. "To judge the poor" in biblical idiom is to intervene on their side, to become their champion. The poem's wit and light touch might render benevolent a king who would otherwise be offended by criticism. The piece is an admirable example of *mûsār,* "discipline; warning," which is etymologically related to the verb *yāsar,* "reprove," in v. 1. In its biblical context, the exhortation is applicable to all who are tempted to turn authority into privilege.

Hymn to the Capable Wife

10 Who can find a capable wife?
    Her worth is far more than rubies!
11 Her husband trusts her judgment;
    he does not lack income.
12 She brings him profit not loss
    all the days of her life.
13 She selects wool and flax,
    and works them with willing hands.
14 She is like a merchant's fleet;
    from far-off lands she brings her food.

15   She rises while it is still night
         to supply provisions to her household,
         portions to her maidservants.
16   She considers a field and buys it;
         from what her hands have gained, she plants a vineyard.
17   She girds herself with strength,
         she exerts her arms with vigor.
18   She enjoys the profit from her trading;
         her lamp is not extinguished at night.
19   Her hand she puts to the distaff,
         and her fingers grasp the spindle.
20   Her palms she opens to the needy,
         her hands she stretches out to the poor.
21   She has no fear for her house when it snows,
         for all her house is clothed in double thickness.
22   She makes coverlets for herself;
         linen and red-dyed wool are her clothing.
23   Her husband is respected in the city gates
         when he sits among the elders of the land.
24   She makes tunics and sells them,
         waistbands she offers to the merchant.
25   She is clothed with strength and splendor;
         she greets the future with a smile.
26   She opens her mouth in wisdom;
         pleasing instruction is on her tongue.
27   She oversees the doings of her house;
         she does not eat the bread of idleness.
28   Her sons rise up and declare her happy,
         her husband proclaims her praises.
29   "Many women act capably
         but you surpass them all."
30   Charm is deceptive and beauty is fleeting;
         it is for revering Yahweh that a woman wins praise.
31   'Extol her for the fruit of her hands,
         let her achievements praise her in the city gates.'"

The poem on the capable or valiant woman is an acrostic poem of twenty-two lines, each line beginning with a successive letter of the alphabet. Both MT and G (which has a different order of sections after chap. 25) end with this poem. The most suitable title is Hymn to (or perhaps Encomium of) the Capable Wife.

The poem is unique in genre, though it has remarkable affinities to the hymn.[3] Its structure is similar to a hymn: an announcement of praise and the naming of the subject, the body or central praise, and the concluding exhortation to the audience to join in the praise. Like hymns to Yahweh the Warrior such as Exodus 15 and Judges 5, it extols the subject's strength, wisdom, and success or "victory." Wolters suggests the poem is a hymn to a warrior that has been adapted to praise a heroic woman: "[Such a hymn] does not dwell on the inner feelings or the physical appearance of the hero, but simply describes the mighty feats of valour which he accomplishes."[4] Indeed, the woman is heroic; her house is a busy farm and factory and she is a wisdom teacher.

The narrator first describes her wonderful deeds (vv. 11–27) and then her own children and husband take up the praise (vv. 28–31). As with most acrostic poems in the Bible, the unity of the poem comes more from its alphabetic sequence than from its narrative logic. There are, however, some formal features unifying the poem in addition to the unity from alphabetic sequence. A chiasm in vv. 19–20 moves the action from the domestic to the public sphere in that the woman's hands that weave cloth open wide to the poor beyond the household gates.

> *ḥayil,* "capable," v. 10a
>   *ba'lāh,* "her husband," v. 11a
>   *ydyh šlḥh* "her hand she puts," v. 19a
>   *kpyh,* "her fingers," v. 19b
>   *kph,* "her palm," v. 20a
>   *ydyh šlḥh,* "her hands she stretches," v. 20b
>   *ba'lāh,* "her husband," v. 28b
> *ḥayil,* "capable," v. 29a

In addition to the chiasm, there are clusters of verses on the same topic: vv. 14–15 are on food; vv. 21–25 are on clothing; vv. 26–27 are on instruction and supervision.

The wife is portrayed in almost superhuman terms. Though the husband and sons are the beneficiaries of her extraordinary capacities, they are not the main topic of the poem. The husband owes all his prominence to his wife, for she has overseen the acquisition of his wealth and given him the freedom to sit among the city elders. His reputation, wealth, and sons witness to her heroic virtue. His praise of her at the end of the poem puts into words what could almost be left unspoken. Her "house" in the broadest sense praises her. Its vitality is entirely the result of her art of governing (= wisdom).

Does the poem have a literary function within the entire book of Proverbs? Some suggest that the highly positive portrait of the woman is placed at the end

---

3. A. Wolters, "Proverbs XXXI 10–31 as Heroic Hymn: A Form-Critical Analysis," *VT* 38 (1988): 446–57.

4. Ibid., 454. Wolters compares David's lament over Jonathan and Saul in 2 Sam. 1:19–27.

to offset the negative portrayal of the foolish woman in chaps. 1–9 and the criticism of women in some sayings. But the positive portrayal of Woman Wisdom in chaps. 1–9 has already accomplished that. Another suggestion is that the praise is modeled on encomia of beloved wives and mothers in Egyptian mortuary texts. Such encomia may indeed have contributed to the rhetoric and ideas of the portrait, but this portrait is anonymous rather than of a particular person. The point of a panegyric is presumably to honor a specific individual.

We propose that it is a portrait of an ideal wife (of a great house) and, on a metaphorical level, a portrait of Woman Wisdom and what she accomplishes for those who come to her house as disciples and friends. Woman Wisdom in chaps. 1–9 sought a permanent relationship to her disciples (8:32–36) and invited them into her house (9:1–6, 11). The portrait has two levels, as do the portraits of the two women in chaps. 1–9. A good wife, who is a gift of God, builds her house. She brings prosperity to all within—her husband, children, servants, and even to those outside—to the poor and those who benefit from her husband's counsel in the gates. If a young man, or, in the context of the entire book, any person, enters into a relationship with Woman Wisdom and becomes her disciple, she will invite that disciple to her house (chap. 9) and make that person "happy" in the fullest sense, bestowing the blessings of children, wealth, renown, and long life.[5] The poem has remarkable affinities to 3:13–20, even to its focus on the woman's hands (3:16 and 31:19–20).[6]

[10] The question "Who can find?" occurs in 20:6 and Qoh. 7:24, with the implication that finding is a miraculous event. She is more precious than rubies, the very same statement that Prov. 3:15 and 8:11 make about wisdom. Proverbs 18:22 and 19:14 are relevant: "Who finds a wife finds a great thing, and enjoys the favor of Yahweh"; "House and wealth are inherited from parents, but a capable wife is from Yahweh."

[11–12] Verses 11 and 12 mention the husband, who does not reappear until vv. 23 and 28–31. The Hebrew consonant *b* (Hebrew *bêt*) is used alliteratively in colon A, *baṭaḥ bāh lēb baʿlāh,* literally, "trusts in her the heart of her husband." So translated, however, colon A is misleading, for the English equivalent "heart" denotes the affections, not the mind. As the parallelism shows, the husband can trust she will handle his affairs efficiently. The word *šālāl* in biblical Hebrew means "plunder, booty," which seems odd to describe income. The versions tried to remove the difficulty by paraphrase: G, *"noble* spoils"; S,

5. For a survey of various opinions with an eloquent argument for the symbolic meaning, see T. P. McCreesh, "Wisdom as Wife: Proverbs 31:10–31," *Revue Biblique* 92 (1985): 25–46.

6. For the patristic interpretation, see C. Magazzù, "L'elogio della 'donna forte' (Prov. 31.10–31) nell'interpretazione patristica," in *Letture cristiane dei Libri Sapienziali* (XX Incontro di studiosi della antichità cristiana; Rome: Institutum patristicum Augustinianum," 1992), 213–34. For the midrash, see B. Visotzky, "Midrash Eishet Hayil," *Conservative Judaism* 38 (1986): 21–25. The midrash on the poem is part of the Shabbat evening ritual when it is recited by the husband to his wife.

"possessions"; T, "and will not be plundered"; V, "and he will have no need of spoil." The usage may be vernacular or it may simply be late Hebrew.[7]

In v. 12a, we have translated the Hebrew idiom ("to render good not evil") in a commercial sense according to context.

[13] Colon A, literally, "she seeks wool and flax," need not mean to shop for suitable material but to oversee its production, that is, growing one's own flax and shearing one's own sheep. Colon B, on the other hand, refers to manufacturing linen and wool cloth, which she does with her own hands (v. 19). In colon B, the phrase is, literally, "at the pleasure of her hands," which attributes to her hands the joy she takes in creating something useful and beautiful.

[14] Having noted the woman's ability to make cloth from her own plants and animals, the poem now depicts her with her eye on the far horizon. The far horizon evokes the picture of a merchant's fleet, bringing food from afar into her larder. It is the only simile in the poem.

[15] The verse is the only tricolon in the poem. In v. 14 the wife imported food; she now distributes it to her household. "House" here and in vv. 21 and 27 means household, including servants. "Allotted portion" in colon C can also mean "task," etymologically, that which is "cut" or decided. Parallelism with colon B suggests taking it as a definite portion of food.

[16] "To consider" implies careful pondering on the woman's part. "To take a field" is to buy it as in Gen. 23:13 and Ezek. 17:5. After purchasing it, the woman plants an orchard of fruit trees, which she acquired by her own earnings, literally, "the fruit of her hands."

[17] To do vigorous work requires an apron or other protective clothing. Putting such clothes on signals to all that she is vigorous. In colon B, the force of the piel conjugation of the verb is "declarative"—she shows her strength through her arms.[8]

[18] The two cola are parallel. Enjoying the profit from her trade and burning the lamp in her house night and day are the same thing. "Profit" (*ṭôb*) in colon A has a commercial sense as in v. 12. A burning lamp is a metaphor for prosperity (e.g., 13:9; 20:20; 24:20). Job 18:6 applies the metaphor to a household: "The light in his tent grows dark; his lamp fails him."

[19] The wife weaves linen cloth from flax and wool from the fleece she has cultivated (v. 13). "Distaff" (*kîšôr*) is the staff for holding the flax, tow, or wool, which, in hand spinning, was drawn out and twisted (spun) into yarn or thread by the "spindle" or round stick (*pelek*).

[20] The same hands and palms so industriously employed in spinning inside the house are now turned to the poor outside the house. A chiasm in vv. 19–20 links her industriousness and generosity: v. 19, *ydyh šlḥh, kpyh* ("her

---

7. So J. Kugel, "Qohelet and Money," *CBQ* 51 (1989): 46.
8. *IBHS* §24.2f.

hand she puts," "her fingers") // v. 20, *kph, ydyh šlḥh* ("her palms," "her hands she stretches"). Deuteronomy 15:7–8 uses the same image of open hands for generosity: "You shall not harden your heart and you shall not close your hand from your kin who is poor. But you shall open your hand to him and lend him enough to meet his need."

[21] The Masoretic pointing of the final Hebrew word in colon B, "dressed in *crimson* (*šānîm*, plural)," ruins the parallel to colon A. The correct reading is supplied by G, followed by S, "double," which interpreted Hebrew *šnym* as *šnayim*, "two, a double amount or portion." G applied it wrongly to the next verse. The point is that even snowstorms, relatively rare in the climate, have been foreseen. She has made the garments of her entire household warm enough to withstand extreme cold.

[22] The Hebrew word for "blankets, coverings" (*marbaddîm*) refers to bed clothes in its only other biblical appearance, 7:16. And in Ugaritic the word is followed by "bed(s)" (*KTU* 4.270.11). The Hebrew word *argāmān* is one of the two Hebrew words for "purple," designating red-purple in opposition to *těkēlet,* blue-purple. Verse 13 speaks of linen and wool. Purple dye was expensive, which suggests all the cloth manufactured by the wife was luxury grade. The woman is elegant and her handiwork is beautiful.

[23] The husband is mentioned for the first time since vv. 10–12 but now called "*her* husband." He only appears again in v. 28 when he praises her. The Hebrew phrase "to be known in" occurs in Isa. 61:9; Pss. 76:2 and 88:13 in the sense of being respected, recognized, praised, which is the meaning here. The gate of the city was the traditional site of community decision making by the male elders (e.g., Deut. 21:19; 22:15). The husband sits among them as a peer, which is the nuance of Hebrew verb in colon B.

[24] For the third time (vv. 13, 22, and here), the woman "makes" (*'āśāh*) something.

[25] As in v. 17, the wife's virtue is expressed by the metaphor of clothing, which is frequent in the Bible; for example, Yahweh girding himself with might. For the second time, strength, a military virtue, is ascribed to a woman, and honor as well. At first glance, colon B does not seem related to colon A. But a closer look shows that her strength enables her to face the future with confidence, as does her "splendor," which pertains to her attractiveness as in Ps. 8:6: "You have adorned [humankind] with glory and *splendor*." She can laugh at the future, like a confident warrior.

[26] Not only does the woman act with vigor and dress beautifully, she also speaks wisely. Her "wisdom" is the art of governing her household. The phrase "instruction of kindness" (unique in the Bible) most probably refers to her instructions to the servants, which she gives with a graciousness that invites their assent.

[27] The "doings" (lit., "goings") in her busy house she closely monitors, which is another way of saying that she does not eat "the bread of idleness," that is, meals that symbolize callousness and self-indulgence. "Bread of . . ." is an idiom occurring elsewhere; to be fed the "bread of tears" in Ps. 80:6 (5E) means to live with painful realities; "the bread of wickedness . . . the wine of violence" in Prov. 4:17 signifies the embracing of a violent way of life.

[28] The movement of the poem changes, and, for the first time, a voice besides the narrator's is heard. The last four lines are praise spoken by the wife's husband and sons. Apart from the lone reference to the husband in v. 23, this is the first time the husband has been mentioned since the opening lines, vv. 10–12. The lines are an inclusio that marks the ending. Further, the last four lines present a logical sequence. Up to this point, the poem has proceeded by way of rapidly changing perspectives (discrete verses), united chiefly by the acrostic mechanism.

Her family performs an act of thanksgiving. To give thanks in the Bible is not simply to say "thank you" but to acknowledge publicly the other's excellence, to bring it to the attention of the community. Husband and son acknowledge as praiseworthy her revering of Yahweh (v. 30b).

[29] Though the versions take the Hebrew phrase in colon A as "to acquire wealth" (and is so taken by Alonso Schökel), its meaning is rather "to succeed, be effective, triumphant," as is shown by comparable usage (e.g., Num. 24:18; 1 Sam. 14:48; Ps. 60:14 [12E]). The second word of the phrase (*ḥayil*) reprises v. 10, "a *capable* wife." Husband and sons acknowledge their wife and mother excels even the most talented woman.

[30] In comparison to the house the woman has built and managed, and especially in comparison to her fear of Yahweh, physical beauty is seen as transitory. It is her house that will endure. Indeed, Wolters believes that the poem is consciously shifting attention from the erotic aspect of the woman, which was customarily praised in the culture, to her heroic courage, strength and wisdom.[9] Proverbs 11:16 suggested that renown and wealth obtained by questionable means are illusory: "A charming woman gets renown, and ruthless men get wealth." Our verse reveals that the woman's virtue comes from her revering God. The book begins (1:7) and ends (31:30) with "revering Yahweh." Metrically, the verse seems to be a tricolon.

[31] Her husband and sons now turn to a public assembly, perhaps the same "assembly" mentioned in 5:14 and 26:26. Though most translators take MT *tnw* as the plural imperative of *nātan*, "to give," the verb is best taken as the piel conjugation of the verb *tānāh*, "to sing, extol," as in Judg. 5:11: "let them chant the powerful deeds of Yahweh."[10] REB nicely catches the spirit of colon B: "Let her achievements bring her honor at the city gates."

9. "Proverbs XXXI 10–31 as Heroic Hymn," 456–57.
10. Ibid., and JPSV.

INDEX OF ANCIENT SOURCES